DRUMCREE

The Orange Order's Last Stand

Chris Ryder and Vincent Kearney

Methuen

10 9 8 7 6 5 4 3 2 1

Published in 2001 by Methuen Publishing Ltd
215 Vauxhall Bridge Rd, London SW1V 1EJ

Photographs © Kelvin Boyes Photography
Map © Irish Times Studio

Methuen Publishing Limited Reg. No. 3543167

A CIP catalogue record for this book is available from the British
Library

ISBN 0 413 76260 2

Typeset by SX Composing DTP, Rayleigh, Essex
Printed and bound by Creative Print and Design (Wales), Ebbw Vale

Contents

Authors' Note

In telling the Drumcree story, we have generally used the convenient terms 'Protestants' and 'Catholics' to denote the two main communities in Northern Ireland because of the different, but sometimes overlapping, interests of Unionists and Loyalists on the one hand and Nationalists and Republicans on the other.

When we set out to trace the origins of the crisis at Drumcree and chronicle the turbulent events there from year to year, we initially underestimated the size and complexity of the task. In completing this book, we must therefore acknowledge the help and assistance of many people, from conflicting standpoints to this deeply emotional issue, who talked to us at length and in detail. Without their considerable frankness, we would not have been able to so comprehensively reconstruct what happened and explain why Drumcree has become such an important and symbolic issue, not only for the people of Portadown, but elsewhere throughout Northern Ireland.

Many of those who helped us with discreet observations and sensitive documents wished to do so anonymously and we gladly acknowledge their assistance here. In listing others, whose names follow, we wish to apologise for any inadvertent omissions.

Graham Montgomery, Melvyn Hamilton, David Trimble MP and First Minister of Northern Ireland, Jeffrey Donaldson MP, Joel Patton, David Burrows, David Jones, Ian Milne, Sir Reg Empey, Ray Hayden and William Thompson MP all helped us to understand and reflect the Unionist and Orange perspective. In particular, we want to make special mention of the the Reverend William Bingham, Denis Watson MLA and the Reverend Brian Kennaway, whose insights and comments were invaluable.

Brendan McKenna and Brid Rodgers MLA were also very co-operative and frank. Dara O'Hagan MLA, Father Brian Lennon SJ, Kevin Henderson, Mick Creaney, Peter Mulholland and Amanda Anderson generously shared their experiences and opinions to explain their side of the story, while Kevin O'Connor deserves our thanks for helping us to find some of the key people we needed.

Others who assisted us were Cardinal Cahal Daly, Archbishop Robin Eames, Canon Charles Kenny, the Reverend John Pickering and Brian Parker. Brian Currin, Don Anderson, Sir Alistair Graham and Richard Gordon explained their roles in the events and provided us with relevant documents. Chief Constable Sir Ronnie Flanagan, Assistant Chief Constable Alan McQuillan, Chief Superintendents Cyril Donnan and Roy McCune, together with Superintendent Kevin Sheehy and the staff at the RUC Press Office, including Amanda, also provided important input to our work. Roger Goodwin at the Army Information Service in Northern Ireland and some military colleagues were frank and incisive in putting the Army's point of view.

Some of the most useful insights we obtained came from the *Portadown Times* man Victor Gordon, who probably knows more about the town and its people than anyone else alive. John Compton and Stephen Kingon of PricewaterhouseCoopers, Chris Gibson, Imelda McGrath of the Northern Ireland Housing Executive, Brendan McAllister of the Mediation Network, David Cook, Harry Castles, Austen Morgan, Chris Anderson and Noel McAdam provided us with many useful ideas and information. Our good friends Richard Ford and Ken Reid are due thanks for reading the manuscript, as is Sandra T, who efficiently transcribed many hours of taped interviews for us.

Once again it is necessary to acknowledge the help of Walter Macauley, whose encyclopaedic knowledge of Northern Ireland, its troubles and people is immense. Yvonne Murphy and her staff who run the Political Collection at the Linen Hall Library also produced material of which we made great use. We must acknowledge the help of Tony Cesari and the *Irish Times* Studio for allowing us to reproduce the map of the Drumcree and Garvaghy Road areas of Portadown.

We also want to thank: Max Eilenberg at Methuen for commissioning this book; Eleanor Rees for her sharp editing skills in processing the text for publication; and our agent, Anthony Goff at David Higham Associates Ltd in London.

Above all we want to express our appreciation to our families for their patience, encouragement and support while everything else took second place to 'the book'.

Vincent wants to thank his wife, Louise, and Vincent, Ronan and Niall, as well as baby Megan, who arrived early, just as the last chapter was being written, for putting up with the lack of attention. His gratitude to 'Nanny' Imelda Faloon, who expertly kept the children constructively diverted, is also acknowledged. Vincent dedicates it to his late grandmother, Annie Sullivan, who unfortunately did not live to see the book she always encouraged him to write.

Chris wishes to thank his wife Genny, for her enduring tolerance, and to dedicate it to his granddaughters, Ciara, who liked the 'com-puter', and Erin, who was also born virtually as the last full stop was being typed.

Chris Ryder and Vincent Kearney
Belfast, April 2001

List of Illustrations

All photographs © Kelvin Boyes Photography

Introduction

Shortly before 10 am on the morning of Sunday 17 March 1985, the 29 members of St Patrick's Accordion Band gathered at Obins Street in Portadown on the annual celebration day of Ireland's national saint, from whom they take their name. As was their longstanding custom, they intended to march the immediate area before departing by bus for a major parade at Cookstown that afternoon. In the early evening, when they returned, there would be another short march before they dispersed into the local clubs and pubs for a night of drinking, singing and dancing – what the Irish call 'craic'. That day there was a new dimension to the commemoration, the high point of the band's annual calendar. After four years of unsuccessful pleading, the Royal Ulster Constabulary, whose unenviable task it was to maintain law and order within Northern Ireland's deeply divided society, had finally relented and given the band clearance to march along Park Road in the interests of what was described as 'good community relations'. So, instead of having to turn back half way along the Garvaghy Road at Churchill Park and retrace their steps, the band would now be allowed to complete a circuit of the neighbourhood.

When Councillor Wolsey Smith heard of the plan he was outraged. In the context of Northern Ireland's rigid sectarian geography, Park Road was a Protestant area, and in his book Catholics, like those in the Accordion Band, had no business marching there. Smith was a prominent follower of the militant Protestant leader the Reverend Ian Paisley, and was both a member of his Democratic Unionist political party and an elder in his Free Presbyterian church. He publicly shared his leader's 'no surrender' views and strongly articulated them as an elected representative on the local Craigavon Borough Council. So that Sunday morning, as the band was forming up and tuning its instruments, Smith had mustered about 100 like-minded supporters and the Reverend Kenneth Elliott, the minister of the local Bethany Free Presbyterian Church, for an impromptu 'prayer service', to make a protest and stop the march, while staying nominally within the law.

Across the town at about the same time, Arnold Hatch, the proprietor of a small engineering firm and an Ulster Unionist councillor, who was also the current mayor of Craigavon, was at home getting ready to go to church. 'The telephone rang and I was asked to go down to Park Road where the residents were concerned about the safety of their homes if the parade was allowed through,' he recalls. When he got there he found Smith, Elliott and their congregation gathered by the side of Park Road, praying and singing hymns. 'The road was not blocked but they had spilled over from the footpath to the side of the road because of their numbers,' he remembers. Hatch now claims he was only there for ten or fifteen minutes. 'I made a short speech through a loudhailer seeking to reassure the residents and telling them that I would contact the police and ask them to ensure that their homes were protected as far as possible.'

A short distance away around the corner, by Woodside Hill at the south end of the Garvaghy Road, there was already a strong police presence. A cordon had been formed across the road by several of the RUC's distinctive battleship-grey armoured Land Rovers and several dozen officers were being deployed. When the band reached the police line it was halted, and the marchers were told by a senior police officer that permission to proceed along Park Road had been withdrawn. The police wanted to avoid any breach of the peace arising from what would inevitably have become a confrontation with the Protestant protestors. When they heard that the parade had been stopped, the prayer meeting erupted in cheers, but back at the police cordon there were prolonged angry exchanges between the leaders of the band and the police before the marchers turned and walked back to the waiting transport in Obins Street. By this time Hatch says he had returned home, called the RUC as promised and then left to attend his own church service at 11 am.

There were no further incidents during the day but that evening, around 6.30 pm, there was great tension when the band returned and set off on its second march. Again the police refused to allow them along Park Road, but this time trouble broke out and some of the band's supporters became involved in stone-throwing attacks on several Protestant homes in the Woodside Hill complex. Three elderly men, aged 66, 80 and 89, who were watching television, were showered with broken glass when stones shattered the window of one dwelling, and in the front room of another, a few doors away, £100-worth of tropical fish perished when a stone fractured their tank.

The day's events produced immediate recriminations. Band leaders accused the police of discrimination and of caving in to the threat of violence from Smith and his supporters. They said they had not broken the law and that the police should have provided protection for them to complete the agreed march route. After all, they pointed out, the police always provided sufficient protection to enable thousands of Orange marchers to pass along Obins Street, also known as the Tunnel, every summer. 'If the Orangemen can parade through the area during the Twelfth then we should be able to parade through Garvaghy and Park Road,' a spokesman told the *Portadown Times*. Much of the Catholic ire was particularly directed at the inconsistency of Hatch, an Orangeman himself, whose tall, gangly figure always singled him out in the ranks of the marchers along Obins Street. 'As the Mayor of Craigavon, supposed to represent all the people, he should have stayed away,' the paper was told. A few days later a group of Sinn Fein protesters filed discreetly into the public gallery at the start of a council meeting before interrupting a discussion about the forthcoming agricultural show with a noisy protest about the halted march. Hatch, who was in the chair, was accused of discrimination against the Nationalist people of Portadown. 'We'll walk over the top of you,' one of them shouted before they were ejected from the council chamber by the police.

Wolsey Smith, the real architect of the confrontation, remained unrepentant. 'The request to re-route the march was a pure act of provocation, designed to annoy the Loyalist people. We were delighted our protest was a success. Allowing the march would have been an unacceptable departure from tradition,' he told the *Portadown Times*. The entire episode prompted Councillor Dan Murphy, a Social Democratic and Labour Party councillor who represented the Catholics in the town, to announce, in grimly prophetic terms, that he was quitting public life. 'I've simply had enough of the sectarianism in local politics. I simply cannot see any hope for moderation.'

Although they appeared of little lasting consequence at the time when compared with the ongoing enormities of the wider communal conflict, which at that point after almost two decades of escalating and ever more violent terrorism had already claimed some 2700 lives, the comparatively minor events that Sunday morning in Portadown would prove to be a turning point of great historical significance. By stimulating dangerous old resentments on both sides, they sowed the seeds for a much more toxic confrontation which would incubate for another ten years or so before finally erupting in a sustained crisis, at nearby Drumcree, which would ultimately engulf the entire community.

Indeed, 'Drumcree' would come to be an internationally recognised byword, symbolising the unyielding intransigence of the people of

Northern Ireland, their pre-occupation with marching, although from opposing standpoints, and the wider political differences that divide them. From 1995 onwards, the course of events provoked by successive July confrontations in the town would destructively ripple far beyond the confines of Portadown. Lives would be lost, the vital tourism industry would be crippled and economic confidence and inward investment seriously compromised. The issues raised by the crisis would defeat the most high-powered efforts at resolution by the British prime minister and a series of professional mediators. The dilemmas it presented would shake some of the most powerful institutions, especially the Orange Order and the Church of Ireland, to their very foundations. Its mishandling of the problem would also play a major part in consigning the beleaguered Royal Ulster Constabulary to the history books. Apart from the incalculable cost, in terms of sundered community relations and consolidated political division, the prolonged crisis forced the British government and taxpayers into massive expenditure to contain sustained public disorder.

At issue is an annual church parade by some 1200 members of the all-Protestant Orange Order and two bands, who insist on what they see as their inalienable civil right to march along the Garvaghy Road in Portadown despite the fact that the Catholic community who live there are overwhelmingly opposed to the passage of the march and believe it is their right not to have to endure it. While many Orangemen regard the Order as a religious and cultural institution, others cherish it as an instrument of supremacy for asserting domination over Catholics. With Britain and Ireland forging ever closer links to cope jointly with the trials and tribulations of their common Northern Ireland problem, these uncompromising Orangemen increasingly see themselves as being politically and culturally emasculated. For them, and for the unruly Loyalist elements who have made common cause with them, Drumcree has come to symbolise this loss. For them, it is the Orange Order's last stand.

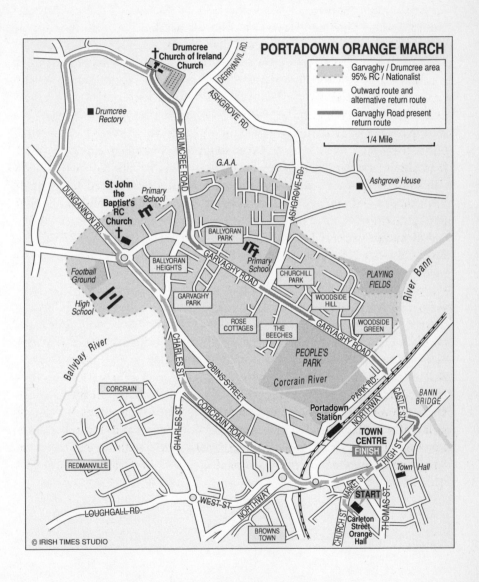

PORTADOWN ORANGE MARCH

Garvaghy / Drumcree area 95% RC / Nationalist

Outward route and alternative return route

Garvaghy Road present return route

1/4 Mile

Drumcree Church of Ireland Church

Drumcree Rectory

DERRYANVIL RD.

ASHGROVE RD.

DRUMCREE ROAD

DUNGANNON RD.

G.A.A.

Ashgrove House

St John the Baptist's RC Church

Primary School

ASHGROVE RD.

BALLYORAN PARK

Primary School

BALLYORAN HEIGHTS

GARVAGHY ROAD

CHURCHILL PARK

PLAYING FIELDS

River Bann

Football Ground

GARVAGHY PARK

WOODSIDE HILL

WOODSIDE GREEN

High School

ROSE COTTAGES

THE BEECHES

GARVAGHY ROAD

Ballybay River

PEOPLE'S PARK

Corcrain River

CHARLES ST.

OBINS STREET

CORCRAIN

Portadown Station

PARK RD.

NORTHWAY

CASTLE ST.

BANN BRIDGE

CHARLES ST.

CORCRAIN ROAD

TOWN CENTRE
FINISH

HIGH ST.

REDMANVILLE

Town Hall

WEST ST.

NORTHWAY

START
Carleton Street Orange Hall

MARKET ST.

CHURCH ST.

THOMAS ST.

LOUGHGALL RD.

BROWNS TOWN

© IRISH TIMES STUDIO

Chapter One
The Vatican of Orangeism

Gaudy banners twisting in the wind; sinewed forearms beating canes on thundering Lambeg drums; shrill flutes; frenzied drummers; sashed, bowler-hatted marchers in their best suits; strutting, buxom ladies in Union Jack dresses; empty bottles and discarded glasses ankle-deep in pubs along the route: some of the commonest sights and sounds associated with Orange marches in Northern Ireland. Orangemen like to present their annual festival as a celebration of civil and religious liberty, expressing their cultural heritage and identity in a spectacle of marching enjoyed by all. The reality can be quite different. The parades that dominate the summer months often do so provocatively and selfishly without regard to the cost in terms of community relations or the public purse. Some of the marches are unmistakably triumphal. Participants see them as a continuing and vigorous manifestation of their Protestantism, Unionism and loyalty to the British Crown. They subconsciously underline divisions and seek to assert ascendancy. Some have likened the way that local lodges parade the limits of their parishes to the way that a tomcat marks out territory, signalling the Orangemen's unyielding belief that they are a powerful majority who will resist any process of change. The marchers say that they have learnt from history the need for eternal vigilance, and their argot is studded with the concept of uncompromising defiance ensuring defence against an enemy. In the complex anatomy of Orangeism, the twin devotion to God and Ulster provides a seamless link between the Protestant religion and Unionist politics.

This longstanding Orange culture in turn provides the basis for equally profitless Catholic, Nationalist and Republican hostility to the Order. The lodges' insistence on marching anywhere at any time, and the bands' habit of playing louder as they pass Catholic churches and neighbourhoods, have helped to thwart any prospect of a mutually respectful relationship. In fact, Catholics see the Order as the all-powerful instrument through which they were consigned to second-class citizenship in Northern Ireland for decades after partition in 1922. The Orange thread, they believe, ran influentially through the Unionist establishment, like a nervous system through a body, from the government and judiciary at the top to the councils and employers denying them jobs and houses at the bottom. Life, they believe, was constantly manipulated to their disadvantage and Orange 'coat-trailing' marches were allowed, and on occasions forced, through Catholic areas, where they were not welcome, in an attempt to demonstrate superiority. Given that the Order was formed to preserve the Protestant faith and later to defend it, Catholics see the Order's regular proclamation of civil and religious liberty for all as a hollow proposition.

These conflicting perceptions are at their most tangible over the attitude to marching bands. While there are many inoffensive silver, brass, pipe and accordion bands who lead Orange lodges when they march, there are also what the Orange community call 'blood and thunder' bands whose boisterous behaviour, partisan tunes and pseudo-military uniforms provide a rallying point for, and a musical expression of, the defiance which is one of the most marked features of Orange culture. Catholics, on the other hand, describe them as 'Kick the Pope' bands. Republicans indeed have come to see them as such a potent form of intimidation that they have in recent years copied the formula and developed their own cadres of musical shock troops, similarly clad in paramilitary-style khaki or often terrorist-like black uniforms. They have also copied the pounding drums and shrill flutes and developed a repertoire of equally partisan tunes.

Marching has long been a predominant feature of life and political expression in Northern Ireland and, as history shows, a consistent source of trouble, violence and regular deaths. The vast bulk of the parades are concentrated into a period from Easter until the end of August, known as the 'marching season', when the weather is usually more congenial for outside activity. The level of parading has risen steadily from 1985, when there were 2120, to 1994, when there were 2792 marches. That year, by comparison, in two major British cities with significant cultural affinity to Northern Ireland and much larger populations, the right to march was more sparingly exercised: 1118 times in Strathclyde, which includes Glasgow, and 425 times in the Merseyside area, centred on the city of Liverpool. From April 1999 to April 2000, for instance, there were 3383 parades in Northern Ireland, 36 of them illegal. This figure includes 536 marches not classified as Loyalist or Nationalist: cultural and religious processions; trade unionists commemorating May Day with a march through Belfast; the Lord Mayor of the city, in common with the civic leaders of many other towns and villages, holding an annual parade, and university students organising 'rag day' parades to assist their fund-raising. However, the overwhelming number of processions are hosted by one or other of what are called the 'marching orders'. On the Protestant, Unionist and Loyalist side the main marching orders are the Orange Order, the Apprentice Boys of Derry and the Royal Black Institution, who together account for 2644 marches of the 1999/2000 total. The Ancient Order of Hibernians is the longest-established marching organisation on the Catholic, Nationalist and Republican side. Their marches are numbered among the 203 by Nationalist and Republican groups. In more recent years a growing culture of band marching, every bit as vigorous as that of their Loyalist counterparts, has flourished among the young activist Republican community, mainly to commemorate episodes during the years of the Troubles such as the introduction of internment in 1971 and the deaths of ten hunger strikers at the Maze prison in 1981. Despite the highly provocative behaviour of some of these bands and marchers – on both sides, it must be stressed – all but a few of the processions pass off without serious incident. In 1999/2000 the police recorded disorder at only twelve parades, although 114 were re-routed and another 24 had conditions imposed, and this has been a consistent and apparently tranquil pattern over the years. However, the handful of contentious parades where disorder actually occurs have, as we shall see when we look at the detailed history of Drumcree, a perpetually potent capacity to bring the whole of Northern Ireland to a standstill and create full-scale political crises. It was always thus.

Confrontations and violent clashes arising from parades stud the history of Northern Ireland over the years. Indeed, in a turbulent eleven months from October 1968 to August 1969, a series of marches and counter-marches by civil rights campaigners and their hardline Unionist opponents overwhelmed the under-equipped and untrained RUC and forced the British government to deploy the Army to prevent all-out sectarian conflict and civil war. In a bid to calm the situation, the authorities imposed curfews (which turned out to be short-lived) on the pubs and bans on all parades save those of the Salvation Army. But so strong was the instinct to march ingrained in the community mindset that the ban proved unworkable and the authorities were forced to relent. As a result, during 1970, in the city of Belfast alone, the hard-pressed police were forced to deploy 13,258 officers to control 51 parades. With ill-concealed frustration the then chief constable, Sir Graham Shillington, wrote in his annual report: 'Many of these events carried enormous danger potential in a city where experience has shown that even minor incidents can generate widespread and vicious rioting. While parades do not represent the sole danger to peace and order, it would nevertheless be a signal contribution if the organisers of such efforts, wherever they may be, were to co-operate more fully with the police in the selection of routes which avoided flashpoints as far as possible.' It was a cry for common sense and moderation that had been made, and ignored, many times before, and it would be repeated in identical terms, and equally in vain, by his successors in the years ahead.

To fully understand why marching is such an important imperative in the interlocking political, religious and cultural spheres of each side of the deeply divided Northern Ireland society, and in Portadown in particular, some people will tell you, in all sincerity, that it is necessary to go as far back as Adam and Eve. However, for our primary purpose, comprehending why a regular Sunday morning church parade which takes place once a year in a modest market town has become such an enduring source of conflict and deadlock, going back a mere three centuries will suffice.

The course of events that was ultimately to culminate in confrontation at Drumcree has its real origins at the Diamond, a cluster of mud-walled, straw-thatched buildings at a crossroads in the Barony of Lower Grange, four miles north of the larger village settlement of Loughgall, in turn closer to what was then the major market town of Portadown. Records compiled by Quakers, dating back to 1665, show that the buildings at the Diamond were occupied by Dan Winter and his sons, who farmed and reared livestock in the adjacent fields. Dan Winter's descendants still live on some of the same land to this day.

Although King William of Orange, with a 36,000-strong multi-national army of English, Irish, Dutch, Brandenburger, Prussian, French Huguenot, Swiss, Swedish and Norwegian soldiers, had overcome the 25,000 combatants loyal to King James at the Battle of the Boyne in 1690, the largest ever military engagement in Irish history, the victory failed to settle the great issues of the day in Ireland, most notably the relationship between what it is best to describe simply as Catholics and Protestants. While the Catholic King had been routed and forced to flee during the twelve-day campaign, the sectarian differences remained and relationships were continually aggravated by a range of other grievances. Catholics felt suppressed by the Penal Laws, which excluded them from celebrating mass or voting, outlawed inter-marriage, restricted their right to education and prohibited them from the professions. Protestants, who had the upper hand (excepting the Presbyterians who were also subject to the Penal Laws), feared that lifting such measures would lead to a loss of political and economic control.

In the latter half of the 1700s a series of rival oath-bound secret societies imposed a reign of terror on rural Ireland. One of the most feared of these mainly peasant-based groups was the Whiteboys, who waged war on the landlords and tax collectors and who took dreadful revenge on anyone who attacked its members. Other groups had names like the Rightboys, Ribbonmen, Thrashers, Peep o'Day Boys and Levellers. Although most were motivated by agrarian grievances, some, especially from the north of Ireland, had a distinct sectarian tinge. Whatever their motivation, however, their crimes were remarkable for their brutality. They would descend on property and plunder food, arms and money before burning the buildings and either killing or stealing the livestock. Those who got in their way were mutilated, raped, abducted or shot, and those who dared give evidence against the attackers were singled out for special treatment. A man who had testified against the organisers of one secret society was later taken from his home, beaten to a pulp with stones and then pitchforked on to a dungheap. His wife was shot through the temple with a pistol.

In 1793, according to another typical horror story, related to the Irish House of Commons by the MP Thomas Verner, a schoolmaster and his family were savagely murdered by a Catholic group known as the Defenders at Forkhill in County Armagh. When houses on the Jackson estate were attacked and the inhabitants shot, the man concealed his wife and declined to reveal where she was. 'The ruffians then put a cord round his throat and so forced out his tongue, which they cut off. His fingers were next cut off joint by joint. His wife, unable to stand the piteous cries, rushed out of her hiding place and she was also barbarously treated. Her breasts were first cut off, then her fingers, joint by joint, and her little son was then mutilated like his father.'

Matters came to a head in 1795 when William, Earl of Fitzwilliam, was appointed Lord Lieutenant of Ireland. Soon after his arrival Henry Grattan, the distinguished orator and parliamentarian, introduced the Catholic Relief Bill to the Irish legislature in Dublin. It was designed to remedy what he had described as a 'pernicious and profligate system which has made Ireland a disgrace before the world'. The British Cabinet objected to the measure, singled out Fitzwilliam, who was in favour of Catholic Emancipation, for blame and promptly replaced him with John Pratt, the Earl of Camden, who took office against a background of widespread disorder and rioting. In May 1975 the House of Commons defeated Grattan's bill 158 to 48, a decision that helped lead to the formation of the United Irishmen, a secret, oath-bound society, with both Catholic and Protestant members, committed to breaking the link with Britain and forming an Irish Republic.

Meanwhile sectarian clashes between the rival secret societies continued unabated, reaching a climax on 21 September 1795. What happened at the Battle of the Diamond that day remains of lasting significance for Protestants. The Orange historian W H Wolsey, in a booklet published in 1923, recalled how Catholic groups firing into and burning houses and driving off cattle had struck fear and terror into the hearts of the Protestants. He describes how the Defenders became so bold that the Protestants had to form themselves into companies to go to market and return in safety. In autumn of that year the Defenders in Monaghan, Cavan and Tyrone were of such numbers that they determined on a grand foray and cattle raid in County Armagh. On 14 September they assembled at Tentaraghan and began systematically to raid and loot Protestant farms in the locality. The Protestants hit back by attacking some of the homes of the Defenders, and four days later there was a serious skirmish when Protestant Peep o' Day Boys exchanged gunfire with Defenders at the Diamond. Undeterred by this, the Defenders marched on past Loughgall and on 18 September a force at least 500 strong took possession of Faughart Hill, which overlooked the Diamond crossroads, where they established camp and hoisted a white flag as standard. Alarmed at this development, the Protestants, determined to defend their homes, assembled within firing range on the Cranagill Hill, which also overlooked the cross-roads, and an uneasy stand-off developed. Efforts to resolve it peacefully seemed to have succeeded when 'articles of amity' were drawn up, but by early Monday morning, after a weekend of sniping and skirmishing between the two sides, the accord melted and a full scale battle erupted. The Defenders' main objective was to seize Dan Winter's cottage, but according to Protestant history, although its thatched roof was fired and the Winters driven out, the land at the Diamond was heroically defended. The Reverend Stewart Blacker, the Dean of Leighlin, diverted lead intended for the re-roofing of his Carrickblacker mansion to be melted and shaped into bullets instead. Peggy Richardson, whose brothers and husband were among the Protestant fighting force, concealed her four-year-old child in a haystack before setting out with two pillow-slips full of gunpowder attached to her petticoat to help relieve the shortage of firepower. Protestant reinforcements soon arrived and attacked the Defenders from the rear, putting them to flight. Wolsey recalls:

> So closely were the Defenders pursued that, in their hurried retreat,
> they left in the hands of the victors plunder of the viler sort: old guns,
> rusty bayonets fixed on poles, pikes, spades, scythes, reaping hooks,

tattered green uniforms, ragged pieces of antiquity in the shape of coats, brogues, wooden crosses, crucifixes, with several white and green flags, which did not do much credit to the artist, one of which however, deserves mention. It was the Defenders' rallying standard: a white ground with a green shamrock border, and on it was painted the Virgin Mary, presiding as a goddess, with a bunch of beads in her hand, and underneath the following inscription: 'Deliver us from these heretic dogs and then we shall be free.' After the dead, numbering about 50, some dressed in clothes plundered from Protestant houses, had been removed and the wounded attended to, according to Orange folklore, the jubilant Protestants assembled in the little field before the wrecked house of Dan Winter, and kneeling around with uplifted hands to heaven, thanked God for his great deliverance. There they vowed to form a society for their mutual defence and protection against such trials as they had just come through.

They called this society the Orange Order, in honour of King William, and closely modelled its structure on the Freemasons, creating a system of lodges based in different localities. Orange history has it that the first member was actually sworn in, pledging brotherhood in loyalty to the monarchy, the constitution and the Protestant ascendancy, at a bush beside the spring well in Dan Winter's garden, but the first formal meeting of the Loyal Orange Institution, as it is also known, appears to have taken place in James Sloan's Inn at nearby Loughgall where there is presently a small Orange museum. Sloan emerged as the first leader, issuing hand-written warrants to the founding lodges. The early membership was drawn heavily from the labouring and artisan classes. Few of the landed gentry joined up, but prominent among the membership in the early days was the Reverend George Maunsell, Rector of Drumcree from 1781 to 1804, establishing, virtually from the very outset, what would prove to be a portentous link. The Order expanded rapidly in its first few months, with district and county lodges being formed among its estimated 2500 members, so its leaders decided to convene a delegate meeting in Portadown to ensure uniformity of rules and practice. They chose to hold the meeting on 12 July 1796, the anniversary of the Battle of the Boyne, and organised a march to coincide with it. A contemporary newspaper report described a march the same day in nearby Lurgan as consisting of 'a motley group of turncoats, Methodists, seceders and high churchmen with a multitude of boys and country trolls cheering the lagging heroes'. Nevertheless, the events of the day initiated what was to be a lasting tradition and firmly established the town of Portadown, together with the landmark shrines at the Diamond and Loughgall, in its immediate hinterland, as the very heartland, or the 'Vatican', of Orangeism.

Given its rapid expansion and the values it espoused, it was inevitable that the fledgling Order would take the Crown side in the abortive 1798 Rebellion and play a part in the defeat of the United Irishmen, who, inspired by the American and French Revolutions, wanted an end to England's role in Ireland. (While modern Republicans claim their line of descent from them, they have never been able to emulate the way the United Irishmen brought together Catholic, Protestant and dissenter under a single umbrella.) Highly exaggerated tales of Orange heroism in the aftermath of the fighting helped swell membership throughout the island of Ireland. Emboldened by the failure of the attempt to create an Irish republic, the British moved to bring in an Act of Union, abolishing the Irish parliament and creating a single government for Great Britain and Ireland. However, the grass-roots members of the Orange Order, especially in the north, were far from unanimous on the merits of this proposal, not least because of existing resentment that a group of politicians in Dublin had earlier succeeded in gaining control of the Grand Lodge of Ireland and moving it from Armagh to the capital. In a bid to preserve unity, the Grand Lodge issued statements in December 1798 and January 1799 advising Orangemen 'strictly to abstain from expressing any opinion pro or con upon the question of a legislative union between this country and Great Britain, because such expressions of opinion, and such discussion in lodges would only lead to disunion'. In practice, the aristocracy, gentry, clergy and professions were in favour and it was the rank and file membership who opposed the measure, fearing it would lead to full Catholic emancipation. Orange lodges in the northern part of the island were the most vociferous opponents. On 1 March 1800, 31 lodges meeting at the Maze, County Down, resolved that the legislative union would be 'the inevitable ruin to peace, prosperity and happiness in this kingdom'. Twelve days later another 36 lodges from Armagh and Monaghan adopted a resolution in similar terms and in defiance of another call for unity, this time from the Grand Lodge of Antrim meeting in Belfast.

The act was passed on 1 August 1800 and became law on 1 January 1801 with the amalgamation of the London and Dublin parliaments. For a time afterwards the rapid expansion of the Order halted and member-ship actually declined. Nevertheless, the Order continued to mark King William's victory every July, regularly provoking trouble in the process, notably in the city of Belfast where the early 1800s were marked by a series of sectarian clashes and riots. The British governments of the time were no friends of the Order and, in 1823, attempted to deal it a fatal blow as part of a measure aimed at discouraging the secret societies who were still responsible for significant lawlessness throughout Ireland. The instrument to contain them was the Unlawful Oaths Act which dragged the Order into its provisions. The lodges' indignation was expressed by a statement from the Armagh County Grand Lodge: 'We feel not less surprised than grieved that Orange associations should be accused of illegal interference in the state, or branded as an intolerant and perse-cuting faction ... Where in this land have the laws been so well enforced and so cheerfully obeyed as in those districts where the Orange association has more power and influence? ... and we call on them to show in all the outrages and rebellious insults which have disgraced the very name of Ireland, where had the true Orangemen been found who were not ranged on the side of these laws?' In 1824, in an attempt to meet the requirements of the Act, the Grand Lodge commissioned the pro-duction of a new constitution and rules which would be legally acceptable to Parliament in every particular, but the legal pinch forced the Grand Orange Lodge of Ireland to ban the 12 July processions that year. James Verner, the Grand Master, appealed to all Orangemen 'to act in the most strict conformity with an order which tends so strongly to show how much the members of the Orange Association are willing to sacrifice to the feelings and even prejudices of their fellow subjects and how desirous they are that no excuses should be left for ascribing any of the disorders that afflict Ireland to their conduct of example'. However, the Grand Lodge was forced to dissolve itself on 18 March 1825 after the passage of the Unlawful Societies (Ireland) Act which proscribed the Orange Order as well as the increasingly powerful Catholic Association. The final meeting of Grand Lodge was held in Dublin and addressed a closing statement to all lodges stating: 'At no period was the Institution in a more flourishing condition, or more highly respectable in the number added to its ranks. Notwithstanding which, the Parliament of the United Kingdom have considered it necessary that all political societies should be dissolved. Of course, our society is included. It therefore becomes our duty to inform you that any lodge meeting after this date commits a breach of the law.' The warning was only partially observed. Many lodges remained in existence and even marched on 12 July, some of the parades causing what had now become customary trouble in Belfast and elsewhere. These activist elements of the Order were predominantly working-class.

The Act was also aimed at curbing the ever more effective activities of the Catholic Association, led by Daniel O'Connell who had emerged as the champion of a militant campaign seeking better conditions for Catholics, whose rights remained heavily circumscribed. The Association's activities, which to the now clandestine Orangemen increasingly threatened to erode the Protestant ascendancy so dear to them, directly contributed to its public renaissance in September 1827, when the Grand Orange Lodge was reconstituted after the act lapsed. O'Connell's intensive campaign succeeded in winning Catholic emancipation in 1829, giving Catholics access to a wide range of state, political and military offices, and clearing the way for O'Connell himself to take a seat in the House of Commons a year later. As MP for County Clare he was the first Catholic to sit there since the Reformation. O'Connell now set a new priority to 'Repeal the Union', an objective which renewed Protestant anxieties about the effects of Emancipation and led many to turn to the Order, in large numbers, for leadership in their determination to contest it and maintain the union. That year, thousands of Orangemen defied a Lord Lieutenant's proclamation banning the July marches. Riots and disturbances erupted in Belfast and eight other towns. Jonathan Bardon's authoritative *History of Ulster* records: 'Over the next few days broken heads and broken windows were of hourly occurrence. There was fierce rioting in Armagh; stone-throwing at Greyabbey; a "fatal recountre" near Enniskillen; Orangemen shot three men in Strabane; at least four were killed at Coalisland; and other lives were also lost at Stewartstown, the Moy and Portglenone (where in that district alone some twenty deaths were reported).'

Dr Henry Cooke, a fiery Presbyterian preacher, emerged at the forefront of those opposing emancipation. In October 1834 he called on a crowd of 40,000 assembled at Hillsborough, County Down, to maintain a united front against Home Rule. O'Connell's work to 'repeal the union' failed to succeed, but the government of the day became progressively more alarmed by the activities of the Order and the constant tension and frequent disorder to which its activities contributed. They were particularly concerned that despite calls for restraint, even from the Grand Lodge itself, what were described as 'the rougher elements' continued to march whatever the consequences. This defiance continued despite the passing of a Party Processions Bill in 1832 and prosecution of some Orangemen. For instance, Colonel William Blacker, who had been present at the battle of the Diamond, was deprived of his commission as a justice of the peace after Lurgan and Portadown Orange Lodges paraded on the lawns at his Carrickblacker house for fifteen minutes on 12 July. Inside the Order, the issue had opened up a major rift. According to the

Order's own account of its history: 'When the question of the right of Orangemen to march in procession was asked many felt that the leaders were far removed from the rank and file in their thinking. It was contended that the leaders were only concerned with the Constitution, Repeal and the situation of the Established Church. The determination of the Orangemen to have their processions and demonstrations took no thought of the effects of these on Westminster and their enemies there and elsewhere.'

At Westminster, however, politicians were so concerned about the Order that a parliamentary committee was established to study its activities and influence. It heard how the leadership was unable to control the membership, and even unearthed signs of an Orange plot to put the Duke of Cumberland on the throne. In evidence submitted to the committee, which shows the unchanging mindset of Orangemen in Northern Ireland over the years, William J Hancock, a Protestant and a County Armagh magistrate, said, 'For some time past the peaceable inhabitants of the parish of Drumcree have been insulted and outraged by large bodies of Orangemen parading the highways, playing party tunes, firing shots, and using the most opprobrious epithets they could invent. A body of Orangemen, wearing Orange lilies, marched through the town ... and proceeded to Drumcree Church, passing by the Catholic chapel though it was a considerable distance out of their way.'

The House of Commons passed its highly critical three-volume report to the King, William IV, who proclaimed on 25 February 1836 that, in line with Parliament's conclusions, he would be 'pleased to take such measures as may be seen to be advisable for the effectual discouragement of Orange lodges and generally of all political societies, excluding persons of a different religious faith, using secret signs and symbols, and acting by means of associated branches'. The very next day, in a preemptive strike to forestall any government action, the Home Secretary was given an assurance by Cumberland that he would 'take immediate steps to dissolve the Loyal Orange Institution in Great Britain'. The northern Irish refused to think of dissolution with Armagh District leading the opposition. Although the Grand Lodge of Ireland voted 79 to 59 in favour of winding itself up on 13 April, many lodges acted as they had done in 1825 and just carried on. Control of the Order passed back to its heartland on 13 June when Armagh County Grand Lodge resolved: 'That the business of the Institution in this country be entrusted, as in the early days, to Grand Lodge of the same until the Grand Lodge of Ireland resumes its function.' Grand Lodge was eventually reconstructed on 15 November 1837 in Dublin and by 1845, the Party Processions Act having expired, the Orangemen were able to demonstrate openly again. The July parades continued throughout the period but the Boyne celebrations had increasingly become a working class affair, inevitably producing disorder and sectarian clashes, which were clearly a source of embarrassment. 'In these days of education and enlightenment,' proclaimed the *Belfast Newsletter* in July 1846, 'Protestantism and loyalty have discovered better modes of asserting themselves than by wearing sashes and walking to the music of the fife and drum.' Nevertheless the sectarian clashes continued, especially in Belfast, where the evolution of the city's industry had attracted large numbers of people to settle. A July 1849 clash at Dolly's Brae in County Down was typical. Thirty people were killed when Catholic Ribbonmen and Orange marchers clashed. Following the incident, in March 1850, another Party Processions Act was introduced. Again the grassroots defied the law and their leadership, continued to mark the Twelfth and provoked the inevitable rioting. By this time, 'hellfire and brimstone' sermons had become customary on Orange platforms, delivered by the likes of Cooke and the Reverend Hugh 'Roaring Hanna', forebears in style and doctrine of the Reverend Ian Paisley over a century later. The practice of putting up arches and bunting across the streets also dates from this time. Although some marchers were prosecuted, the magistrates and the police tended to turn a blind eye to demonstrations which remained within Protestant localities, but, as the events of 12 July 1867 illustrate, the Orange Order remained capable of putting large crowds on the streets when its cause demanded it. That day, William Johnston of Ballykilbeg, who was opposed to renewed legal curbs on Orange marches, led 100 Orange lodges, with 40,000 people as participants or spectators, in procession from Newtownards to Bangor. Johnston and 23 others were charged. They subsequently pleaded guilty and were fined but Johnston insisted on going to prison, serving a few days short of two months before his release on 27 April 1868. Ten thousand people and bands were at the prison gate that day to greet him and bonfires were lit on many of the country hills that night. Grand Lodge disapproved of Johnston, showing yet again that it was out of step and sympathy with rank-and-file opinion.

No great issue dominated the middle years of the nineteenth century, but the Order suffered a setback in 1869, the year after William Ewart Gladstone came to power and secured parliamentary approval for the disestablishment of the Church of Ireland. Gladstone, who had earlier said, 'Ireland forces upon us these great social and great religious questions, God grant that we may have courage to look them in the face and to work through them,' now declared that it was his 'mission to pacify Ireland'. Thereafter the central theme of his political career was to create Home Rule for Ireland by re-establishing an Irish legislature in Dublin. Protestants, and the Orange Order, were fundamentally opposed to the concept. They envisaged it as a Catholic-dominated body challenging their ascendancy and economic power, which, moreover, would open a window of opportunity for those who were continually clamouring for an end to the union and the creation of an independent Ireland. Over the coming years and into the early part of the twentieth century, these fears would galvanise the Orange Order and see it emerge as the crucial power-broking force in the new politics of Ulster Unionism.

The Grand Lodge of Ireland entered the fray against Home Rule in December 1885 by calling on all lodges to demonstrate. Gladstone's first Home Rule Bill fell in June 1886, when it was defeated 343 to 311 in the House of Commons. That month the worst sectarian rioting of the century erupted in Belfast docks and spread throughout the city. By the time the disorder subsided in September, 31 public houses had been wrecked, 32 people had been killed (including seven shot by the police), 377 were injured and 442 arrests had been made.

Gladstone lost the general election, fought on the issue, in July and went into opposition. While he remained committed to the policy of Home Rule, it was not until 1893 that he had the opportunity to introduce the legislation for a second attempt. This time, while the bill was passed by the Commons, it was rejected by the House of Lords. Throughout this period, as the threat to the union evolved, the Order was once more fully respectable and the middle classes, aristocracy and politicians again filed into its ranks. Lord Randolph Churchill, a leading member of the British Conservatives, whose father, the eighth Duke of Marlborough, had been Lord Lieutenant of Ireland, was a powerful opponent of Home Rule and famously inspired an Orange audience at a rally in the Ulster Hall, Belfast on 23 February 1886, when he declared: 'Ulster will fight. Ulster will be right.' In a letter to Gerald Fitzgibbon, the Solicitor General in Ireland in 1877 and a leading Freemason in Dublin, Churchill wrote, 'I decided some time ago that if the Government of Her Majesty went for Home Rule, the Orange Card would be the one to play. Please God it may turn out to be the Ace of Trumps and not the Two.' The defeat of the first bill was greeted by bonfires on the hills around Belfast and seven years later, before the second bill was introduced in February 1893, the Order again went into action to campaign against it. Orange delegates and members were among the 12,000 people who attended the inaugural Ulster Unionist Convention in Belfast's Botanic Gardens on 17 June 1892 which led to the formation of Unionist clubs throughout the north of Ireland.

Colonel Edward Saunderson, the wealthy land-owning MP for North Armagh and a prominent Orangeman, struck a characteristic chord of uncompromising defiance when he declared soon afterwards that even if the Home Rule Bill passed the House of Commons 'it will never pass the bridge at Portadown.' The following month, Gladstone returned to power after the general election and formed the fourth administration of his marathon 61-year parliamentary career. In February 1893 he brought in the second Home Rule Bill, prompting an estimated 100,000 members of the Orange Order to demonstrate their continued opposition with a four-hour march in Belfast on 4 April 1893.

Having seen off Home Rule again for the present, the internal tensions between the working-class rank and file in the Order and the middle-class and aristocratic members were re-kindled. In 1901 Thomas Henry Sloan, a trade unionist who worked in the Harland and Wolff shipyard in Belfast, emerged as leader of the Belfast Protestant Association, which drew its members from the Belfast Orange lodges. After its co-founder Arthur Trew was jailed for twelve months for inciting a riot at a Catholic Corpus Christi procession, Sloan, also the Master of a Lodge, took over. He heckled the County Grand Master of Belfast, Colonel Edward Saunderson, at the 12 July demonstration at Castlereagh the following year, but although he accused Saunderson of voting against the inspection of Catholic convent laundries, where females worked in sweatshop conditions, Sloan had little concern for the unfortunate workers. His real gripe was that the leadership of the Order cared little for the concerns of its predominantly working-class membership. Sloan was charged with unbecoming conduct and brought before the Belfast County Lodge's disciplinary committee. He stood as candidate in the 1902 by-election for south Belfast against the official Unionists whom he attacked for too willingly giving in to Catholic and Nationalist pressure. Sloan was suspended for two years from the Orange Order, and three lodges which had supported him had their warrants withdrawn by the Imperial Grand Lodge. On June 11 1903, some 8000 people attended a meeting in Belfast and agreed to form an Independent Orange Order. They organised their own 12 July demonstration at Dundonald that year, attended by approximately 500 members. (The Independent Order still exists to this day and holds its own Boyne commemoration rally, regularly addressed by the Reverend Ian Paisley, but it has a very small membership.)

In the great course of events in Northern Ireland in the early 1900s, Sloan's rebellion was only a minor sideshow, but it did highlight the importance for the Orange Order and Unionists of maintaining a united front. On 22 October 1904, with the threat of Home Rule still hanging over them, a conference of Unionists in Belfast therefore passed a resolution suggesting that the secretary of the Irish Unionist Parliamentary Party be directed to summon a preliminary meeting to discuss the advisability of founding a central Ulster Unionist Association. On 2 December, at this meeting, it was resolved: 'That an Ulster Unionist Council be formed, and that its objects shall be to form an Ulster Union for bringing into line all local Unionist associations in the Province of Ulster with a view to consistent and continuous political action; to act as a further connecting link between Ulster Unionists and their parliamentary representatives and to settle in consultation with them the parliamentary policy, and to be the medium of expressing Ulster Unionist opinion as current events may from time to time require; and generally to advance and defend the interests of Ulster Unionism in the Party.' The Ulster Unionist Council was constituted formally at a meeting in the Ulster Hall, Belfast on 3 March 1905 with a membership of not more than 200, of which 100 would be nominated by local Unionist associations, 50 nominated by the Orange Order and 50 co-opted as 'distinguished Unionists'. This body included leading Orangemen of the day: the Earl of Erne (Grand Master of Ireland and County Master of Fermanagh), Colonel Robert H Wallace, Walter H H Lyons and Edward M Archdale (all three Deputy Grand Masters), Sir James Stronge (Deputy Grand Master and County Master of Armagh), William J Allen (Deputy Grand Master of Armagh) and Colonel Edward Saunderson, MP, the first leader of the Ulster Unionist Parliamentary Party at Westminster, Deputy Grand Master of Ireland and the Deputy County Grand Master of Cavan.

Although the Order's marches continued to be a persistent source of sectarian disorder in Belfast and elsewhere, including Portadown, it was a reflection of the Order's great influence and standing that it could still secure such a significant place in the new body which was to steer Ulster Unionism through the crises of the next fifteen years and lead to the foundation of the state of Northern Ireland. Events gathered pace after Herbert Asquith retained power at the January 1910 general election. During the campaign, speaking at the Royal Albert Hall in London, Asquith, who as Gladstone's home secretary had supported the unsuccessful Home Rule cause, publicly pledged to put the proposition forward again if elected. Unionists and Orangemen, who were to play a key role, immediately began to ready themselves for the clash they now knew to be inevitable. At this point there were three strands of Unionism; the Ulster Unionists led by James Craig, a millionaire businessman whose wealth was founded on the family whiskey distillery and who was a dominant force in the Unionist Council and the Order; the Irish

Unionists, under the leadership of Edward Carson, the distinguished King's Counsel who used his formidable powers of oratory to good effect in the courts and the Commons, where he sat as the MP for Dublin University; and the British Conservatives and Unionists under the future prime minister, Andrew Bonar Law, who was Canadian-born but of Ulster descent. A month after the election, two of these strands were woven together when Carson accepted the leadership of the Ulster, as well as the Irish, Unionists. Asquith's commitment to bring in Home Rule legislation had to be postponed, however, while he wrestled with a continuing constitutional crisis brought about after the House of Lords rejected the 1909 budget. The situation forced another general election in January 1911 which again returned Asquith to power. By the end of August, having secured legislation removing power over money bills from the House of Lords and preventing it from imposing a veto of more than two years on bills coming from the Commons, Asquith was ready to turn his attention to Home Rule.

Within a month, on 23 September, a crowd said to have numbered up to 100,000 people attended a rally at Craig's palatial home, Craigavon, overlooking the lough on the eastern outskirts of Belfast, to receive Carson. The event marked the beginning of an all-out confrontation with the British government over Home Rule. 'We must be prepared,' Carson told the vast crowd, 'the morning Home Rule passes, ourselves to become responsible for the government of the Protestant province of Ulster.' On 6 December, the Ulster Area of the Orange Institution became a temporary Grand Lodge with Colonel Robert H Wallace as Provincial Grand Secretary. Within a month he had applied to magistrates in Belfast for authorisation of drilling by Orangemen and opened a register of Orange brethren with military skills. The permission was usually obtained with ease. Most of the magistrates were Unionist-minded and only two were required to sign each application. On Easter Tuesday, in another massive show of force, a crowd estimated to number 200,000 attended a rally at Balmoral showgrounds in Belfast, where they heard Bonar Law declare, 'Ireland is not a nation but two peoples separated by a deeper gulf than that dividing Ireland from Great Britain.' The platform party included Carson and a delegation of 70 English, Welsh and Scottish MPs. With the Unionists now actively planning to form a provisional government and to resist Home Rule by force, if necessary, the political temperature was already soaring when Asquith finally introduced his bill in the House of Commons on 11 April 1912. It was just three days before the shock news that the Belfast-built liner, Titanic, had struck an iceberg on her maiden voyage to New York and sunk with the loss of 1490 of her 2201 passengers and crew.

The campaign against Home Rule was first directed from the Unionist Council office at Mayfair Buildings, Arthur Square, but in mid-1912 the need for more accommodation prompted a take-over of the Old Town Hall in nearby Victoria Street, redundant since the opening of the new City Hall in Donegall Square in August 1906. That July, addressing a Unionist rally at the Churchill family home, Blenheim Palace in Oxfordshire, the recently appointed Conservative leader, Andrew Bonar Law, considerably legitimised Unionist planning for a provisional government, which was already underway in the Old Town Hall. 'I can imagine no length of resistance to which Ulster will go which I will not be ready to support,' he said. Preparations were also being made there for the signing of 'Ulster's Solemn League and Covenant', largely the work of James Craig and based on the Scottish Covenant of 1580. The Standing Committee of the Unionist Council had met at Craigavon on 19 September, when the text was finally ratified and the 28 September designated as 'signing' day. Prior to that, a series of demonstrations were held throughout the north to explain the significance of the Covenant and encourage people to come and sign. On that Saturday, also called 'Ulster day', all commercial activities were suspended and from early morning churches were crowded with worshippers 'invoking God to be with them in the solemn obligations they were about to undertake', according to contemporary accounts. In Belfast the Loyalist population marched in formation, the Orange Brethren wearing their sashes and regalia, to the City Hall where they were received by the Lord Mayor and members of the Corporation. Sir Edward Carson was the first to sign. After that the crowd was admitted, 500 at a time through the front entrance, to sign at tables placed along the corridors of the building, nearly half a mile in length, before being ushered out at the rear. Altogether, that day throughout the north, 471,414 men and women signed 'Ulster's Solemn League and Covenant', some in their own blood.

> Being convinced in our consciences that Home Rule would be disastrous to the material well-being of Ulster as well as of the whole of Ireland, subversive of our civil and religious freedom, destructive of our citizenship and perilous to the unity of the Empire, we, whose names are underwritten, men of Ulster, loyal subjects of His Gracious Majesty King George V, humbly relying on the God whom our fathers in days of stress and trial confidently trusted, do hereby pledge ourselves in solemn Covenant throughout this our time of threatened calamity to stand by one another in defending for ourselves and our children our cherished position of equal citizenship in the United

Kingdom and in using all means which may be found necessary to defeat the present conspiracy to set up a Home Rule Parliament in Ireland. And in the event of such a Parliament being forced upon us we further solemnly and mutually pledge ourselves to refuse to recognise its authority. In sure confidence that God will defend the right we hereto subscribe our names. And further, we individually declare that we have not already signed this Covenant. The above was signed by me: God Save the King.

Unimpressed by this passionate expression of Unionist opinion in Belfast, the House of Commons in London approved the Home Rule Bill on 16 January by a comfortable margin of 367 to 257. A Carson amendment seeking to exclude Ulster from its provisions had earlier been defeated. Within days the Unionists announced the formation of the Ulster Volunteer Force, a 100,000-strong body of men aged from seventeen to 65, who had already been drilling openly for some time. Many of these men were recruited through the network of local Orange Lodges. At the same time, the Unionist Council put into action a secret operation to procure a large quantity of arms and ammunition so that they could fulfil the threat to resist the imposition of Home Rule by force. Money was no object. As the crisis had intensified, the wealthy gentry and businessmen had inundated the Council with donations and offers of help. Much of the UVF drilling, for instance, took place in the grounds of their homes and estates throughout the north.

The unveiling of the Unionists' private army coincided with the defeat of Asquith's bill in the House of Lords on 30 January, when only 69 peers voted in favour and 326 opposed. The bill returned to the Commons the following July, where again it was passed, by 352 votes to 243, and a week later on 15 July it was once more rejected by the Lords, 302 to 64. By this time the Unionists were totally committed to ensuring that the northern part of the island was excluded from Home Rule, and so, in September, a 500-strong delegate meeting of the Ulster Unionist Council voted to establish a provisional government of Ulster, to be chaired by Carson. Faced with such an open challenge to its authority and the ever more likely prospect of serious conflict in Ireland, with parallel efforts being made by Irish Republicans to raise and arm their own force of Irish Volunteers, Asquith's government announced a ban on the importation of arms into Ireland in December 1913. Early in 1914, during a fund-raising expedition to the United States, Patrick Pearse, forecast that 'before this generation has passed the Volunteers will draw the sword for Ireland. I do not know how nationhood is achieved except by armed men.' Far from being satisfied with what was, in reality, only a limited measure of Home Rule, Pearse was speaking for an activist group who not only wanted to create an independent Irish nation but who also opposed any Unionist secession from it.

In March 1914, with the war drums so audibly pounding, Asquith's government sought an undertaking from the British Army, whose main Irish garrison was at the Curragh some miles west of Dublin, that it would be prepared to act in Ulster and enforce the Home Rule legislation in the teeth of Unionist resistance. What happened next is politely referred to as the Curragh Incident, but it is more accurately described as the Curragh mutiny. Faced with an instruction from the War Office to prepare plans for the protection of arms depots in Ulster, Major-General Sir Hubert Gough, who had earlier served in India and South Africa, chaired a meeting of 56 officers at the Curragh on 20 March. Although they were informed that any officers who lived in Ulster would not be asked to act there, all others would be required to carry out their orders or be dismissed. Faced with this choice, they decided they would rather resign their commissions rather than move against the opponents of Home Rule. Gough, who said he would personally prefer to fight for the Unionists rather than against them, then travelled to London to report directly to the War Office. There he was sympathetically received by General Sir Henry Wilson, a County Longford-born Unionist sympathiser who openly professed his Orange links and had advised on the formation of the UVF. Asquith decided to avoid confrontation and attempted to brush off the issue by sending a message to Gough that it had all been a mis-understanding. By this time, the UVF emissary, Frederick Crawford had been to Hamburg and procured 35,000 rifles and 5 million rounds of ammunition, which were clandestinely landed from the freighter *Clyde Valley* at Larne, Bangor and Donaghadee on the night of 24/25 April. The weapons were quickly dispersed to pre-arranged hiding places, many of them in Orange Halls, by members of the UVF. A month later, on 25 May, the House of Lords' power of veto for two years having finally expired, the House of Commons again approved the Home Rule Bill. The Unionists then used their support in the Lords to have a Government of Ireland (Amendment) Bill introduced giving each of the nine counties of Ulster the individual right to seek temporary exclusion from Home Rule. On 8 July, the bill was amended to permit Ulster to remain permanently within the United Kingdom.

Before the Lords' decision, however, King George V called a conference at Buckingham Palace in an effort to break the deadlock and avert what was promising to be a violent episode. The danger was underlined by yet another monster protest, with a gathering of 150,000 Orangemen at Craigavon and, on 10 July, the declaration of a Provisional Government and the convening of its first meeting in Belfast. The possibility of compromise was therefore remote when the leaders of the government and the main political parties (Liberal, Conservative, Nationalist and Unionist) gathered at the Palace on 21 July. The King met each delegation daily to monitor the progress of the discussions but there was little surprise when the conference broke up inconclusively after three days. Two weeks later, on 4 August, the declaration of war on Germany overshadowed the Irish deadlock and provided an opportunity to stand back from the brink. So although the Government of Ireland Bill was then passed, conceding partition to the Unionists, both Unionists and Nationalists then consented to another bill postponing the implementation of Home Rule until the end of what would be the First World War. The King signed both bills into law on 18 September 1914.

As a mark of their loyalty and commitment to the Crown, the Unionists rallied to the British cause. Many members of the UVF promptly enlisted in the British forces where they formed the 36th Ulster Division. During the Battle of the Somme, fought across the poppy fields of northern France in the early days of July 1916, 5522 of them perished in a single day during which they took more than 500 prisoners and won four Victoria Crosses, Britain's highest gallantry award, made only in wartime. Unionists regarded the sacrifice as the most telling demonstration there could be of their loyalty to Ulster, Empire and the British Crown, but their hopes that it would quench the Home Rule cause were in vain. Many of those who fought and died at the Somme were actually volunteers from the southern counties of Ireland, but there were other nationally-minded Irishmen, like Pearse, who now judged that 'England's difficulty was Ireland's opportunity' to strike for complete independence and who used the nation's preoccupation with the World War to camouflage their own violent plans.

A few months before the Somme, on Easter Sunday, 23 April 1916, in Dublin, a group of armed Irish Nationalists took over the main post office and displayed a proclamation declaring the formation of an independent Irish Republic. The Rising attracted little public support and was easily put down within a few days by the British army. Indeed its leaders were jeered as they were arrested and taken away to prison. However, their speedy execution was deeply resented and the anti-British feeling this stimulated was soon transformed into popular support for the new Irish Republican Army and Sinn Fein ('Ourselves Alone'), its political wing. By 19 January 1919, when there was an election to the British parliament,

Sinn Fein had become a major political force, winning 73 of the 103 Irish seats. Instead of taking their seats in London, the members announced the setting up of a new Irish parliament in Dublin. The same day, at Soloheadbag, in a remote corner of County Tipperary, an eight-strong IRA 'flying column' ambushed two members of the all-Ireland police force, the Royal Irish Constabulary, who were escorting a horse-drawn cart delivering gelignite to a quarry. The constables were killed and their weapons and the explosives captured. The attack marked the beginning of what is now called Ireland's War of Independence.

In October 1919, the worried government in London posted General Sir Nevil Macready, the Commissioner of the Metropolitan Police and a veteran of the Boer War, to Dublin to direct a campaign of repression against the IRA uprising and stabilise the situation. With the RIC demoralised and in disarray, the cutting edge of his force became 7000 ex-soldiers, veterans of the war recruited in 1920, who became known as the Black and Tans because of the khaki army trousers they wore with dark green police jackets, a consequence of uniform shortages. Together with 1400 auxiliaries, ex-officers formed into 100-strong companies and paid the then astronomical bounty of £1 a day, they imposed a reign of terror and reprisal throughout the country, but without significant success. The IRA campaign was unstoppable and had steadily undermined British authority in Ireland. By the end of 1920, against this violent background, Britain sued for peace and parliament in London passed another Government of Ireland Act. Although it again conceded partition, which satisfied the Unionists in the North by allowing them to remain under Britain's wing, its provisions for limited devolution to the new Dail in Dublin fell far short of the full-blooded independence for the whole of Ireland demanded by Sinn Fein and the IRA. The Act thus failed to halt the violence, which intensified into a cycle of bloody reprisal and counter-reprisal. By the time a truce was agreed, with some difficulty, in July 1921, 418 RIC members and 146 British soldiers had been killed, as well as at least 80 civilians, men, women and children. The British government moved to resolve the worsening situation by underlining its commitment to partitioning the North, and offering an improved, but still limited form of self-government to the South.

The Dail unanimously rejected the British offer but agreed to negotiate. This triggered a major split within the IRA and when a treaty was finalised in December 1921, recognising the partition settlement, a cruel civil war erupted. Hardliners led by Eamonn de Valera rejected the partition treaty and insisted on an all-Ireland settlement, but they were eventually crushed by the new government, led by Michael Collins, which took office in Dublin. It was bedevilled by widespread bitterness and political recrimination over the merits of the settlement, an issue that scarred and still divides the country's political system today. Throughout this period the violence was mainly confined to the southern and western counties of the island, but the Unionists in the North were deeply alarmed. Their earlier belligerence had persuaded the British government to abandon Home Rule and concede their demand for partition, but they feared that if the IRA secured power they would eventually overwhelm the North and there were fears that the British government might not come to their assistance. Furthermore, the extent of partition and the exact line of the new North-South border had still not been finalised. Nevertheless, when King George travelled to Belfast to open the Northern Ireland parliament at Belfast City Hall in June 1921 there was evident relief that Home Rule had been defeated and the union and Protestant ascendancy maintained.

The Orange Order had been pivotally involved in the successful campaign, expediently transcending the layers of class and conventional politics. Through days of great crisis and insecurity, common membership of the Order had inextricably bound Unionists together, from the leadership all the way down to the humblest Ulster Volunteer. The Order sums up its contribution as follows:

> From the outset of the campaign against Home Rule the Orange Order had taken a responsible part. There was a high standard of leadership utterly dedicated to the service of the Unionist and Protestant cause. The Grand Masters had been men of consequence, namely the Earl of Enniskillen, the Earl of Erne, Sir James Stronge, W.H. Lyons, and Sir Edward Archdale. They presided over brethren who responded to good leadership and who were concerned to back that leadership against all enemies. It is certain that without the Order the fight for the maintenance of the Union would have been lost.

Carson declined to lead the new Unionist government and stepped aside to make way for James Craig, who became the first prime minister of Northern Ireland the day the Belfast parliament first met. Thereafter, the Order was rewarded for its support by being given an unprecedented position of power and patronage which lasted for some 50 years, until the Belfast parliament was prorogued in 1972 and replaced by direct rule from London. During this time, as prime mover in forming the Ulster Unionist Party, the Order was politically invincible. In 1932, Craig, who had been honoured as Lord Craigavon of Stormont in 1927, confirmed its status in the pecking order when he said that he was an Orangeman first and prime minister second. According to Kevin Haddick Flynn, the Orange historian, 138 of the 149 Unionist MPs who sat in Stormont between 1921 and 1968, and all of the prime ministers during that time, were members of the Order. During these years the Order cut a triumphalist path across the landscape of Northern Ireland and its sometimes breathtaking bigotry and intolerance was openly tolerated and encouraged by the religious and political establishment. Prime ministers and senior churchmen, invariably wearing the Orange sash, walked in its lengthy processions and articulated unswerving anti-Catholicism and Britishness from its platforms. Those who deviated from the path were ostracised and expelled. With banners flying and bands playing, the Order invariably won regular confrontation after confrontation with Catholics about its right to march what it calls 'the Queen's Highway'. But as the winds of political and demographic change swirled around Northern Ireland in the years after the outbreak of the Troubles in 1968, the Order's power and influence inevitably came under scrutiny and it was, ironically, at Drumcree in Portadown, the very Vatican of Orangeism, a few miles from its Loughgall birthplace, that it encountered, in the late 1990s, what has turned out to be the defining trial of its strength.

Chapter Two

Disponendo me non mutando me

There was no hint of the long years of turmoil to come in the pages of the *Portadown Times* in the summer of 1968, the last summer of 'normality', as it has been described. The front page of the 'pre-Twelfth special edition' on Thursday 11 July was dominated by news that a family had been left homeless after their thatched cottage in Drumallyduff was gutted by fire. Another small item noted that 'for the second time in the past month' Portadown public park had been the target of vandals. On inside pages, the paper reported that work was to start on a major Garvaghy Road improvement scheme and remarked that 'motorists will not be sorry to hear the news – the potholed road is one of the worst in the country.' Another newsworthy item was the visit of the Portadown Cactus Society to Larne, where they viewed over 1000 plants. The letters page was devoted to missives about whether women should wear hats and trouser suits to church. Eleanor and Esme Boyle from Portadown congratulated the Reverend W Craig, who had spoken out against the practice, which a number of other ministers had supported: 'We think it disgraceful that these ministers set at nought the Word of God. How can they stand up in their pulpits and tell women it doesn't matter about hats. We wonder what sort of Gospel message they preach. If each of these ministers would read I Corinthians 2 they would surely realise the difference it does make. As for trouser suits, we shudder to think what will happen next!' A feature entitled 'Police News' urged people to 'Be Sure Before Shooting' after a valuable racing pigeon was hit by hail from a shotgun whilst flying over waste ground at the Bann. Police asked that 'gunmen make sure exactly what they are aiming at'. An advertisement in the same edition informed Orangemen and their supporters that roll call for the marchers would be held at Carleton Street Orange Hall at 8.45 am the next day. The paper also recorded that at the pre-12th service at Drumcree parish church the previous weekend, J A Fullerton of the Lord's Day Observance Society had warned more than 1000 Orangemen that Protestant traditions were under threat from indifference and complacency.

The following week, the *Times* printed an eight-page picture special of the bands and marchers. The front page, which in later years would be dominated by reports of clashes at the July parades, carried the headline 'No Jobs for the Boys', revealing that there was little prospect of work for 240 teenage youths who had left school during the summer. The only sign of trouble came in a court report recording that a man from Ballyoran had been fined £1 for spitting at a police car. By the standards of Portadown's often turbulent history, the late 1960s were halcyon days of relative tranquillity.

Although there is evidence of early pre-Christian settlement in the area and authoritative testimony that it was later fought over by rival Irish chieftains, the rich Armagh land was not put to any real productive use until the plantation of Ulster in the early seventeenth century, when James I of England dispossessed the native Irish and granted English and Scottish settlers their lands. There are conflicting accounts of how the name came about. Some authorities say it is derived from the Irish *Port-na-dun* ('Port of the fortress') but another insists *porta* means a gate and *down* describes an artificial hill or some type of earthwork. Whatever the correct explanation, while the land was granted in 1610, the real development of the town really begins in 1631, with the initial impetus coming from the Obins family, who that year acquired the land, built an Elizabethan-style mansion and sited twenty tenants in the Ballyoran area, close to the the line of the street that today bears their name. With its strategic position, straddling the Bann River which meanders northwards from its source in the Mourne mountains through Lough Neagh to the point where it enters the sea at Coleraine, County Londonderry, and close to the apex of three counties, Armagh, Down and Antrim, the Obins recognised the area's potential as a trading place and secured a patent for a fair and market at Portadown in 1631, about the same time the first bridge was built across the river.

From time to time the Obins, like the other settlers, suffered at the hands of the dispossessed Irish fighting to retake their captured lands. A rising took place throughout Ulster in October 1641 and within days the rebels were in control of many settlements in Tyrone and Armagh. Obins Castle was among those captured and up to 200 settlers (historical accounts vary) were driven into the Bann, where they were either shot or drowned. Hamlet Obins, who had escaped the sacking of Portadown in 1641, returned in 1652 to reclaim the estates which eventually passed to his son Anthony. He contributed greatly to the further development of the town in 1703 by carrying out the first survey and promoting the project to build a canal linking the Bann to Newry and the sea, which was completed in 1741. Another generation took over the estate in 1750, and Michael Obins in turn made a lasting mark on the town's history by establishing a linen market in 1762 which laid the foundations for the major local industry for years ahead, followed in 1780 by a grain market which utilised the canal. Around this time, Portadown also became well known for the manufacture of cider, produced from the extensive plantations of apple trees which remain a significant feature of the Armagh landscape and lead many still to call it the 'orchard county'.

Michael Eyre Obins inherited the family estate after his father died in 1798, but some years later, in 1814, he entered Holy Orders, settled in England and sold the Portadown interests to the Sparrow family of Tandragee. One of them, Millicent, married Lord Mandeville in 1822. He later succeeded to the family title, becoming the sixth Duke of Manchester and landlord of Portadown and Tandragee. The Mandevilles' benevolence to the town had its positive side: they donated land for schools and a church. However, they also bequeathed their coat of arms and, in the light of subsequent events at Drumcree, a somewhat prophetic motto: *Disponendo me non mutando me* – colloquially, 'You can bend me but you can't break me.'

By the late nineteenth century the town was expanding rapidly and its industry and commerce thrived. In 1828 the first Town Commissioners were appointed, followed by a Town Clerk, a Scavenger and a Town Inspector, who was instructed that at all meetings of the Commissioners and on market days he must wear a blue frock coat with red collar, a black leather belt and sword and a black hat with a silver band, and carry a long staff with a gilt head. The Commissioners, who also became responsible for lighting the town in 1845, were replaced by a council after the passing of the Local Government Act (Ireland) 1898. By the early years of the next century, the town had its own gas and electricity companies and, after 1906, fresh running water piped from the Mournes with the completion of an £80,000 construction project. A contemporary guide book boasted: 'The town is one of the cleanest and healthiest, the health statistics being most satisfactory. Its progressive Council and efficient officials are fully alert to the importance of proper sanitation and clean and wholesome meat and milk supply.'

Early development of the town had been greatly assisted by the erection of the first stone bridge over the Bann in 1764, but after this was washed away by floods the following year and several subsequent structures collapsed, a new granite bridge was built on firm ground and the river diverted to flow under it. To keep pace with increased usage the

new bridge was widened in 1923. The Ulster Railway, later the Great
Northern Railway of Ireland, radiated from Belfast and reached Seagoe in
1842. That year, William Makepeace Thackeray, the distinguished,
Indian-born nineteenth-century novelist and author of *Vanity Fair*,
visited the town and wrote: 'The little town of Portadown with its comfortable, unpretending houses, its squares and market place, its pretty
quay, with craft along the river, a steamer building on the dock close to
mills and warehouses, that look in a full state of prosperity, was a
pleasant conclusion to this ten miles drive, that opened at the newly
opened station.' Six years later a railway bridge was built over the Bann
and the line was extended to Armagh and subsequently Enniskillen and
Clones.

Portadown became an important railway junction in 1855 with the
completion of the line to Dublin. It is said the Duke of Manchester
insisted on it being routed through Portadown for his own convenience
rather than along a more direct route to the east. Portadown junction was
later linked to Omagh and Strabane (with a narrow gauge railway
connection to Letterkenny, Donegal and Killybegs) and Londonderry. As
a result the station, with its grand arched façade, four platforms and
extensive marshalling yard, became a key exchange point for mailbags,
newspapers and all manner of livestock, freight, produce and parcels,
earning Portadown the epithet 'the hub of the north'. These good communications links were also helpful in establishing Portadown as an
important centre for linen production. In its heyday, with the advent of
steam power and the important asset of an unlimited supply of Bann
water for boiling and bleaching, there were seven large weaving
factories, some with as many as 500 power looms, operating in the town.
Alongside them were a series of hemstitching establishments turning out
fine linen handkerchiefs, tablecloths, bed sheets, pillow cases, clothing
fabric, suit linings and furnishing fabrics. According to a 1920s guide to
the town, 'the manufactures of the mills and factories within its
boundaries are famed to the ends of the earth.'

A raft of smaller support and service enterprises, such as iron and brass
foundries, grew up on the back of the railways and the linen industry.
Over the years, cider production was joined by whisky distilling and
brewing. There were a number of millers producing animal feed and a
range of smaller industries associated with farming and agriculture,
packing and distribution of eggs, butter, poultry and apples and curing
ham and bacon. The area also became well known for its horticultural
nurserymen and its rose growers, like Sam McGredy who exported
worldwide and won an international reputation for his fields of colourful

blooms at the Garvaghy Road, which attracted hundreds of admiring visitors. By the end of the Second World War the town's population had reached 16,300, compared with 12,000 just before the war in 1937. When the first General Census in Ireland was taken in 1821, there were 167 families in the town, between them numbering 933 persons. Things began to change rapidly after the years of the Second World War. The growth of vehicular traffic on the roads helped throttle the railway freight business and passenger numbers dived sharply as motor cars became more widely available. Eventually all the lines closed with the exception of Belfast–Dublin, and the once busy station became semi-derelict before it was demolished and replaced with a modern facility in the early 1970s. The linen industry experienced a similar decline in the 1950s and '60s as cheaper man-made fibres captured its traditional markets. Famous linen brand names closed down or diversified in a bid to survive.

One in ten of the workforce was unemployed in March 1963, when a weary Lord Brookeborough, one of the Unionist and Orange founding fathers of Northern Ireland, stepped down as prime minister after twenty largely stagnant years. He was replaced by the moderate Captain Terence O'Neill, who boldly pledged to 'transform the face of Ulster'. Soon afterwards O'Neill launched a major initiative to revitalise the rapidly decaying town, and nearby Lurgan, which had also suffered from the rundown of the linen industry. The plan was conceived by Sir Thomas Matthew in his 1963 Belfast Regional Survey and Plan which suggested merging the two towns into a new conurbation, creating a modern commercial, industrial and residential base to relieve the pressure on Belfast, and set for it a population growth target of 100,000 by 1981. 'Handled with imagination,' he said, 'it could become an asset to be talked about in the industrial boardrooms of London, Paris and New York.' The first stretch of motorway opened and extensions were headed in the direction of the £140-million, 100-square-mile new town. 'Lurport', as it was initially named, would spearhead and symbolise a new era of prosperity based on the white-hot advancing technologies and industries of the late twentieth century.

But imagination was a quality sadly scarce in parochial Northern Ireland, where the Sixties notably failed to swing, and the project became immersed in controversy from the very outset. When the new town was formally designated in 1965, the Unionist administration named it Craigavon, in memory of the first prime minister. Catholics, unsurprisingly, failed to see such a one-sided gesture as being any sign of the brave new world, equally shared with Protestants, to which O'Neill paid much public lip service. The Catholic MP Gerry Fitt called the naming 'a calculated insult', and Austin Currie, an up-and-coming Nationalist, said, 'To call this new city after someone who is looked upon by over one-third of the population as an arch-bigot is something that ought to be abhorred.' At this time the minority community was becoming more vociferous about what they saw as years of disadvantage and organised discrimination against them. Apart from opposing the name, they protested that locating such a prestigious economic development in a pre-dominantly Protestant area rather than in the second city, Londonderry, or Derry as they preferred to call it, was unjustified. Conditions in parts of Portadown were also appalling. Although it had just won the Best Kept Town award for the third time, and the mayor, Tom Newell, called on people to keep their 'keen sense of civic pride to ensure that Portadown maintains its place as one of the most progressive towns in the province,' in March 1970 an inspector for the NSPCC refused to enter run-down Catholic-occupied slum houses at Charles Street after finding dead rats on the streets and an open sewer.

The new town project thus got off to an inauspicious start from which it never fully recovered. Nationalists accused the Unionist government of wilfully locating it to their own advantage for selfish, political and religious, rather than proper social and economic reasons. The chief town designer resigned soon after beginning work on what it had been said would be a 'pedestrian utopia' and produced his own blueprint for an expanded Belfast and Londonderry and the development of Armagh, the ancient ecclesiastical capital of Ireland, as a major administrative centre. There were protests against the project by everybody from farmers, who resented the loss of their homes and prime land, to councils in Belfast and elsewhere who feared their areas would be starved of jobs and investment in favour of the new town. One farmer delayed work on a £6.5 million Goodyear tyre plant for months because he was only offered £12,500 for his land. Together with other farmers, he maintained a 24-hour vigil to stop bailiffs ejecting him before the 'Battle of Ballinamoncy' was settled with an offer of £20,000. By May 1969, Brian Faulkner, as minister of development, was on the defensive. Without the planned growth of the project, he claimed, Portadown and Lurgan would have remained small market towns with scattered industry. Already 400 houses had been built and there were plans for 1000 a year thereafter, but despite the availability of a special grant of up to £500 to encourage families to relocate there from Belfast, few were willing to do so and blocks of flats and rows of new houses stood vacant. Soon afterwards the Craigavon Development Commission, appointed to create the new town, revealed that 1 million square feet of factory space had been provided, creating

2500 new jobs, and that a similar amount of space was planned. However, such was the criticism of the project that Faulkner faced calls for a public enquiry in the Stormont House of Commons. Earlier it had been revealed that only 70 out of 9700 unemployed people in Belfast, Newry, Strabane and Enniskillen had expressed any interest in moving to the new town and taking a job at the Goodyear plant. In 1973, when local government was re-organised, the commission was wound up and replaced by Craigavon Borough Council.

The new town concept remained officially alive for another five years until the government quietly buried it with the epitaph that 'the altered economic climate, changed forecasts of population growth and the need for greater emphasis on the problems of the decaying inner areas of existing cities' had caused a change of policy. By then the area between Lurgan and Portadown, which had been earmarked as the heart of the new city, was a wasteland. Although the British Army had commandeered hundreds of houses to accommodate soldiers' families, over 600 houses, which had cost almost £1 million to build, were still lying empty, most derelict and deteriorating having been extensively vandalised. Families were leaving the area at the rate of twelve a week. Although Protestants and Catholics had earlier co-existed in mixed streets for a time, the onset of the Troubles and upsurge in violence had caused those who wanted to stay to divide themselves by religious and political affiliation, and to advertise in the local papers to swap houses and move into one or other of the new ghettoes they created. From both sides of the divide the social services agencies were then overwhelmed by an avalanche of problems such as domestic violence and child battering. On one occasion an aborted foetus was found in an ornamental lake. Meanwhile the lengthy housing waiting lists in Lurgan and Portadown were testament to how even the local people wanted nothing to do with the new city.

However progressive, industrious and visionary the Obins family and others had been in founding and developing Portadown and making it prosper, the history of Portadown is far from idyllic. Indeed the Orange Order and its activities are inextricably linked to the town, its history and, in relation to the deadlock at Drumcree in the late 1990s, its very future. Although Portadown remained its heartland, the relationship was always acrimonious, especially between the Order and the town's minority of Catholics, and its connection with the parish church at Drumcree came to be an enduring source of crisis.

According to one of history's most renowned preachers, there was nothing God-fearing about the town on 10 April 1767. On that date, John

Wesley, the founder of Methodism, recorded in his journal: 'At one I preached at Portadown, a place not much troubled with religion.' When he visited again, four years later on 28 June 1771, he preached on the street to what he this time described as 'a serious and well-behaved congregation.' Whatever caused Wesley's first observation, there had been Christian worship in the area as far back as the sixth century and there were certainly several thousand loyal and devout Protestant citizens around ten months after the Battle of the Diamond when the fledgling Orange Order organised its first Battle of the Boyne commemoration march in Portadown on 12 July 1796. The delegate meeting convened in conjunction with the march welded the 23 local or private lodges into Portadown District LOL 1, a designation designed to indicate that 'the members of the District regarded that body as a superior lodge, their loyalty being primarily to the Portadown area rather than to their own private lodges,' in the words of 'The Orange Citadel', the official history of Orangeism in the town. From its very outset, therefore, parading was established as a central principle and activity of the Orange culture and the Portadown District was proudly positioned at its forefront. Indeed, the Order claims as a matter of historical record that parades were a feature of the life of the Protestant community, 'as an appropriate medium to witness for their faith', for many years prior to the formation of the Orange Institution.

Given this fusion of religion and politics, it was therefore not surprising that before long Orangemen would choose to parade in formation to worship. At the time there were no churches in the town itself – the first place of worship for any denomination was the Methodist Chapel built in 1802 and St Mark's (known originally as St Martin's) Church of Ireland Parish Church was not built until 1826. However there were two parish churches in the adjacent countryside: Seagoe to the east and Drumcree to the west. Ruins on the Seagoe church site date back to the sixth century and it is reputed that St Patrick once worshipped there. Across the river, the origins of Drumcree ('ridge of the branch' in old Irish) church can be traced back to the twelfth century. The present church, incorporating the tower and spire of its predecessor, was built and dedicated in 1856, as it stands today, a major landmark on a hillside. Earlier, in July 1807, a column of Orange brethren, headed by men on horseback, had marched out from the town to the church, which was bedecked with flags. They were greeted by the rector, the Reverend Stewart Blacker, a member of LOL 176, who conducted a service and preached to them. This is the first recorded instance of an Orange service being held at the church, and, in the light of the ultimate crisis, it has become an article of faith for the Portadown Orangemen that, with occasional interruptions, the march and service has been repeated on an annual basis ever since. Over the years the practice also developed of marching out along what is presently Obins Street, then the main arterial exit route from the town to Dungannon and the west, and returning along what is now Garvaghy Road, which in those days was a narrow country lane meandering across agricultural land, and then along 'The Walk' (now Castle Street) to their assembly point. After the Orange Hall was built at Carleton Street it became the base for the District and the starting and finishing points for its marches. It is to this long-established routine that the Orangemen of Portadown attribute what they now see as their inalienable right to march to Drumcree church along the 'traditional' route.

'The Orange Citadel' says that during what it calls the years of crisis, from 1825 to 1845, when the Order faced sustained efforts at suppression, it was 'the Orangemen of County Armagh who remained unbowed and unbeaten in the face of adversity and took the lead in maintaining Orangeism and the Orange identity'. Apart from the illegal parade on Colonel Blacker's lawn in 1833, the Portadown Orangemen broke the law again when they proceeded to Drumcree church on 5 November for a service to commemorate the failure of Guy Fawkes to blow up the Houses of Parliament in London, the famous Gunpowder Plot. There was more defiance when they marched again on 12 July in 1834 and 1835. That year, however, when the authorities discovered plans for another march to flout the law on the next day they drafted in the 33rd Foot Regiment and the 2nd Dragoons from Newry to prevent it. The Orangemen then formed up in Lurgan but, on the instructions of the magistrates, were confronted by 'a force of horse, foot and police' at Edenderry Bridge. Colonel Blacker then intervened and persuaded them to disperse.

Although there was periodic defiance of the law in the years after that, it was not until the Party Processions Act lapsed in May 1845 that the Boyne victory could again be legally celebrated. The Portadown parade that year prompted Lord Gosford to write to Dublin Castle, the seat of British power in Ireland: 'I have this moment seen Mr Singleton RM, who informs me that, on Saturday last, 80 Orange Lodges, 60 stands of colours, each with fife and drums, 1800 Orangemen, wearing scarfs, and accompanied by 10,000 persons, marched in procession through the town.' Three years later, the 12 July period was marked by the ringing of the church bell and a service at St Mark's, with 769 present and the proceeds of the collection totalling seven shillings and two pence. Reflecting the temperance streak that courses through Orangeism, the

Portadown District passed a resolution in 1849 forbidding lodges from meeting for their business in a public house and preventing publicans from holding the position of master of a lodge.

The Order now entered another turbulent period of its history, much of it arising from events in and around Portadown. In 1850, a year after the clash at Dolly's Brae, the Party Processions Act, curtailing parades and empowering the confiscation of arms and emblems, was put back on the statute book. Again the law had little impact on what was now proudly dubbed the 'Orange Citadel' of Portadown and the customary marches and church parades continued. In 1860, after riots associated with July Orange marches at Newtownards, Lurgan and nearby Derrymacash, the authorities rushed through more restrictive legislation, but this did little to curb what was now routine defiance of the law by the Orange Order, frequently resulting in rioting in Belfast and other places, until it began to be more rigorously enforced at the end of the decade.

A clear sign of a crackdown came on 1 July 1869 when four unarmed police constables stamped out a bonfire at the junction of Killicomaine and Gilford Roads in Portadown. The fire was lit by a group of children to burn the effigy of Governor Robert Lundy, in Orange folklore regarded as an arch-traitor for wanting to surrender the besieged city of Derry to the Catholic King James in 1689 in the skirmishing leading up to the Battle of the Boyne. One of the constables stated that lighting a bonfire was illegal and called on the children to disperse immediately but a large crowd of adults soon gathered and began to argue with the police who threatened them with imprisonment if they did not disperse. The crowd began to throw stones at the police who were forced to return to the safety of the Royal Irish Constabulary Barracks in Woodhouse Street. Soon afterwards virtually the entire station party, eight or nine officers, emerged to deal with the angry, stone-throwing crowd, now swollen by hundreds of Orangemen who had earlier been at a Lambeg drumming match. Unable to control them, the police retreated and Sub-Inspector Nunan gave the order for the police to open fire on the protesters. The first volley, fired in the air, had little effect in dispersing the crowd and a second volley was discharged. A young Protestant, sixteen-year-old Thomas Watson, a porter at the railway station, who had just finished his evening shift and was going home, was standing in a shop doorway when he was hit in the chest and fatally wounded. Nearby, nineteen-year-old William Girvan, a Catholic from Coalisland, was seriously injured. After these shootings, the disturbances intensified and continued well into the night.

Thomas Watson's funeral procession to Seagoe cemetery a few days later attracted a huge crowd of onlookers. At least twenty Orange lodges, clad in full regalia, walked behind the hearse. The incident, which later became known as the 'Fatal Affray', created considerable concern and controversy. Questions were asked in the House of Commons, letters appeared in the national newspapers and the police officer, who had given the order to open fire was later charged and tried for manslaughter at the Dundalk Assizes. Nunan was found not guilty, much to the consternation of the *Portadown News*. 'The police certainly acted in the matter with great indiscretion and imprudence,' it commented on 16 July 1870, adding, 'Sub-Inspector Nunan has been – well – tried at the Dundalk Assizes, and a jury of his fellows have brought him in 'Not Guilty' of the manslaughter of poor Watson. We believe however that any impartial man that reads the evidence … must say that the verdict was such as might be expected from a Dundalk jury.'

Shortly after this episode and William Johnston of Ballykilbeg's 'Right To March' campaign, the Party Processions Act was again repealed and Orangemen were once again able to openly celebrate the anniversary of the Battle of the Boyne without fear of arrest. The annual round of marches continued without noteworthy incident after that until 1873 when a group of Canadian brethren, including Brother Oronhyoteka, a Mohawk Indian chief, attended the July demonstrations and spoke from the platform at Armagh. That evening, however, there was a deeply significant incident. The Portadown Orangemen returned from Armagh at 6.30 pm and marched through the town before they dispersed. The homeward journey of three lodges, comprising 86 Orangemen in total, took them through the Catholic 'Tunnel' area, so-called because of the deep, stone-lined cutting which linked Woodhouse Street to Obins Street under the railway lines heading west out of the town, which was itself the main road thoroughfare in the same direction. What happened when the parade, with flags unfurled and drums and fifes playing, reached there was described by the *Portadown News* on 26 July in the following terms:

> They got the length of River Lane without the least molestation and it was beginning to be hoped that the inhabitants of this unenviably notorious locality would manifest for once a forbearance, peculiarly foreign to their training and inculcations. At this place, most wanton and unprovoked, but eminently characteristic assault – characteristic insomuch as it was of the most dastardly and despicably sneakish description – was made upon [the Orangemen] from the backs and windows of the houses with stones, brick-bats; large pieces of broken crockery and every conceivable description of missile, all of which

were thrown with a violence and continuity perfectly compatible with the skulking poltroonery that dictated such a plan for waylaying a number of peaceable men whose only crime was that they were Protestants and loyal subjects.

According to the paper, the Orangemen soon recovered from their surprise and gave a good account of themselves before regrouping and completing their march. Recording the same incident, the *Belfast Newsletter* reported how 100 police with fixed bayonets confronted an Orange mob. When a sub-inspector struck a horse with his sword to stop it breaking the police lines, the air was black with stones thrown at the police. They were ordered to charge and in repeated clashes several people were injured and one killed by the police bayonets. The sub-inspector was felled by a brick on the head and given a severe kicking by a section of the mob as he lay on the ground. Only the intervention of a crowd from a public house, who dragged him inside for safety, prevented him from further injury. The entire clash appears to have been futile for, according to the report, the Orangemen formed up and marched through the Tunnel 'without either giving or receiving the slightest offence as the riot raged. A number of civilians, as well as police, were injured in the clash, the first recorded incident of Orange marchers being attacked in the Tunnel.

It is worth explaining at this point that ever since the days of the Plantation landlords had created 'Irish quarters' as they developed their estates and towns. Invariably these came to be occupied by the native Irish Catholics and gave rise to the practice of segregated Catholic quarters as the urban population expanded with the growth of industry and manufacturing. Thus in Belfast Catholics and Protestants settled in different areas, delineating the rigid sectarian boundaries that persist today. In Portadown the Catholics settled in the 'Tunnel' area, which became a veritable ghetto, and an equally persistent location for communal conflict. Catholics came to believe that Orange marches through 'their' area were simply designed to assert ascendancy and keep them in their place.

The next notable landmark for Portadown District came in 1873 when the foundation stone for a new Orange Hall was laid in Carleton Street. When the building work finished two years later, the District, which had previously held its meetings in the Technical School, now had its own headquarters to conduct its business and hold social functions. In the years up to 1914, in tandem with the Home Rule crisis, the Order built fifteen other halls in and around Portadown, many of which later became outposts for the UVF and repositories for the illegal arms landed in 1912.

Portadown Orangemen played their full part in the successive Home Rule Bill protests, one of them, eighteen-year-old flax weaver Samuel Giffin, losing his life as a result. On 1 January 1884, he was one of a large contingent of Orangemen who travelled by train from Portadown to a rally in the village of Dromore in County Tyrone. When they arrived a crowd of counter-demonstrators had gathered and were being kept apart from the Orangemen by a party of Royal Irish Constabulary officers and Hussars. Trouble flared as the Orangemen were returning to the railway station and Giffin was among a group who broke away and charged towards the nationalists. The police and soldiers fixed bayonets and during the clash Giffin was injured and taken to a local house, where he died eight days later as a result of a bayonet wound. As with Watson, some years earlier, the Orangemen turned out in force for the funeral procession of their 'fallen Brother' to Seagoe cemetery.

The year 1890 marked the bicentenary of the Battle of the Boyne and the Portadown District travelled by train to Dungannon for a 'monster' rally to mark the occasion. The *Portadown and Lurgan News* later described it as 'one of the largest and most enthusiastic gatherings of Loyal men ever held in the province of Ulster on the Twelfth'. Two years later, the July marching period coincided with the general election, with Gladstone bidding to form his fourth administration and revive his aim of introducing Home Rule. Tension was clearly high and there was serious rioting at the Tunnel. The next year, passions about Home Rule were still running high among Unionists and Nationalists, during July as the country waited to see if the House of Lords would support the Commons in passing the Bill. However, a large force of police and troops was drafted into Portadown during July and there was no repeat of the clashes.

In the light of future events it is worth noting that in 1903, the annual Orange demonstration was held, without trouble, at Ashgrove in the Garvaghy Road area of the town. Two years later, Patrick Faloon, a 36-year-old Catholic father of four, was watching an Orange parade pass through Obins Street when he was confronted by Thomas Cordner, a Protestant factory worker, who produced a revolver and shot him. The injured man tried to get away but was pursued, shot in the back and died in his Curran Street home shortly afterwards. Two Royal Irish Constabulary officers apprehended the gunman, but as he was being led to the Barracks a crowd of Orangemen attempted to rescue him. Prolonged rioting between the police and several hundred Orangemen then started and that evening the police blocked the mouth of Obins Street to prevent another Orange parade going through the Tunnel area.

By this time, it had become the established custom to erect arches across the street at up to a dozen points in the town and festoon the routes of the various Orange feeder parades and main marches with lines of red, white and blue bunting. From 1910, when it was erected, every Twelfth they even draped an Orange sash around the statue of Colonel Edward Saunderson, the town's MP and an Orangeman, who had died four years earlier. By the early 1900s, fears of Home Rule were once again uppermost in the minds of the Unionist community and the topic dominated the speeches at the Twelfth demonstrations in Armagh in 1911 and in Tanderagee the following year. As before, the Orange Order was at the heart of events and when it came to founding local units of the Ulster Volunteer Force, colloquially labelled 'Carson's army', its leaders and members were at the forefront. Stewart Blacker, a veteran of the North-West Frontier and Boer War in South Africa whose ancestors had been prominent Orangemen, took local command of the UVF, together with Graham Shillington and William Wright, who would both later become Masters of Portadown District.

The outbreak of the First World War in August 1914 postponed the introduction of Home Rule. In common with Orangemen and Ulster Volunteers elsewhere, the Loyalists of Portadown voluntarily flooded into the armed forces, altogether some 2200 of them. Most joined the 9th Battalion Royal Irish Fusiliers, commanded by Lieutenant-Colonel Stewart Blacker and Major Graham Shillington, who already had many of the men under their leadership as UVF members. According to 'The Orange Citadel', Portadown 'brethren served in every theatre of the Great War, from the retreat from Mons to the carnage of Ypres and from the mud-soaked trenches of the Somme to the heat, sun and death of Gallipoli.' During what was called 'the war to end all wars' 239 Portadown men were killed in action, 44 died from their injuries, 40 perished from sickness and two were accidentally drowned. Another twenty were listed as missing (believed killed). Of those who returned home from the battlefronts, 61 suffered shell-shock and 473 were wounded. Some were decorated for gallantry: one received the Distinguished Service Order, eight were awarded the Military Cross, two with bar, and one soldier was decorated with the prestigious French award for bravery, the Croix de Guerre. Another fifty Portadown combatants were also decorated with Distinguished Conduct and Military Medals. It was, however, the casualties inflicted on the 36th (Ulster) Division at the Battle of the Somme in July 1916 that caused most trauma. In the words of 'The Orange Citadel':

The 12 July 1916 was to be like no other in the history of the Orange Institution. Only eleven days previously the manhood of Ulster had taken part in the Battle of the Somme where they had been killed in their thousands as they charged towards the German trenches. Soon after, the long casualty lists began to arrive in the town with almost every home having someone, a father, brother or son, killed or wounded at the Somme. It was a sad day in the history of Ulster. Many of those serving were, of course, Orangemen, who met, in lodge assembled, on the eve of the great battle. Some members wore their sashes over their uniforms as they went into battle.

As a consequence of the casualties, the Twelfth demonstrations were cancelled across the province. Flags were flown at half-mast and blinds were drawn in virtually every household. The *Portadown News* of 15 July reported: 'For the first time within the recollection of the oldest Orangeman in Portadown there was no demonstration in connection with the anniversary of the Battle of the Boyne, the lodges of the District complying with the request of the Grand Lodge of Ireland that there should be no celebration this year.' Speaking of a hastily-arranged church service to mark the tragedy, the paper continued: 'There was a large attendance and the service was of a very solemn and impressive character. The flag of the Empire and the flag of Ulster, draped in mourning, were displayed. In the course of his address, Canon Moeran paid a warm tribute to the soldiers of the Ulster Division who had fought so valiantly in defence of the flags.' It is a measure of the distress the casualties caused in the town that Portadown District decided not to make any formal record in its minute books. Nevertheless, the great sacrifice is still vividly recalled by the entire Orange Order and Unionist community as evidence of its unsurpassed loyalty to the Crown and Britain during the war and afterwards. While the loss of life was undoubtedly significant, the Order conveniently forgets that there was no undue monopoly of loyalty or suffering in Northern Ireland. Southern Irishmen had also fought and died in British uniforms, and there were many, many more streets in the big industrial cities of northern England where the telegram boys went from door to door delivering bad news after the Somme and the other bloody battles of the Great War.

Hardly had the loyal sons of Portadown returned after the Armistice in November 1918 than Ulster was engulfed in yet another conflict, the Irish war of independence. Surprisingly, however, despite the rampant lawlessness and anarchy throughout the island, Portadown, for once, was a relative oasis of peace. The town, in fact, remained largely untouched by the violence although a local Orangeman, Special Constable William McKnight, died after being caught up in an IRA ambush on 3 May 1922. McKnight was a member of a patrol halted at a bridge that had been blown up at Corbanaghan, near Cookstown in County Tyrone, when IRA gunmen, lying in wait, opened fire. Wounded in the abdomen, he died the next day. The dead constable was one of many former Ulster Volunteers, Orangemen, and survivors of the trenches (he had been awarded a Military Medal), who had joined the Special Constabulary when it was raised by the new Unionist administration in Belfast in 1921, to help ensure that the Irish Republican Army was not able to thwart the exclusion of Northern Ireland from what would soon emerge as the Irish Free State. Unionist and Orange history attributes much of the credit for the defence of the north to the 'B Specials', as they were widely known. In fact there were few of the Specials who were not also Orangemen and many platoons drilled and mustered in local Orange Halls. So, in the terms of Unionist history, 'Brother' David Rock, a leading Portadown Orangeman, who was the Specials District Commandant in the town, is given much of the credit for keeping the peace in Portadown during the tense years of the early 1920s, especially after a young Catholic was shot dead in reprisal for McKnight and widespread rioting in the town seemed inevitable.

With the advent of the Unionist-dominated government for Northern Ireland and partition secured, the Orange Order moved into a lengthy period where its power and influence reigned supreme. Its new-found virtuousness was underlined in 1928 when the distinguished artist Sir John Lavery, then aged 72, set up his easel in rooms above the Classic Bar to paint the Twelfth procession making its way through Portadown. (The resulting work now resides at the Ulster Museum in Belfast.) The inter-war years were largely uneventful, with Portadown District's now time-honoured rituals being fully observed: marching to church services and 'the field' for the annual ceremonies; passing resolutions of loyalty to the King, Constitution and reformed Protestant religion; and, from time to time, unfurling new lodge banners, or street arches which were becoming ever more elaborate and colourful. One, first erected at Corcrain Orange Hall in 1937, had a 60-foot span while another, inaugurated the same year at Edgarstown, was 50 feet wide and 30 feet high. However, this folksy picture painted by the Order conceals the constant underlying tensions between the two communities and the regular occasions when they flared into confrontation and violence.

The Armagh County Twelfth demonstration in 1938 was the last until the Second World War concluded in 1945. Again the 'sons of Ulster' sought to demonstrate their loyalty to King and country by joining the British forces, but not in the same numbers as in 1914. Inevitably some of them paid the supreme price, including a number of members of Portadown District. When the Order resumed its Twelfth marches in 1945, with a demonstration at Shamrock Park, Portadown, many of the marchers wore their sashes over their military uniforms and mention was made of the gaps left in the ranks of many lodges by the deaths of fallen servicemen.

According to 'The Orange Citadel', portraying the Order as the epitome of respectability, the years after the war saw a great influx of new members from the professional classes, doctors, solicitors, ministers, teachers and businessmen, who:

> [...] associated closely with their working class brethren who worked in the town's factories. This period was, arguably, the least trouble-some time to have been an Orangeman in Portadown District and indeed throughout Ireland as a whole. At this time there was little or no hostility shown towards the Orange Order from any quarter whatever. The Order was regarded as a noble and honourable body whose aims reflected those of the Protestant community in general and as such gained a large measure of support from those outside the organisation. To be a member of the Orange Order, at this time, elevated a man in the sight of his peers. There was also no controversy over traditional parade routes. All parades in the town, including those through the 'Tunnel', passed off peacefully right up until the start of the Troubles with no sizeable police presence needed to escort the marchers. Usually the total number of RUC officers present at Orange demonstrations amounted to one policeman at the front of the parade and one to the rear. Due to the small number of cars and vehicles then on the roads, traffic control was not as yet a major problem. All these factors surely made this 'A Golden Age' of Orangeism.

It may well have been, but sectarianism continued to scar the face of Portadown. A number of band members and supporters were injured when a lorry was driven through the St Patrick's Day parade in Obins Street in 1948. In August 1952 a motorcycle crashed into a parade, and a car was driven through another procession by the band in 1954. Such ugly manifestations only served to inspire the unrepresentative minority who harboured the Republican dream and were willing to resort to violence to achieve it. Although the IRA had largely been in hibernation since the end of the Second World War, when they had tried in vain to violently exploit the situation in Northern Ireland, they had not been entirely dormant. The Catholic Church had already condemned IRA membership and declared it a mortal sin. There had been a flurry of threats and small explosions at the time of the coronation of Queen Elizabeth in 1953, mostly directed at cinemas showing news-reels of the ceremony. The police had said that they were on full alert but there was distinct embarrassment in Banbridge, County Down, some eleven miles from Portadown, when the Picture House was blown up while the local sergeant was curled up asleep in the back row. The first sign of more serious IRA preparation for hostilities, however, came on the afternoon of 12 June 1954 when fifteen men in a borrowed cattle lorry entered Gough Barracks, then a substantial British army base in Armagh, overpowered the guards at the armoury and escaped with 670 rifles, 27 Sten guns and nine Bren guns. Later in the year, on the Saturday night of 17 October, the IRA tried to repeat their success. A party of some nineteen young men got off the Londonderry–Belfast train at Omagh. They all had single tickets and no baggage. At 3.15 the next morning they were part of a large group of armed men who forced their way into the military barracks in the town. The guard force was alerted and in the ensuing gun battle four members of the garrison were wounded by gunfire; a fifth was beaten about the head with a revolver butt. Many of the attackers fled in a waiting lorry, but the police rounded up eight of them before they could get away and they were later sentenced to long terms of imprisonment.

Everything thus pointed to arming attempts for a new IRA offensive, but before they left their starting blocks, a breakaway group called Saor Uladh ('Free Ulster') attacked a police station on the border and a number of customs posts, losing a member, shot dead by the RUC, in the process. The IRA offensive 'Operation Harvest' was finally launched on 11 December 1956. That night there were ten attacks on targets throughout Northern Ireland, including bombing a BBC transmitter at Londonderry, burning a courthouse at Magherafelt, firing a B Special drill hut in Newry and bombing an army barracks in Enniskillen. Several bridges were also severed. Next night two police stations at Lisnaskea and Derrylin endured gun and bomb attacks. On 30 December the attackers returned to Derrylin, opening fire from across the border and shooting an RUC constable dead. After the attacks, the Irish government in Dublin threatened stern action if the campaign continued, although a minister at the Foreign Office in London recorded that the Irish ambassador was 'more voluble than convincing' when called in to discuss the situation. In Belfast, Prime Minister Brookeborough asserted his determination to crush the campaign but, in reality it rapidly fizzled out after its opening fury. By 16 October 1958 the ongoing IRA campaign was past its peak with 229 incidents to date and damage worth £700,000. There were only 27 incidents in 1959 and 26 in 1960. The IRA was responsible for 50 incidents in 1961, 46 of them involving explosives. The campaign was finally called off on 26 February 1962 when the IRA called a unilateral ceasefire.

In all there had been 605 outrages since 1956, leaving sixteen people dead: six RUC officers and ten IRA members. Another 32 people had been wounded. Security operations had cost some £3 million, while damage had exceeded £1 million, and 160 people suspected of Republican sympathies had been interned without trial for varying periods. The IRA had been humiliated by the Catholic population they claimed to represent, who had not, as they hoped, risen in support of their campaign. Even the traditional sectarian hotbeds in Belfast had remained dormant. What was happening instead was the emergence of a new Catholic middle class, in many respects a direct result of the 1944 Education Act which made university education more accessible. As the report into the origins of the troubles, prepared by the Scottish judge Lord Cameron, would later say, Catholics were no longer 'ready to acquiesce in the acceptance of a situation of assumed (or established) inferiority and discrimination'. As an alternative to violence, the traditional instrument of change, their principal weapon was research, carefully documenting the realities and injustice of the disadvantage and discrimination long endured by Catholics, to make a case, principally to the British government, for overdue reform.

The Campaign for Social Justice, established in 1964, and then the Northern Ireland Civil Rights Association, formed in 1967, produced the material, and Gerry Fitt, a former seaman and the only non-Unionist among the twelve Northern Ireland MPs at Westminster, together with a cadre of sympathetic British Labour MPs, used it to good effect. It drew attention to the inequities in what the *Sunday Times* memorably described as 'John Bull's political slum', a portrait of inequality that was a damning indictment of the way that Unionists, under the all-pervading influence of the Orange Order, had behaved. In terms of employment, public appointments, the allocation of housing, electoral practice and the drawing of administrative boundaries, the invariable objective was to ensure Protestant advantage and supremacy. The words 'Catholics need not apply' or 'Protestant labourer wanted' were common in notices advertising jobs. Bad housing conditions were compounded by unfair allocation procedures where those in the greatest need did not get priority. Electoral boundaries were unequally drawn and the franchise was unfair. In the city of Londonderry, the Catholic majority were always ruled by a Unionist majority on the council because of the way the electoral boundaries were rigged, and in the county of Fermanagh, where the population was evenly divided, the elected council almost permanently consisted of 35 Unionists and seventeen non-Unionists. The council's power and patronage was exercised accordingly. Of the 372 people it employed, Protestants numbered 332 and held all the top jobs. Of 75 school bus drivers, only seven were not Protestants.

Over the years since partition, there had been countless examples of such imbalances, some articulated and defended by the most prominent personalities, senior members of the government, Unionist party or Orange Order and, frequently, all three. In 1925, for instance, Sir Edward Archdale, the minister of agriculture, charged in parliament with employing Catholics in his ministry, replied: 'I have 109 officials and, so far as I know, four of them are Roman Catholics, three of whom were civil servants turned over to me, whom I had to take on when we began.' Speaking from an Orange platform on 12 July 1933, John Andrews, a future prime minister, answering a charge that 28 out of the 31 porters at the newly constructed Northern Ireland parliament building at Stormont were Catholics, replied: 'I have investigated the matter and I have found that there are 30 Protestants and only one Roman Catholic – there only temporarily.' Dawson Bates, the minister of home affairs, responsible for the police, was another government minister with such a prejudice against Catholics that he made it clear to his Permanent Secretary that he did not want even the 'most juvenile clerk or typist, if a Papist, assigned for duty to his ministry'. In 1934, in another anti-Catholic episode, Bates wrote to a senior colleague advising him not to use the telephone to his office as he had discovered the telephonist was a Catholic.

Such bigotry was endemic, commonplace and endorsed from top to bottom of the Protestant community. Again in 1934, Basil Brooke (later Lord Brookeborough), another future prime minister, addressing Derry Unionist Association, said: 'I recommend those people who are Loyalists not to employ Roman Catholics, 99 per cent of whom are disloyal. I want you to realise that, having done your bit, you have got your Prime Minister behind you.' A day later, in the Northern Ireland parliament, when asked to repudiate the remark, James Craig (Lord Craigavon), the prime minister, refused: 'There is not one of my colleagues who does not entirely agree with him, and I would not ask him to withdraw one word he said.' The entire Catholic community was still being branded as an enemy of the state as recently as 1955. Brian Faulkner, another future prime minister as deeply steeped in the rituals of the Orange Order as he was senior in the Unionist party, proclaimed: 'The government must ask themselves whether it were safe to employ in government service people who openly advocated treason.' However, some of the most uncompromising Unionism and unshakeable bigotry came in the distinctively bellowing voice of the Reverend Ian Paisley, the Moderator of his own Free Presbyterian Church, who would later emerge as one of the most significant politicians of his time. Addressing the Independent Orange Order rally at Loughgall, the founding shrine of Orangeism, on 13 July 1969, he said: 'I hate the system of Roman Catholicism, but, God being my judge, I love the poor dupes who are ground down under that system. Particularly I feel for their Catholic mothers who have to go and prostitute themselves before old bachelor priests.'

The 1960s were years of liberation and great social change in Britain and around the world. The rapid spread of television and the immediacy with which it could bring events into people's homes had a profound effect, even in Northern Ireland. Some Orangemen and Unionists spotted the opportunity, and the dangers, that were inherent in the scale of Catholic apathy to the IRA's pyrrhic campaign, but this perceptive and visionary minority was all too tiny. The philosophy of 'not an inch' and 'no surrender', so deeply hammered into the majority mindset, would quickly squander the moment, with terrible, but avoidable, consequences. So, from the outset of O'Neill's term of office, the hardliners in the party and the Order insisted there was no need for reform and determined there would be no change. As his cousin Phelim O'Neill soon found, anyone who broke ranks would be publicly ostracised. Although he came from a classic Unionist background – his father, Lord Rathcavan, was the first Speaker of the Northern Ireland parliament – O'Neill was far from the stereotypical 'big house Unionist'. Unencumbered by his inheritance or the baggage of history, he often said that whether one happens to be a Protestant or Catholic is nothing but the accident of birth, and he was an especially fierce critic of those from both sides of the community fomenting trouble. 'I must say that I do not know why it is but I am sure the time must come when the sensible people in Northern Ireland, regardless of their religion, will to some extent unite, make their presence felt and stop allowing themselves to be led by people who prey on their emotion,' he told the Stormont parliament.

Phelim O'Neill was at the forefront of the handful of realists and visionaries who knew that change was necessary, that divisions must be bridged, that reconciliation ought to be given greater priority. In line with this philosophy he then took what was, by the standards of the time, the daring step of attending a cross-community service in the Catholic church in Ballymoney during a civic week in 1966. As a result, the full wrath of the Orange Order, of which he was a member, fell upon him. Eventually the matter reached the Grand Orange Lodge of Ireland in June 1968 and he was expelled. In public he said he had no regrets, he had done the right thing at the time and would do it again in similar circumstances. Privately, it was a source of great amusement to him that the local Orange Hall, in which he was so reviled, was built on his land and thereafter he did not bother to disguise his contempt for his tormentors: 'Talking to some of one's constituents is as rewarding as addressing one's pigs in their sty,' he would say.

The simmering discontent in Northern Ireland finally came to a head in the latter half of 1968, a year of momentous historical significance with the Russian invasion of Czechoslovakia, the assassinations of Martin Luther King and Robert Kennedy, the student riots in Paris and the world-wide protests against the United States' involvement in the Vietnam war. The civil rights campaign in the United States was, in fact, the major catalyst inspiring the campaign for widespread reform in Northern Ireland which was led by a broad church of Republicans, Liberals, Socialists, Catholics, Protestants and even a prominent Communist, who came together and formed the Northern Ireland Civil Rights Association in January 1967. Their aim was to work for reform exclusively within the Northern Ireland set-up, presided over by the Unionist-controlled Stormont government, not to foment an uprising or pave the way for Irish unity. For the first time in Northern Ireland's troubled history a significant number of Catholics and moderate Protestants worked together in the civil rights movement to create a better state of affairs for all. The main demands were for measures to bring an end to religious discrimination, and the catch-cry 'one-man, one-vote' was chanted at the civil rights marches. The other main demands were for the disbanding of the all-Protestant reserve police, the B Specials (membership of which heavily overlapped that of the Orange Order), and the repeal of the Special Powers Act, which permitted the Northern Ireland government to impose unfettered emergency security measures.

If these long overdue reforms had been implemented they might have provided a durable basis for long-term peaceful co-existence between Catholics and Protestants in Northern Ireland, where at this time there was no significant demand for Irish unity although many Catholics continued to cherish the aspiration. However, the blinkered hardliners within the Unionist administration, heavily influenced by the uncompromising Orange Order and fearful of losing ground and power to the growing band of intransigent followers of Paisley, scorned the over-whelming case for reform and tried to use the ill-trained and inadequately-equipped police force to crush the protests. With the pro-reform British prime minister, Harold Wilson, breathing down his neck, the Unionist prime minister, honourable but helpless Terence O'Neill, who had been derided for his weakness in advocating reform from the very day he succeeded Brookeborough, was facing yet another in a series of plots designed to thwart his plans and undermine his leadership. A series of explosions at water and electricity installations in and around Belfast, carried out by extreme Protestants but carefully attributed to the IRA to create a sense of crisis, had already destabilised him. Given Portadown's status as the very epicentre of uncompromising Unionist and Protestant defiance, it is highly appropriate that the conspiracy which finally sowed the seeds of O'Neill's downfall was hatched there on 3 February 1969, when twelve extreme Unionist MPs gathered at a hotel in the town for what has become known as the 'Portadown parliament'. A few days earlier they had all signed a document calling for a change of leadership. O'Neill retorted that it was not a change of leadership they wanted but a change of policy away from the reforms now being demanded by an ever tougher Wilson. 'I will not back down. I will not trim my sails. I will do my duty,' he said. A statement after the meeting explicitly called for him to go to bring an end to five years of crisis and restore party unity, considerably weakening his position. That evening, in a bid to head off such a virulent challenge to his authority, he decided to appeal over the heads of the politicians directly to the people and called a general election for 24 February. After what he called the 'crossroads election', O'Neill's leadership was endorsed by his parliamentary party but the deep fissures in Unionism soon opened again and within weeks he was gone, leaving Northern Ireland sliding steadily into the abyss of violence that would consume it for the next three decades. This time, unlike the first troubles from 1920 to 1922, Portadown would not be bypassed. It would, instead, be firmly in the eye of the storm.

Chapter Three
Together We Progress

Of all the Orange parades to Drumcree parish church over the years there was undoubtedly none more provocative nor bizarre than that on the Sunday morning of 9 July 1972. After weeks of rising sectarian tension in the town and violent threats to halt the annual parades, hundreds of members of the self-styled Ulster Defence Association, clad in masks and military uniforms, formed a phalanx around the bowler-hatted Orangemen of Portadown District to ensure their march was not impeded. Under the eyes of the legitimate security forces, who chose not to intervene, they escorted the Orangemen through the Tunnel into Obins Street. At one point in Obins Street, they even formed a guard of honour along the edge of the pavements for the marchers to pass. As a body, the Catholics of the area regarded the episode as 'coat-trailing' on an epic scale, and in the resentful aftermath a cadre committed to the culture of terrorism that was so damagingly gaining ground on both sides now chose to counterpoint it violently.

Three days later, in the early hours of 12 July 1972, as the traditional 'eleventh night' bonfire parties were breaking up, a young Protestant, nineteen-year-old Paul Beattie who worked as a butcher at Sprott's bacon factory, was walking with his father, David, along Churchill Park in the Garvaghy Road area of Portadown. They had just escorted a friend home and were making their way back to their own residence at Castle Avenue. As they passed a pedestrian access way between numbers 290 and 292, they were confronted and stopped by four men, one of whom was armed and who shot Paul twice at close range, killing him. 'I told them they may as well shoot me as they had killed my son,' the father recalled later. Within a few minutes, RUC Sergeant Richard Barker arrived at the scene where he saw the young man's body lying on the footpath. Because of rising tension among the crowd which gathered after the incident, he quickly arranged for the corpse to be removed to the Lurgan and Portadown hospital for post mortem examination. In response to rumours that Paul had been murdered because he was a member of the loyalist Ulster Defence Association, both his parents and the organisation issued statements emphatically denying it.

Later in the day, in the lull between the morning and early evening Twelfth marches, Ralph Henry, a 33-year-old former policeman who was a member of the UDA, had embarked on a tour of some of the town's pubs and was making no secret of his views about the murder. According to people who remember seeing him that day, he said, in one pub: 'There'll be a taig (Catholic) shot for this.' Brandishing a diary in which he claimed to have a list of prominent Catholic businessmen, he also advised a Protestant man to get out of the Catholic-owned pub in case he was shot by mistake. Around 8 pm, Henry reached McCabe's Bar in High Street, where he was well known and had indeed been barred for a time two months earlier after causing a disturbance. He left soon afterwards when a barman in the TV lounge refused to serve him, but returned around 10.45 pm, shortly before closing time. He recognised a man who was employed in the textile factory where he also worked. 'You're a Prod?' asked Henry, to which the man nodded. Asked about his drinking companion, a Catholic, the man replied that he was also Protestant, 'to avoid any trouble'. Henry then talked about avenging the Beattie murder and produced a black hood. Holding it in his hands with his fingers through the eyeholes, he said, 'I'm going to clean this bar out. When you have got your orders all that matters is carrying them out. Wife and family don't matter.'

Moments later, Henry pulled the hood over his head, produced a revolver and walked through from the lounge to the public bar shouting: 'Don't move. Everybody back away from the bar.' One of the customers, 52-year-old William Cochrane, was singled out and shot in the head at close range with the words: 'This is for Paul Beattie.' Henry then retraced his steps and turned to the proprietor, Jack McCabe, who calmly told him there was money in the till if that was what he was after. 'It isn't that, James. It's you that I want,' replied the gunman, before raising the weapon to the back of McCabe's head and firing a shot at almost point-blank range. As McCabe slumped to the ground, fatally wounded, Henry ran out.

The killing of Cochrane was an act of futile revenge, for the unmarried victim, like Beattie, was a Protestant. In fact he had served for a time in both the Army and the Navy, and had then returned to live in the town with his brothers. Jack McCabe, aged 48, who lived at Renmore Avenue in Portadown, was a Catholic and a prominent member of the business community in the town. As well as operating a couple of public houses, he ran a wholesale wine and spirit business and, at the time of his death, was building a large warehouse on an industrial estate on the outskirts of Portadown to cope with its expansion. He was also an active member of

Rotary and other charitable groups and the vice-chairman of the management committee of the new £7.2 million Craigavon Hospital, which was then under construction. Thousands lined the streets for both funerals and it took two cars and two lorries to carry the wreaths which accompanied Beattie's coffin to Seagoe cemetery.

Henry was arrested in Portadown later on the evening of the double killing and charged with drunkenness and then murder. When he came to trial, several bar staff and customers said they recognised the hooded gunman as Henry because they had seen him in the bar earlier wearing identical clothing. The trial collapsed twice because the juries were intimidated, but Henry was finally found guilty after a third hearing and Lord Justice Jones sentenced him in February 1974: 'You have been convicted of a crime for which there is only one sentence. This is one of the worst cases I have met in the course of my professional career and accordingly I sentence you to life imprisonment.' As he left the dock, Henry raised a clenched fist and shouted 'No surrender.' The case was a legal landmark, for it played a key part in the decision, not long afterwards, to introduce 'no jury' hearings for people charged with serious terrorist offences.

Although there had already been close to 450 deaths elsewhere in Northern Ireland since the outbreak of the troubles almost four years earlier, these three violent murders in the space of 24 hours were the first in Portadown and, as a senior police officer would eventually tell the Coroner, the first in the area for 40 years. The *Portadown Times* described it as 'the darkest day in the town's history'. The deaths were, however, the inevitable consequence of a rising tide of tension and violence in the town where deep sectarian rivalries were long-established and had always smouldered dangerously under the surface.

The first incidents in Portadown actually came early in 1971, when incendiary devices were found in a number of shops and factories and 6000 bales of hay were destroyed in an arson attack at a farm in the Drumcree area. The local *Times* reported on 12 February that 'peaceful Portadown this week got its first real taste of terrorist activity. Suddenly, disastrously, peaceful Portadown finds itself embroiled in the mad turmoil. Suddenly we find ourselves experiencing something of the terrible events that are now all too commonplace in the Falls, Ballymurphy and the Shankill.' The mayor, Alderman Tom Newell, appealed for calm, and Brian Faulkner, minister of development, praised the town for its community relations, saying: 'Well done Portadown. I must praise the lead it is giving in keeping calm.'

The growing human cost of the escalating violence was brought home to Portadown on 27 February 1971 when 32-year-old Constable Robert Buckley was one of two RUC officers murdered by gunmen from the recently formed Provisional IRA during disturbances in the Ardoyne area of north Belfast. Although he was married with two children and had settled in Belfast, the dead policeman was a native of Portadown where the tragedy of his death touched many who knew his family. Despite the deteriorating situation, the customary Twelfth events passed off without serious incident, but there were now regular outbreaks of rioting and fighting between rival groups from the Catholic Obins Street and mainly Protestant Edgarstown areas, which continued throughout the year.

Two landmark events dominated the early months of 1972: 'Bloody Sunday' in Londonderry on 30 January, when fourteen unarmed civil rights marchers were shot dead by British soldiers; and the prorogation of the Northern Ireland parliament and government and the introduction of direct rule from London on 24 March. In Portadown, however, it was the ever important issue of marching that dominated affairs. In August 1971, following the introduction of internment without trial, the Belfast government introduced a ban on all parades in a bid to defuse tension and remove what had become routine occasions for triggering disorder. The Central Armagh Protestant Unionist Association, which owed its allegiance to the Reverend Ian Paisley (who had carved out for himself a notorious reputation for his fire and brimstone anti-Catholic preaching and political brinkmanship and oratory which stopped just short of outright incitement to violence), called on all Loyalists to defy the ban on parades, and convened what proved to be a stormy meeting at Corcrain Orange Hall on 18 January. The main speakers were the Reverend Ivan Foster and the Reverend William McCrea, both Free Presbyterian ministers and budding politicians. Although the ban was roundly condemned, cooler heads prevailed and the following weekend the *Portadown Times* leader column praised the Orange Order for its 'commendable restraint' and its local officials for being 'only too well aware of the dangers of making inflammatory statements'. (The ban was lifted later in the year.)

For their part, Catholics in the town had failed to support the campaign of civil disobedience as part of the civil rights campaign and, for instance, continued to pay their rent, rates and other bills to public organisations despite such action being taken by Catholics elsewhere. The *Times* recorded on 11 February that the majority of the town's 'peace loving Roman Catholics' had shown they wanted nothing to do with the civil disruption. By now there were signs that the troubles were beginning to affect the local economy. Sam McGredy, whose grandfather, also Sam, had founded the world famous rose-growing business in the Woodside nurseries on the Garvaghy Road in 1880, decided to relocate in New Zealand. Although only twenty jobs were lost from the nurseries, the withdrawal, around the same time, of a precision engineering firm to England, because of loss of confidence by its customers in Britain, was a mark of the social and economic debility now facing Northern Ireland as a whole. Undeterred by the gathering gloom, however, the ladies of Drumcree parish were feverishly knitting and sewing in advance of the annual garden fete, the proceeds of which were intended to raise some of the £10,000 needed to renovate and modernise Carleton Street Orange Hall.

The pending fall of Stormont brought the hardline Unionist William Craig to the fore, and he chose Portadown for the first of a series of Hitler-style events at which he and others made inflammatory speeches and inspected lines of men wearing military uniforms and clothing, their faces masked or hooded. More than 10,000 attended the rally on 11 March, which, for the first time, brought the Loyalist paramilitaries onto the streets in large numbers. Later that month, Craig's Vanguard movement, in which David Trimble, the future Unionist leader and Portadown MP, cut his political teeth, organised a two-day general strike throughout Northern Ireland as part of their protest campaign against the shutdown of Stormont. With sympathisers in key positions in the power stations, the organisers were able to interrupt electricity supplies and force shops, offices and other workplaces to close whether or not they fully supported the protest. Even with this advantage, however, more conventional strong-arm tactics and intimidation were used to enforce the strike. Thus there were ugly scenes in Portadown, where the town was sealed off by masked men who hijacked vehicles to use as barricades. Catholic-owned businesses were looted and burned and a detachment of troops was quickly deployed after residents erected barricades in a number of areas, including Churchill Park and Garvaghy Park, to hold back roaming Loyalist mobs.

The experience was traumatic for the town. The editorial in the *Times* captured the sense of shock: 'Portadown has always prided itself on its community relations. While other towns have been torn asunder by civil strife, Portadown set an example and built itself a reputation envied by every town in the country.' For a time church and civic leaders came together to try to end the trouble, convening an emergency peace conference, which was held in the RUC station. Father Francis McLarnon, in an open letter to his Catholic parishioners, said that they had all been tried severely during the days of tension but 'have already had ample evidence of the sympathy of the great bulk of their Protestant neighbours'. In some neighbourhoods, Protestants and Catholics had united to keep gangs out and protect their neighbours from intimidation. In another, Catholics, who were able to buy supplies of bread and milk in Obins Street, brought extra back to distribute among their Protestant neighbours. A group of women from Edgarstown, a staunchly Protestant housing estate, helped the McKeever family clean out the downstairs lounge of their public house in West Street after it had been fire-bombed. Protestant neighbours also helped two Catholic families in Union Street by launching a fund to replace their furniture, burnt by a mob during the Vanguard strike. Coming towards Easter and the start of the annual marching season, community leaders met in a local church hall to thrash out a peace formula and set up local peace committees in potential flashpoint areas such as Churchill Park and Corcrain.

Despite these initiatives, Portadown was being steadily sucked into the widening conflict. On Sunday 14 May, a 50lb bomb contained in a small van exploded in Thomas Street, causing damage to property but no injuries. It was the first such bombing in the town. The night before a 200-strong branch of the UDA had been formed at a word-of-mouth recruiting meeting and, on the evening of 31 May, wearing their masks and military uniforms, 100 of them took to the streets and drilled openly in the Edgarstown estate. Soon afterwards such drilling intensified and the UDA began erecting barricades in several country towns, including Portadown, causing confrontation when the army was deployed to remove them, and provoking fighting between rival groups.

While these events were unfolding on the Loyalist side of the divide, a group of people from the Obins Street and Parkside areas had formed a committee earlier in the year to campaign against Orange marches continuing to pass through the predominantly Catholic area. On 7 April the 'Portadown Resistance Council' issued a hard-hitting statement calling for the re-routing of the Twelfth parades away from the Tunnel area. This was the first time Catholics had ever made an organised effort to stop parades. The Orange Order, which in those days marched through the area several times over the period, rejected the call. Seemingly oblivious to the turbulent history of parades in the town, it said the parade had taken place for many years and had offended no one. However the UDA struck a more belligerent note and issued a statement saying it would not heed a threat 'from the IRA' and warned there would be repercussions for local Catholics, especially women and children, if the traditional parades did not go through as scheduled. In a bid to halt the church parade on Sunday 9 July, the two wings of the Republican movement, the Official and Provisional IRA (the latter temporarily observing a fragile truce), had pragmatically joined forces. During the night they blocked both ends of Obins Street with large barricades made up of cars, boulders and concrete blocks and built a number of smaller obstacles in between. Soon after dawn, army and police chiefs approached leaders on both sides in a bid to negotiate a compromise solution, but the Nationalists refused to remove their barricades and Orange leaders would not concede any change to their intended journey. As a result of the deadlock a troop of soldiers, with bulldozers and heavy lifting equipment, was ordered in at 9 am to clear and secure the route, some two hours before the parade was due to leave Carleton Street Orange Hall. The police and military deploying from both ends of the street encountered fierce resistance, came under a barrage of missiles and became involved in hand-to-hand fighting with some of the angry residents. Two people suffered heart attacks during the prolonged encounter in which the security forces fired rubber bullets and CS gas and only managed to subdue the disorder fifteen minutes before the parade was due.

When it arrived, the parade was led by a UDA detachment which preceded the Orangemen under the railway bridge and into the Tunnel. Masked and uniformed men, carrying a UDA flag, were cheered by Loyalists as they marched in, the cheers soon giving way to sound of broken glass from the earlier disorder crunching beneath their feet. They halted 100 yards inside the Tunnel, at the start of Obins Street, and told police they would not go any further. The commander ordered his men to form a guard of honour and told them: 'We go on through if one shot is fired.' Then more than 1000 Orangemen, with District Master Herbert Whitten, the Unionist MP for Central Armagh, among the front ranks, walked on as the UDA men stood to attention.

Shortly afterwards the two wings of the IRA called a joint news conference in a house in Obins Street. It was addressed by four masked men who revealed that the Orange Order had refused to negotiate about the parades the previous evening and produced a joint statement accusing the RUC and Army of 'collaborating with the UDA' to allow the 'coat-trailing' parade to go through. Calling for the coming parades on the 12 and 13 July to be re-routed, the statement said there was 'no option but to defend this area against further provocation' and warned the 'UDA that action would be taken against them if they entered the Obins Street area again.' It was against this background that Paul Beattie was shot dead in the early hours of 12 July, undoubtedly by Republican gunmen who have never been brought to justice.

In the past passions had usually subsided after the Twelfth period, but they did not do so that year. The IRA exploded a 150lb bomb in Woodhouse Street on 15 July and then derailed a freight train between Lurgan and Portadown on 21 July at almost the same time as 22 people were killed and many more injured in a wave of nine explosions in Belfast which became known as 'Bloody Friday'. Over that weekend, a terrorist arms cache was found in the Tunnel area: seven rifles, a Thompson sub- machine gun, fifteen grenades, fifteen bombs and detonators and 30lbs of gelignite as well as ammunition and medical supplies. Thirteen men and two juveniles were arrested for questioning. The UDA maintained its 'no-go' area until 21 July when the army mounted 'Operation Motorman', at the time the largest land-based operation since the end of the Second World War, to open up the Republican areas in Belfast and Londonderry and get the Loyalist paramilitaries off the streets in an attempt to restore law and order. In Portadown the UDA avoided direct confrontation and removed its own 'no-go' area.

The evil effects of unbridled paramilitary rule became evident on 4 August when the body of Felix Hughes, a 40-year-old Catholic father of six, was found in the Bann river near Watson Street. He had been badly beaten and tied to a mattress, which was weighted down with heavy stones. Hughes, a welder in the Unidare factory who lived in the Killicomaine estate, had been abducted by Loyalists on July 15, the night of the bomb in Woodhouse Street, and his body was believed to have been in the water for three weeks. Another Catholic was found dead in the river shortly afterwards. On 31 August, the body of Eamon McMahon, a boxmaker who had been missing for several days, was discovered by a mother and her child out walking. It was later established that a piece of heavy cord or clothes line had been tied around his neck before he was beaten unconscious and dumped in the water to die. The next night a Catholic-owned shop was burned during overnight rioting by Protestant crowds who attacked security forces and burned vehicles.

The IRA was responsible for the next murder, four days later. Fifty-four-year-old Victor Smith, a Protestant, was a well known barber who served part-time as a lance-corporal in the Ulster Defence Regiment. He was the first person to die as the result of an explosion in Portadown when he took the full force of a 50lb car bomb which detonated as he drove past the corner of Bridge Street and High Street. The device, abandoned in a Jaguar car outside the Catholic-owned McGurk's Bar, went off without warning, blowing his car over, turning it into a fireball and trapping him inside with no chance of escape. The bar was also extensively damaged but the owner and her son, who were in the premises at the time, escaped injury. An RUC patrol saw two men running away from the car containing the bomb and opened fire on them, but failed to capture them. Smith did not normally use that route coming off duty from the UDR base at Seagoe to his home in Jervis Street, but that evening he had taken a detour to drop a colleague home.

The eighth person to be murdered in Portadown in twelve weeks died on 4 October when Loyalists threw a hand grenade into a Catholic home at Deramore Drive at 11 pm while the family was watching television. Patrick Connolly, a 23-year-old bricklayer, was killed and his mother and his 21-year-old brother were injured. With murder, sectarian clashes and general lawlessness now commonplace, and fear at large among both sections of the community, at the end of October publicans in Portadown decided to begin closing their premises at 10 pm, the first place in heavily bibulous Northern Ireland to restrict opening hours in this way.

By the end of the traumatic year of 1972, there had been 467 victims of the Troubles, causing the chief constable, Sir Graham Shillington, to reflect in his annual report: 'The seemingly endless spiral of death, destruction and human suffering tends to make all but the most resolute despair of restoring peace to our strife torn community.' The effects of deaths such as these on the particular community from which the victims came cannot be underestimated in understanding how the traditional partisan tensions in Portadown escalated into the nakedly sectarian conflict that would dog the town and disfigure its reputation for decades to come. The quasi-judicial investigation by the Scottish judge Lord Cameron, published in 1969, analysed the origin of the troubles among Catholics as follows:

> The immediate causes of the outbreaks of violence [...] arose from a wide variety of sources. Some and not the least powerful, as we have found, are deep-rooted in the continuing pressure, in particular among Catholic members of the community, of a sense of resentment and frustration at the failure of representations for the remedy of social, economic and political grievances. What was considered by many Catholics and others who had been pressing for certain political reforms was the failure or delay of Government to match promise and performance, introduced an element of disappointed expectation into the political atmosphere in the early summer months of 1968.

If anything the sense of Catholic grievance had intensified since. Although the British government had finally begun implementing the promised reforms, such as abolishing the hated B Specials, the security response to the violence had created new levels of alienation. The police invariably turned their backs on Protestant crowds, often turning a blind eye to people armed with sticks and cudgels, during confrontations, and to the minority community the overwhelmingly Protestant force appeared to be taking sides. There had been a short honeymoon period between Catholics and the Army after it had taken to the streets in 1969, but its robust tactics had created hostility and the perception that the soldiers, like the police, were anti-Catholic. Hardline Catholics believed, and moderate Catholics feared, that the security forces at best turned a blind eye to the activities of Loyalist paramilitary gangs or, at worst, actively collaborated with them. When internment without trial was introduced, with an initial swoop on some 400 suspects in the early hours of 9 August 1971, the fact that not a single Protestant terrorist suspect was arrested caused the rift between the security forces and the Catholics to become a gulf which, even thirty years later, would still not be properly bridged. In Portadown, where marching, in particular, remained such a live issue, the generally hostile attitude of Catholics toward the security forces was compounded by the unwillingness of the police to use their powers to re-route loyal marches away from their areas, and, in Catholic eyes, the way the police repeatedly used their muscle to force the marches through.

For their part, according to Cameron, Protestants had 'equally deep-rooted suspicions and fears of political and economic domination by a future Catholic majority in the population'. There was nothing new about this sense of insecurity. It had fuelled the great Home Rule crises among their forebears over the preceding century or so and, once they had secured partition, encouraged Protestants and their leaders to actively use their power to keep Catholics down and in their place, lest they be overwhelmed. Reforms, however justified by the factual evidence, justice or any other yardstick, must be resisted in case they were misinterpreted as weakness. The B Specials, the police and, indeed, the Army must be totally supported as a safeguard against the IRA causing insurrection and leaving the Protestants to the unpredictable uncertainties of a Catholic-dominated united Ireland.

In the final analysis, reflecting a real fear that Britain could tire of its Northern Ireland problem and unilaterally withdraw, many Protestants acquiesced in the formation of paramilitary groups, such as the UVF in 1912, to provide a last line of defence. At this time there was much talk of going it alone as an independent Northern Ireland if this worst-case scenario ever materialised. So the IRA 'economic' bombing campaign of the early 1970s, designed to weaken Britain's resolve to stay in Northern

Ireland, was seen as striking at both the wellbeing and prosperity of the Protestant community and its principal political aspiration to stay British. Similarly, the sustained attacks on the security forces, especially the RUC and the locally recruited UDR, and the murder and maiming of their personnel, were seen as an effort to remove the Protestant defence capability. So, in staunchly Loyal communities in towns like Portadown, the death of brave and reliable men and women serving in the security forces tore at the very heart of Protestant emotions. Any compromise, pragmatism or conciliation could therefore prove to be fatal and must be resisted. Since marching was for so long one of the most tangible ways in which this political culture and belief was demonstrated and expressed, no quarter could be given there either. As Cameron concluded: 'The friction generated by these differences, fears and resentments produced tensions which undoubtedly played an immediate and continuing part in producing the agitations which led to the violence of 5 October [1968] and thereafter.'

While the year 1972 had been marked by great political change, it also saw the beginnings of a process of social upheaval that would have long-lasting consequences for all the people of Portadown. In the late 1950s Portadown Borough Council decided on a policy of rolling slum clearance to replace the very high number of small, unfit, often over-crowded terraced houses in increasingly dingy streets just off the town centre. They were to be replaced by newly-built modern homes clustered in estates. At the time a house with an inside toilet, hot and cold running water, constant heat and light and a patch of garden was the height of luxury. The first development took place at Woodside, about half a mile from the town centre at the southern end of the Garvaghy Road, then a semi-rural thoroughfare bordered by fields, the world-famous rose-growing nurseries and a small number of whitewashed cottages. The council constructed a number of three and four-bedroom houses, finished either in red brick or grey render, with the first tenant families getting the keys in 1956. Similar developments followed at Brownstown and Killicomaine. As replacement houses became available large areas of old-style street housing were demolished to make way for more new houses and commercial development. The Churchill Park estate, for instance, also off the Garvaghy Road, was built in 1968, mainly to accommodate people moving from the Castle Street, Bridge Street and Francis Street redevelopment area. Its award-winning, futuristic design of flat-roofed houses finished in grey brick proved highly popular with the early residents. The development programme was to have a dramatic impact in future years when the mixed population changed. As 'The

Orange Citadel' states: 'Where once Orangemen had walked along the Garvaghy Road to the gaze of no one, they now walked past housing estates which were almost exclusively Roman Catholic and who resented the parade.' In response to the civil rights campaign, local councils, like Portadown (whose record was far from the worst), were stripped of their housing powers in 1971 and replaced by the centralised Northern Ireland Housing Executive, which met for the first time on 13 May. Its remit was to introduce and enforce a standardised points system for the allocation of houses, based strictly on need, and to accelerate the house building programme with a target of completing 73,500 new homes by 1975. The Executive thus took over and completed the Ballyoran Park Estate, still further along the Garvaghy Road, providing highly acclaimed red-brick and pebble-dashed dwellings, and the redevelopment of the Edgarstown area.

As we have seen, the government had already sought to revitalise the area, including neighbouring Lurgan, by creating the new city of Craigavon, but even financial incentives had not persuaded people to move there in large numbers. Instead they preferred to live in new housing on the outskirts of the original town and, in the more relaxed atmosphere of the 1960s, many, especially the newly married with young families, were prepared to cross the traditional sectarian divide and live side by side with those of the opposite religion. The violent events of 1972, however, put a swift end to this cautious integration. In one week, as a result of Loyalist intimidation, 50 families fled the Killicomaine estate: half the Catholic population in the area. By the end of the year, another twenty had gone. Protestants were also targeted and five narrowly escaped being burnt to death in their Churchill Park fish and chip shop in February 1973. The owner, Harry Riddell, and four members of his staff were trapped inside when a gang blocked all the escape routes and set it on fire. Throughout the town a similar retaliatory pattern of what is now called 'ethnic cleansing' took place. Apart from families of 'the other sort' being ordered out or fleeing voluntarily, shopkeepers, bar owners and other businesses were drawn into the net. Bakers, milkmen and even window cleaners received warnings and threats which they ignored at their peril.

Despite the growing tide of violence and sectarian friction, some efforts were made to halt what rapidly turned into a two-way exodus, with families arranging exchanges between themselves. Protestants and Catholics in the Garvaghy Park housing estate joined together and formed a residents' association 'to prevent the estate from becoming a ghetto' and said they wanted to maintain 'the excellent community relations' that had existed since the 100-dwelling estate was built in the 1960s. Such initiatives proved to be in vain, however, and in the succeeding years intimidation would drive isolated Catholics, a fifth of the town's 20,000 population, away from Corcrain, Brownstown, Clounagh and Killicomaine to extend the sizeable Catholic ghetto along Obins Street, northwards from the town centre, and along both sides of the Garvaghy Road, where the Housing Executive provided new and modernised housing. The population movement, founded on naked sectarian imperatives, was so complete that the entire parish of Edenderry was virtually deserted after the parish priest's house was attacked with hand grenades and the church set on fire. The Catholics then built a new church at Garvaghy Road, St John the Baptist, to serve the increased population, together with schools.

Just as housing provision had been shaken up as a response to the civil rights campaign, so too was the system of local government. Health, education, roads, libraries, water supply and a whole range of local government services were handed over to new boards and agencies. The old urban, rural and county councils were replaced by a streamlined network of 26 district councils, whose principal functions were to empty dustbins and bury the dead, until they could prove their competence to manage the entire range of services efficiently and without discrimination, an evil previously practised with equal enthusiasm by the old councils whether under Unionist or Nationalist control. When the Craigavon Borough Council came into being late in 1973, under the terms of this new system, and chose the sentiment 'Together We Progress' as its motto, it seemed to herald a new era of constructive cross-community co-operation. As it turned out, nothing could have been further from the truth, for the new council, under the joint control of the Ulster and Democratic Unionist parties, emerged as a hotbed of Old Testament zealotry and set new standards of discrimination and bigotry in a land where neither had ever been in short supply.

Within its first couple of years Craigavon Borough Council imposed Sabbath shutdowns on the swimming pools in Lurgan and Portadown and a new £400,000 recreation centre at Brownlow. A request for a £25 donation to buy a caravan to be raffled to provide facilities for old people was turned down because of opposition to gambling. Even the Jehovah's Witnesses were refused when they asked to use the swimming facilities on Sundays to carry out baptisms. Attention then turned to a civic golf centre, which was also closed on Sundays despite the fact that it raised a third of its annual £18,000 income from Sunday players. The council then ran up a bill of £748.23 in little over six months employing two officials to take the names of up to 150 golfers who defied a large 'no trespassing' sign and continued using the facility despite the ban. A plan to fence the complex was drawn up but quietly abandoned because councillors feared the £70,000 it would cost would create too much of a public fuss. In due course a boating lake and artificial ski slope were also voted out of bounds on Sundays. Some councillors wanted to go even further, citing scriptural quotations in support of their demand to shut down swings in the public parks, tennis courts, and soccer, gaelic football, hockey and rugby pitches. There were also regular clashes when the council was asked to approve the availability of alcohol at functions on council premises, with inconsistent outcomes, usually depending on how many turned up at the meetings. The council persisted with its 'Lord's Day observance' policies despite the fact that a poll found 981 out of 1000 people questioned were in favour of opening the recreation centre. The *Belfast Telegraph* chided the council in an editorial on 16 July 1974: 'Vast amounts of money have been spent on these facilities, not all of it raised by the people of Craigavon, and one of the reasons is the hope that it will keep young people off the streets and out of mischief. The councillors need not imagine that all these idle hands will be joined in prayer.' The sectarian nature of the decision was highlighted by the *Portadown Times* on 5 July: 'The decision to close the pools comes as no surprise to anyone with even an inkling of how local politics operate ... Somehow some councillors got it into their tiny minds that the Protestants wanted the pools to remain closed and that the Catholics were queuing up for the first dip.'

There were more overt signs of bigotry. In February 1975 the council joined with 35 other objectors and voted to oppose a planning application for a Catholic church hall at Ballyhannon on the outskirts of Portadown. Later, in 1977, it voted thirteen to six against signing the Fair Employment Agency's declaration of principle and intent to prevent discrimination in employment on grounds of religion or politics. The council was also opposed to simultaneous moves to bring the law on abortion and homosexuality into line with the rest of the United Kingdom. When the Armagh team won the Ulster Championship in 1977, a Unionist councillor opposed a motion congratulating the team because 'the Gaelic Athletic Association was imbued with the ideals of a united Ireland'. The council also rejected an invitation to take part in the 'It's a Knockout' television programme, in which towns from all over the United Kingdom and Europe competed against each other, because it was to be recorded on a Sunday, and a bid to stage world champion water-skiing was also turned down for the same reason. A Catholic community group seeking a grant for its work was questioned about expenditure of £37 sending mass cards as marks of sympathy. There was more trouble in 1978 when the council insisted that the Union flag should fly along the Netherlands colours at an international table tennis tournament despite the fact that the sport's ruling body forbade the display of any national emblems. In the end the matches were played after agreement was reached that national flags would only fly outside the sports centre but not be displayed inside.

Local newspapers conducted polls and interviews from time to time, all of which indicated that there was far from unanimous support for the policy from among the local community and ratepayers. Yet councillors brazenly persisted in defending their actions. Writing in the *Belfast Telegraph* in June 1976, in an article littered with biblical references and scriptural interpretation, Alderman James McCammick, then Mayor, said: 'There are within every community those who need to be given standards on which to base their manner of living and as responsible, democratically elected members, we are obliged to preserve those reformation principles handed down at tremendous cost.' The council's messianic efforts were, however, called into question in December 1978. At the conclusion of a 14-month investigation, the Fair Employment Agency found the Council guilty of religious or political discrimination when it appointed a Protestant with inferior qualifications to those of a Catholic applicant to the post of outdoor recreation officer. The landmark case, the first of its kind, went to the county court, where the council was vindicated, but the original verdict of discrimination was finally confirmed by the Court of Appeal. A second case, with a similar outcome, caused the council to suffer a serious snub in July 1979. Days before a delegation was due to leave for a ceremony to set up a 'twinning' arrangement with the Californian city of Santa Rosa, the hosts abruptly cancelled after hearing details of the 'anti-Catholic' record of the council in a letter from the Catholic man in the second case. He revealed that there was not a single Catholic among the senior staff of the Council and that in the Recreation Department, where the two cases of discrimination took place, all the 24 staff were Protestants. Other 'anti-Catholic' gestures he recorded were the unwillingness of the Council to pass a resolution of sympathy after Pope John Paul I died in 1978 and its refusal to be officially represented at the opening of a new Catholic church.

Councillor David Calvert, a Paisleyite of uncompromising views, was frequently at the heart of the sectarian controversies in the council. In October 1979, he provoked a walk-out by three SDLP councillors when he asked 'if the Roman Catholic system of worship is within the parameters of Christianity?' On other occasions over the years, police had to intervene when council meetings became overheated and escort councillors and others from the scene. By this time, the threat of court action by the Catholic SDLP party was causing the 'no Sunday opening' policy steadily to crumble, although the diehards, like Calvert, who would narrowly survive a terrorist assassination attempt in 1987, continued to fight all the way. The council was by then well embroiled in a matter which would explicitly expose their partiality and heavily punish those directly responsible for it.

The saga began on 6 November 1978 when the Council agreed in principle to lease seven acres of land at North Street, Lurgan, to St Peter's Social and Recreation Club. The 400 club members intended, at their own expense without burdening ratepayers, to transform the derelict site, formerly occupied by a pet food factory, into a sports complex with an athletics track, sports pitches and a well-equipped clubhouse for use by young people. Negotiations were begun with the District Valuer and he communicated the details of an agreed deal to the Council in a letter dated 4 September 1979. A month later the full council was asked to approve a 99-year lease at the peppercorn rent of five pence a year with the club paying the council a premium of £14,000. The councillors voted thirteen to ten, by a show of hands with two abstentions, to reject the deal. At that point, Councillor Calvert proposed a 'procedural' motion to rescind the provisional agreement to lease the land which was approved by an identical margin. St Peter's, the council clearly underlined, was not getting the site at any price.

Not for the first time, the now notorious council had divided on sectarian lines, turning on the sports club because it drew its members from the Catholic community and was affiliated to the all-Ireland Gaelic Athletic Association, a body established in 1884 'for the preservation and cultivation of our national pastimes and for providing amusements for the Irish people during their leisure hours'. In practice the GAA fostered the sports of handball (played in a high-walled enclosure), hurling (a more robust form of hockey) and gaelic football (a cross between soccer and rugby). The Association therefore ranked high in Unionist demonology, with some justification, it must be said, for its rigorous exclusivity – anyone playing other sports was excluded or expelled – and its ban on members of the 'Crown forces' (the British armed forces and the Royal Ulster Constabulary) from membership or participating in any GAA activity.

Shortly after the council's decision, the club chairman, Barry Derby, indicated it would be taking legal advice. In the event, the club decided the best way to seek a remedy was to make a formal complaint to the

Commissioner for Complaints (Ombudsman) in Belfast, whose office has been established with powers to remedy inefficiency and injustice. A formal letter of complaint was submitted on 26 October 1979, and after a thorough investigation by his staff the Ombudsman determined in September 1980 that the council was guilty of maladministration and discrimination. 'Up to a certain point it is reasonable and natural that … public representatives should work and vote to defend the interests of those to whom they owe their election. However, in the present case … the likely adverse effect of the project on the real interests of the Protestant community in Lurgan turns out to be so unsubstantial that I must regard the Council's decisions in this matter as discriminatory.' Expressing 'great regret that it should be so sharply divided along sectarian lines on the issue', he concluded, 'the only way in which there could be a fair settlement of the Club's grievance was by the Council proceeding with the making of the leases.'

Although the council voted to 'accept and take the necessary steps to comply with' the Ombudsman's report, it showed little urgency in doing so. Indeed its subsequent actions, which dragged on for well over three years, were so far from being in line with the letter and spirit of the vote and the recommendation that the club's eight trustees decided to go to court in July 1984 to seek an order for compliance and compensation. In making an order for the council to enter into the lease and awarding the club damages in October 1984, Judge Frank Russell QC ruled that the Council had deliberately adopted a course of action to cause delay and, in so doing, had attempted to impose 'unreasonable and onerous provisions' in the lease. Reviewing the course of events, the judge said:

> It has been known to the Council throughout this transaction that the Club intended to spend very considerable sums of money in bringing this site (which as I have indicated was as long ago as 1980 categorised by the Commissioner as a dump and eyesore) to a condition which would permit sporting activity to take place on the site. Notwithstanding this the Lands Committee of the Council on 23 February 1983 resolved 'that the term of the lease be 5 years without provision for renewal thereafter'. The effect of this would be that the Club would be unable to make any, let alone any effective use of the site, for no tenant would spend money on premises they would have to vacate after so short a period. The term of the lease for a period of five years was confirmed by a Council meeting held on 20 June 1983. Following advice from counsel, a meeting of a special committee held on 1 February 1984 instructed the Borough Solicitor to prepare a lease for a

22-year term and the lease approved by the Council at a special meeting held on 5 March 1984 confirmed that the lease should be offered for a term of 22 years. The fact that it took the Council three and a half years to agree on such a fundamental matter as the proposed term of the lease is a measure of its approach to the implementation of the Commissioner's recommendations.

The judge was also critical of the grudging terms in which the Council implemented the Commissioner's recommendation when it finally approved the draft lease on 5 March 1984: 'That this Council being consistent with the former decisions of Council again confirms its opposition to St Peter's GFC Social and Recreation Club obtaining a lease for the former Windsor Foods Lands, but nevertheless recognises the law of the land in relation to this matter and in order to comply with the legal advice of the Borough Solicitor, reluctantly accepts this proposed lease.' He went on to say:

It is impossible to deduce ...whether or not the actions ...were a result of a deliberate policy decision by certain members of the Council. No member of the Council chose to give evidence so the Court is left in the dark as to what motivated the Council to act as it did; a charitable observer might attribute the delay and procrastination to incompetence; a less charitable and more objective observer would attribute the delay and procrastination to malice and ill-will on the part of certain members of the Council, but for the purpose of this judgement it is sufficient if I say that the effect of the Council's actions over the past four years has been to delay matters as effectively as if there had been a specific policy decision by certain members of the Council to delay the implementation of the Commissioner's recommendation for as long a period as possible.

The judge went on to cite examples of the Council's bad faith in attempting to impose, through the lease, what he termed 'many unobjectionable provisions which, in my judgement, are not only unreasonable or onerous but which are designed to be unreasonable or onerous'. These included proposed covenants which would have restricted the club to using the ground for 'ball games', prohibited the construction of an athletics track and even prevented it from constructing changing or washing facilities. It was also proposed that the club should be required to construct 'a wall of a minimum height of at least eight feet, and up to twelve feet in parts', with 'bent arms with barbed wire on the top thereof, such wall to be rendered rough-cast and the plans of the said wall to be approved of and the wall erected to the Council's satisfaction and to be maintained and kept in good order, repair and condition.' Its purpose was to prevent spectators viewing games from neighbouring higher ground and the proposed condition added that: 'In the event of the said wall not being of sufficient height ... the Trustees shall raise said Wall to such a height as will prevent spectators having a view into the demised premises.' The court heard evidence from a quantity surveyor that the 645 metres of wall required would cost at least £71,468 to build. The judge commented: 'When one considers that the Council's stewardship of this land has thus far consisted of allowing a derelict dump to become progressively more derelict and overgrown and when one further considers that the grounds of Brownlow House where they overlook the site are themselves derelict and overgrown the Court can only conclude that the purpose of the covenant relating to the wall was to impose so severe and so uncertain an expense on the Club that the Club would feel unable to accept the obligation and would refuse to accept the lease.'

As part of this course of deterrence and obstruction, the council also sought to make further mischief by imposing conditions about the flying of flags, always a contentious issue even in the most tolerant of circumstances. On 24 February 1983 the council's lands sub-committee instructed the council solicitor to submit to them a draft lease which prohibited the flying of flags or emblems and, the following May, the committee approved a clause which read: 'The Trustees or any person using the said demised premises or any member of the said Club or said members, friends, guests or visiting team shall comply with the terms of the Flags & Emblems (Display) Act (NI) 1954.' However, this general clause was significantly refined at a meeting of the council on 20 June when a proposal to amend the covenant was passed: 'That in relation to prohibition of the flying of flags and emblems specific reference be made in the lease to the Eire tricolour.' After some wrangling the final version of the lease contained an injunction 'Not to permit the flying of any flag other than the Union Flag'. The judge said: 'I have no doubt that the clause was designed to be offensive and I treat its late insertion in the draft lease as yet another example of the Council's hostility both to the Club and to the granting of a lease to the Club.'

In conclusion, the judge added: 'If the Council had acted fairly and speedily after it had accepted the Commissioner's recommendations in September 1980 the damage to the Club would have been relatively small. I am satisfied that the Council's maladministration has resulted in expense and damage which extends to the present. Accordingly I award the Club the sum of £107,763 by way of damages.' Turning to the question of relief, he commented that 'the Council had not acted in good faith and nothing before the Court (including the failure of the Council to offer any explanation to the Court of its conduct) leads me to conclude that the council would change its course of conduct in the future if it was left to its own devices. In my judgement justice can only be done to the Club if the Council is directed to enter into a lease with the Club,' and he so ordered, also awarding costs against the council.

Despite the damning indictment of its attitude and tactics, the council chose to challenge the amount of damages that had been awarded. The claim was heard by the Lord Chief Justice, Sir Robert Lowry, who delivered judgement on 25 November 1986, and made it clear from the outset that he endorsed and entirely agreed with Judge Russell's findings. Lowry also rejected new inferences that the club's plans were far too ambitious and beyond its financial resources – 'I was satisfied that the Club was a strong, well-organised and viable institution, of good standing in the community and in the eyes of banks, credit unions and suppliers of drink.' However, he did accept evidence from surveyors and others about the cost of the proposed sports development and how it was calculated and accordingly revised the damages payable by the Council downwards to £100,064. Costs were again awarded against the Council, and it eventually handed over the ordered sum, plus £29,871 interest and £37,352 legal costs, on 2 April 1987. When its own legal expenses of £58,432 were added, the council's campaign against the club cost a total of £225,719, expenditure that was subjected to an extraordinary audit when the local government auditor came to examine the council's books. As a result of his investigation, he decided there had been wilful misconduct on the part of seventeen councillors whose actions in deliberately frustrating the granting of the lease amounted to unlawful discrimination, and surcharged them personally to reimburse the council. One of the councillors had died in the interim, but the other sixteen appealed the decision and lawyers argued the matter before Lord Justice Carswell for five days early in 1989. When he delivered his judgement on 27 February, he did not disagree in any substantive way with the views of the two other judges but he did waive the surcharge on four councillors, Sydney Cairns, James Gillespie, James Forsythe and Ian Williams. In respect of the others, he held that councillors David Calvert, Gladys McCullough, Arnold Hatch, Mary Simpson, Philip Black, Frederick Baird, Alan Locke, Robert Dodds, Wolsey Smith, Cyril McLoughlin, Samuel Gardiner and George Savage were indeed guilty of misconduct, but he reduced the joint surcharge imposed on them to a total of some £90,556, including some legal costs. In addition they were all barred from council membership for five years.

Once the councillors had decided they would not mount an appeal to the House of Lords, the Reverend Ian Paisley, leader of the Democratic Unionists, and James Molyneaux, leader of the Ulster Unionists, chaired the launch, at a Belfast hotel in April 1989, of an appeal to raise £150,000 to meet their bill. 'I appeal to people to dig deep and forward the money needed,' said Paisley. The councillors themselves remained unrepentant. In a prepared joint statement read to a news conference in the Craigavon Civic Centre on 11 April, the day they were required to stand down from the council, they claimed to have suffered a great injustice and accused Tom King, the secretary of state, and the Northern Ireland Office of allowing terrorism to rage unchecked while unleashing the full force of the law against them. 'For us to do other than we did would have been to betray those who elected us and as honourable men and women, this we could not do.' The deputy mayor, Jim McCammick, also defended the group, who had given 157 years' service between them to the community, and said that nobody in his or her right mind could say that there had been discrimination. With seven of the twelve councillors concerned also members of the Orange Order, a special collection was taken at the County Armagh Twelfth demonstration in Keady that summer. At that point, according to the local MP, Harold McCusker, about half the £150,000 target had been raised. The St Peter's development was finally completed and opened in August 1990, twelve years after it was first mooted, by Peter Quinn, the president of the GAA, with an inaugural match between teams from Armagh and Down.

In the intervening years of the late 1970s and early 1980s Portadown regularly figured in the headlines recording the ongoing Troubles. William Craig was back in town at a large rally on 19 June 1973, railing against a British government White Paper outlining proposals for a return to self-rule for Northern Ireland. The British government wanted arrangements whereby Protestants and Catholics would jointly share and exercise political power. A copy of the document and an effigy of its principal author, the secretary of state William Whitelaw, were set on fire by Craig as thundering Lambeg drums were played. Later in the year, a Dublin–Belfast train was hijacked south of the Irish border in County Louth and sent driverless to Portadown where it crashed, but no explosives had been put on board. Like everywhere else in Northern Ireland, Portadown was paralysed during the Ulster Workers Council strike in May 1974, through which Loyalists brought down the groundbreaking power-sharing executive installed at Stormont the previous January. At the height of the strike, 10,000 people attended a major demonstration in the town and a pub was destroyed in a bomb attack during days of widespread intimidation and violence. In one incident, during a power cut, a gang of youths rampaged through the town centre singling out twelve Catholic-owned premises which were extensively damaged and looted. Shortly afterwards, £1 million-worth of damage was caused when firebombs exploded in Corbett's store. A number of police officers and soldiers were killed by terrorists in the locality over these years, and as tit-for tat sectarian tensions ebbed and flowed with the course of political events and security incidents elsewhere, Portadown emerged at the heart of what became known as the 'murder triangle'.

As ever the annual marching season proved to be an inevitable tension-booster, with Nationalists consistently focusing on the unacceptability of the annual marches through the Tunnel and along Obins Street. Seamus Mallon, a former teacher from Markethill, County Armagh, had now come on the scene as an elected representative for the Social Democratic and Labour Party, and was in the forefront of those who persistently agitated for an end to what he called these 'provocative coat-trailing exercises'. The Orange Order equally fiercely defended its traditional route through the area, not least because it feared any concession would lead to demands for route modifications and the variation of the numbers of marches.

The trouble generated by the Tunnel situation in the 1970s and early 1980s was reasonably manageable for the security forces by the brutal standards of the Northern Ireland conflict at the time. In 1974 the RUC deployed on average 130 officers to escort each parade, but of course some of the more troublesome marches demanded a much heavier police and army deployment. In a reference to events in Portadown, the chief constable's annual report for the year records: 'Parades were held by both republican and loyalist organisations and local band parades showed an increase over the previous year. A marked tolerance was shown by all sides and generally they passed off in a peaceful manner.' In fact a quiet protest took place as 900 Orangemen and three bands returned from the Drumcree church service, when a group of young people in the Churchill Park housing estate stood in silence with their backs to the procession, until it had passed only a few feet away.

There was a more sinister and dangerous effort to halt the march a year later. As hundreds of Orangemen gathered outside the Orange Hall at Carleton Street for the parade to Drumcree on 6 July, the police and army were responding to anonymous calls warning that bombs had been planted in houses along the route. At great personal risk the security forces searched the entire parade route and located two devices, one containing 5lbs of explosive, the other 10lbs, in derelict houses in Obins Street, which were set to detonate whilst the parade was passing. They were defused by an army bomb disposal team and the parade went ahead, just fifteen minutes late. A year later, the chief constable's annual report commented for the first time on the burden of the large number of parades during the marching season every year. Sir Kenneth Newman, who had come from Scotland Yard to help rebuild and reorganise the RUC after the trauma of 1969, wrote: 'No serious incident took place but the fact that some 14,860 police officers had to be transported to events throughout the province gives some indication of the heavy demands made on the overstretched resources of the force.'

Although there were no serious incidents arising from the Twelfth marches over the next few years, successive chief constable's reports reflect the evolution in police thinking about the scale of policing required to deal with parades. From 1978 onwards, the report contains tables detailing the ranks and numbers of officers required to police Orange demonstrations. On 12 July, for instance, one superintendent, three chief inspectors, twelve inspectors, 58 sergeants and 195 constables were sent to the predominantly Catholic village of Keady, near the border, to ensure that the Armagh county demonstration passed off without trouble. When Newman, who had given the RUC back its self-confidence and laid new foundations for its future efficiency and effectiveness, left Belfast to become one of Her Majesty's Inspectors of Constabulary and commandant of the Police Training College at Bramshill in Hampshire at the end of 1979, he was replaced by his deputy, Jack Hermon, a local man, who had also played a key role in revitalising the force. In his first annual report, for 1980, there was the clearest possible signal that a major change of policy on the parades issue was being shaped: 'It is worth mentioning that all too often large numbers of police personnel have to be deployed to deal with politically inspired parades and demonstrations, many of which pose a serious threat to public order. It is unfortunate, after the experience of more than a decade of violence and civil disturbance, that such activities have not been abandoned in favour of less inflammatory forms of political expression.'

Chapter Four
Tunnel vision

When Jack Hermon was a young police officer he was once sent to deal with an emergency call reporting a brawl between rival teams and spectators at a football match. Chided by an onlooker for not immediately wading in to separate the combatants, Hermon forthrightly explained that if he intervened they would simply bury their differences and join forces in beating the daylights out of him as a police officer. He thought that it was better to let them fight themselves to an exhausted standstill and then arrest them. The incident illustrated Hermon's instinctive understanding of the Northern Ireland people, their complex chemistry and character and the necessity for patient and practical pragmatism in dealing with them. It was an important personal asset that would come into play in the early 1980s when Hermon resolved to deal with the flashpoints which perennially turned the marching season into such a burden for the police and a trial for much of the community.

Hermon's conventional Protestant upbringing, and his ascent through the ranks of the RUC during years when Orange and Unionist influence in the force was considerable, marked him out as an unlikely challenger to Orange ascendancy. He was, however, a trailblazer and ever since the Hunt report in 1969, which recommended fundamental reform of the force, he had been at the forefront of efforts to re-train and re-structure the overwhelmingly Protestant and male force to operate with greater impartiality and sensitivity in a deeply divided society. Tackling the marching problem, which cut to the very heart of the divisions in society, was an important and overdue task deserving priority and action.

Born at Islandmagee, County Antrim, in November 1928, John Charles Hermon studied accountancy for three years after leaving Larne Grammar School before switching to a police career and joining the RUC in 1950. His first posting, as a junior constable, was to the small village of Eglinton in County Londonderry. With his boundless energy and enthusiasm he enjoyed walking ten-mile beats across the mountains to places inaccessible by vehicle or bicycle. The old hands teased him for his zeal but that stopped when they were forced to walk the same beats to serve his summonses for the absence of dog licences and the like.

Hermon's life-long concept and vision of police intimately involved with the population was acquired in that close-knit rural community where they patrolled without weapons and protective equipment and knew everyone on their 'patch'. There was early evidence of Hermon's self-confidence when he put a ticket for obstruction on the car of the local magistrate after several warnings went unheeded. In 1957 he was promoted to sergeant and posted to Coalisland, County Tyrone, to replace a sergeant who had been the victim of an IRA booby-trap bomb. It was in this period that Hermon's instincts for impartiality and even-handed application of the law were honed. In difficult circumstances he sought and made what were to prove lasting friendships with members of both the Protestant and Catholic communities. His political antennae, which were to be more crucial than anyone could then have imagined, were also finely tuned there.

Hermon was clearly marked out as a high-flyer in 1963 when he was sent to Bramshill Police College, the first RUC officer ever to attend. On his return he was promoted to head constable and posted to Hastings Street police station on the western fringe of Belfast city centre, where he became notorious for his stern, disciplinarian approach. The 1964 Divis Street riots dominated this period and brought about his first encounter with Ian Paisley, who was to become a long-running critic and opponent. The handling of the affair left an indelible impression on Hermon of the evils of direct political manipulation of a police force. From that point he was no longer in the mould of the traditional RUC officer class. But, demonstrating his skills for in-house politicking, he skilfully concealed his real views and did not allow them to damage his promotion prospects.

From Belfast, Hermon returned to Tyrone, this time to Cookstown, on further promotion as district inspector. After a year he moved to Enniskillen as deputy commandant of the Training Centre, later taking charge in 1969. In late 1970, after the Hunt report, he was made chief superintendent and became the RUC's first training officer, charged with implementing the Hunt reforms. It was an awesome task to develop training schemes for the force while it was simultaneously trying to expand and cope with the worsening civil disorder and terrorist violence. He performed well, masterminding the huge recruiting intake and laying the foundations for the modern RUC and Reserve.

In April 1974 Hermon was appointed assistant chief constable and as well as supervising the training function he became involved in community relations work, building up a large branch with the twin aims of bridging the Protestant–Catholic community divide and bringing the force into close contact with both communities. He played a highly personal role, opening up lines of communication with church leaders, businessmen and other groups to create a two-way dialogue on the future of the RUC at a time when its role and shape was being widely debated. The then Secretary of State, Merlyn Rees, was mesmerised by him the first time they met. Rees was a man for thinking out loud and developing policy through discussions with his advisers. One of his favourite techniques was to hold dinner parties at Stormont House and then 'chew the fat', as he put it, over the brandy and port. Hermon was invited to one of these dinners at this time when Rees was preoccupied with policing and the future of the RUC. When the decanters began to go round the table, Hermon, whose political instincts were probably sharper than anyone else present, delivered a lengthy dissertation on the philosophy of policing, penal policy, the political future of Ireland and the role of the RUC therein. It was a veiled bid for the top job and an early exposition of the radical Hermon agenda, and it worked. When he had gone, Rees remarked to one of his officials: 'Well, at least we've got a future chief constable.'

Soon after Newman became chief constable in 1976, Hermon was advanced further and appointed as one of his two deputies with responsibility for the control of RUC operations. He sat on the Bourne committee, the only RUC member, and played a significant role in writing 'The Way Ahead', the blueprint that 'Ulsterised' security policy by reasserting the RUC's prime responsibility for maintaining law and order by beginning the process of withdrawing the army to barracks. Newman departed at the end of 1979. Hermon took over in the new year and set out to achieve the principal goals he had defined, especially building enough trust with the Catholic community to obtain support for the RUC and attract Catholic recruits.

Before long Hermon had become a uniquely controversial figure, certainly by comparison with all his predecessors as chief of police. After repeated brushes with Paisley, who was a British and European MP, he closed his door on politicians, scarcely bothering to disguise his contempt for the way they exploited the RUC for their own ends and hijacked the newspaper headlines to parade their self-importance. Unionist leaders, unsurprisingly, had little good to say of him; Paisley conducted an unremitting 'Hermon must go' campaign and always drew loud applause from his audiences and congregations when he bracketed the then prime minister, Margaret Thatcher, 'Mrs Traitor', and her 'puppet' Hermon in a conspiracy 'to sell Ulster out into a united Ireland'.

More than any other factor Hermon valued his operational

independence from political direction and his accountability only to the law and the courts. He deplored the Unionist call for 'control of security', for it really meant a return to the bad old days of Stormont when the force was run by the Unionist Party. He knew that any such control would involve one-sided application of new anti-IRA laws, which would in effect be anti-Catholic. The strong Unionist reaction to Hermon was rooted in this, for the Unionists resented the fact that Hermon was so vigorously his own man and would not be told what to do. On the Catholic side, Hermon's image was equally controversial. A number of influential Catholic politicians and churchmen, who had unpublicised access to him, gave discreet, private support to the force, and regarded him as the most sensitive police chief the province had ever had. But he was more widely regarded as the latest in a line of repressive police bigots prepared to tackle the Catholics and pussyfoot with the Protestants.

Inside the force he attracted the same extreme reaction; his officers all respected him but either liked or hated him. All but a few feared him to the point where they kept their private views to themselves. He was not popular, either, among the security mandarins at the Northern Ireland Office. His straight-talking, often passionate approach and his blunt, though private, criticisms of the way some issues were handled were taken with less than good grace by ministers and officials in Stormont Castle who grumbled behind his back about his supposed inability to see where policing stopped and politics began. In the context of divided Northern Ireland such diverse and contradictory perceptions of the man suggested that his policies were probably right. Since he had positioned himself in the centre of the whirlpool and taken criticism from all sides, a case for his impartiality and fairness could be argued. He was paying the price of 'policing such a divided society,' recalled one of his colleagues. 'The best he could hope for was a grudging respect.'

Hermon remained aloof and unmoved by the stir he caused. Like all visionaries, he was imbued with a tangible sense of purpose and confidence which often bordered on the arrogant. He was convinced of the rightness of his policies and the need to force them through, whatever his critics or the faint-hearts said. 'Popularity is not my business. Command is,' he said frequently as he single-mindedly pursued his carefully planned course. He placed his faith in the good sense of the overwhelming majority of the community, a concept he trusted implicitly. Colleagues, who remember their own nervousness at certain points, talk now about Hermon's instinctive understanding of the Ulster character and his shrewd judgement, founded on good information from the network of contacts he had cultivated in both communities. 'There were dangerous times when I did not share his faith or judgement,' admits one. 'But I have to say he was proved right. Every time we approached the abyss, it moved.'

The community polarisation caused by the 1981 hunger strikes, and the sustained street disorder that followed, so stretched the RUC on the ground that Hermon was forced to bide his time before approaching the marching abyss. However, he continued the conditioning process about the necessity to do so, first flagged in his 1980 report. In 1981 Hermon reported that the cost of policing the parades and ensuing disorder was £12 million, 'resources that could more productively be deployed for the benefit of all'. A year later there were congratulations and thanks for those who had exercised 'maturity and responsibility' leading to a drop in the number of parades. There was no direct reference to the problem in 1983 but the 1984 report, published in early 1985, put the subject very firmly on the public agenda for that year's marching season: 'I feel bound to say that the objective of community reconciliation is not helped by the defiant insistence of some sections of the community on parades and routes regardless of circumstances, and by some insensitive, provocative bands and demonstrations and the tensions they cause. The insistence on parading in circumstances which made undue demands on the security forces and pose a threat to public order, is a grave and increasing cause for concern.' A timely parliamentary question arising out of the report elicited the information that it had cost £2 million and required the equivalent of 39,000 police officers to control 2400 demonstrations during a six-week period that year.

In the aftermath of the hunger strikes, there had been a sea change in the British government's policy towards Ireland. Alarmed by the prospect of Sinn Fein emerging as the dominant political voice for Catholics – a clear danger, the Thatcher government in London was gravely warned by the Irish prime minister, Dr Garrett FitzGerald – tentative discussions had begun about a far-reaching political understanding to create not only constructive political interaction between the two communities in Northern Ireland but also to forge a much more formal mechanism for inter-governmental co-operation. The news of this hopeful political dialogue quickly filtered through the ranks of the SDLP, who were given to understand that the talks would deal comprehensively with ways to promote truly equal treatment and conditions for everyone in Northern Ireland and find means to remedy a whole range of Catholic grievances, not least unwelcome marches. With Hermon's ongoing strictures about the overdue need to tackle them also firmly imprinted in her mind, Brid

Rodgers sensed a major opportunity emerging to draw high-level political and police attention to solving the long-festering parades issue in Portadown. Rodgers, born in the Donegal Gaeltacht, had settled in Lurgan, half a dozen miles from Drumcree, after her dentist husband had bought a practice there. She became involved in the civil rights movement and then the SDLP, gaining the posts of general secretary, then chairman, and emerged as one of only a handful of women in frontline politics. So, as a keen supporter of the St Patrick's Accordion Band, or the 'Tunnel band' as it was known in the town, she encouraged them to test the water to see if indeed the times were changing.

The band was formed in 1932 by a group of enthusiasts in the Obins Street area. An early picture shows 21 men and a boy, in suits, shirts and ties, wearing their only item of uniform, white peaked caps. One of its earliest influences was a former sergeant-major in the British Army, who had drilled the band and introduced a number of British marching tunes into its repertoire. The military link was continued when Michael Henderson, a former sergeant-major in the Irish Army, took over. During an association with the band that lasted almost 45 years, he too put much emphasis on drill and took great pride in its musical prowess and marching ability, especially later when his son, Kevin, and three grand-children joined the ranks. Although its membership was exclusively Catholic, the band enjoyed good relations with Protestant bands in the neighbouring Corcrain and Edgarstown areas, lending and borrowing each other's instruments for their annual high days. St Patrick's lent their kit to the Orangemen for the Twelfth parades and borrowed from them for their own main events, the St Patrick's Day parade on 17 March and the Ancient Order of Hibernians demonstrations in mid-August. It also took part in Republican commemoration marches at Easter and played before and during matches at the local GAA grounds. There was no doubt about what was the most important event of the year: the annual St Patrick's Day march commemorating Ireland's national saint, from whom the band took its name.

However, from the band's point of view, the celebrations had long been blunted. The police always prevented them from completing a circuit of the Catholic part of Portadown by marching outwards along Obins Street from the Tunnel and back by the Garvaghy Road, because that route would have taken them along Park Road, an enclave of Protestant residents. Another stalwart of the band was Mick Creaney, the chairman. A member for 40 years and one-time bass drummer, he recalled: 'I remember my father told me when I joined the band that my old pair of shoes would last me a long time for all the walking I would be allowed to do.' The prohibition was all the more frustrating because the band, like the other residents of Obins Street, had to stand by and watch the police and army facilitate the Orange marches every year. At that time, apart from the Drumcree church service, the Order's time honoured rituals involved the lodges coming into town, the main march and the lodges going home again. Indeed the residents complained that the only time Obins Street was ever cleaned was the week before the Twelfth, when teams of council workmen were dispatched to weed and sweep the road and pavements in preparation for the marches. The police would also order residents to remove their cars from the street to give the marchers an unobstructed passage. Their anger was further deepened by the way the bands, especially the drummers, became more frenzied as they passed the parochial house, where the local priests lived, and the sight of some of the Orangemen and their followers breaking away from the parade to urinate against its walls.

For years, like many of the residents, the band had sent a letter of protest to the police objecting to the Orangemen getting through the Tunnel and along Obins Street, but each year it was ignored. However, in early 1983, encouraged by Brid Rodgers, Michael Henderson's son Kevin, the secretary of the band, wrote making applications for a St Patrick's Day parade. Against the changing political background, the band believed that it would now become increasingly difficult for the police and government to justify Orange parades through the area each July if the Catholic band were not allowed to parade the route it wanted. Although Rodgers and Henderson were turned down after a meeting with the police in 1983, they refused to give up and began a letter-writing campaign seeking support for their cause. On 16 January 1984, they wrote to the chief constable and the secretary of state, copying the letters to senior politicians in Britain, the Irish Republic and the United States. In the letters, Henderson complained about the refusal to let the band parade along Park Road and accused the RUC of 'religious and political discrimination' against the band. Complaining about Orange marches through the area, he said, 'these parades are highly provocative to the Catholic community, they are protected by the RUC and Ulster Defence Regiment and, on such occasions, the Catholic community are confined to their homes almost in curfew style.' He added that the Catholic community were verbally and physically assaulted by the UDR 'especially on their way to and from mass'. The UDR was an almost totally Protestant, locally recruited regiment of the British Army, which Catholics generally regarded as nothing more than a revamped version of the hated B Specials.

An RUC Assistant Chief Constable replied to Henderson's letter on 12 March, justifying the restriction on the parade route because extending it 'would lead to a heightening of tension in the town and would probably give rise to public disorder, possibly resulting in injury to persons or damage to property.' Referring to the passage of Orange parades, the RUC's spokesman said: 'I am sure you must realise that in this case the police are simply allowing the bands to follow the long established traditional route over which the parades have taken place for many years.' An equally discouraging reply came from an aide to Neil Kinnock, the Labour Party leader, stating that he could not deal with the issue because 'there is a very strict rule in the House of Commons that one MP may not deal with the problems of another MP's constituents.' A furious Henderson wrote back, saying he could not abide by that rule because his MP was Harold McCusker, an Ulster Unionist and Orangeman who played a Lambeg drum and actually took part in the Obins Street parades. Henderson said, 'I feel it would be an entirely futile exercise to ask him to make representations on behalf of the Catholic people of Portadown, particularly because of the insistence of the Orange Order on the right to have their parades march through 100 per cent Catholic areas whilst a band belonging to the Irish tradition is forced to remain inside the Catholic ghetto. It is the strong opinion of my committee and indeed of the whole nationalist community in Portadown that a continuation of the practice of forcing Orange parades through a wholly nationalist area will have very serious implications.'

On 8 March 1984, Brid Rodgers, who had since been appointed a member of the Irish Senate, wrote to the band, saying: 'I have put the case of the proposed band route most strongly to the minister for foreign affairs and have also expressed my concern to the Taoiseach about the situation particularly in view of the latitude which is allowed to the July March. I have now been informed by the department of foreign affairs that representations have been made on the matter to [secretary of state] Mr Prior's office.' Peter Barry, the Irish foreign minister, who was shocked by what she told him of the state of affairs in Portadown, vowed to put intense pressure on the British government to make sure the situation was not allowed to continue.

The following May there was a markedly more sympathetic response from the British Labour party, when Peter Archer, the opposition spokesman on Northern Ireland, said he had written to the secretary of state 'to express my disquiet at the apparently unequal treatment between the two communities'. These powerful representations failed to win any concession in 1984, but in 1985, as the two governments reached the home straight in their protracted negotiations leading to the Anglo-Irish Agreement, it was a different story. The RUC commanders in Portadown finally relented and indicated that 'in the interests of good community relations' the band could walk its chosen route on St Patrick's Day. The only conditions imposed were that band members alone could take part, without accompanying supporters, and that only the flag of St Patrick would be permitted. The police didn't want an Irish tricolour inflaming what was always going to be a testing situation. Michael Henderson was ecstatic. Brid Rodgers recalls: 'He couldn't believe it when we were told the police had given permission to walk the whole route. For years the band had just walked up and down the street.'

This time the police had granted permission for the band to complete a circuit of the area, walking from the Tunnel at the south end of Obins Street, along King Street and Park Road, through the small Protestant enclave, where many of the houses were anyway lying derelict, and back to the main nationalist area of Portadown, along the Garvaghy Road, Corcrain Road, and Obins Street to the starting point. The 29 band members recall forming up, with some 50 supporters, on what was a bitterly cold morning, watching their breath form vapour in the air, stamping their feet on the frosty ground to keep warm. News of the original police decision to permit the march had provoked an outcry from Unionists who had called a 'prayer' meeting in Park Road to coincide with the intended parade. A short distance away around the corner, by Woodside Hill at the south end of the Garvaghy Road, there was already a strong police presence. A cordon of RUC Land Rovers had been formed across the road, and several dozen officers were deployed. When the band reached the police line it was halted and the marchers were told by a senior police officer that permission to proceed along Park Road had been withdrawn. The police wanted to avoid any breach of the peace arising from what would inevitably have become a confrontation with the Protestant protestors. When it heard that the parade had been stopped the prayer meeting erupted in cheers, but back at the police cordon there were prolonged angry exchanges between the leaders of the band and the police.

Henderson, who was 69 at the time, strode angrily through the police lines and had to be restrained from walking up the street to confront the protesters, especially Arnold Hatch, the mayor, who, as an Orange member, was always in the parades through Obins Street. Kevin Henderson remembers his late father's disappointment: 'He was absolutely devastated. Some people living in the area said they didn't believe we would ever get down Park Road, but my father believed the police would make sure the parade got through. Although he had been in the Irish army he was a quiet person and very religious. On that day I thought he was going to be arrested. He was furious and accused the police of failing to do their job.' Mick Creaney was also very angry: 'As far as we were concerned this was the Orange Order stopping our parade. He may not have organised the protest, but the fact that Arnold Hatch was there was enough. The Orangemen walked through our area every year and now they were stopping us walking around our own area for the first time.' As word spread that the parade had been blocked, a crowd gathered. One of the onlookers was a young man with Republican tendencies, Brendan McKenna, who had been staying over at his wife's home in Parkside just off Obins Street. For him, and for the Catholics of Portadown, the blocking of the parade was to have a lasting impact.

The police action was discussed at a heated meeting between senior RUC officers and representatives of the band in the police accommodation at the Mahon Road barracks on 16 April. Notes of the meeting record the delegation telling police that 'if the criterion of the RUC was to choose the action that led to the least breach of the peace this was suggesting that the nationalists should be prepared to cause a greater threat of a breach of the peace on the 12 July [sic] and the Protestant band would be re-routed.' Some weeks after the incident, Hatch invited the band to take part in the annual Mayor's parade through the centre of Portadown the following May, the first time they had ever been asked to participate. The band committee met in St Mary's Hall to discuss the invitation but decided not to accept. 'We were worried about our safety because we felt the band would be attacked by Loyalists in the town centre,' recalls Creaney. 'We were also still very annoyed at the way we had been treated. We reckoned that Hatch realised he had made a big mistake and had invited us to try to recover the situation. We declined because we had not been allowed to walk on St Patrick's Day, which was very important to us.'

Looking back, Brid Rodgers believes the blocking of the St Patrick's Day parade was the catalyst for the controversy that has surrounded marches in Portadown ever since and helped set the scene for the confrontations at the Tunnel the following year. 'That was the day that turned the whole thing. That was the day the Nationalist community said they had had enough. Many of the residents said afterwards that the Orange Order would never parade in their area again,' she says. Kevin Henderson agrees. 'When they stopped our parade that day it was like taking the pin out of a hand grenade,' he says. The explosive effect would become all too clear the following year, in 1985, when Hermon decided the time had finally come to carry out his long-signalled intention to deal with the effects of provocative marches. The timing of the move, with speculation about the contents of the emerging Anglo-Irish Agreement stoking up Protestant fears by the day, was deeply unfortunate and plunged the RUC into what would turn out to be a more searching ordeal than even its collapse in 1969 or the onslaught it faced on the streets during the 1981 hunger strikes. Unionists promptly accused Hermon of dancing to Dublin's tune in seeking to regulate some of the traditional marches. Subsequently the issue was exploited out of all proportion, causing serious Protestant disaffection with the RUC for the first time in its history.

When Hermon began planning to deal with marches several years earlier, he had no idea that when he made his move that the inherent historic sensitivity would be so acutely aggravated by unforeseeable political developments. Given the scale of the marching season in Ulster – 1450 Loyalist and 450 Republican parades were scheduled in 1985 – the number of flashpoint parades, at less than fifty, was pretty small. But such was the emotional and political background to them that there was a real danger of any RUC action resulting in hardliners resisting re-routing, tempers rising and trouble spreading elsewhere throughout the community. Thus great store was set by secret talks with leaders of the Orange Order and other march organisers in a bid to achieve agreed compromise and remove the need for direct police action. The initiative met with some success. In some places, marchers agreed minor re-routings or conditions about the conduct of bands and marchers to minimise disruption and provocation. In Lurgan the marchers agreed to parade on one side of a traffic island known as 'the Knob', rather than spread out the full width of the road, at a point leading to a Catholic area.

While his divisional commanders, in each locality, had pursued such voluntary compromises, Hermon had been building up alternative resources for what he foresaw as a decisive summer in getting to grips with contentious marches, preferably by agreement but if necessary by confrontation. The force could now muster 3500 men and women, deployed in formations known as MSUs (Mobile Support Units). Drawn from every police division in Northern Ireland, these units were commanded by an inspector with two sergeants. They operated from four armoured Land Rovers, each containing a squad of six constables, who were all highly trained in co-ordinated public order tactics, with the equipment and mobility necessary to operate in strength, at short notice, anywhere in Northern Ireland. Their worth had been proved during the traumatic days of the hunger strikes and their skills had since been honed further in both training and operational roles. Among senior RUC men there was confidence that if they had to fight with provocative marchers they would win.

Hermon saw it as vital to the future of both the RUC and the atrophied political process in Northern Ireland that tackling the running sore of provocative marches should be recognised as an RUC achievement. But so fundamental was the principle at stake that the secretary of state, Douglas Hurd, emphasised that Hermon could call on as many soldiers as he needed. There was by no means unanimity in the senior echelons of the force either about the policy or the strategy. Some senior men feared being caught in province-wide confrontations with the majority Unionist population while the IRA exploited the overstretch with violent consequences. At a series of planning meetings in the pine-panelled conference room on the third floor of police headquarters in Belfast, Hermon soothed their fears and placed his faith in what he invariably called 'the good sense of the law-abiding majority'. As the marching season approached, several senior men who did not share this faith quietly crossed their fingers under the table.

With tension soaring and threats of defiance coming from the Loyal Orders, there was constant police contact at local level in a bid to bypass the inevitable hotheads and secure support for the limited re-routing from Hermon's 'law-abiding majority'. It worked in nearly all the 50 target locations where population movement, redevelopment and other physical changes, such as the repositioning of roads, had transformed the religious mix of an area and made previously accepted parades unwelcome. There were also some forms of direct action. In one place, Catholic residents opened their windows and played recordings of Republican songs at full blast, which they claim to this day helped to encourage the Orange marchers into a negotiated re-routing. Elsewhere bunting and banners were cut down during the night and Orange arches damaged. From time to time parades were also fired on by IRA gunmen and on other occasions bombs were planted on or near contested parade routes.

In most places, however, the traditional 'not an inch' Unionist mentality persisted, and in the absence of local compromise the police were forced into open confrontation. The first encounter came at the overwhelmingly Catholic village of Castlewellan, County Down, on 27 June when a parade through the village was banned. Marchers were halted at a cordon of Land Rovers and minor skirmishes developed during which 22 police and two civilians suffered injuries. Prominent among the protesters were local Paisley supporters, including a woman councillor who climbed up on a police vehicle and screamed abuse. Next morning their leader addressed himself to the situation at a news conference in Stormont. Returning to his familiar anti-Hermon theme, he said that he had been approached by officers who were 'sickened' by what they were being asked to do. He claimed that many had refused to enforce the Castlewellan ban and that hand-picked teams of Catholic police officers had been formed to do what he called 'Dublin's dirty work'. According to Paisley, there had been a Garda observer present as well 'to take stock'. Then, in a significant outburst, studded with further typical belligerence and exaggeration, Paisley mapped out the ground on which the battle for the hearts and minds of the community was to be fought over the next eighteen months: 'If the RUC are going to push the tricolour and Dublin down our necks and be used as the stooges of Dublin, then the whole might of Protestant resistance will be brought against them. If they are going to put us into the Free State in a clandestine way, and the RUC is going to be the weapon, then the RUC and anyone who stands in our way is going to be opposed. It's going to be a battle to the death. The time has come for the police to choose whether to be for Northern Ireland or against it.'

That evening there was more trouble when police prevented a crowd of 4000 from parading through Gortalowry, a Catholic estate on the outskirts of Cookstown, County Tyrone. An angry Protestant woman spat 'black bastards' at the policemen holding the line, and said, 'I never thought I'd say it but I wish the IRA would shoot them all dead tomorrow.' Next day in the town's Protestant Monrush estate a crowd of stone-throwing Loyalists attacked a house occupied by two young policewomen and damaged the nearby residence and car of a part-time reservist. On 11 July a crowd of 30 broke away from a bonfire party and attacked the home of a retired RUC man. He had settled there after the IRA had bombed his home in Coagh eleven years earlier. It was a grim omen of worse to come, and inevitably the spotlight switched to Portadown. At the time the Tunnel was a dreary place, a ghetto shared by some 70 families, its walls scarred by IRA graffiti, with a dirty scrap-yard, Denny's pork and bacon plant and a furniture factory side by side with blocks of badly-kept modern flats and several rows of terrace houses, many bricked up. With the advent of the motorway network, a new internal ring road and the pedestrianisation of the bridge under the main Belfast–Dublin railway, it was hard to argue that it was anything but 'coat trailing' for the marchers to insist on the traditional route. The access under the bridge, now confined to pedestrians, was so low and narrow that the parades had to lower their flags and banners, walk through in almost single file and reform on the other side.

Throughout their entire consideration of strategy to reform the Ulster marching season, the RUC knew that Portadown would be the seminal battle. In the early days of July the leadership of the Orange Order frantically tried to distance itself from Paisley and the troublemakers who fuelled the tension by spreading a tide of unfounded rumours through the Loyalist community. A typical scare began with a newspaper story that RUC volunteers were being sought to learn the Irish language. The claim was true. However, it did not reflect preparations for integration with the Garda Siochana, the police force of the Irish Republic, as the scare-mongers shrieked. Instead it was for the very solid operational reason that as IRA activists made more and more use of the Irish language the RUC needed officers fluent enough to deal with them. But a militant faction within the Orange Order in Portadown would not be placated. As tension mounted over what action the RUC would take, they organised a monster Orange Rally on 3 July to protest at 'the denial of our civil rights to walk the Queen's highway'. The rally passed off without incident but tension remained high. Three days later the RUC announced its policy. Urging people not to play into the hands of either the IRA or the UVF, who were manoeuvring to exploit the situation, the RUC said that a church parade would be allowed through the Tunnel next day, Sunday, but that the other parades on 12 and 13 July would not. The church parade passed off with only minor scuffles between the police and local Catholic protesters, who were pacified by the efforts of Father Brian Lennon and his Jesuit colleague, Father Eamon Stack. The clashes were an opening ritual. Everyone knew that the real test would come on the Friday morning, the Twelfth. Not for the first time, there was friction between the Grand Lodge and the District with the Grand Secretary saying the Order would abide by the police decision and the local 'Parade Action Committee' saying it would not.

On Thursday evening, as the traditional bonfires blazed, nearly 1000 police were drafted into Portadown. A battalion of the Queen's Own Highlanders set up tents in the public park adjacent to Obins Street and commandeered the local parish hall. At dawn, as the RUC blockaded the area with their Land Rovers, the Orangemen began to gather at their halls and soon the sound of bagpipes being inflated and tuned and drums being beaten and stretched contributed to the rising tension. The Orangemen had no clear strategy. Some wanted to recognise change and go on with their celebrations. Others wanted to 'converge' on Portadown as a protest. The minority of hotheads wanted to storm the police barricades and march through. Shortly before 8 am the police took up positions by their vehicles as the bands and marchers began to form up. Then, to the strain of their stirring anthem, 'The sash my father wore', Loyal Orange Lodge 7, the appropriately named Breagh Leading Heroes, a cadre of craggy-faced, middle-aged men in black bowler hats and their Sunday-best suits, walked up to the police line and stood marking time as a senior police officer confirmed that they would not be allowed to march through. The confrontation lasted two days and there were sporadic clashes with the police during which plastic bullets were fired. On the evening of the Twelfth there was more concentrated rioting for two hours in the town centre as the police held back a stone-throwing mob from the Tunnel area. Inside, the Catholics briefly abandoned their hostility to the security forces and women poured out of their houses with cups of tea and platefuls of sandwiches for the soldiers waiting in reserve. At the end of the two days, 28 policemen had been injured but no marchers had broken the ban. More importantly, the soldiers had not been directly involved. The RUC had coped on its own.

It was a signal step for Northern Ireland and by the beginning of September, as the marchers traditionally put away their sashes and bowler hats until the spring, the RUC was quietly satisfied. The marching issue had been joined without serious conflict and even the most diehard Orangeman knew that things would never be the same again. The final count confirmed Hermon's confidence in the good sense of the majority of the community. Out of a total of 1897 Loyalist and 223 Republican parades, only three had been banned and 22 re-routed. However, the achievement was not without cost, for 260 members of the force had suffered injuries. Their impartiality was underlined by the arrest figures – between 27 June and 9 August, 468 Loyalists and 427 Republicans were charged with offences connected with public disorder. In Dublin, Dr Garrett FitzGerald praised the RUC for the evenhanded way they had policed the marches. Although his words marked a distinct change in Dublin's traditional attitude to the force, they played into the hands of those angry Protestants who had by then firmly smeared the force as 'tools of Dublin'. Such sentiments intensified after the formal signing of the Anglo-Irish Agreement at Hillsborough on 15 November 1985, which led many Protestants to turn viciously on the RUC for the first time in its history.

The first intimidation had come during the summer in Cookstown and Portadown, when police homes were attacked to mark disapproval of the RUC's role in halting and re-routing marches. This resentment intensified in the weeks after the Agreement was concluded, and early in 1986 fifteen police homes were attacked in a single evening, eight of them in

Portadown. The attacks had reached epidemic proportions by the end of March. Further anti-police feeling was stimulated in Portadown after the Secretary of State banned an Apprentice Boys' march through the town on 31 March, Easter Monday, on the advice of the chief constable. In ensuing disturbances 100 plastic baton rounds were fired at Loyalists in the town centre by the police, one of them wounding twenty-year-old Keith White, who was involved in the rioting and who died two weeks later. Within days of the clash there had been 45 attacks on police homes and families. On 4 April in Lurgan, when Lady Jean Hermon, the chief constable's wife, called on families who had been intimidated, a crowd gathered and threw eggs and tomatoes at her. Many police officers and their families had narrow escapes. One family group was watching television when petrol bombs were hurled into their living room; a part-time woman reservist and her mother escaped from their home with their clothes on fire after their door had been battered down and petrol bombs thrown, only to be greeted by a jeering crowd. Another reservist was shot in the hallway of his North Belfast home. Other officers woke to find their homes ablaze or full of smoke and had to run for their lives. One father devised a game to see which of their three young children could get out of the house first when mammy or daddy ordered it. The intimidation was even more subtly carried out by the graffiti writers. 'Join the RUC and come home to a real fire,' they wrote on the gables. 'Buy and die,' was daubed on homes abandoned by police families. To placate the fears of the force, the chief constable set up an emergency housing unit at the Belfast headquarters. In towns like Portadown, where it was most necessary, officers were provided with extinguishers, blankets and fire-fighting advice. Those who wished to move were accommodated in police quarters and helped to safeguard their belongings until a new dwelling was obtained. The camaraderie of the RUC was the most telling tactic as the police 'family' rallied to protect those at risk. By June the attacks began to peter out after sustained condemnation from Protestant church leaders and other responsible opinion, but by the end of the year there had been 564 incidents and 120 police families had had to abandon their homes. As many as 111 families were attacked or threatened more than once. The weapons used against them ranged from daubed slogans to bricks, petrol bombs and shots. 'It is only by an act of God that we did not sustain fatal casualties,' one senior man remarked.

The Easter clashes at the outset of the marching season meant there was to be little respite for the RUC, and once again Portadown proved to be an incendiary flashpoint. Anticipating trouble, the RUC had laid down conditions for the 1986 Drumcree church parade going ahead on Sunday morning, 6 July. The main restriction was confining the march to members of Portadown District, which proved to be a prudent precaution when thousands of potential marchers from all over Northern Ireland assembled outside Carleton Street Orange Hall that morning well before the 10.30 am scheduled start. Among them were members of the Ulster Clubs, a militant paramilitary grouping that had come to the fore during the recent anti-Agreement protests, and George Seawright, a Scottish-born loyalist who had built a sufficiently strong base on Belfast's Shankill Road to secure a seat on the city council and in the Stormont assembly. After he had gleefully called for Catholics to be consigned to incinerators, upon hearing that some parents had objected to 'God Save the Queen' being played at cross-community school concerts, even the Reverend Ian Paisley's Democratic Unionists found his views unpalatable and drummed him out. Seawright has been known ever since as a 'burn again Christian'. The Portadown District officers, anxious to comply with the police ruling, were deeply embarrassed by his presence that morning, but because he was a member 'in good standing', and they lacked the fortitude to exclude him and his Belfast henchmen from the march themselves, they instead delayed its start and asked for an urgent meeting with the police. Shortly afterwards, two of Portadown's most senior RUC officers, Chief Superintendent Bill Stewart and Superintendent William McCreesh, accompanied by a sergeant, arrived at the hall. They reminded the Orange leaders that only local members would be allowed on the march and agreed a plan for the marchers to walk through police lines in single file so that Seawright and others could be weeded out.

With the march now an hour late, the crowd outside had grown restless and there were fears that the police were inside conveying news of a ban. Sensing the change of mood, the police officers enquired about leaving by a back entrance but there was none and one of them joked about borrowing bowler hats to slip away safely. Their apprehension was not misplaced. As soon as they stepped back into Carleton Street, they were set upon and subjected to a violent assault. Blows and kicks were aimed at them and some marchers struck them with their rolled-up umbrellas. Other Orangemen came to their rescue and helped the officers push their way through the crowd to the end of the street where their car was waiting. (Next morning Stewart was found to have a fractured skull.) Soon afterwards the march set off and in Woodhouse Street, near the entrance to the Tunnel, Seawright, who was to be shot dead by the extreme Republican INLA the following November, was pulled from the ranks. The move caused an angry reaction and there was hand-to-hand fighting between the police and the marchers, who again used their umbrellas as weapons. A short time later, in the vicinity of the parish church, a crowd of Orangemen wearing regalia overturned a police Land Rover. Later the Order excused the 'unfortunate' incident by claiming that 'in the midst of what was a highly volatile situation a policeman had stepped over the parameters of professionalism by seeking to taunt Orangemen by use of a physically obscene gesture.'

After the service, the Orangemen formed up behind a pipe band and paraded back towards Garvaghy Road. At Ballyoran, police Land Rovers were drawn up to form a barrier to keep a distance between the marchers and the residents, some of whom had been holding a tea party in the middle of the road as a form of protest. They dispersed quietly as the parade approached and turned left into Garvaghy Road but a crowd of Catholics who had gathered on high ground began chanting 'Burn us now' when they spotted Seawright in the ranks. He had managed to give the police the slip and rejoin the march. Soon the bitter verbal exchanges between residents and marchers evolved into violent clashes with the police and there were running battles for a time. During these exchanges, a dart thrown by someone in the Nationalist crowd stuck in a policeman's neck. Although the march reached Carleton Street without further serious incident, hundreds of marchers and other Loyalists then returned to the Tunnel bridge to vent their anger on the police. Altogether thirteen police officers were injured.

The Portadown District leaders met in Carleton Street Orange Hall the following Thursday evening to take stock, and afterwards made an appeal for calm at the main demonstrations two days later. Harold Gracey, the recently appointed district master, read a statement condemning the violence and criticising the police. He also claimed that senior civil servants from the Department of Foreign Affairs in Dublin had been in the Tunnel to observe the parade. Despite all that had gone on the previous weekend, he mouthed a sentiment that would become all too drearily familiar in years to come: 'For over 150 years the Orangemen of Portadown have walked through Obins Street each July on their way to morning services at Drumcree parish church, without giving offence to anyone.' Gracey, who was to become a central figure in the events of the years ahead, is a stereotypical Orangeman, fiercely proud of Portadown's figurehead position within the Order. It would become his pre-occupation to avoid going down in history as the man who lost the 'Vatican of Orangeism' to the enemy. With his father and mother having been members, Gracey was steeped in Orange and Unionist history and tradition from birth and has held virtually every local office in the institution. Continuing the tradition, he is never prouder than when his own son and two grand-children, whom he is said to adore, accompany him on parades. Associates say Gracey, a retired Northern Ireland Electricity employee, is single-minded, determined, quiet, private, courteous, family minded, not overly religious and enjoys a drink.

Violence did erupt in the town centre on the evening of the Twelfth, as 32 lodges from Portadown District returned from Armagh. Bottles and stones were hurled at police as the marchers made their way along the main street. At one point a Land Rover with a senior police officer on board was halted by the crush of marchers and onlookers. At that point the leader of a band shouted 'Protestant Boys', causing the senior officer to leap from the vehicle and order other police to arrest him for provocative behaviour towards the police. 'I don't think so, Sir,' replied one of them. 'He was only shouting the next tune to the rest of the band.' When the parade retraced its way back through the town centre, there was more serious violence as the crowd turned more viciously on the police. One Land Rover was overturned and set alight, shrouding the town centre in choking black smoke. Plastic baton rounds were fired as police in riot gear moved in to rescue their colleagues and disperse the crowd.

Although there were ugly scenes in Portadown again over the next few days, including an RUC Land Rover being overturned and set on fire in the town centre, the defiance had begun to melt. There was the beginning of a sullen acceptance that the agreement was not to be overturned and contentious marches were not going to be allowed free rein in the future. An uneasy peace had been secured over the Twelfth when the police permitted eight lodges who would normally have marched the Tunnel to proceed instead along Garvaghy Road. The police banned a march from going through the Catholic part of Keady on 8 August and easily contained the rioting that resulted. At the end of 1986 Hermon was able to report that although greater manpower than ever before had been deployed to police the year's 1950 marches (170 down from the previous year), all but 67 had gone off without incident or disorder.

After a march-free winter a new Public Order regulation came into effect on 11 April 1987. Based on a similar act recently brought into effect in the rest of the United Kingdom, it gave the police tougher powers to control and direct processions. Formal notification had to be given of all events except funerals, and the Flags and Emblems Act, which specifically banned the display of the Irish tricolour, was repealed. In future the test would be whether flying any flag would cause a breach of the peace. The introduction of a new band contract by the Orange Order was supposed to curb the excesses of the 'Kick the Pope' or 'blood and thunder' bands, but it was never effectively enforced by Grand Lodge and many bands still do not know of its existence. By the terms of the contract they were to be subjected to tighter control by parade organisers, their repertoire of provocative tunes and behaviour was to be curbed and they were banned from drinking in transit to demonstrations and at them. Paisley and other Unionists thundered that the new Order was 'a recipe for civil war'. They called a 'Day of Defiance' to mark its introduction but it proved to be an embarrassing flop. Even Paisley in his Ballymena stronghold could only muster a handful of protesters and it was clear that, for the time being at least, the sting had gone out of the Unionist opposition.

The marching season of 1987 was the most peaceful for years, with disorder at only 26 of the 1976 parades, but, inevitably, there was more trouble in Portadown. Although local Orange leaders had informally conceded that they would no longer march along Obins Street at all, the rituals of protest and defiance still had to be observed, not least to assuage the militant Loyalist elements who had so violently attached themselves to the Order's cause. While those on the Nationalist side also realised that the Tunnel was now out of bounds and would remain so, they also went through the motions of dissent, collecting a 1300-signature petition which was sent to the secretary of state in support of yet another plea for the prohibition of 'these provocative and sectarian shows of strength'.

The security forces thus mounted a massive show of strength, drafting in 1000 police and 3000 troops on Drumcree Sunday to enforce the ban imposed on the route. When the full operational plan was received by the police in Portadown one senior officer went through it itemising the details of the massive deployment: a wall of scaffolding and corrugated iron to be erected across Woodhouse Street to prevent marchers or demonstrators even approaching the entrance to the Tunnel; the installation of closed-circuit television to photograph rioters for later identification and prosecution; the tasking of a spotter plane to help co-ordinate operations on the ground. 'Christ,' he said, 'the next thing they'll be sending us a submarine to patrol the River Bann.' The Orange Order announced that it would hold a protest adjacent to Corcrain Orange Hall if the parades were prevented from marching along Obins Street. Other lodges pledged to travel to Portadown to support them after holding their own local parades. If necessary they 'would take to the fields' to reach the town. In the event, Gracey handed over a formal protest to the police blocking the northern end of Obins Street and the parade went on its way along Garvaghy Road where, as the *Portadown Times* reported, 'there was a minimum of confrontation with a massive security forces presence.'

The following year, 1987, the Orangemen did not parade to the Drumcree church service, choosing instead to stage a protest and hold an open-air religious service in Woodhouse Street. The authorities had again mounted an elaborate security operation to halt them. This time the Army's barricade across the street consisted of heavy sheet steel, fifteen feet high, topped with coils of barbed wire, because rioters had all too easily torn down the corrugated iron the previous year. Speaking to the assembled brethren, Gracey denounced the decision to ban the parade through Obins Street, linked it all to the evils of the Anglo-Irish Agreement and claimed the Orange Order was being used to move support from Sinn Fein to the SDLP. Across the town, the Drumcree Faith and Justice group, which owed some of its origins to the local H-block hunger strike committee, had arranged a carnival at Ballyoran Park to protest against the march and had hired a folk group, Highland Paddy, for the occasion. Around 300 turned out but the protest was not necessary. For the first time since the war years, the Order chose not to go to the church. The Twelfth itself was peaceful, with police escorting the Orangemen along the Garvaghy Road, walking between rows of Land Rovers. Afterwards they hailed the good behaviour of the marchers, saying 1987 could well be a blueprint for the future. The only other notable incident that year concerned an unfortunate soldier, helping to put up the Woodhouse Street barrier under the watching eyes of a battery of television cameras. He was disciplined by his commanding officer for spray-painting 'hallo mum' on the steel.

By now it was abundantly clear to the Orange Order that the tradition of marching along Obins Street had finally come to an end. A survey carried out by the Faith and Justice Group found 1324 adults, a clear majority, in Obins Street and Garvaghy Road wanted this outcome. The outward journey to Drumcree and the country Orange halls would now take them along a parallel route to Corcrain and beyond, with, they believed, a return journey along the Garvaghy Road. As the Portadown District claimed publicly in July 1986, a permanent deal had been struck with the police to enable eleven lodges and three bands to traverse the Garvaghy Road in exchange for surrendering the custom of passage along Obins Street on both 12 and 13 July, although there was no understanding at that point that the Drumcree church parade the previous Sunday would be included. The pact had been sealed, the Orangemen believed, during their negotiations with the local police and endorsed at a summit between the Upper Bann MP, Harold McCusker, and the chief constable, Jack

Hermon, at which they claim to have been given a verbal assurance that the Garvaghy route was henceforth non-negotiable. 'I was in on the negotiations with the chief constable and the solution that Garvaghy Road should be the route came from Jack Hermon, not from me or Jim Molyneaux or Martin Smyth who were negotiating on behalf of the Orangemen,' said McCusker, who died from cancer in 1990. To confirm their perception the Orangemen point to a subsequent public statement from the RUC, which said, 'Unlike the Tunnel area, Garvaghy Road is a main thoroughfare in which Catholics and Protestants reside.' Police officers involved at the time now claim that there was no specific undertaking given about the Garvaghy Road but that it was said parades were generally not banned or re-routed from main thoroughfares. Neither, according to the police, was there ever any formal or informal assurance given that the Garvaghy route was permanent. These conflicting beliefs would prove to be of lasting significance.

While the decision to ban and curtail the parades through the Tunnel was greeted with relief by the residents, Rodgers and others argued that the alternative route, the Garvaghy Road, was potentially more explosive because more Catholics lived there. However, unlike Obins Street, where some 70 front doors of catholic-occupied houses opened directly onto the street where the procession passed, the three overwhelmingly Catholic housing estates at Ballyoran, Garvaghy Park and Churchill Park were set back a distance from the main road. The SDLP accused the police of capitulating and condoning the 'complete domination of the Nationalists in Portadown,' and Brid Rodgers warned Hermon that he was making a grave mistake. 'I remember telling the police that they were just storing up trouble for future years. They were going to have to suffer a lot of pain for re-routing them away from Obins Street, so I argued that they might as well do it right and tell them the alternative was the Northway, which did not contain any Catholic housing. When they rejected that I warned that it would come back to haunt them.'

For their part, the police were in no mood for further confrontation at that time. Having been battered for two successive summers by Loyalists in Portadown and across Northern Ireland as part of the campaign against the Anglo-Irish Agreement, they were relieved when the Order accepted the alternative route. 'We were glad to get it over with and breathe a sigh of relief for the time being,' recalls one senior officer. 'While it was a big issue for a couple of weeks every year, nobody ever mentioned it in between.' The *Portadown Times* summed up the situation in an editorial soon afterwards: 'One of the lessons which has really hit home these last two years is that there has not been enough talking between the main parties concerned. What a pity present divisions in Portadown would appear to rule out talks involving the representatives of the Protestant and Orange majority community on the one hand and the Catholic and nationalist community on the other.' By failing to resolve the conflicting understandings about the Garvaghy Road, heed Brid Rodgers' perceptive warning or encourage cross-community dialogue in the town, the authorities had left a live wire dangerously exposed in a still highly inflammatory environment. It was only a matter of time before it would spark into life again, more damagingly than they could ever have imagined.

Chapter Five
Drumcree: the last stand

Shortly before 11 am on 8 November 1987, a 40lb bomb concealed by members of the IRA in St Michael's Reading Rooms in Enniskillen exploded without warning, bringing down the building, killing eleven people and injuring 63 more. They had gathered there, next to the town's war memorial, for the annual Remembrance Sunday service commemorating the dead of the two world wars. Instead of standing in silent tribute, however, other spectators and servicemen and women clawed through the rubble with their bare hands in a frantic effort to rescue the casualties. The bombing proved to be a defining moment of the Troubles, for it stimulated the beginning of far-reaching political exchanges that would develop over the next decade, albeit at a painfully slow speed, into a comprehensive peace process.

The scale of the revulsion was so overwhelming and widespread that John Hume, the leader of the SDLP, judged the time was right to initiate talks with Gerry Adams, one of the most influential voices in the Republican movement. Hume and Adams soon enunciated a new agenda, based on political advance towards Republican objectives, but only by peaceful means. Given the centuries of distrust of Britain within the Republican constituency, which had been consolidated during the years of conflict, there was much to be done on both sides to change traditional mindsets and nourish what was already being called the peace process. But it gathered real, albeit for the time being secret, momentum after Peter Brooke took over as Northern Ireland Secretary in July 1989. Brooke judged there was a new 'window of political opportunity', but he was not after a short-term fix. He wanted to build on the 1985 Anglo-Irish Agreement, which had, for the first time, given the Dublin government a highly influential role over events in Northern Ireland. His real aim was to forge new political arrangements redefining, more fundamentally than at any time since partition in the early 1920s, the complex triangular relationship between London, Dublin and Belfast.

If progress was to be made, above all, Brooke reasoned, the violence must be halted. In a surprise move, marking his first hundred days in office, he sent a remarkable public signal to the IRA that if they renounced violence then the government would be 'imaginative' in dealing with them. The message was secretly reinforced through intermediaries to the IRA, the first signs of flexibility since the collapse of a ceasefire in 1975. Brooke then set out methodically to pummel the politicians and gunmen from a state of weary deadlock into a clear effort to find solutions. The strategy was pursued along parallel paths. In public there were 'talks about talks' with the Irish government and the four principal political parties in Northern Ireland. There were regular exchanges with the IRA, first through Catholic clergy as intermediaries, later also through the SDLP leader, John Hume. In both processes, however, there was only inch-by-inch progress from the shackled positions of Irish history.

On 26 March 1991 Brooke finally lined up the parties and two governments for discussions and hopes were high that come early July the parties would be signing an historic new agreement. The prospects of being frozen out of a political breakthrough were not lost on the IRA who, for the first time, began what was to be a protracted policy change, from what William Whitelaw called the 'absurd ultimatums' first presented in 1972 to the highly pragmatic Republican policies that had since evolved. But when the first round of Stormont talks quickly became bogged down Brooke halted them, reasoning that an orderly end to the first inter-party contact for sixteen years would enable the process to be rekindled again. By the end of 1991 a new round of 'talks about talks' was under way.

More significantly, a deep understanding was being forged between the two prime ministers, John Major and Albert Reynolds, who jointly adopted a problem-solving posture with both the politicians and the IRA, with whom both were now deep in secret dialogue. But there was great frustration at the IRA's unyielding posture, despite Brooke spelling out explicitly that Britain had no long-term economic or strategic interest in Ireland. After the general election of 1992, a new Northern Ireland Secretary, Sir Patrick Mayhew, took the chair when the talks resumed at Stormont that April. In July, now including the Irish government, they moved briefly to London, the first time that all the constitutional parties to the Irish conflict had sat around the same table for more than 70 years. After a summer holiday, more new ground was broken when the Ulster Unionists took part in discussions at Dublin Castle, the first time they had ever ventured south. These talks ended inconclusively in the autumn of 1992, but, Sir Patrick said, 'things are never going to be the same again. Historic watersheds have been reached and left behind us as we have moved on.'

Both strands of negotiation now moved into private and largely secret phases until John Hume and the Sinn Fein leader Gerry Adams dramatically announced they had agreed a formula for peace in late 1993. The two prime ministers instantly swooped on the potential deal and, in the aftermath of one of the worst ever bouts of tit-for-tat sectarian savagery in Ulster during the autumn, the Downing Street Declaration was signed that December. From then on both governments worked assiduously to draw the strings of the public and private peace processes together. The IRA fought hard for concessions to persuade its members to support an open-ended ceasefire. The constitutional politicians fought equally hard not to concede anything in advance. With firm under-standings finally put in place in August and September 1994, the IRA and Loyalist paramilitary groups both declared open-ended ceasefires. The declarations were the most carefully nurtured and hard-won components of a joint drive by the British and Irish governments over several years to end violence in Ulster and create a durable political settlement.

By the standards of the mid-1980s the intervening marching seasons in Portadown had been relatively quiet, although far from models of restraint. In 1988, the police and army once again flooded the town with personnel and closely escorted the march along the Garvaghy Road. In sharp contrast to the unyielding attitude he would adopt a decade later, Harold Gracey said: 'We have come to accept that this is the way things will be. At the end of the day we had to abide with the police decision and we had no plan to stop at the Woodhouse Street barrier as we did last year. All we wanted to do was to get to church as peacefully as possible.' Commenting on the Twelfth that year, the editorial in the *Portadown Times* on 15 July stated: 'The lessons seem to have been learned and the smile is back in Portadown for 12 and 13 of July. The town enjoyed its most peaceful marching season since 1985, relatively free of the tension and street disturbances that marred the celebrations in the past three years.' The following year, with the hottest Twelfth weather since 1955, the marches again went off without major incident. RUC officers recall the split-second timings they had developed to minimise the opportunity for trouble. Their Land Rovers were kept well back until the last moment and then, as soon as the marchers had cleared the Catholic part of the Garvaghy Road, they were quickly pulled out again. 'The idea was to get it all over with the minimum of fuss. The more we hung around, the more we were a tempting target, so we got in and got out again pretty fast,' recalls one MSU officer.

But the lack of trouble was far from a sign that the Garvaghy Road residents had withdrawn their opposition to the march or even acquiesced at its passage. Brid Rodgers and other political figures continued to protest to the British and Irish governments about the situation, which was periodically discussed by the Anglo-Irish conference of ministers at its regular meetings. The principal community opposition to the march was now being expressed through the Drumcree Faith and Justice group which also incorporated the People Against Injustice Group, formed in 1985 as part of the backlash against the banning of the accordion band march by the police. One of the prime movers was Father Brian Lennon, a Jesuit priest who had come to Portadown and, with the blessing of Cardinal Tomas O'Fiaich, established a Jesuit outpost at Churchill Park in 1980, which was named Iona House. In a policy change for the order, Lennon's mission was to reside in the community and tackle issues of injustice and inequity in a peaceful, non-violent way. 'The idea was to live in a poor area and work to reduce class gaps, north–south gaps and Protestant–Catholic gaps,' he recalls. 'The aim was also to challenge violence, totally, strongly and consistently and to use prayer as a political weapon, which Catholics had never done before.'

Lennon, who came from the south of Ireland, before moving to Portadown had spent the four years since his ordination working with the Irish School of Ecumenics. He had his first encounter with the RUC during the annual Catholic bonfire night on the eve of the internment anniversary on 8 August 1981, at the height of the hunger strikes. 'I watched police fire about 150 plastic baton rounds. I couldn't believe it was happening. I had no pre-bias against the RUC but it was not a congenial first encounter.' From the outset he adopted an active and prominent role among the Catholics of Portadown, on occasion urging radical and reconciliatory gestures on them. He had, for instance, argued, albeit unsuccessfully, that St Patrick's band should accept the mayor's invitation to take part in his annual parade despite their disappointment in 1985. Once the focus of the march protests had switched from Obins Street to the Garvaghy Road, it was Lennon who came up with the idea of holding tea parties in an attempt to channel the hostility and prevent it becoming violent. Every year as the march approached, they allowed themselves to be removed from its path. At the same time, the group talked to the RUC and other interested parties about the strength of feeling against the march, but it singularly failed in repeated attempts to open up dialogue with the Orange Order itself.

Against this unsettled background the 1990 and 1991 Twelfth parades took place without serious upheaval. The Orange Order handed in its now ritual protest letter to the police about being denied the route along Obins

Street, the residents' tea party was removed and the police escorted the march along the Garvaghy Road. A senior police officer recalls that the event had become a one-week wonder. 'There would be a whole flurry of concern and protest in the week beforehand, we would muster huge resources to push it through and after the seven-minute march – I timed it one year – everybody would go home and forget about it until the next July. I used to think it was a terrible waste of public money and police time but at least there was only minimum disorder and no lives were lost although we had to keep increasing the numbers we drafted in year by year to make sure of that.'

However, following four violent deaths, there was a very different mood in the Garvaghy area in the run-up to the 1992 march. Towards the end of June, following a telephone call to the *Irish News* in Belfast, Irish police went to a remote headland at Mullaghmore, County Donegal, where they dug up a shallow grave and removed a female body. It was quickly confirmed to be that of Margaret Perry, a 26-year-old civil servant from Churchill Park in the Garvaghy Road area, who had last been seen outside an off-licence almost a year earlier on 21 June 1991. The grim discovery was quickly overtaken by another. Early on 1 July, the naked bodies of three men, all with links to the area, were found abandoned by roadsides in south Armagh, within a ten mile radius, close to the border.

The four violent deaths were all connected and related to the relentless undercover war fought across an invisible front line between terrorist organisations and the security forces in Northern Ireland. With top-grade intelligence being the lifeblood of police and army efforts to deter and detect the gunmen and bombers, vast human and financial resources were invested in placing and cultivating 'agents' able to provide inside information about the sources of money, the location of arms and explosives hides, the identity of key terrorist activists and the plans they were making to target and attack lives and property. Given the damaging blows that such agents had regularly inflicted on the activities of both Republican and Loyalist organisations, it was not surprising that they conducted vigorous and constant internal checks on their members and treated mercilessly any 'informers' or 'touts' who were unmasked. The IRA was particularly active and ruthless in protecting its internal security and maintained special teams to do so. Loyalty tests and traps were constantly being set for its members and anyone who came under suspicion would be taken away for 'debriefing', a cruel euphemism for a session of violent interrogation invariably accompanied by torture. In the past such practices had included the use of electronic cattle prods and submerging the suspect in a bath of scalding water.

Against this background, therefore, it was not surprising that, in 1991, Gregory Burns, aged 34, married with three children but separated from his wife, panicked when his girlfriend, Margaret Perry, discovered that he was acting as an informer. Burns, whose 21-year-old brother Sean was one of three unarmed men shot dead by the RUC in November 1982, giving rise to controversial allegations of a 'shoot-to-kill' policy, had been recruited after being turned down for a place in the Ulster Defence Regiment. So, together with two friends, 29-year-old Aidan Starrs, who had served an eight-year prison sentence for being in possession of hand grenades, and Johnny Dignam, who had earlier been prominent in the campaign against the marches along Garvaghy Road and was more recently acting as Sinn Fein spokesman in the area, Burns abducted Perry. According to post mortem findings, she was murdered soon afterwards with blows to her head, and her body was concealed in a shallow grave. Although the men were questioned by RUC detectives investigating her disappearance, they were released without charge. The IRA was not, however, bound by such legal niceties as having to obtain verifiable evidence, and so, after some twelve months' work, when its 'counter-intelligence' team was ready, the three men were rounded up for a 'debriefing'. Starrs was captured while attending a commemoration ceremony at the grave of Wolfe Tone, the eighteenth-century leader of the United Irishmen. Dignam told his wife he was going with Starrs to buy lottery tickets and was never seen again. Burns was taken from his new girlfriend's home by masked men.

Post mortems carried out after their naked bodies – a pointed act of humiliation – were discovered twelve days after their disappearances revealed that each had been shot twice in the head and also showed clear signs of torture: marks on the back of Burns' right thigh were consistent with cigarette burns, and an oval burn under Starrs' left arm was likely to have been caused by a hot poker. Before they murdered them, the IRA interrogators extracted written confessions from the men, which were later sent to their families. In his final testament, Dignam, 32 years old and a father of two with a pregnant wife, who had once been imprisoned for explosives and firearms offences, wrote: 'I am writing this letter to apologise for all the pain and heartache I have caused you. I have only a matter of hours to live my life. I only wish I could see you and the kids one last time but, as you know, this is not possible.'

With the Drumcree church parade due to pass at the end of a week which had seen the entire Catholic community in Portadown shocked by the sheer brutality of the murky episode, the Faith and Justice Group cancelled the now customary tea party as a mark of sympathy for the families of those involved. The Orange Order was also asked to cancel its parade but refused. There were no incidents on the outward journey to the church, where the rector, the Reverend John Pickering, thanked the Orangemen for giving the proceeds of the collection to the church roof repair fund. After the service, the Orangemen formed up with their new MP, David Trimble, at their head. (He had been elected for the Upper Bann seat in 1990 in succession to Harold McCusker.) As the procession made its way along the Garvaghy Road, surrounded by police, scuffles broke out and three bandsmen were injured. Residents later claimed that some Orangemen had shouted abuse about the three dead men but the Order, claiming the trouble had been orchestrated, issued a statement saying none of their members had said anything to offend the bereaved families. By contrast the Twelfth parade was reported to be 'quiet and untroubled' with only a handful of people turning out to watch it pass along the road.

Whatever the insensitivity of the Portadown Orangemen in pressing on with their march, it was nothing compared to the behaviour of another set of Orange marchers in Belfast on 8 July, an incident that was to have great significance in accelerating what had become ever more impatient Catholic demands to bring an end to contentious marches. Earlier in the year, on the afternoon of 5 February, two Loyalist gunmen entered a busy betting shop in the Catholic-populated lower Ormeau Road area of Belfast. When they had ceased firing what was later calculated to have been 44 shots, four people lay dead, one was fatally wounded and declared dead on arrival at hospital, seven were wounded and another three, although uninjured, suffered deep shock. Within minutes the first police and ambulance officers at the scene found the premises choked with gunsmoke and the floor awash with blood. The five murder victims, staff and customers, all from the close-knit community in the immediate locality, ranged in age from fifteen to 66. But the blow these hate-filled killings caused was compounded by the marchers the following July. As they passed the betting shop and the mouths of the streets where the friends and families of some of the victims lived, with unprecedented offensiveness some of the marchers raised the five fingers of their hands, and there were shouts of 'Five-nil', and 'Up the UFF,' a reference to the outlawed Ulster Freedom Fighters who admitted carrying out the killing. Sir Patrick Mayhew, who had recently arrived as secretary of state, said it was behaviour that 'would have disgraced a tribe of cannibals' and, as we will see, would have lasting consequences.

The betting-shop killings were but one of a series of vicious tit-for-tat sectarian attacks of a ferocity not experienced since the 1970s. Although the secret peace process and inter-party political negotiations were stealthily, but slowly, unfolding at this point, they had also been accompanied by a serious upsurge in IRA economic terrorism and renewed Loyalist violence. Much of it was designed to demonstrate that neither Republicans nor Loyalists were in the negotiations from anything other than a position of strength and could wage their wars indefinitely if need be. Typical of many IRA outrages at the time was an attack on Craigavon police station on 12 December 1991, when a 2000lb bomb devastated not only the police station but a church, school, houses and other buildings nearby. On 5 March the following year, a 1000lb device caused widespread damage to premises along the main street of Lurgan while on 22 May 1993 an estimated £8 million-worth of damage was caused to the commercial heart of Portadown when a similarly sized bomb, abandoned in a stolen van, went off. Few premises escaped at least superficial damage and many others had to be pulled down and rebuilt, a process encouraged by the formation of a voluntary group called Portadown 2000 to lead and promote the regeneration of the town. The attack, in the very heartland of Orangeism, was seen by Loyalists and the Order as the latest in a long series of deliberate attempts to provoke and undermine them, and further reinforced their sense of hurt, isolation and persecution. 'The Orange Citadel' says: 'It was clear that, to nationalists and republicans, Orangeism was the complete antithesis of their ideological aspirations and was in fact the bedrock on which the protestant and British people of Northern Ireland relied for direction and support. This hatred of the Orange Order and all it stood for manifested itself in the large number of purely sectarian attacks made upon the members and meeting places of the institution.'

Over the years, apart from opposition to their marches, the Orange brethren of Portadown and its hinterland had indeed suffered repeated acts of violence and intimidation. During the years of the Troubles at least five members of the Portadown District lodges had been murdered and many more injured. For instance, 73-year-old Robert Whitten, a member of Prince of Wales LOL 56, was shot by a sixteen-year-old gunman on 1 March 1977 in an attack which was also intended to murder his brother, Herbert, the Portadown District Master, and died three months later. There had been a sustained pattern of attacks on Orange Halls, by far the most serious that at Tullyvallen, located in a remote rural setting near Newtownhamilton in County Armagh. Members of the Guiding Star Temperance Lodge were holding a routine meeting on the evening of 1 September 1975 when two masked men entered and began firing indiscriminately with machine guns. Other gunmen outside the hall shot in through the windows. Four members of the lodge died instantly, including William McKee, 70, and his 40-year-old son, James. A fifth man died two days later and six other lodge members were wounded. Before leaving the scene the terrorists planted a bomb, aimed at members of the security forces arriving in the follow-up to the incident, but it was spotted and safely defused. Some years later, in November 1977, when a 22-year-old man was convicted for driving the killers to and from the scene, a judge commented on the evidence given by the survivors of the Orange Hall attack: 'I have heard soft-spoken men from County Armagh whose friends were killed or wounded give their evidence quietly, with sadness in their eyes and with real dignity. They will not submit to violence or the threat of violence. They are determined to live as their forefathers have done before them, not to be deterred by violence, believing that peace and normality will return.' It was a perceptive and accurate analysis of just how deeply the trauma of the killings had been seared into the mindset of all Orangemen and how it reinforced their traditional uncompromising steadfastness in the face of those considered enemies. 'People underestimate the impact of 30 years of violence on the Orange and Unionist psyche,' says Jeffrey Donaldson MP. 'Many Protestants have literally felt under siege for many years, particularly those in rural areas where they have been under attack from the IRA. The Orange Order is particularly strong in those areas, where Protestants believe Republicans have been engaged in a form of ethnic cleansing. So, after thirty years of conflict and attacks by Republicans, the opposition to parades was seen as another Republican tactic in their strategy to undermine the identity and heritage of the Protestant community.' The Reverend William Bingham, a Presbyterian minister and leading Orangeman, holds similar views: 'In the eyes of the vast majority of the Orange Order, the IRA and Sinn Fein spent 30 years engaged in a sectarian campaign to kill the Protestant people and eradicate their culture and heritage. Incidents like the Tullyvallen Orange Hall killings, when those killed were targeted for the very reason that they were Protestants and Orangemen, had a traumatic impact on the institution and the wider unionist community.'

Against this backdrop, the recent town centre bombing had further aggravated the shared sense of persecution among the Portadown Orangemen. That summer, when the Faith and Justice group published the results of a survey which found that 90% of Catholics in the Garvaghy Road area objected to the parades, it was therefore dismissed by the Order and its members as another rigged instrument of torture. In a bid to assert equality with Protestants, who festooned much of Portadown with bunting, painted the kerbstones and lamp standards in sequences and hoops of red, white and blue and straddled many thoroughfares with arches, the group applied to erect a similar arch across the Garvaghy Road, to be decorated with Irish symbols and inevitably painted the green, white and orange of the Irish tricolour. The Portadown Orangemen considered the move as a further provocation and were apoplectic at the prospect of having to parade under such an arch, a possibility which caused the police to step in and prohibit its construction on the grounds that it would cause a breach of the peace.

In the light of these worrying pre-march skirmishes, a large force of police and troops was again drafted in for the Drumcree church parade on 9 July, but it passed off peacefully, apart from a few hostile remarks shouted by people standing on the footpath at upper Garvaghy as the Orangemen passed. The following week, police chiefs praised the parade organisers and residents for their behaviour after what they described as the most peaceful marching season in the town for years. A police spokesman said: 'There was scarcely an incident in the Twelfth season in Portadown this year, which was the most enjoyable we can remember. There was common sense and reason shown all round and the tensions predicted in certain quarters failed to materialise.' However, away from what was for once a peaceful Portadown, the security forces in Northern Ireland and Britain were facing an upsurge in Republican and Loyalist terrorism. While it was, of course, a summer of concern because of the violence, it was also, for the first time in some quarter of a century, a summer of hope with the ceasefires imminent. However, in the years to come, while they brought about a measure of peace, albeit a guarded and fragile one, in the rest of Northern Ireland, its ancient marching tensions condemned Portadown to an unprecedented period of turmoil. Jeffrey Donaldson summed up why the issue assumed such importance: 'Drumcree came to symbolise for the Orange Order as a whole something that was very important to them – the constant undermining of their culture and identity. If Portadown District, seen as a bastion of Orangeism, lost out then there was little hope for Orangemen in other parts of Northern Ireland where there were contentious parades. If Republicans could take on the Orange Order in Portadown and win then they could win anywhere. The feeling was that the real agenda was to drive the Orange Order off the streets. It became about much more than a stretch of road in Portadown. Drumcree became a symbol of Protestant civil rights. It was regarded by many Orangemen as the last stand.'

Chapter Six
Drumcree One

The leaders of the Portadown Orangemen were singing 'God Save the Queen', the final hymn of the service in the front pews of the Drumcree parish church, a short time after noon on Sunday 9 July 1995, when they received alarming news. David Burrows, who held the rank of deputy district master in the Order's complex hierarchy, had, as was customary, arranged to make contact with a senior police officer at that point to let him know the service was coming to an end and the march would soon be forming up to head for the Garvaghy Road. The police officer simply thanked him for the call. Almost immediately Burrows watched as several police Land Rovers down the hill started to move, but not in the direction he expected. George Robertson, who held the rank of district lay chaplain, was told to run up the central aisle from the church door to whisper to the leaders what the police were doing. Denis Watson, at that time the deputy county grand master, recalls: 'We walked out of the church and immediately knew there was going to be a problem. The police were blocking the small bridge at the end of the narrow road from the church leading towards the Garvaghy Road. We realised then that a decision had been taken to block the parade.'

The Orangemen were thrown into immediate disarray. After almost 200 years of marching to Drumcree on the Sunday before the Twelfth, and despite all that had transpired in the dozen previous years, they had never made any contingency plans to deal with that eventuality because they had never contemplated the march being halted. The subject had actually been raised before the parade left Carleton Street earlier that morning. Melvyn Hamilton, a civil servant by profession and a member of the Grand Lodge of Ireland, who had been invited to attend the parade and service as a guest of Portadown District, asked senior members what their plans were if it was stopped. It quickly became clear they had none, so shortly before they set off Hamilton, a deeply religious man who was an elder of the Presbyterian church, asked District Master Harold Gracey and his senior officers to pray for a peaceful parade. Standing together in the hall, they bowed their heads as he led them in prayer.

Moments later, about 10.30 am, with District Master Harold Gracey, David Trimble MP and a colour party from Ex-servicemens' LOL 608 at their head, some 900 marchers accompanied by two accordion bands moved off from the Orange Hall. There was significant tension during the outward march. Although thousands of supporters waved flags and cheered on the Orangemen as they left the town centre, many of the marchers were nervous about what would happen next. They were all too aware of the rising agitation among Catholic residents who lived along the homeward route to have that part of the parade diverted. The residents had provocatively applied to hold a march of their own at the same time. Shortly before 12.30 pm, after the service ended, the Orangemen had filtered out and formed up for their planned march. This would take them down the hill along Drumcree Road, across a small stone bridge, and along another narrow rural stretch before reaching the first Catholic-occupied houses of the Ballyoran estate and turning on to the built-up stretch of the Garvaghy Road itself.

Within a few minutes, however, faced with a cordon of police Land Rovers formed up on the bridge, they were brought to a halt and advised the parade was not being permitted. With many of the Orangemen impatiently marching on the spot behind them, Gracey and Trimble went forward, asked to speak to the senior officer and protested vociferously about the decision. Many of the marchers still thought the police were lined up to escort them along the Garvaghy Road as they had done previously. Despite Gracey's indignation, the police were unyielding, and he turned to address the crowd: 'The brethren of Portadown will not be moving, let it be hours, let it be days, let it be weeks. We are for staying until such time as we can walk our traditional route down the Garvaghy Road.' Eventually he walked back up the narrow road towards the church where, some of the onlookers remember, he looked visibly shocked. 'Drumcree One' had begun.

With the terrorist ceasefires almost a year old, the absence of violence had transformed the general mood in Northern Ireland. After years of pessimism and despair the hope in the air was tangible. Plans for extensive regeneration and investment to counteract the effects of the Troubles were gathering pace and powerful benefactors including the government of the United States and the European Union had signalled both moral support and funding. A new majority, regardless of their background or ingrained prejudices, wanted to ensure that the years ahead would not be as bad as those just past. In the new spirit of the peace process, the use of politics rather than violence was now overwhelmingly accepted as the way to build a better society based on principles of reconciliation, tolerance and diversity. Moves to negotiate the most comprehensive and radical redefinition of the British–Irish relationship, the governance of Northern Ireland and Belfast–Dublin links since partition in the early 1920s were already under way. Everything was on the table, it had been said.

All of this made Protestants very fearful. Ever since the abolition of the Stormont parliament they had seen their once-absolute political power being steadily whittled away and had watched the growing influence of Dublin over events in Northern Ireland with alarm. While an end to IRA violence was welcome, the emergence of what was described as a 'pan-Nationalist front' comprising Republicans, Nationalists and the Irish government was most unwelcome. With Dublin primarily blamed for the wave of restrictions on Orange marches over the preceding decade, the prospect of hundreds of convicted IRA prisoners gaining early release as a result of the ceasefires and more curbs on parades chilled their bones. In any case, with 1995 marking the two hundredth anniversary of the Battle of the Diamond and the bicentenary of the Orange Order, and a programme of commemorative events planned in the 'county of the Diamond', they were more determined than ever to defend their civil and religious liberty, and so any possibility of giving up the traditional route along Garvaghy Road was unthinkable. On the other hand, for the Catholic residents of the area, implacably opposed to Orange marches constantly taking place without their consent, there was a feeling that the new era of peace opened the door to a negotiated resolution of what was for them the most pressing political issue of all. The winds of change blowing across the political landscape of Northern Ireland that summer significantly bypassed Portadown.

Earlier in the year, there had been a series of meetings among the residents to discuss the issue and develop a more purposeful strategy to bring an end to the tension, misery and regular violence which for them marred every summer and turned what should have been the most carefree month of the year into an annual ordeal. It was widely accepted that the tea parties and folk festivals organised by the Faith and Justice Group in an attempt to channel the protests and to prevent them becoming violent had run their course. In May a decision was taken to amalgamate a number of tenants associations in the area with the Faith and Justice Group and operate jointly as the Garvaghy Road Residents Group. It is important to recognise that, while there were Sinn Fein members and supporters involved, reflecting the political profile of the community, it was much more broadly constituted. The first chairman was Malachy Trainor, but he stepped down after a week in case his new-found prominence turned him into a target for Loyalist terrorists. They had already murdered two of his brothers and his mother, Dorothy Trainor, a Protestant married to a Catholic, who was shot dead by the UVF on April 1 1975 as she walked home with his father to Churchill Park on the Garvaghy Road, after a night out at the British Legion Club in Thomas Street. He was badly wounded but survived. Ronald, Malachy's brother, a member of the Irish Republican Socialist Party (IRSP), was killed by a Loyalist bomb thrown into his home at Ballyoran Park in December 1975, while another brother, Thomas, who was a member of the INLA, was one of two men shot dead by the UVF as they walked along Armagh Road in Portadown in March 1978.

Brendan McKenna, the young Republican who had watched the St Patrick's band being stopped by the police back in March 1985, swiftly replaced him as chairman. McKenna, an abrasive, single-minded and obsessive character passionately opposed to everything represented by the Orange Order, would become one of the pivotal figures in the years ahead. Still viewed by some as an outsider because he had spent his formative childhood and teenage years half a dozen miles away in Lurgan, he rapidly became a hate figure to his opponents and a hero in the local community. An Irish speaker who prefers to use the Irish language version of his name, Breandan MacCionnaith, he met his wife, Philomena McCoy from Obins Avenue, in 1975 at a dance in the Lurgan Catholic Association. Then, at the height of the troubles, Catholics from Portadown often went to nearby Lurgan for entertainment, considering the centre of their own town too dangerous because the pubs were frequented almost exclusively by Protestants. As the romance flourished, McKenna began travelling to Portadown on a regular basis and settled there after he and Philomena were married in 1977. They moved into a house in the Parkside area of Obins Street with their four children, three girls and a boy, and still live there.

McKenna, then aged 24, was arrested in 1981, and later imprisoned, for his part in a bomb attack in Portadown town centre. At 5.28 pm on 6 August the police had started checking cars in Thomas Street, Portadown after receiving a warning telephone call. They quickly spotted a green Ford Cortina with its wheels sagging from the weight of explosives on board. In another tell-tale sign of a bomb they could also smell the fumes of the deadly 'Anfo' mix, as the bomb disposal experts described the home-made explosive, made of ammonium nitrate fertiliser and oil, which was characteristic of IRA bombs. Not everyone wanted to be evacuated, though, and the police had to draw batons to clear drinkers from a Loyalist-frequented pub in the immediate vicinity, a task achieved a few minutes before the device exploded at 6.08 pm causing extensive blast and structural damage to buildings over a wide area of the town centre. The army later estimated 300lbs of explosive had been detonated. Meanwhile other police had checked the registration number of the bomb car, OMD829Y, to trace the owner, who lived in Churchill Park. Two officers, armed with rifles, were quickly despatched there. When the first knocked on the door, McKenna ran from the back of the house into the arms of the waiting second officer, who also retrieved a gun and balaclava discarded during his rapid exit.

Six days later McKenna was charged with conspiracy to cause an explosion. In due course, his role in the operation was revealed when he was jailed for six years at Belfast Crown Court after being convicted of carrying a firearm with intent, false imprisonment and hijacking on August 5 1981. The court heard that two masked men burst into the house in Churchill Park and demanded the keys of the family car. A gun was produced and one of the men made off in the car while McKenna held the family of three hostage for almost three hours. Judge William Doyle, a Catholic who was himself later murdered by the IRA, said McKenna had been convicted by the 'most cogent evidence' and described the offences as 'horrifying'. These days, the Orange Order frequently points out that it cannot speak to a man who bombed the British Legion premises, some of whose members lead the church parade to Drumcree, which now honours those who died at the Battle of the Somme. In fact, the Legion was not the target; it was one of more than 40 buildings damaged when the car bomb exploded outside the offices of the local Credit Union, a Catholic organisation, in Thomas Street. It was planted there because it was the narrowest part of the street, thus ensuring maximum damage. Earlier that year a similar bomb had been abandoned at Magowan Buildings in the town, again planted at the narrowest part of the street. The bombings were part of an IRA strategy to inflict maximum damage on the commercial hearts of the main towns in Northern Ireland.

Under the leadership of McKenna and Father Eamon Stack, a Jesuit priest working with Fr Lennon, who had been elected as joint spokesman, the residents' group quickly adopted a far more pro-active and aggressive approach to the marching issue. They wrote to the Orange Order and police requesting meetings and had a number of meetings with the RUC, but the Order never even responded to the letter. They also wrote to Secretary of State Sir Patrick Mayhew, asking him to follow the precedent set by his predecessor Douglas Hurd, who had endorsed the prohibition of Orange parades from the Obins Street area in the mid-1980s. An official from the Security Policy and Operations Branch of the

Northern Ireland Office replied: 'Decisions on the routing of parades are an operational matter for the RUC.' The group organised a petition of people living in the area and gathered 1200 signatures calling for the Orange parades to be re-routed. As 12 July drew closer they also filed notice to the police for a march to go to the Orange Hall in Carleton Street at 10 am to hand in a letter of protest on July 9, the day of the Drumcree church service. Their plans were outlined at a news conference where the group expressed the expectation that the police would stop the planned march but, in so doing, highlight the offence Orange marches caused to the people of the Garvaghy Road. Father Stack, who conceded the police were in an impossible position, said, 'The Orange Order doesn't seem to realise the hurt and inconvenience these parades cause with people hemmed into their houses and not allowed out while the parades are forced through.'

The group said it was seeking an accommodation with the Order through face-to-face talks and without it any marches through the area between Drumcree Sunday and the Twelfth would be unacceptable. As they expected, permission was refused, although the police did offer the residents the opportunity to go there between 6 am and 8.30 am, well before any of the Orangemen arrived. This was rejected; the association insisted it wanted to hand in the petition as the unwelcome parade was about to start. Although the Order had not responded to the residents' letter, the news conference prompted a statement saying that the church parade to Drumcree parish church was the oldest recorded service in the history of the Orange institution and for almost 200 years the Orangemen had paraded with dignity to and from the 'mother' church at Drumcree causing no offence. The statement pointed out that the outward route was originally along Obins Street and then back by Garvaghy. 'It is only since the troubles and the subsequent demographic changes in the Garvaghy Road area that there has been some opposition to these annual Orange parades.' The statement concluded: 'Always conscious of the feelings of the local residents of the Garvaghy Road, the Orange Institution has been at pains to avoid confrontation and to conduct themselves with the utmost decorum as befitting a religious organisation parading to and from divine worship.'

Portadown District also outlined what it called the 'five compromises' made over the previous ten years: no Orange or Royal Black Institution parades now pass through Obins Street; only two Orange parades pass along the Garvaghy Road, one returning from Drumcree Parish Church and the other on the morning of the 12 July; only a limited number of bands take part in the two parades; bands are permitted only to play hymns or suitable march music, and bands do not play when passing the Roman Catholic Chapel. What the Order did not say was that in its statutory notice served on the police for the Drumcree church parade it still listed Obins Street as the outward route, causing the police to issue a formal re-routing taking the parade along Northway and then towards Corcrain. The residents were deeply disappointed by the uncompromising and dismissive tone of the Orange statement. There was more concern three days before the church parade after police removed twenty tattered Irish tricolours that had been flying from lamp standards along the Garvaghy Road for the previous four months. The operation, which appeared to them to be a necessary preliminary to the marches being pushed through yet again, was described as provocation 'by a police force that is the backbone of the Orange Order'.

In line with their new militancy, on the morning of 9 July, at the same time as the pre-march prayers were being recited in Carleton Street, McKenna and several hundred of the residents began marching from the community centre at Ashgrove Road, intending to go down the Garvaghy Road and onwards to the town centre. They knew well they would be stopped, for allowing them to parade close to where thousands of Orangemen had gathered would only have resulted in violence. The police moved quickly to block their path by putting a line of Land Rovers on the Garvaghy Road, near the junction with Woodside Green, and serving them with notice that they could proceed no further. While they were thus prohibited from marching, they were not specifically told that they must get off the road, so up to 500 of them sat down in front of the Land Rovers to await developments. McKenna then read out the letter intended to be delivered to Carleton Street, calling on the Orangemen to voluntarily re-route the inward march 'going through an area where it was not wanted and remove one of the greatest causes of community tensions in Portadown'. At that point the police were outnumbered by the size of the crowd and powerless to remove them from the path of the Orange parade in time without the use of what would have been condemned as excessive force. This was the key factor in the police decision to halt the Orange march after the conclusion of the church service and create what was, by all the precedents at that time, to be a lengthy stand-off.

As soon as Harold Gracey had retraced his steps back up Drumcree Road to the church, Hamilton, the most senior member of the Order present at the time, asked what he intended to do. In his view the only options were to turn and go back to Carleton Street the way they had come or to stay at the church for a few hours to see what happened.

'Harold had been caught by surprise,' recalls Hamilton. 'There were no plans for people to stay there, no arrangements for food to be brought in and none of the officers had brought extra clothing.' With the Orangemen now milling around outside the church waiting for instructions, a carnival atmosphere quickly developed as the bands that had accompanied the parade to the church marched up and down the road outside the church playing familiar Orange tunes. Meanwhile Hamilton contacted John McCrea, the grand secretary, and asked that he and the Reverend Martin Smyth, the MP for South Belfast and grand master of the Order, come to the church. Both refused, an action that would lead to bitter recrimination. As the afternoon wore on and news of the situation spread across Northern Ireland, car-loads of supporters began arriving with supplies of food and blankets. Tents were pitched in the field across the road and soon gas stoves and barbecues were alight. The church hall was quickly turned into a canteen and women began producing a ceaseless flow of tea, coffee and sandwiches. Leaders of the Order established a meeting place in a back room of the hall to consider their next moves but grass roots feeling was already clear: they would stand their ground for as long as it was necessary to complete the march as planned back along the Garvaghy Road. Some prominent Orangemen already believed that might take some time.

For their part, the residents remained blocking the carriageway on the Garvaghy Road until mid-afternoon, fearful that if they left the police would change their mind and push the march through after all. They were delighted and surprised by the turn of events. They had expected the RUC to clear them off the road and hoped to score a propaganda victory with pictures of the rough policing that would entail. In June, Father Stack had first asked the Mediation Network to assess the prospects of achieving an agreed settlement of the dispute, but when they advised such an outcome was unlikely at that time they were instead asked to send observers to the Garvaghy Road as independent witnesses to record the course of events for future use. The Mediation Network was an independent body, established in 1991 with funding from the Northern Ireland Community Relations Council, 'to assist reconciliation in our society by supporting a culture in which conflict is dealt with constructively' by the provision of training in community relations, conflict intervention and, in particular, mediation – third-party intervention to help resolve disputes. It would play a key role as events unfolded but, in the meantime, after police assurances that the march would not be forced through, the residents dispersed and went home.

By the evening, Harold Gracey's call for Orangemen throughout

Northern Ireland to come and support the protest was drawing an ever-increasing response. Graham Montgomery, a teacher at Friends' School in Lisburn and a member of a lodge in Moira, who had watched the parade leave the Orange Hall in the morning with his father, returned to Portadown after lunch and joined the growing crowd on Drumcree hill. He remembers the first hours of the protest as being reminiscent of a scout jamboree with a very relaxed atmosphere. 'People were arriving to show solidarity and also out of a curiosity value,' he recalls. Meanwhile across the rest of the town and further afield in different parts of Northern Ireland, other sympathisers had begun blocking roads and picketing police stations.

Hamilton, Watson and a number of district officers then decided to hold an open-air evening prayer service, mainly to keep people occupied and reduce the chances of confrontation with the police. So at 8.30 pm marchers were assembled again outside the church and paraded down to the police lines where the Reverend Percy Patterson, the county grand chaplain, and the Reverend John Pickering, Rector of Drumcree, led them in prayer. But the mood changed soon after the Reverend Ian Paisley – who had conducted his customary pre-Twelfth open air service at the Diamond birthplace of the Order earlier in the day – arrived at around 10.30 pm with around 100 supporters and addressed the crowd.

Darkness had now fallen and with it arrived more sinister elements, in large numbers, many carrying bags of drink. Stones, and the empty bottles, were soon being thrown at the police as a cadre of stewards appointed by the Portadown District struggled to keep control. Several of them were hit by objects aimed at the RUC lines. Montgomery knew things were getting out of the Order's control when he overheard a protestor at the front line declare himself as a representative of the Ulster Volunteer Force. Later he challenged another protestor, this one wearing an Orange collarette, who was preparing to throw a stone at the police, but all he got for his responsible action was a violent punch in the stomach from his brother Orangeman. In a bid to quench the escalating trouble, the Portadown officers requested Paisley to go down the hill to talk to police and appeal for calm. According to the account of the evening in 'The Orange Citadel', Paisley pledged support for the struggle and advised the Orange demonstrators to 'exercise restraint even under the greatest provocation'. His oratory worked for a time and he left for Belfast to attend a meeting with deputy chief constable Blair Wallace. By the time Paisley returned in the early hours, with the unwelcome news that the RUC was standing firm and the march was not proceeding, sustained violent clashes with the police had long resumed and continued well towards dawn on the Monday morning, 10 July, with officers coming under a constant barrage of missiles as they tried to contain Orangemen and their supporters from breaking through. Using the darkness as cover, many made repeated forays to reach the Catholic area across the adjoining fields. Concerned at the ferocity of the protests, and fearing that Loyalist paramilitaries would attack Nationalists in the town, Father Stack overnight contacted Brendan McAllister, the head of the Mediation Network, and asked him to make representations to the Orange Order for a meeting to discuss the halted parade.

That Monday morning all the parties to the confrontation met separately to take stock of the situation. Overnight there had been intermittent contact between the Order and Assistant Chief Constable Freddie Hall, the senior police officer at the scene. The Orangemen walked through the police cordon, which was still in place at the bridge, for a series of face-to-face meetings. The police wanted a full-scale meeting with the Portadown District officers, but Gracey would not agree. Eventually, under pressure, he relented but insisted the meeting must be in Carleton Street, a venue the police were still wary of since the previous occasion when one of their number had suffered a fractured skull. A meeting did take place at 11 am, attended by Gracey and other senior Orange figures in the town who had mustered considerable political muscle to support them. The Ulster Unionist leader James Molyneaux, David Trimble, the local Upper Bann MP, and Jeffrey Donaldson, soon to be an MP, all three members of the Order, took part in the talks. Donaldson recalls them as being frank but unyielding on both sides. 'They mainly dealt with how the protest would be policed rather than how a parade might be able to take place,' he says. In the mean time Hamilton and Watson were drawing up plans for a massive rally in a field at the back of the church hall that night, well away from the police cordon at the bridge, in an attempt to keep control of the protest and prevent more clashes with the police by reducing the opportunity for violence. Senior police officers welcomed the idea and gave assurances that they would not stop anyone travelling to the event, providing they did not cause trouble. The police feared that trying to stop large numbers getting to the area of the church would only result in more serious violence and draw them into confrontations over a wider area. All through the day, as crowds converged on Drumcree in ever-increasing numbers for the evening rally, the number of sympathetic street protests continued to increase. Country towns, villages and key road junctions across Northern Ireland were blocked and traffic brought to a standstill.

The most serious incident was the blockade imposed on the key ferry port of Larne where lorries and cars, many containing families departing for their annual summer holidays, were trapped in a ten-mile tailback. Roy Beggs, the local Unionist MP and an Orangeman, was among those protesting and was later fined £1350 for public order offences. The security forces were powerless to confront those causing the trouble or remove the hijacked articulated transport vehicles being used to block the road. There was no military armoured heavy-lifting equipment deployed in the town and none could be got through from the Royal Engineers' depot at Antrim, where it was based, because of the disruption. This indeed was the most telling measurement of the way the RUC had underestimated the scale of the problem they would face. In what was the first summer of peace, they were in any case reluctant to deploy soldiers. Getting the military presence off the streets, as a sign of normalisation, had been one of the key factors in putting the terrorist ceasefires in place and nobody would have welcomed any development that would expose the fragility of the peace process.

By 7 pm on Monday, when the rally behind Drumcree church had been planned to start, thousands were still trying to reach the location on foot, having had to park a considerable distance away because of the large attendance. The organisers decided to put the speeches back for an hour, leaving a number of bands and the thundering Lambeg drummers to entertain those waiting. The great drums, three feet in height and almost the same wide, each with names like the 'Craigavon Challenger' and 'Earl Kitchener the avenger', date back to the seventeenth century. They weigh about 40lb and demand Herculean neck muscles to carry them and powerful wrists to beat out the rhythms with Malacca canes. The drum cylinder is usually made of oak and the heads with goatskin, treated by each drummer with his own secret potion to harden and stretch it. One of the most striking features of the Orange culture was the endurance drumming contests when two drummers would go head-to-head, playing incessantly until their wrists bled and one gave up. That night the intricate rhythms of the Lambegs, 'the war drums of the Orange Order' as one enthusiast described them, could be heard over a wide area in the still summer air.

When the speeches finally got under way, the crowd, which had swollen to well over 50,000, heard Portadown District Master Harold Gracey, David Trimble, Jeffrey Donaldson and Ian Paisley repeat their demands to complete the march and pledge to stay at Drumcree until they were allowed through. Despite the hopes of the organisers that there would be no violence, the police came under attack before the speeches had even ended, causing them to fire plastic baton rounds in return. A series of running battles then developed between the police and several thousand Orange supporters who had not dispersed after the rally, and spread to the surrounding fields with rioters, many wearing Orange collarettes or sashes, making repeated forays to outflank the police and reach the Catholic Ballyoran area. A number of marshals appointed by the Order were hit and injured as they tried to form a buffer zone between the troublemakers and police, who fired further volleys of plastic baton rounds as well as using dogs to contain them.

Unknown to the mass of the crowd, the Orange leaders and politicians had already agreed to engage in a mediation process earlier in the day, provided it did not entail any face-to-face talks or contact with the residents. Molyneaux had flown to London after the morning meeting with the police and used his standing as a party leader at Westminster to talk to the prime minister, John Major, and the secretary of state, Sir Patrick Mayhew. Early in the afternoon, Trimble, Gracey and Donaldson came down the hill from Drumcree church hall, slipped through the police cordon at the bridge and got into a police minibus parked nearby. There Assistant Chief Constable Hall and other senior police officers were waiting for them. Donaldson recalls that this time their tone was in sharp contrast to the earlier meeting. 'Now the focus was on how a parade could take place,' he remembers. The police encouraged the delegation into seeking a means to resolve the stand-off by engaging with Brendan McAllister, from the Mediation Network, who had already been asked to become involved by Fr Stack on behalf of the residents. McAllister had talked to ACC Hall after the stand-off began on Sunday and again met him before the minibus meeting to initiate a process of what McAllister later described as 'crisis mediation'. After the Orange delegation had returned to Drumcree hill, McAllister made contact with Donaldson by telephone, and that afternoon and evening, with the assistance of his colleague Joe Campbell, he moved between representatives of the Orange Order, the Garvaghy Road Residents Association and the RUC trying to weld the components of an accommodation together. With the pounding drums and shrill bands playing away outside, one of the meetings took place with the participants sitting on the chancel steps in the church, the only quiet place they could find.

After the evening rally, when Gracey, Trimble and Paisley and others had passed through the police cordon, they were taken in a convoy of police cars, ironically along the disputed stretch of the Garvaghy Road, to Edward Street RUC station in the town centre to continue negotiating. At around midnight, the breakthrough came when the police started to talk about how many Orange marchers it would be safe to bring down the road. '200 or 400?' one asked. The Orange delegation seized on the remark, realising there was at last a strong chance the parade would be allowed to take place. After some discussion, the Order said it would agree to a silent parade, with no music, and would ensure that only members of the district took part, with supporters left behind at Drumcree. The talks were conducted against the noisy background of up to 5000 Loyalists and bandsmen marching up and down through the nearby town centre. At one stage a police officer, who could not be heard over his radio, went into a phone box to call the station. When he was spotted by the demonstrators, a Lambeg drum was wedged against the door of the phone box and he was subjected to a noisy ordeal for a time. The officer covered his ears and the crowd laughed.

Finally, at about 1 am, according to the Orange understanding of what was to become a hotly disputed account of events, an agreement was reached for the march to go ahead. With mobile phones playing an ever more important role in the proceedings, the details were passed back to those at Drumcree hill and the lodges began to assemble in anticipation of the march finally proceeding. Trimble, Donaldson and Paisley went back to the church to help segregate the Portadown Lodges entitled to march from the others, while Melvyn Hamilton and George Patton, the Orange Order's executive officer, went to address a rowdy loyalist crowd gathered at the police cordon leading to the Garvaghy Road. There they encountered the Reverend William McCrea, the mid-Ulster MP, who had been hit on the head by one of the objects thrown at the police. Even though it was now well beyond 1 am crowds began to gather at the Protestant end of the Garvaghy Road and in the town centre to await the marchers.

News of the imminent march reached the residents of the Garvaghy Road shortly after midnight, when Brendan McAllister came back to the residents from Edward Street RUC station and said he believed there was a possibility that the police were working on a deal with the politicians and Orange representatives to get the parade down the road. As he was speaking, the Orange delegates were in fact beginning to brief their members that there would be a parade. Alarmed, McKenna and Stack convened an emergency meeting of the residents' group in the community centre on Ashgrove Road. They also sent members of the group to knock up key supporters and alert reporters, many of whom were staying in houses in the area. As far as they were concerned, there was, as yet, no agreement to which they were party. Soon afterwards, matters took a decidedly ugly turn when around 400 people, some armed with cudgels and iron bars, staged a sit-down protest on the Garvaghy Road.

At that point, a number of police Land Rovers, which had been facing the Loyalist protesters at Drumcree, turned around and began driving up the road towards the residents. A senior police officer climbed from one of the vehicles and told McKenna the protestors would have to get off the road. With a crush of television crews, photographers and reporters now crowded round the residents, the police were now facing a potential public relations disaster: removing the residents would require force which would once more expose the police to the charge that they always favoured the Orangemen. They therefore decided to play for time by delaying the expected march and put the mediators back into play.

When word of the new delay reached the Orange leaders at Drumcree hill, they accused the police of losing their nerve again, just as they believed had happened on the Sunday morning when the residents originally blocked the road. They learned by mobile phone calls from people watching events on the Garvaghy Road that the police were engaged in an uneasy stand-off with those blocking the road and did not seem to be getting ready to clear the road by force to permit the march. They were also puzzled when convoys of police Land Rovers, which had earlier turned away and driven towards the Garvaghy Road, returned to their original positions. Trimble at first thought the police plan had changed because the noisy celebrations of some on the hill had alerted residents to what was going on. Paisley had made a speech describing the decision as a great victory and then led the protestors singing hymns, which worried Trimble because the singing was bound to be heard on the Garvaghy Road. Soon afterwards he went to the rectory, where John Pickering let him use his phone to call Molyneaux in London. John Major, Mayhew and Annesley then received calls from Molyneaux, while Trimble called RUC headquarters and urged them to do something because he was concerned that protestors who had been told to go home on the basis that an agreement had been reached would feel betrayed if the parade was again blocked and would react violently. Hamilton remembers conversations with police officers at this point when they were clearly wavering about their ability to put the march through. Soon afterwards he collapsed from a combination of exhaustion and stress and had to be driven home to recover.

Donaldson recalls: 'My clear recollection is that the police said a parade could take place early the following morning and it was just a matter of them working out the logistics. When dawn broke that morning, we began to get concerned. The police had not contacted us to discuss logistics for the parade and there were no signs that the police were being mobilised for such an operation'. Another meeting was set up in the police minibus where there was some tough talking. 'I recall telling Freddie Hall that there had been a clear expectation given to the Orangemen that there was going to be a parade and here we were on the eleventh of July, with the traditional eleventh-night bonfires due to take place. I said we had tried to give leadership and had tried to keep people calm during the night but really if the police reneged on their commitment to facilitate a parade then we felt that the situation would get out of control and that any leadership role that we might have would be totally undermined. I think that was the make or break point', says Donaldson. With no progress evident, some time after 5.30 am, the Orange team actually issued the police with an ultimatum that all contact and talks would cease if the promised march was not under way by 8 am.

The unfolding situation in Portadown was, in fact, being monitored very closely by the RUC chief constable, Sir Hugh Annesley, and his most senior commanders at police headquarters in east Belfast. There they were already deeply concerned about the collateral effects of the Drumcree stand-off, especially the continuing blockade at Larne, and the increasing likelihood of becoming entangled in a second confrontation between residents and marchers, this time at the lower Ormeau Road in Belfast, where opposition to the Loyal Orders had become entrenched in the aftermath of the disgraceful taunts about the betting-shop murders during a march in 1992. In particular the police dreaded the possibility that the Orange Order would carry out its threat to divert the main Twelfth demonstrations, with an estimated 60,000 marchers, from all over Northern Ireland to lay siege to the area if the 'feeder' parade, comprising the lodges from Ballynafeigh district, was not allowed to march along the Ormeau Road on the way to linking up with the main Belfast parade. Apart from opening a second front, which would have stretched police resources to breaking point, there were fears that the Order would escalate protests at other points across Northern Ireland with serious potential for inter-community disorder.

Just as the Mediation Network had been working to resolve the deadlock in Portadown, so a married Quaker couple from England were involved in trying to broker a deal to avoid a crisis at the Ormeau Road. Although there is a substantial native Quaker community in Northern Ireland, which runs family visitor centres at the prisons among other worthwhile projects, the joint British and Irish committee which established a Quaker House at University Avenue, Belfast in 1982, often opted to import couples to operate from it. In the past, Cornish, English and American as well as Irish couples have worked there. Their task was to provide a haven, a neutral venue, to encourage people who would not normally meet to come together to discuss and explore their differences. They saw their main role as facilitators rather than mediators but they were prepared to undertake that task if asked.

The couple who resided and worked at Quaker House in the summer of 1995 (the Quaker workers usually prefer to remain anonymous) had been in Belfast for about two years and their first experience of parades was shortly after their arrival when they were invited to Portadown to observe the tea party on the Garvaghy Road. 'We couldn't really believe that such strong feelings existed,' they remarked afterwards. Their real involvement in the parades issue developed from their attendance at a meeting in the Ballynafeigh Community Development Association at the start of January 1995, where they met some local members of the Orange Order. Some time later they met Gerard Rice, the spokesman for the Lower Ormeau Concerned Community, through a contact made at Conway Mill, a community development centre from which Sinn Fein conducted much of its activity. The Quakers tried to prepare the ground to bring the two sides together, but Rice's record – he had been imprisoned for IRA membership and arms offences – proved to be a stumbling block and the Orange representatives would not talk to him. Eventually Noel Liggett, the district master, took a huge personal risk and managed to win the approval of a sufficient number of lodges, first for talks about talks, then for face-to-face contact, under the auspices of the Quakers at a house in south Belfast. While this courtship was developing over several months, the Quakers worked on the terms of a possible agreement to resolve the marching issue by compromise. With others, they typed up a list of every possible solution, from the practical to the impractical, such as the idea of the marchers going around the lower Ormeau by river on a boat from the bridge to the city centre, which was given to both sides at the end of one difficult meeting which seemed to have ended in impasse.

From the outset it was recognised that an important factor was to get both sides to understand the position of the other and thus bridge the gulf of misunderstanding between them. As in Portadown, the residents did not fully appreciate the nature of Protestant democracy which in the Ulster Unionist party, the Orange Order and many religious denominations alike is from the bottom up. In the Order, local lodges cannot be given instructions by Grand Lodge. In the Church of Ireland, the local select vestry runs the parish, not the bishop or archbishop. A councillor or MP is selected by each constituency branch in the Unionist Party, not imposed by the leadership. Similarly, the Protestant side sees a pan-Nationalist front ranged against it and fails to distinguish the sometimes fundamental differences between the Catholic church, the SDLP and the

IRA – and its political front Sinn Fein – who do not always agree on issues affecting them.

With the moment of truth for both main parties to the conflict on the Ormeau Road fast approaching, the Quakers convened separate meetings with the residents and the Orange representatives at their house on the evening of the day the Drumcree stand-off began. Next day consecutive meetings took place between deputy chief constable Ronnie Flanagan, Gerard Rice and John Gormley for the residents, and Robert Saulters, then the senior Orangeman in Belfast, and Noel Liggett. At first all were in separate rooms considering a draft agreement, with the Quakers shuttling between them. Flanagan, who showed great skill in pressing both sides to face reality, later helped the Quakers to bring them face to face for a final meeting, which he chaired. Rice and Gormley agreed to the draft in principle but said they would have to take it back to a public meeting of the residents for approval. The two Orange Order men said they would also accept it, at which point the Quakers went back to their word processor, removed the word 'draft' from the heading and printed out copies of the formal 'agreement' that had now been reached. Rice and Saulters, who was the Belfast county grand master, shook hands. The ground-breaking agreement read:

> The Ballynafeigh District Orange Lodge believes in democracy and in everyone's right to enjoy civil and religious liberty. This means that all sections of the community must be free to express their religious and cultural traditions. The Lower Ormeau Concerned Community like-wise accepts that all have a right to express their religious and cultural identity. Both parties, however, recognise that, in the exercise of these rights, all sides must be sensitive to the wishes and concerns of others. It will take time for the deep wounds suffered by many living along the whole of the Ormeau Road to heal; both parties are committed to assist that process.
>
> Accordingly the Lower Ormeau Concerned Community and the Ballynafeigh District Orange Lodge agree that:
> * The Ballynafeigh District Orange Lodge will walk down the entire length of the Ormeau Road on the morning of 12 July 1995;
> * The Ballynafeigh Black Preceptory will walk down the entire length of the Ormeau Road on the morning of 26th August 1995;
> * In future, parades of any description will take place along any part of the Ormeau Road between the Ormeau bridge and the railway bridge only where agreement has been made beforehand between the parade organisers and the people of the Lower Ormeau Road. Only an open,

public meeting of Lower Ormeau residents can give such agreement
on behalf of the people of the Lower Ormeau Road;
- The Lower Ormeau Concerned Community and the Ballynafeigh
District Orange Lodge will either initiate or strongly support moves
to improve appreciation and understanding of the culture and
traditions of the people living on the Upper and Lower Ormeau
Road;
- This agreement has been satisfactorily verified in the presence of the
Quaker representatives and representatives of the RUC.

Flanagan was well satisfied with the morning's work, which he considered had produced a formula with the potential to defuse not only the
looming confrontation on the Ormeau Road but also the rapidly
worsening one at Drumcree. He folded his copy of the document and put
it into the inside pocket of his jacket. It was still there, some hours later,
in the early hours of Tuesday morning, while he was travelling along the
M1 motorway from Belfast to Portadown to see if he could defuse the
new impasse that had been reached on the Garvaghy Road. Ever since the
2 am confrontation, talks involving local police, the residents and the
mediators had continued, with the protestors still blocking the road. With
the Orange 8 am ultimatum also in play there was a growing sense of
urgency. Gradually the outline of an agreement did begin to emerge, but
precisely what was said, understood and agreed to is still hotly disputed
to this day and any goodwill that was generated by the mutually
pragmatic end to the stand-off instantly dissolved. Indeed what happened
next only served to heighten the deep levels of resentment and distrust
that already characterised the dispute.

After the last minibus meeting, Donaldson phoned Molyneaux in
London to bring him up to date. Molyneaux then made calls to Annesley
and Mayhew. Shortly afterwards, Molyneaux rang Donaldson to say that
Annesley had given the go-ahead for the parade. Flanagan and Blair
Wallace, the other RUC deputy chief constable, were already on their
way to Portadown to oversee the final stages of the negotiations and
police operation. Their presence was a sign of just how much was at stake
for the RUC itself and for the community at large. They went onto the
Garvaghy Road itself to take over command from weary colleagues, some
of whom had been almost constantly on duty since early on Sunday
morning.

When the highly personable Flanagan, who was building a reputation
for being approachable, open and pragmatic, got talking to McKenna he
pulled the Ormeau document from his inside pocket and told him they

were within a whisker of clinching peace on the Ormeau Road but that if they couldn't do a deal in Portadown first then it wouldn't work. McKenna was ready to help. He suggested the police should lift and remove the residents from the road to signify they did not fully consent to the parade passing. Flanagan was doubtful. He pointed out that televised images of them being carried away by the police, however passively, would send the wrong signals to the Ormeau. Eventually it was agreed that the members of Portadown District alone would walk along the road, with no music, while the residents would stand quietly, their backs turned to the marchers. The police presence was to be minimal, with no riot gear worn, and officers would stand along the roadside alternately facing the residents and the marchers to underline police neutrality. Furthermore, there was to be no march along the road the next day. Both sides finalised a verbal agreement at about 9 am, clearing the way for the march to proceed. 'The Orange Citadel' records its passage as follows:

It was shortly after 9.00 a.m. that Portadown District Lodge members were informed that the parade would go ahead along its traditional route of the Garvaghy Road. The one condition attached was that only Portadown District members would be allowed to parade. The brethren were requested to move back up Drumcree Hill away from the police road block to allow them to remove the Land Rovers. This was done. Shortly after 10.30 am Portadown District Lodge formed up on Drumcree Hill behind their District Standard. Following the removal of the police road block and under the instruction of their Worshipful District Master the parade moved off on its return journey to Carleton Street Orange Hall, to the applause of the visiting brethren. On a damp grey morning the only sound to break the silence was the noise of eight hundred marching feet as the Orangemen of Portadown District started along the Drumcree Road on the return route to Portadown, 46 hours late. The parade turned left onto the Garvaghy Road where a crowd of less than one hundred nationalist protesters stood across the road at the old Mayfair factory. As the brethren approached, the protesters moved to the footpaths and stood in silence as the parade passed by. No words or comments were exchanged. To the sound of marching feet the Orangemen passed the silent protesters, up past Woodside Hill along Parkmount towards the town. As the parade rounded the right hand bend at the carpet factory entrance and came within sight of those waiting at the Shillington Bridge a cheer went up. At Park Road corner there were remarkable scenes with the waiting crowds cheering and waving flags. The cheering continued as the parade, now joined by bands, visiting brethren, Bro. David Trimble and the Rev. Ian Paisley, proceeded through the town centre to Carleton Street Orange Hall. The town was at a stand still as cheering shoppers, workers and friends welcomed the Orange brethren home. No police presence was evident in the town centre, the police having been recalled to barracks. On arrival at Carleton Street the Orange brethren applauded the Portadown District Master as he made his way down the Orange ranks. Bro. David Trimble and the Rev. Ian Paisley, with linked hands, also walked along the ranks to cheers and applause. Following these scenes the road blocks were removed from roads throughout the Province. Other planned demonstrations, protests and actions formulated should the parade not have gone through were stood down. The Drumcree Sunday Orange parade that should have taken a maximum of fifteen minutes to pass through Garvaghy Road was finally over after an unprecedented 48 hour delay. The Portadown Orange brethren, with the support of brethren and friends from throughout the province, had shown what could be achieved by people power in what was largely a peaceful stand-off.

There was a collective sigh of relief across Northern Ireland as the tension quickly evaporated and the agreement was widely hailed as a victory for common sense. As the last marchers left the Garvaghy Road, some residents even clapped and waved. Assistant Chief Constable Hall was reported as saying he was confident the Drumcree agreement would stick, ending years of conflict between the Orange Order and the residents of the Garvaghy Road during the July marching season. Speaking afterwards, McAllister said: 'The Orangemen and Nationalists have confirmed my own belief that across our community there is a wisdom and maturity which can prevail in the midst of difficult conflict.' Within a matter of hours, however, such high hopes and any spirit of compromise or accommodation had vanished. After the passing of the march, the residents, some watching in the community centre, others in their homes, were outraged when they saw the television pictures of Trimble and Paisley joining hands and marching triumphantly into Carleton Street at the head of the parade. Their indignation soared when they heard Harold Gracey and others give a series of television and radio interviews insisting there was no deal with the residents. The final insult came as they watched Paisley hail the passage of the march as 'one of the greatest victories during the past 25 years for Protestantism in Northern Ireland'.

Brendan McKenna says: 'People were furious when they saw Trimble and Paisley acting like they did and talking about a great victory for the Orange Order and saying they would continue to walk down the road. Within a matter of hours people in the area had gone from being jubilant to being in complete despair.' That night, McKenna and Stack convened a meeting of the coalition at Iona House, the Jesuits' residence. The sixteen coalition members who attended were tense and angry. In addition to their outrage at the remarks by Gracey, Trimble and Paisley, they were now convinced they had been misled by Flanagan. 'As far as we were concerned, the issue was quite clear,' recalls McKenna. 'People here were convinced there was a deal because we had told them we had been given an assurance by the police that there would be no future parades without their consent. That assurance was given by Ronnie Flanagan. It was on those terms that we agreed to the march coming down with the residents staging a peaceful protest. As far as we were concerned when that march came down people here were waving goodbye to the Orange Order once and for all. That was why some people waved as the parade left the road. If we hadn't believed that we would not have agreed to the parade.'

As the recriminations crashed back and forth, the next day attention was focused on the Ormeau Road in Belfast where the Quakers' painstakingly-constructed agreement had been undermined by events at Drumcree. The Ballynafeigh District banner had been spotted on television being paraded at the police cordon during the Monday night rally and the triumphalist scenes after the parade had caused similar outrage among the Ormeau residents. With a high-profile Republican presence signalling IRA disapproval, a parade by consent was therefore overwhelmingly rejected at the second of two public meetings in the area. As a result, early next morning, the RUC deployed hundreds of officers to block residents in their homes to enable the 150 Orangemen from the Ballynafeigh lodges, with their four bands, to parade along the disputed stretch of the Ormeau Road. Some protesters attempted to stop them from reaching Ormeau Bridge and vehicles were hijacked and burned as they clashed with police. Rioting followed.

The marching controversies also triggered off a wave of tit-for-tat sectarian arson attacks. Among the properties damaged were 61 Orange halls and 25 Catholic churches. Yet despite the major community convulsions caused by these two marches, disorder only occurred at thirteen out of a total of 3500 parades during 1995 (2581 Loyalist and 302 Nationalist). Only twenty parades were re-routed and two had other conditions placed upon them. In his annual report, Sir Hugh Annesley again referred to the 'effect contentious parades can have on our relationship with the community. There remains much confusion in the public mind about our role in this area. I repeat again that we are not a licensing authority for parades: We are guided in our decisions by the simple parameters of whether serious disorder, serious disruption to community life or serious damage to property are likely outcomes if notified processions are allowed to take place. It is in everyone's interest that all those involved continue their efforts to eliminate contention and controversy.' But such efforts continued to be bedevilled by the ongoing controversy over the hotly disputed terms on which the Drumcree stand-off was ended. McKenna's position was publicly supported by the Mediation Network in a detailed formal statement issued later as what it called 'a matter of professional integrity'. It stated:

We remained on the Garvaghy Road and relied on the chief super-intendent to engage with the Orange Order. We were present when Brendan McKenna informed senior RUC officers of the Garvaghy Road group's intention to allow themselves to be physically removed from the road by police if the Orange parade recommenced. As police began to liaise with Orange leaders concerning arrangements for the parade, we were joined at the scene by deputy chief constables Flanagan and Wallace. Mr Flanagan briefed us on the worsening situation elsewhere in Northern Ireland with delicate negotiations concerning parades on the Ormeau Road and a blockade of Larne. Mr Flanagan advised us that the way in which the Garvaghy Road dispute was concluded would have direct implications for the situation elsewhere. An angry scene between police and protesters could worsen the Ormeau marching dispute and even destabilise the ceasefires. It would be crucial that Garvaghy Road residents voluntarily remove themselves from the road without being constrained by the police. We advised Mr Flanagan to share these observations with the leader of the Garvaghy Road group, Brendan McKenna. Subsequently Mr Flanagan repeated his views to Mr McKenna and Fr Eamon Stack in our presence. Mr McKenna agreed to request the protesters to remove themselves from the road on sight of the oncoming parade. As Mr McKenna left to speak to the crowd, we observed to Mr Flanagan that the mood of the crowd was such that Mr McKenna would have difficulty persuading the protesters to accede to his request. Brendan McAllister observed that Mr McKenna would have more chances of success if protesters knew there would be no march on Garvaghy Road in 1996. Mr Flanagan replied that there was no question of marches

going where there was no consent from the community. We now
believed that there would be no further marches on Garvaghy Road
without the residents' consent. This statement was witnessed by Mr
Campbell. We then moved to hear Mr McKenna address the crowd.
When he asked them to clear the road, numbers of protesters heckled
him and refused his request. Mindful of the deputy chief constable's
assessment of the possible consequences, for the wider situation in
Northern Ireland, Brendan McAllister spoke to the crowd, advising
them to trust Mr McKenna's leadership and encouraging them to
engage in a dignified silent protest. As the parade drew near, the
protesters complied with these requests with a discipline which is a
matter of public record.

The differing perceptions of precisely what was agreed on the
Garvaghy Road early that July morning were to have long-term repercussions. Suspicion and animosity deepened as the residents believed
both the RUC and the Orange Order had broken their word. It also had a
profound impact on the way the coalition conducted future talks.
Rosemary Nelson, their solicitor, advised them to keep a written account
of all meetings with government officials, the police and mediators. In
subsequent years, note-takers attended all meetings and prepared
minutes. Before each subsequent meeting could begin, the residents
insisted on agreeing minutes of their previous discussions, which were
carefully stored away to protect their position in any future controversies.
Sir Hugh Annesley had earlier disowned the residents', and the
Network's, version of events when they met him at the Lurgan RUC
station some weeks after the event. At the time, and ever since, Ronnie
Flanagan himself has also consistently denied misleading the residents'
representatives or giving any assurance about future marches in the terms
claimed. He points to news bulletins that evening, in which no such claim
was made by the residents, and and insists the only march he agreed to
halt was that of the Twelfth, the next day.

For its part, the Orange Order insists that it did not sign up to an
agreement that stipulated there would be no further parades along the
road. 'That was never mentioned as a possibility in our discussions. We
were dealing purely with the parade that year. There was no discussion
with the police about future years,' says Donaldson. Although he was
centrally involved in the talks to end the stand-off, he did not walk in the
parade because he was not a member of Portadown District. In a radio
interview shortly after the marchers had left the church, he described it as
'a victory for common sense'. Donaldson also believes that Paisley and

particularly Trimble were unfairly maligned for their 'jig' after the parade. 'The incident was deliberately misinterpreted. I think it was entirely spontaneous. I don't think it was intended to be a display of triumphalism. People were just relieved that a very dangerous situation had been resolved and that the parade had taken place. I think it was grossly overplayed by Nationalists, by the Garvaghy Road residents, who used it as an excuse to entrench their position. The incident was then used to cast David Trimble in a critical and negative light and I do not think that does justice to the role he played in helping to keep the situation calm and in helping to bring about a resolution.'

Another senior Orange figure agrees: 'Hindsight is a wonderful thing. I think what they did was simply express the feelings of everyone in the town that an immense pressure had been lifted. I don't think there was any offence meant to anyone. It was not planned, it was just a spontaneous act. Everyone had been wound up very tight and this was seen as a great relief. For many it was like the ending of the siege of Derry. It was viewed as a very historic moment in the history of the Orange Order. It was a sense of relief rather than victory.' Trimble insists the gesture was entirely spontaneous as the parade arrived in Carleton Street and the crowd shouted for Paisley and Trimble to come forward. 'If I had had someone with me at that time who had told me about the television cameras it would not have happened. People have to appreciate that the state of mind of those there, including myself, was that we had come back home. The view that it was a triumphant march is just not true. It was a feeling of great relief,' he says.

However negatively it was seen through Catholic eyes, the 'jig' and his role in Drumcree soon paid a rich political dividend for Trimble, a university law lecturer. At the end of August, Molyneaux, whose leadership was increasingly coming under challenge, finally announced his resignation as leader of the Ulster Unionist party and the long-serving John Taylor, who had been a junior minister at Stormont when direct rule was commenced in 1972, quickly emerged as favourite to replace him. The Ulster Unionist Council convened in the Ulster Hall in Belfast on 8 September to make its choice. After two preliminary ballots, Trimble, the outsider, convincingly defeated Taylor by 466 to 333 votes and was appointed leader. The Upper Bann MP had not been considered a powerful contender and his victory was largely due to the support of the 120 Orange Order delegates and the large number of Order members among the others. One of those he defeated was the Reverend Martin Smyth, the grand master of the Orange Order, who had been heavily criticised by members of the institution for not giving enough support to the Drumcree protest.

Before the year end the Portadown District decided to strike a medal for those who had taken part in the stand-off. The £10 'Siege of Drumcree' medals, the proceeds of which were to fund improvements to Carleton Street Orange Hall, gained an unusually esoteric value when they were unveiled, for the word 'siege' had been wrongly spelt 'seige'. The district officers decided to make a special presentation of medals to some of those who had played a prominent role in bringing the episode to, for them, a successful conclusion. However, Melvyn Hamilton, their guest at the church service, who had driven himself to the point of exhaustion trying to keep the protest peaceful and negotiating to get the parade through, was excluded. He was dismissed as a coward for suggesting that returning to Carleton Street by another route was an option. After collapsing, he was driven home to Waringstown and put to bed. Five hours later he was woken by his wife, Pamela, and watched on television as the parade went down the road. He shook his head in disbelief when he saw Trimble and Paisley joining hands and walking along Carleton Street. 'I was very disappointed,' he says. 'I don't think it was triumphalist. I think it was a spontaneous reaction because of the emotion of the occasion but I knew right away that it was a big mistake and would make the situation worse for the following year.'

Chapter Seven

Thugs in sashes and Orange feet on the

Garvaghy Road

'Can I say at the outset, brethren, I'm a sectarian bigot and I'm proud of it. There's nothing to be afraid of in those words. It's only two little words and they're only words of the English language. Sectarian means you belong to a particular sect or organisation. I belong to the Orange institution. Bigot means you look after the people you belong to. That's what I'm doing. I'm a sectarian bigot and proud of it.'

The words of Brother David Dowey, delivered from a written paper, standing at a lectern draped with the union flag, on the stage of the Ulster Hall in Belfast on the evening of 14 November 1995. They were greeted with rapturous cheers, whistles, foot-stamping and applause by a capacity Orange audience of some 1200, all clad in sashes. They had responded to an invitation from the steering committee of a new grouping called the 'Spirit of Drumcree' to attend the rally in one of the great shrines of Ulster Unionism. Dowey, an Orangeman since 1971, a member of the committee and a civil servant by profession, went on to explain their purpose. 'This is a movement, an initiative, put together by ordinary grassroots Orangemen absolutely sick to the back teeth of no leadership from the Grand Lodge.' Referring to the Order, he said: 'We have very strong religious principles and we stand by those and abide by those, right to the day we die, but it is essentially an organisation set up to defend the Ulster Protestant people and it's about time they started doing that.'
   Turning to the issue of Drumcree during his 45-minute address, he reminded the audience that in 1850 William Johnston of Ballykilbeg led the opposition to the Party Processions Act. To more rousing applause, he stated: 'If we are to face up to the parades issue it might well be that we'll have to take a similar stand. We have to show the authorities that we're not prepared to bend the knee. So you will have to be prepared, brethren, I think, to get your hands dirty.' Looking ahead to the summer of 1996, Dowey added, with more applause: 'Brethren, I don't like to say this, and

I don't mean to scaremonger, but my own personal feeling is that next year the government will use the troops against us. Are you prepared to stand fast?' Above shouts of 'Yes' from the audience he warned that 'a time will come soon, very soon, when we will have to defend ourselves physically. As distasteful as it may seem, brethren, that will have to happen. But remember, it's how the Order was founded, it was founded in violence to defend the Protestant people.'

Turning again to the weakness of Grand Lodge, he criticised the Orange leadership for refusing to hold a mass rally in support of the Drumcree protest, similar to that held outside Belfast City Hall to protest against the Anglo-Irish Agreement in 1985, because of fears that there could be trouble. 'If Grand Lodge were so concerned about the breaking of a few windows in Belfast city centre they should have taken us up the Falls Road where a few more broken windows wouldn't have mattered anyway,' he said. Returning to his sectarian theme, he urged the audience to 'keep Protestant money in Protestant areas' and added: 'We should take a tip from our forefathers who, whenever they were building their towns and cities, they made an Irish quarter, outside the walls. That's where they belong, outside the walls.' (Later his employer, the Northern Ireland Civil Service, suspended him and, after an investigation, he received a formal written reprimand and a warning as to his future conduct after it was decided he had breached his Conditions of Service Code.)

Earlier, the Ulster Hall audience had heard Brother James Brown, District Treasurer of Sixmilewater, County Tyrone, read an extract from Psalm 27 before being asked to stand for a prayer. Standing at the lectern, with his hand on his bible, he intoned: 'Father, we pray that all that is said and done in this gathering tonight will redound to the honour and glory of thy great name.' Recalling how their forefathers had banded together and formed the great Orange Institution 'to safeguard themselves from Popery', he prayed on: 'Surely, Father, nothing has changed in our day and generation. The Church of Rome is still the same, seeking to destroy and to subjugate and take us back to pre-Reformation days. Our aim is to see this great organisation on fire for God and united together to meet the future in the days that lie ahead.'

Cameramen and journalists were not allowed to remain in the hall to hear the addresses. They had been admitted to film the preliminary formalities when a flute band in caubeen hats, smart red tunics and blue trousers formed up on the stage, which was decorated with an arch bearing the words 'Spirit of Drumcree'. High behind them the hall's famous organ had been draped with the banner of Holdfast LOL 1620, and in front of them the table and the lectern for the speakers were covered with union flags. Applause for the band was still going on when the doors at the back of the hall opened and two Lambeg drummers, one in each aisle, waddled the length of the hall with their unwieldy instruments, thundering out the sort of tribal rhythm guaranteed to send shivers of excitement up and down Orange spines. They were followed by a bowler-hatted colour party, three flag bearers and two escorts carrying swords upright, who paraded to the front of the hall before planting the flagpoles in holders at the side of the platform. Among the audience was Harold Gracey and other members of Portadown District, many of them with 'Siege of Drumcree' medals pinned to their jackets and sashes. He was given a standing ovation. It was at this point that the press and television were asked to leave and the no-holds-barred addresses began.

The principal speaker was Joel Patton, who earned his living as a market gardener and was a notably militant Orangeman of the old not-an-inch school. Patton set out the demands of what was essentially a pressure group during his 45-minute oration. These were later put to the vote and adopted as policies. The demands were: that the Grand Master, the Reverend Martin Smyth, should resign immediately; that Grand Lodge should introduce elections on the basis of 'one Orangeman, one vote' for principal positions in the Order; that it should initiate within three months an annual congress of Orange delegates elected by private lodges; that an immediate directive should be given banning voluntary re-routing of any traditional Orange parades; that the Order should give an immediate undertaking not to enter into or support any talks with Sinn Fein-IRA, and that it should announce its immediate disaffiliation from the Ulster Unionist Party. (The Order was entitled to send 120 delegates to meetings of the Ulster Unionist Council which elects the party leader and makes policy.) The rally ended with more music and drumming before the crowd, far more than the organisers had anticipated, dispersed back to their cars and buses to journey back to their homes all over Northern Ireland. Indeed the starting time had had to be delayed for fifteen minutes to allow them all time to enter the hall. Outside, as they waited, the Reverend Brian Kennaway, Graham Montgomery and other members of the Order's education committee handed out leaflets challenging the group's claims about the inadequacies of the Orange institution.

The origins of this raucous 'Spirit of Drumcree' rally lay in the stand-off a few months earlier. Patton had been one of those who quickly answered Gracey's call to go to the church and support Portadown District in their bid to get down the Garvaghy Road. He was adamant it was their inalienable right to do so. As he waited around, sipping tea from plastic cups, he was amazed at the number of fellow members who bemoaned the state of the Order and criticised what they saw as a distinct lack of leadership. They exchanged phone numbers and agreed to meet in more comfortable surroundings to further discuss what could and needed to be done. Once the post-Twelfth holiday period was over, Patton took the initiative and began contacting them. The man who earned his living propagating plants was now sowing the seeds of protest.

At first they met in small groups in each other's houses and sifted through lists of lodge members, identifying those who they believed shared their views and would want to support them. A month later 40 of them attended a four-hour meeting at the Burnside Orange Hall in County Antrim. Many of them had played active roles in the campaign against the Anglo-Irish Agreement or were linked to the Ulster Clubs that emerged at that time. Patton himself chaired the meeting, which discussed the leadership and direction of the Order, its relationship with the Unionist party, what it should be doing tactically about Drumcree and other issues. Encouraged by the debate Patton and his caucus decided to organise a second meeting and bring more people into their circle, again by invitation only. This time, in September 1995, some 150 gathered at Tamnamore Orange Hall near Dungannon, where they were addressed by Patton and John McGrath, a senior Orangeman from County Antrim. That night they decided to call their group 'Spirit of Drumcree', although some of those attending wanted a name that suggested they were addressing the weaknesses of the entire institution, not just the problem at Drumcree.

The group then decided to break cover and launch itself against the establishment of the Order by holding a rally at the Ulster Hall. In preparation for the big event they convened a series of smaller meetings throughout Northern Ireland in order to drum up more support, including a well-attended one at Craigavon Civic Centre. However, Patton's delight at the turn-out for the Craigavon meeting was tempered by the fact that few of those attending were from Portadown District. 'I thought that was very strange. It had been well advertised through the Orange grapevine, but Portadown kept it quiet and didn't really support us. Harold Gracey and a small number of district members turned up at the Ulster Hall rally but at no time in the Spirit of Drumcree's history did we receive support from Portadown District officers. It seemed that they wanted nothing to do with us. They wanted our support but wanted to keep total control of the protest themselves and did not want any interference.'

Nevertheless the two elements, Portadown District and Spirit of Drumcree, joined together on 2 October to stage an unruly protest when Grand Master Martin Smyth was one of 320 people from both sides of the border, including clergy, politicians and members of the business community, who attended a United Prayer Breakfast in the Drumsill Hotel, Armagh. Others who ran the noisy gauntlet of shouted abuse were Cardinal Cahal Daly, the Catholic Primate of All Ireland, Ulster Unionists Roy Beggs MP and Jim Nicholson MEP, and the Reverend Roy Magee, the Presbyterian clergyman who had had been instrumental in the talks brokering the 1994 Loyalist ceasefire. The protestors handed in a leaflet to the breakfast organisers accusing Smyth of hypocrisy for 'engaging in a joint spiritual effort with those who seek to overthrow Ulster'. Smyth dismissed the protest: 'There is an element in our community who will always be opposed to Christians coming together. This is the kind of event which can bring people together under the authority of God to try to bring the nation back to Christ.'

The existing factional rivalries within the Order, exacerbated by the creation of the Spirit of Drumcree group, erupted on 13 December when the education committee, which contained some of the most visionary and progressive members of the institution, submitted a highly critical report of the rally to a meeting of Grand Lodge in the House of Orange, the organisation's headquarters at Dublin Road, Belfast. After distributing leaflets outside the Ulster Hall, Kennaway, Montgomery and five others had gone in to the event and were appalled at what they heard. Their report set the committee on a collision course with both the hardline and conservative elements in the organisation and triggered off a period of internal turmoil that would still be raging unresolved within the Order some seven years later. Patton was not deterred by the immense opposition to his group because he was convinced that not only the future of the Orange Order was at stake but the very union with Britain. 'I happened to believe that the primary objective of the residents' groups being set up was not to stop parades. Their primary objective was to force us into dialogue with Sinn Fein-IRA.'

Meanwhile Portadown District also made its position clear to Grand Lodge. Gracey called for the Spirit of Drumcree group to be disbanded. For the time being Portadown was loyal to Grand Lodge because it wanted nothing that would deflect attention from its single-minded battle with the Catholic residents for the right to walk along the Garvaghy Road. Another senior figure in the Order said: 'The predominant feeling within Orangeism was that we were right and so we didn't have to explain our position to anyone. So we were not very active in the media or in planning ahead. As time went on we realised that was not the case and that 1996 was going to be a problem.'

While these events were unfolding, in stark contrast, McKenna and his associates were very actively thinking about what would happen in July 1996 and what they would do in the meantime to promote their case. They were now in close contact with similar groups which had been formed in other parts where contentious marches had already become or were looming as an issue: Bellaghy, a small village in County Londonderry with a 97 per cent Catholic population; Londonderry, where the annual Apprentice Boys march in August caused tension on its passage through the exclusively catholic part of the city; Dunloy, another almost totally Catholic village in north Antrim, and Newtownbutler, a mainly Catholic village in County Fermanagh, close to the border.

Unionists and the Orange Order have always believed that the Republican movement was the hidden hand behind the formation of residents' groups and deliberately orchestrated the confrontations over marches from 1995 onwards as part of a post-ceasefire strategy to build their political power base in Catholic areas, at the expense of the SDLP. In support of this theory they point to secretly tape-recorded remarks made by Gerry Adams at Athboy in County Meath during a 'closed' session at a Sinn Fein conference on 'Conflict Resolution Processes', when he said: 'Ask any activist in the North, did Drumcree happen by accident, and he will tell you "no". Three years of work on the Ormeau Road, Portadown, and other parts of Fermanagh and Newry, Armagh and in Bellaghy, and up in Derry. Three years of work went into creating that situation and fair play to those who put the work in. They are the type of scene changes we need to focus on and develop and exploit.'

With McKenna and Rice both having served prison sentences for IRA activity, and other convicted persons elsewhere so prominent in the anti-march campaigns, the case would seem to be beyond doubt. However, while some official sources uphold this view, a larger number of others in the police, the Catholic communities affected and the SDLP have all told us that, contrary to the interpretation put on the words of Adams, the IRA did not conceive a strategy to manipulate the marching issue through the residents' groups and that, while they did make some efforts to influence it in places, they were often rebuffed and forced to work with churchmen and rival political and community leaders in each locality. One Republican source told us that 'McKenna was always his own man. We could never tell him what to do and many times he wouldn't even talk to us at all.' Dara O'Hagan, a Sinn Fein Assembly member whose father was one of three top IRA figures who escaped from prison in Dublin in 1973 in a hijacked helicopter, says: 'What Adams was doing was stating the reality. The opposition to Orange parades was always there, Sinn Fein did not have to manufacture the situation or manipulate people in the

Nationalist community or residents' groups to protest at the marches. There has always been deep-seated antagonism and injustice, and there has been organised protest at various periods over the years.'

In the autumn of 1995 the residents' group in Portadown changed its name to the Garvaghy Road Residents Coalition and initiated a series of meetings with politicians and a range of interested parties. They met Archbishop Robin Eames, the Church of Ireland Primate of All Ireland, whose own diocese, of course, included the parish church at Drumcree. He said he hoped to be able to persuade the Orange Order to sit down in a face-to-face meeting to resolve the issue. They wrote to Sir Patrick Mayhew, the secretary of state, and to the Irish government setting out their views. Three letters were sent to Trimble, the local MP, but he did not respond. Another person who came into view at this time was Dr Mo Mowlam, the MP for Redcar in the north-east of England, who had recently been appointed shadow secretary of state for Northern Ireland. With John Major's Conservative government becoming ever more deeply embroiled in allegations of sleaze and corruption, and the confident expectation that Tony Blair's reformed Labour party would comfortably win the coming general election, her importance as a potential secretary of state was recognised. So during her regular fact-finding visits to Northern Ireland they made a pitch for her sympathy and ensured she was kept abreast of developments.

The efforts of the Quakers and the Mediation Network to broker deals, which had foundered in 1995, were the first occasions when professional mediators had ever been used to work with both sides. Despite the fact that there were vast reservoirs of antagonism and distrust to be drained, they played a role in defusing the crisis at Portadown and came close to getting a written agreement signed and implemented on the Ormeau Road. There were thus strong and indeed justified hopes that, in the end, with more trust-building and experience, this approach might well succeed. This feeling was quite marked within the Northern Ireland Office, where there was only a sense of dread about the coming Drumcree and a distinct lack of alternative ideas, or even the political determination, to resolve it. There was therefore some relief at the end of 1995 when the Garvaghy Road residents endorsed an approach from the Mediation Network to co-operate with them in a new, though ultimately unsuccessful, effort to build a process which would lead to a consensus with the Orange Order.

Other efforts were made to bring the two sides to the dispute into direct contact as a pre-requisite for finding a lasting solution. A month or so after the parade, Kennaway, Montgomery and Richard Whitten agreed to attend a secret meeting with representatives of the Garvaghy Road Nationalists. The contact was arranged by a Jesuit priest Kennaway had previously met while in Dublin delivering a lecture about the Orange Order. Before attending, though, Kennaway decided to get cover from more senior members of the Order, so he visited Jeffrey Donaldson, a deputy grand master, at home and briefed George Patton, the Order's executive secretary. Neither raised any objections. The meeting, chaired by the Dublin Jesuit in a house at Tandragee, County Armagh, ended fruitlessly and, for Kennaway, on a sour note. Instead of the anticipated tirade against the Order and parades on political and ideological grounds, he was stunned when one of the delegation of residents objected to how the Orangemen dressed, saying parading in suits and bowler hats was a form of social discrimination because most Catholics living in the area were unemployed and could not afford such fine attire. When the Orangemen pointed out the anguish caused by IRA terrorism, not least the recent bomb in Portadown, the encounter quickly went downhill. The production of a tribal map, coloured orange and green, showing how proposed long-term development would further isolate Portadown Orangemen from Drumcree church was the last straw and the now mutually antagonistic meeting broke up.

Evangelical Contribution on Northern Ireland (ECONI), a bible-based reconciliation group established in 1987 to co-ordinate and develop an evangelical response to communal divisions in Northern Ireland, also tried to bring the two sides into contact by bringing Father Stack and Sister Laura Boyle, from the Garvaghy side, to a dinner with the Reverend William Bingham and Denis Watson, both prominent Orangemen, which was held in the home of one of ECONI's members in the leafy suburbs of south Belfast. Again polite exchanges of views failed to ignite into the constructive and wider engagement that would be necessary to resolve the differences between the two sides. By Easter 1996, the traditional start to the marching season, it was clear that the Loyal Orders were in an utterly uncompromising mood. The collapse of the IRA ceasefire in February, and the murder of two shopkeepers in an explosion, which also caused £100 million-worth of damage, at Canary Wharf in the London Docklands, together with the government's subsequent efforts to restore the ceasefire and draw Sinn Fein into the stumbling political talks, caused uncertainty and resentment with suspicions of appeasement hardening the Loyalist mood. The high-profile role of the Irish government in the political process in Northern Ireland exacerbated anxieties that a political initiative was being shaped which would sweep away partition, leaving the northern Protestants abandoned by Britain and at the mercy of the Irish Republic. There was a growing feeling that a stand had to be taken against all the concessions, appeasement and weakness. This was not confined to the members of the marching orders; it was shared by some of the influential, but normally apathetic, business and middle classes, who were generally of Unionist sympathies.

Against this gloomy backdrop the RUC was prudently planning to deal with whatever disorder would inevitably follow, if the peace-building initiatives failed. It formed and trained 75 Divisional Mobile Support Units, and virtually every able-bodied man and woman in the force was drafted into the effort. From their own intelligence gathering, police commanders knew there was little likelihood of a deal to defuse the crisis, and what slim opportunity there was steadily diminished as what was now called 'Drumcree Sunday' fast approached. When the police decided to halt the first of the season's marches along the Ormeau Road, a lengthy stand-off developed and there were ugly clashes. The mediators working in Belfast, Portadown and Londonderry were still unable to make any progress. In most cases the Loyal Orders simply refused to meet them, claiming that the IRA was orchestrating the discontent and that residents' groups were phoney front organisations. Any meeting with the residents, or their representatives, was also out of the question, for those who did not have records of direct IRA involvement were seen as IRA 'puppets'. The open involvement of the Jesuit priests in the Portadown situation was a further obstacle. In terms of Orange demonology the Jesuits were to the Catholic church what the SAS was to the British Army, their elite stormtroopers. There was, in fact, some unease among the more moderate residents in the affected areas that they were having to stand shoulder to shoulder with Republicans, but in the affected communities, opposition to the parades was unanimous and uncompromising and, most certainly, not confined to people with Republican links or sympathies. Given the failure of mediation to break the deadlock and the atmosphere of political discontent and rising frustration on the Protestant side, the scene was therefore set for serious trouble.

As the marching season gathered momentum through the spring, prominent figures on the Orange and Unionist side hammered away at the point that their civil rights and religious liberties were being compromised to appease the IRA. They also made no secret of their intention to use force of numbers to overstretch the police and create a crisis if they did not get their way over the Drumcree march. There was now a general recognition by ministers and officials at Stormont Castle, inside the RUC and throughout the Nationalist community that the marching question had now been elevated to the forefront of the Unionist political agenda. Ideally, it would have been treated as a local problem and kept low-key but in the contemporary political circumstances, where the Unionist community increasingly saw the situation as a matter of fundamental principle, that was no longer possible. It was abundantly evident that there would be no substantial political progress and the resulting communal upheaval would not be extinguished until the business of the Garvaghy Road routing was settled.

Sir Hugh Annesley, the chief constable, and his most senior advisers were therefore faced with the classic Northern Ireland political dilemma. With no middle way evident, whatever course of action was adopted would alienate one side by pleasing the other. Over the preceding 30 years, Annesley, a Dublin-born Protestant, had risen steadily through the ranks of the London Metropolitan Police to Deputy Assistant Commissioner, and then moved to Belfast as head of the RUC in 1989. Drumcree 1996 was to be his last big test in Northern Ireland, for he had already announced in May that he would retire the following November. He well knew that pushing the march through again would attract criticism from the entire Catholic community and cause great damage to the long-fragile police relationship with them. According to police intelligence reports, there were active preparations being made for wider communal conflict and disorder in other Catholic areas throughout Northern Ireland if the march went through. Halting the march would thus protect the RUC's improving, but still cautious, reputation for even-handedness among Catholics but incur the wrath of the Protestants. The police also knew there were hardline elements in the Orange Order and also, despite the ceasefire, within the Loyalist paramilitary underworld who were actively manoeuvring to overwhelm the police and draw them into a confrontation with the massed ranks of the Protestant community on the scale of 1974. Then the Ulster Workers Council general strike had succeeded in bringing northern Ireland to a standstill, made possible by a combination of deliberate police inaction and impotence because of the extent of the disorder. A similar putsch in 1977, led by the Reverend Ian Paisley, was, by contrast, vigorously opposed by police and troops and put down. (By contrast in the summer of 1996, large-scale military reinforcements were not available. With 11,000 soldiers committed to peacekeeping duties in former Yugoslavia, post-Cold War manpower cuts and a serious shortage of recruits, the Army was suffering from serious overstretch.)

Several parallel efforts to avert the looming confrontation by initiating dialogue and finding local accommodation continued as the days remorselessly ticked away towards Drumcree Sunday, which this year fell on 7 July. The Orange side remained unyielding in refusing to meet the residents, who were still rigidly opposed to the march going through. Annesley and his officers had engaged in talks with both sides and monitored every move for weeks in their own bid to work out a compromise. A large map of the area had been prepared, and police officers shuttled between the sides, marking possible combinations of new routes in coloured ink, but still without convincing either side to reach an agreement. On Wednesday 3 July the residents met Flanagan, who gave them a grim assessment of the security situation, warning that intelligence reports indicated Loyalist paramilitaries were preparing for major violence throughout Northern Ireland. The residents were alarmed, but insisted they would not agree to a parade under those circumstances, which they viewed as tantamount to blackmail by the Order and its supporters. They reminded Flanagan that back in the 1980s troubles, his predecessor Hermon had ordered the arrest of more than 60 prominent Loyalists to defuse tension and pre-empt attacks on Catholics.

The RUC's senior commanders gathered in Belfast on Friday 5 July to take a decision on whether or not the march should go through and to finalise their strategy, knowing that their decision would have far-reaching consequences for the RUC and the Northern Ireland community. The police were by now thoroughly dissatisfied with the obligations the law imposed on them in respect of marches. Most people did not understand that the only test that had to be applied to a proposed march was a strictly legal one: would it lead to serious public disorder, serious damage to property or serious disruption to the life of the community? The judgement was for the chief constable alone, without political interference or direction although the Northern Ireland Secretary had power to prohibit a demonstration if it would impose undue demands on the police or military. Many believed the police licensed or even approved marches, and unscrupulous political leaders were all too ready, all too often, to misrepresent the subtlety of the police position, exploit a ruling and use it to stoke up hostility against them. That Friday afternoon, recognising the decision would impose a great ordeal on the force, the staff associations, the Superintendents Association and the Police Federation, were the first to be told that Annesley had decided to halt the march. As instructions went out to every police station to muster the newly trained force of Mobile Support Units to enforce the decision, a news conference to make the announcement was called for the following morning.

Speaking in the conference room at RUC headquarters, Annesley said:

'I greatly regret that despite all the efforts of the RUC, and many others, it has not proved possible to resolve the conflicting views, especially about the Orange Order Parade along the Garvaghy Road. Following extensive consultation I have concluded that to allow the Orange Order Parade along the Garvaghy Road would be likely to occasion serious public disorder. Accordingly, I have earlier this morning given directions that conditions are to be imposed on the organisers to prohibit this part of the proposed route. Similar conditions have been imposed on the Garvaghy Road Residents Coalition in respect of their proposed march into the centre of Portadown. The decision I have made is under Article 4 of the 1987 Public Order legislation and I hope all those involved will peacefully comply with this legal requirement. There are no winners in violence, only losers. Even at this late stage, it is not too late for an accommodation to be reached. For the well-being of all concerned, I sincerely encourage both sides to re-appraise their stance in pursuit of a peaceful resolution.'

McKenna and other members of the coalition were in the community centre that Saturday when Annesley announced his decision to re-route the march. They were surprised and delighted by his comments. 'We couldn't believe it,' recalls McKenna, putting a more than favourable interpretation on what the chief constable said. 'He referred to the fact that the Orangemen were not wanted on the Garvaghy Road, which was exactly what we had been saying for a number of years. It sounded like he was reading from our script.'

Soon after dawn the next morning, the customary tranquillity of a Portadown sabbath was shattered as relays of helicopters clattered into the Drumcree area, dropping off clusters of police officers and soldiers equipped with all the paraphernalia of riot control including long plastic shields, protective helmets and plastic baton rounds. Each carried a white cardboard box containing drinks, chocolate, fruit and sandwiches, a sign that they were prepared for a long stay in the fields between the parish church and the Garvaghy Road housing estates. Overnight the Army had erected a barbed-wire cordon along the fields on either side of the confrontation point at the bridge by the edge of the graveyard adjoining the church. Nearby the Army had established a field hospital, portable toilets had been brought in for the police and soldiers and arrangements had been made to provide 4000 meals a day. For the time being the bridge remained open, but a phalanx of police officers with armoured Land Rovers was drawn up a short distance away, ready to move onto the bridge and close the road. Further back some soldiers were positioned in reserve at Mahon Barracks, a couple of miles away, where a tented city had been erected to provide sleeping and eating areas for the thousands of personnel drafted into the town. The nerve centre of the big security operation was also located there in the series of inter-linked portable buildings, with anti-mortar fortifications on the roof, which served as a headquarters for what the RUC called South Region. Along the corridor from the ACC's office in the complex, in the map-walled command room usually used to run anti-terrorist security operations along hundreds of miles of the Armagh, Fermanagh and Tyrone border, live television pictures were being beamed from the front line at Drumcree and a series of desk officers monitored messages and issued instructions by telephone and radio. In one corner of the room, sat the military liaison team, their dark khaki uniforms contrasting with the RUC's rifle-green. The television pictures were also being beamed back to the force command room at headquarters in Belfast.

Down at Carleton Street, the Orangemen had also begun to gather from an early hour. At 9.15 am Harold Gracey addressed a news conference during which the terms 'no compromise' and 'no surrender' figured prominently. They were still to the fore some time later when he addressed the marchers from an upstairs window of the Orange Hall that Sunday morning before they set off, also pledging that the Orangemen intend to stay at Drumcree for however long it took. This time he added the oratorical flourish that 'Drumcree' was their 'Alamo', a reference to the role emigrant Ulster Presbyterians played in taking land from the native American Indians in the nineteenth century. One of the most famous of this stock was Davy Crockett, 'the king of the wild frontier' whose family roots lay in Tyrone and Donegal. He died at the Alamo, a fortress on the San Antonio River in Texas, on 6 March 1836, when around 150 soldiers fighting for Texan independence from Mexico were overrun by a 4000-strong Mexican force. Jeffrey Donaldson, who had been invited to parade as a guest of Portadown District, turned to a group of senior Orangemen listening and said: 'Somebody should point out to Harold that the Ulstermen were massacred at the Alamo. It was a defeat.'

Moments later, the long column of 1100 Orangemen and two accordion bands formed up and marched out into the town centre, heading towards Drumcree, but the outward journey was not incident-free. A police vehicle loaded with officers was driving in towards Portadown when it met the parade, spread out across the entire width of the road, and had to pull over to the side. Sensing trouble, Nigel Dawson, a district officer and steward, resplendent in his best suit, bowler hat and white gloves, stepped out of the parade and made frantic signs urging the police to turn and drive out of the path of the parade. The vehicle remained in position and within minutes was surrounded and being rocked from side to side by some Loyalist spectators. One policeman suffered facial injuries. As they tried to pull open the doors, Orange stewards intervened and enabled the police vehicle to get safely away, an action which, it was promptly acknowledged in an RUC statement, had prevented more serious injuries. The crowd then turned on a BBC television camera crew and a photographer was attacked. Soon after this incident, on their way past the Brownstown estate, a stronghold of Loyalist paramilitaries where a large mural had been painted on a gable wall pledging solidarity with the marchers, they passed a number of white memorial crosses stuck in a grass verge. They were trophies. stolen by Loyalists from a memorial in the centre of the fiercely Republican village of Crossmaglen, and were intended as a clear sign that local Loyalist paramilitaries were taking a keen interest in the outcome of the Drumcree march.

At 11 am, with the bells of Drumcree church ringing to summon the congregation to prayer, the RUC moved into position to block both ends of the Garvaghy Road. A trio of Land Rovers was driven into position to block the bridge across the road at Drumcree and cadres of officers formed a line directly behind them. Behind this advance party, more police and Land Rovers were formed up. By this time the marchers had arrived at Drumcree and were filing into their seats for the 11.30 service, which, because of the immense interest and unprecedented attendance, was relayed by loudspeaker to hundreds of spectators waiting outside. Just before it ended at 12.40 pm some of them started to move into the graveyard beside the church, which provided a good vantage point for what was to follow. Others moved farther down the road and into the fields beside the now blocked bridge, over a dried up stream which had become the routine point of confrontation. A few minutes later, accompanied by David Trimble and a band, the first cadre of Orangemen, ruddy-faced countrymen in their best suits, Orange sashes, white gloves and bowler hats, some carrying swords, marched the couple of hundred yards down to the police line and stopped inches from the grim-faced officers. Gracey, who was also at their head, was allowed through to make his protest to the police. Soon afterwards, the large number of Orangemen gathered in the vicinity of the church, were addressed by Trimble over the loudspeaker system: 'Dublin are giving the orders. In a few hours time the rest of the province will show their support', he said. An hour later he was joined by the Reverend Martin Smyth, Grand Master of the Orange Order, who had been notably absent a year earlier, and they held a press conference stating they had already compromised enough and would not do so today.

While these preliminaries were going on, a communications and control room, set up in the church hall and thenceforth referred to as the Drumcree Bunker, had gone into action. Equipped with laptop computers, fax machines, telephones, televisions and videos, it was designed for monitoring news reports and responding quickly to inaccuracies or hostile reports. It had been organised by Denis Watson, one of a small group set up to plan for the 1996 stand-off which had held regular meetings at Carleton Street over the preceding months. Among the plans they had talked about was bringing the entire Twelfth demonstration to Portadown if the parade was not allowed down the Garvaghy Road, or staging mass demonstrations in a number of other areas. As in 1995, one of the early arrivals at Drumcree was Joel Patton, this time with members of his Spirit of Drumcree group in tow. When he visited the Bunker he was far from impressed by what he saw and found Watson was trying to get a phone system set up while Gracey was giving a succession of media interviews. 'When we arrived in Portadown district officers were telling everyone they had detailed plans, but we soon realised there was no master plan. Their only plan was based on pressure of numbers. They believed that large numbers would force the government to back down,' says Patton.

Although he had been involved in an incessant propaganda war with Grand Lodge, using the media to vent his anger at what he saw as a lack of direction, Patton and other members of his Spirit of Drumcree group had also drawn up plans for protests they believed would bring Northern Ireland to a standstill, but they decided they would only put into operation protests which had the backing of Grand Lodge and Portadown Distinct. Patton told Watson there were Orangemen ready to take protests on to the streets elsewhere, which he believed would be all the more effective and reduce the possibility of violence if they were approved and organised. He warned that if protests were allowed to happen in a spontaneous way they would soon get out of control. By this time his mobile phone was ringing constantly with Spirit of Drumcree members either looking for instructions or reporting that hardliners had already begun to organise protests, when they learned there were no advance contingency plans to throttle life in Northern Ireland, by blocking main roads, key junctions and other locations like Belfast International Airport. Patton then took it upon himself to broaden the protest by phoning Spirit of Drumcree members and giving instructions. 'We knew people in various areas were ready to take action so we wanted to ensure it was organised. We were not in a position to issue a rallying call to Orangemen and to tell them what to do because we didn't have enough influence, but when some members of the Order asked for advice, we suggested tactics to them.'

Meanwhile events had begun to escalate at the police cordon by the bridge. In mid-afternoon there was a clash after Martin Smyth approached the barrier accompanied by a band. Some stones and bottles were thrown at the police while a demonstrator tried to scramble past them through a hedge at the side of the road. After heavy skirmishing broke out at the police cordon, more units, clad in riot gear, were moved forward and a firework was thrown among them. Some time later, Ian Paisley arrived at Drumcree and also made his way to the cordon, where he was cheered by the crowd and delivered a typically apocalyptic address: 'I do not promise an easy victory this time. It was easy last year. Now we've all the power of the British government against us aided and abetted by the skunks from Dublin. We are fighting for the promise of the life to come and that's worth fighting for and that's worth dying for.' In the opening shot of what was to be a highly personalised campaign of intimidation directed at the police officers, Paisley added that the police should remember they cannot live in Garvaghy Road. The clear inference of the remarks was that the RUC should not oppose the march or they would be driven from their homes in Protestant areas, precisely the situation many had faced in 1985 and 1986.

As the afternoon and evening went on, a rota of Orange lodges and bands from all over Northern Ireland had begun arriving at Drumcree, forming up outside the church and marching down to the police cordon before joining the rapidly growing crowds who had begun a vigil in the field beside the church. The air was thick with the smell of frying food from the mobile catering vehicles that had arrived and opened up for business. There was an almost constant musical accompaniment from the many bands and, from time to time, music and announcements crackled out across the field from the loudspeaker system that had been set up. Again, beside the Drumcree Bunker in the church hall, an army of women was turning out plates of sandwiches and salads. Jeffrey Donaldson remembers the carnival atmosphere, with families standing on the hill eating picnics and enjoying the constant parading up and down to the police cordon. Across the fields adjacent to the church, the police, who were still at the forefront of the operation, snatched some sleep when they were relieved from spells of standing at the cordon and along the barbed wire entanglements that now snaked across the fields. They lay on the grass or rested wearily against the sides of their vehicles. By nightfall, however, there was no rest and the carnival atmosphere had evaporated. A crowd of at least 4000 subjected them to a constant hail of stones, bottles and fireworks, which continued into the early hours of Monday despite the efforts of Orange stewards to halt it. Elsewhere in the Portadown area at the same time, other sinister men were engaged in an even grimmer escalation of the conflict.

At 11.50 pm on the Sunday night, a taxi depot in nearby Lurgan received a call asking for a car to the Centrepoint bar on the Portadown Road out of Lurgan. Part-time driver Michael McGoldrick, aged 31, a Catholic mature student who had graduated from Queen's University in Belfast two days earlier with a degree in English and politics, was despatched to pick up the passenger. He was never seen alive again. The next morning at 7 am, soon after dawn, his body was found some eight miles away at Montiaghs Road, Aghagallon, slumped over the driving wheel of the light blue Toyota Carina he had been using as a taxi. He had been shot twice in the back of the head. His parents heard that their only son, married with one child and a pregnant wife, had been murdered while they were watching television in their holiday caravan at Warrenpoint in County Down. His father later described how they screamed and shouted with grief. 'It was our only son, our only child. I ran out of the caravan. I remember going down on my knees and hitting the ground with my fists.' Later he added: 'Fire and brimstone speeches have featured too much in this situation. Their loose talk has cost this young fellow his life. It could have been any innocent young lad. We do not want any retaliation.' The callous killing confirmed the RUC's intelligence and worst fears that a faction of the outlawed Ulster Volunteer Force in Portadown had renounced the almost two-year-old Loyalist ceasefire and was going to engage in sectarian murder to reinforce the protest at Drumcree. The following day an anonymous fax was sent to the Residents Coalition office: '1 dead, 5,999 more to go'. (Five years later, although 1200 people have been interviewed and a number of suspects questioned, no one has been charged with the murder.)

Over the next three days, as the stand-off continued, there was sustained violence at Drumcree. Police fired plastic baton rounds to repel repeated attempts to break and cut through the barbed wire entanglements. The Army at first repaired the breaches but then moved in force to strengthen and extend them across the fields. During the Monday afternoon they also moved to fortify the bridge. While several units of police surged forward across the bridge, Royal Engineers moved in behind them, putting in place heavy concrete blocks – 'dragon's teeth', as the soldiers call them – and more coils of wire. Having created a 'buffer zone' they then withdrew, firing plastic baton rounds at a mob who had subjected them to a heavy barrage of stones and bottles while they covered the military work party. All the time 'Drumcree tourists' were arriving in buses and cars to walk from the church to the bridge and then join the vast crowd constantly gathered on the hill. The situation was not without its humour. At one point, some of the Loyalists raised a make-shift banner on which they had scrawled: 'It must be war. Kate Adie's here.' The BBC news reporter, a veteran of many conflict situations, was among the vast crowd of media personnel who had set up base with their satellite trucks just behind the police blockade at the bridge and were beaming live pictures of the clashes round the world. Although the confrontation had started on a positive note between the Order and the media, who were offered tea and scones in the church hall, the relationship speedily deteriorated and camera teams and journalists were soon told it would be 'inadvisable' to venture into the Orange ranks. Two foreign photographers who ignored the warning were attacked and ended up in the ditch in front of the police lines.

Elsewhere in the Portadown area and further afield throughout Northern Ireland Orange sympathisers blocked roads by hijacking and burning vehicles. Suspect devices were planted on the railway near Portadown, bringing the Belfast–Dublin cross-border train service to a symbolic halt. As the week wore on, factories and shops were set ablaze and progressively more ugly intimidation developed. A virtual siege was thrown around the mainly Catholic Armagh village of Markethill, preventing bread, milk, mail and all other supplies from being taken in. Among those confined by the picket was the SDLP MP Seamus Mallon, who was taken out in an army helicopter so he could travel to parliament in London. Hospitals, which were already on full standby to treat casualties of the violence, found their capacity reduced when staff could not get in because of public transport disruption and the blocked roads.

While individual members of local lodges and the Spirit of Drumcree members were prominent in causing civil disruption, the cutting edge of violence was supplied by hardline members of the UVF, disillusioned with the ceasefires and the subsequent course of political events which they saw as underlining the Loyalist position. Their figurehead was Billy Wright, aged 37, who was known as 'King Rat'. Although the police could never sustain serious charges against him, they had good grounds for suspecting that he, and a small band of equally fanatical associates, were responsible for at least twenty chilling sectarian murders and massacres in mid-Ulster over the previous several years, causing the area to be named the 'murder triangle'. Wright was very much a marked man and, apart from constant police attention, had survived six IRA attempts to murder him. In an interview with one of us that year, Wright discussed plans for attacking targets in the Republic from a safe house in the Dublin area. He was going to target the tourist industry, he said, which was a mainstay of the Irish economy and he talked clinically of shooting a few tourists, or exploding bombs without warning in bars or restaurants, in order to plunge the country into crisis by damaging international confidence that it was a safe place to visit. With thousands of people crossing back and forward across the Irish border each week Wright believed it would be easy to operate from a base in the Republic. He also had more fanciful ideas, such as poisoning reservoirs, but they were not taken seriously by other Loyalist groups, although no one doubted either Wright's ability or his willingness to carry them out.

The violent clashes and the naked sectarian hatred unleashed in 1996 reached a scale not seen since 1969. A large number of schools, churches and houses were attacked and burned. Belfast's international airport was sealed off and at one point an undertaker collecting a body had to remove a crucifix from a coffin to get it past the Loyalist vigilantes blocking access to the complex; the priest escorting the funeral party was so frightened of being attacked that he removed his clerical collar. In parts of Belfast, Catholic and Protestant families who had moved into mixed areas in the more relaxed atmosphere that quickly followed the ceasefires found themselves under threat, and the sight of refugees fleeing from their homes, their belongings piled in vans and lorries, once more became commonplace. At one location in north Belfast, fifteen Saxon armoured vehicles loaded with troops had to be deployed to hold an angry mob at bay while Catholics rushed to empty their homes.

Over the loudspeakers at Drumcree, the police were subjected to a relentless cycle of intimidation. According to RUC sources, individual officers were named and offensive personal remarks called out. One woman officer was taunted about a recent miscarriage; married officers were heckled or jeered about the safety of their wives and families at home. One officer was confronted at the barbed wire by a fellow elder from his church and informed that he and his family would no longer be welcome to worship there. A youth wearing Orange regalia exposed himself to some female officers. Elsewhere, police families came under attack in their homes in many Protestant areas. In one seaside village a mob stormed the house and armed police had to take the officer, his wife and their two-year-old son to safety. Other police families had to flee their homes as mobs threw bricks, rocks and petrol bombs. One evening Flanagan got a call on his mobile to ring home urgently. When he did he was told there were a cluster of Orange pickets outside his house in Bangor. His teenage son asked whether he should go out and talk to them. 'I said, no, I'll tell you what to do, son, get the video camera and go up to the bedroom and get as good footage of them as you can to see who these people are. I've joked about that since. I said I went round and smashed all their windows. But, legally, when we explored it, for the offence of intimidation to be complete, I need to prevent you doing something you want to do or I need to force you into doing something you don't want to do. So that was never tested. Nobody from the family ever actually went out and was prevented, although they were all blockaded across our driveway and you couldn't get in or get out.'

With the entire 13,000-strong RUC now working on a twelve hours on, twelve hours off basis, officers who had been expecting to be deployed at Drumcree for at most 48 hours found themselves virtually living in the field during the time they were on duty and sleeping in a tent at Mahon Road barracks when they were resting. Their deployment was indefinite, was all they were told. (Some policewomen, desperate for a change of underwear, asked one of the regular cleaning staff to visit the local branch of a chain store on their behalf. However, one of them wryly complained to male colleagues afterwards that the highly functional garments purchased on her behalf were a far cry from the more exotic lingerie which she customarily wore on and off duty.) Some officers were indeed withdrawn from Portadown only to find themselves drafted into other equally volatile flashpoints elsewhere.

As night followed violent night, crowds of Orangemen continued to flock to Drumcree in solidarity, and the destruction continued throughout Northern Ireland, with the police caught between rampaging mobs. Sometimes they struggled to confront the lawlessness, but there were many instances where they stood by as spectators. The Spirit of Drumcree group claims: 'There were a number of areas where the police spoke to protestors and said they would not attempt to remove them from the road providing the protest was peaceful.' Graham Montgomery says, 'I remember being stopped by the army and being told I couldn't go any further because protestors were blocking the road. When I looked past them I could see three people, one of them carrying a Union flag, standing across the road. I couldn't understand why they weren't just told to get off the road.' There was also much anecdotal evidence, from the Catholic side, of police failing to keep roads open or intervening to prevent intimidation. Brid Rodgers recalls, 'It was not just the perception, it was what was happening on the ground. There were police officers standing watching women and children blocking roads and not doing anything to move them. The experience of Nationalists over thirty years of violence was that they would not have been allowed to behave in that way. If they had blocked roads they would have been removed with force.'

Despite the most extensive army support on the streets since the ceasefires, it was clear by the Wednesday night that the RUC was over-stretched and exhausted and that there was insufficient military support to keep the roads open, protect the community and disperse the mobs. By then the police had made 87 arrests, mainly in Portadown and Belfast and fired 339 plastic baton rounds during clashes which caused over 450 assaults on RUC officers. Some 86 people, including firefighters and 49 police officers, suffered injuries during the attacks, among them a nineteen-year-old man hit by a baton round during disturbances at Drumcree. Another casualty was a 70-year-old Catholic priest, treated at hospital for the effects of smoke inhalation after arsonists put a ladder against the window of his church and set it alight with petrol bombs. Police also recorded more than 100 cases of families being subjected to intimidation. It was apparent that the scale and intensity of the disturbances had taken the RUC and Northern Ireland Office by surprise. That same evening, announcing the commitment of two more army battalions to assist the police, secretary of state Sir Patrick Mayhew admitted the police were indeed stretched to the limit and 'having a very hard time' from the effects of 'severe abuse' and intimidation. Mayhew, who had earlier in the week announced his coming retirement from parliament and politics, came under fire for complacency and misjudging the seriousness of the crisis when he later rounded on a television interviewer and said, 'I say, cheer up for heaven's sake. Why always gloom away and take the most extreme view? Cheer up.' In a mischievous intervention the same evening, the Reverend Ian Paisley told the crowd of around 16,000 at Drumcree: 'We see a light at the end of this tunnel. We are moving in the right direction.' The RUC Chief Constable Sir Hugh Annesley and senior police were falling out over the handling of the Drumcree situation and the situation in the north in general, he claimed. 'And we all know what happens when thieves fall out,' he added.

As the fourth day of the crisis drew to a close, and with the traditionally dangerous pre-Twelfth drinking around the bonfires due the next night, July 11, imposing a progressively more important deadline, efforts to find a way out of the impasse accelerated dramatically. The probability of thousands of Orangemen descending on Portadown on Friday evening, following the main Twelfth marches, added further impetus to the search for a solution. If the issue remained unresolved, as in 1995, yet comprehensive lines of communication between the parties had been opened and maintained from the outset of the confrontation on Sunday morning. At one stage Donaldson was standing on Drumcree hill, between protestors hurling stones across the barbed wire lines at the police, when his mobile phone rang. The caller was Ronnie Flanagan, who was in a helicopter directly overhead and could see Donaldson on the ground below. Donaldson, who was involved with the organisation of Orange marshals to help stop troublemakers, asked him to move the security forces back out of range of the rioters and to create a wider buffer zone.

At the same time David Trimble was at the heart of a far more carefully calculated initiative to find a way to bring the crisis to an end. Apart from the fact that the Protestant community judged the parades controversy to be part of an IRA strategy, opposition to meeting residents' groups hardened because the likes of McKenna and Rice would not step aside. They argued that it was a matter for the residents, not the Orange Order, who should represent their interests. The Reverend William Bingham, who had been on holiday in France in 1995 when the stand-off developed and had followed events on BBC Radio 4 news bulletins, remained at home in 1996 and was centrally involved in the deliberations in the church hall as the week passed. 'We were absolutely adamant that we would not meet the Garvaghy Road residents face to face. There were two reasons: firstly, that it was a civil right to walk down the road and you should not have to ask permission to exercise a right; and secondly, we felt there was a significant influence by Sinn Fein-IRA on the coalition. In the eyes of the vast majority of the Orange Order, the IRA and Sinn Fein spent 30 years engaged in a sectarian campaign to kill the Protestant people and eradicate their culture and heritage. Incidents like the Tullyvallen killings, when those killed were targeted for the very reason that they were Protestants and Orangemen, had a traumatic impact on the institution and the wider unionist community. We felt it was completely pointless to try to have a discussion with people who clearly do not want us, not just on the Garvaghy Road but in the whole of Ulster. For us it was like asking the Jews to strike a deal with Adolf Hitler. I realise the Holocaust was on a different scale and would not attempt to compare the two, but in the tenseness of the situation at that time, that was the way many Protestants viewed it. We felt the IRA would have been quite happy to gas us, to kill us, if they got the chance, so why would we think of entering negotiations with someone who has been a member of the IRA.'

Bingham's reasoning was widely shared, but Trimble hoped that he could find a way to bypass the opposition by plugging into another, well-established channel for cross-community dialogue: that between the leaders of the four main churches, Church of Ireland, Presbyterian, Methodist and Catholic. In particular he hoped that the very warm and close relationship between Archbishop Eames, the Church of Ireland leader, and his Catholic counterpart, Cardinal Cahal Daly, who presided from twin cathedrals overlooking each other and dominating the skyscape of Ireland's traditional ecclesiastical capital, Armagh, could be used to lubricate arms-length contact between the marchers and residents. The MP well knew this was an essential prerequisite to any easing of the situation. He outlined his views to Eames by telephone on Monday and met him on Tuesday before flying to London to meet the prime minister, John Major, the next day. (In the context of Drumcree, an exasperated Major would later say: 'What happens in Northern Ireland is not acceptable. If it happened in Surrey or Sussex we would not tolerate it.')

The Archbishop, an avuncular figure who would come to describe the ordeal of Drumcree as his annual Calvary, was already thinking along similar lines. He was under pressure from influential quarters within the church, especially in the Irish Republic, to close Drumcree church hall and graveyard to the protestors in a bid to stop them dragging the entire Church of Ireland into disrepute in the eyes of the world. Eames was hidebound by the governing structures of the church, which prevented him from directing how local parishes conducted their affairs and curbed his authority over individual clergymen. The real power resides with the parishioners, who elect a Select Vestry to exercise it on their behalf. In the Drumcree parish, as all but a couple of the fourteen-strong vestry were also members of the Orange Order, any intervention by Eames would have been, at the very least, unwelcome. All he could do, therefore, was conceal his frustrations and work tirelessly, as he did, for an amicable accommodation, although he did make the somewhat impractical suggestion to the police that they should consider putting screens in the way of the television cameras so that every time the news programmes crossed to Drumcree the silhouette of the parish church on the hill would not be used as a backdrop by reporters.

Eames first learned of the serious crisis that had flared up in 1995 when he saw a news bulletin on the screen on the back of an aircraft seat as he flew into Perth in Western Australia from Singapore. On returning home a week later he was appalled when he discovered the full extent of what had gone on and condemned it roundly. 'My recollection is, my impression is, that between '95 and '96 everybody went to sleep until almost the eve of the march. I certainly didn't go to sleep because I feared '96. You see, through this entire episode I'm getting information from many, many sources, not least the Garvaghy Road people. So I'm aware of the build-up, possibly better, in many cases, than some of the political players. After '95, after this U-turn, or whatever it was called, I was getting information that the Orange Order were beginning to say, right, we got down this year, they better not try to stop us next year. If you remember, prior to July in '96, there was a tremendous build-up in the political scene in Northern Ireland and things were beginning to boil. The southern [government] influence was beginning to be felt and people were saying the show-down will be the first Sunday in July at Drumcree,' he recalls.

That morning, Eames was on his way to Youghal in County Cork to fulfil an unavoidable engagement, but his mind was really on what was happening at Drumcree. 'I had my mobile phone open all the time with my people who were at Drumcree, bringing me up-to-date. They were there until 7 pm that night. As in 1995 the Orange Order used the premises at the church hall for feeding the Orangemen and the hall for sleeping and meetings. That is the first time that I was conscious that they were actually getting such co-operation from the Select Vestry.' So, even before talking to Trimble, Eames was very alert to the need to find some means of getting a deal to end the crisis, not only in the interests of his own church but the entire community beyond. Over the next 24 hours he talked to a large number of people apart from Trimble, including members of his own church and Catholic clergy among whom were Father Brian Lennon and the Cardinal. 'There was nothing really in the field of mediation and I got in touch with Cahal Daly and said I feel desperately that we ought to try and do something, are you willing?' The Cardinal, a distinguished scholastic philosopher, who had heard the worsening news from his office in Armagh, had already cut short a busy week-long visit to Austria, lecturing, preaching and visiting churches and universities, because of the grave situation. He flew from Zurich to Dublin on the Tuesday evening and arrived at Ara Coeli, his Armagh home, at about 1 am on Wednesday.

Earlier on Tuesday, Trimble was part of a joint deputation of Unionist MPs who had an hour-long meeting with John Major in his room at the House of Commons. Ever the incisive lawyer, Robert McCartney pointed out to him that not since the Manchester martyrs of the mid-nineteenth century had British forces fired live rounds on the population and citizens of the United Kingdom in order to maintain public order. 'I said: What are you going to do if, come Thursday, there are ten thousand Orangemen there and they decide that they are going to break through the barricade and move? How are you going to stop them? Well, he did not say.' McCartney pointed out that present policy, if carried to its logical conclusion, was that the soldiers and the RUC would use live rounds on Orangemen. After the meeting, again in apocalyptic mode, Paisley warned the crisis at Drumcree was now 'a powder keg. The prime minister unfortunately believes that the chief constable did right, and until the prime minister changes that, I cannot see any resolution to what is going on. The chief constable looked at it and said that if they go down the road there is going to be civil commotion. But he didn't look at the other side. He didn't look at the civil commotion that was going to take place if he did not allow them down the road. We have just a foretaste of that already. The situation can only be resolved by the prime minister and the Northern Ireland secretary telling the chief constable he has made the wrong decision and that it should be reversed. There is no other way forward.'

Trimble was significantly more measured, saying that he did not think the strength of feeling on the issue in Northern Ireland had been appreciated in London. 'I hope they do so now and I hope they also realise we do need to have a decision very quickly on this,' he said, specifying 48 hours as the limit. 'The problem is how to find a way forward when at present there isn't anyone in the Nationalist area to deal with.' However, he added: 'I have said that following the meeting with the prime minister, I would be willing to meet the leaders of the four main Churches in Northern Ireland – that would of course include the leader of the Catholic church – to see if we can find a way forward in this.' Having put down a significant marker and opened the way for Eames and Daly to begin work, Trimble went off to rendezvous with his wife, Daphne, whom he first met when she joined his law class, to change and attend a glittering, white-tie state banquet being given by the Queen at Buckingham Palace to honour the South African president, Nelson Mandela. When news of his attendance reached Portadown, it led to criticism. In the eyes of the Orange Order, who saw themselves in the same mould as white South Africans, Mandela was far from an inspirational figure. Bingham explains: 'While he was regarded by most of the world as a hero, he is viewed by many Protestants and Orangemen as a terrorist and the feeling was that Trimble should not have gone to the dinner.' Trimble could see no conflict of principle, nor even any irony, in attending a dinner to honour a man many of his community regarded as a terrorist while at the same time insisting that the Orange Order could not talk to Brendan McKenna.

Overnight, against the backdrop of the continuing violence, events were moving swiftly to find a way to bring the two sides into contact, under the auspices of the church leaders. The question of a venue was quickly solved when the management of the Ulster Carpet Mills plant, at the south end of the Garvaghy Road, agreed to allow the use of their boardroom and some offices to facilitate the dialogue. (The family-owned business, founded by George Walter Wilson in 1938, is presently operated by his three sons, Walter, John and Edward, and sends its high-quality carpets from the Garvaghy Road plant all over the world. Among the prestige premises they have carpeted are the London Ritz, the Waldorf Astoria in New York, Hong Kong's Mandarin Oriental and the Mount Nelson in Cape Town, as well as numerous office blocks, airports and luxury cruise ships.)

While Trimble was flying back from London on the Wednesday morning, a day of preparatory exchanges for what would become known as the 'carpet mills talks' was already under way. At 9.15 am, McKenna, Stack and others from the Residents Coalition travelled to Armagh to see Eames. After a half-hour discussion they rushed back to the community centre in Portadown to meet John Steele and Stephen Leach, two senior officials from the Northern Ireland Office, who had telephoned the previous day and asked for an off-the-record meeting. They told them it was their view that a parade was going to be necessary to resolve the dispute – 'getting Orange feet on the Garvaghy Road', as it was articulated by Steele. The conversation represented a significant change of approach on the part of the government. Only 48 hours earlier on Monday, the day after the parade had been stopped, Brid Rodgers had rung Mark Durkan, who was one of the SDLP's main negotiators in the ongoing political negotiations at Stormont, and told him of tension and nervousness in the area caused by rumours that the parade was going to be forced down the road. Durkan went to see Sir Patrick Mayhew, the secretary of state, who assured him there was no need to worry as 'they will go down that road only when there is agreement and no other way.' Another community leader, exploring the protection of the Nationalist interest the previous day, was given an equally gung-ho reassurance by Mayhew. He was also told that the parade would not be pushed through and that, in an unprecedented step over the entire duration of the Northern Ireland crisis, police officers from Britain would be brought in if necessary to relieve the RUC in non-troubled areas so that the force could muster its maximum strength to hold the line at Drumcree. Now, however, they wanted a solution, however expedient or pragmatic. 'It was typical of the Brits,' recalls one former Northern Ireland-born official. 'When the going got tough, any principles they had just went out the window.'

However much the government had begun to wobble behind the scenes, the residents were still in an uncompromising mood. McKenna said any parade was out of the question because of the widespread violence being conducted in support of the protest. He compared the situation on the

Garvaghy Road to that of a black community in London, surrounded by white fascists, being told that there would be no government pressure on the black community to allow the fascists to parade through their area. One of their visitors that day was Mo Mowlam, who had flown in from London, been helicoptered down to Mahon Road barracks and then driven down to the community centre, which was the nerve centre for opposition to the parade. By now, having made several visits, she knew the residents well and was brought up to date on the situation as she saw it.

Earlier that morning, the Orange Order had also been given a strong indication that the pressure was working. The previous evening, Watson had called and asked for a meeting with Flanagan. It was arranged they would meet at the House of Orange in Dublin Road, Belfast. Watson travelled to Belfast with Kennaway, in his camper van, which Kennaway had taken to Drumcree instead of his car so that he could sleep in it. Others, including David Burrows, the deputy district master, travelled to Belfast separately. For some of the delegation, it was the first time they had left Drumcree since Sunday and they were shocked by the sight of road blocks and the charred remains of cars. Inside the House of Orange they prepared tea, coffee and scones while waiting for Flanagan. In his typical low-key way he had driven himself from police headquarters through streets littered with the debris of days of rioting and destruction, parked inside the police station at Donegall Pass and walked round the corner to the meeting. The talk was about various means of getting the problem resolved and at one point Flanagan asked what would be the best time for the parade to go down the road. He did not say anything explicit, but Watson and Kennaway were left with the clear impression that Annesley's unyielding position was going to change and that a parade would go down the road the next day. Kennaway was so confident of this that as soon as the meeting was over he phoned his family and told them to get ready to go off on their planned trip to the Fermanagh lakelands, where he was to address the Twelfth rally at Kesh, because 'this time tomorrow things should be sorted out.' On the way back to Portadown, along the motorway, David Burrows called Gracey and told him to get the district officers together for a meeting. Although a breakthrough seemed imminent, tensions between Portadown District and the county were at crunchpoint. That same evening, county officers including Denis Watson took part in a meeting at Carleton Street Orange Hall where they discussed the drastic action of suspending Portadown District's warrant because of their artifice in recent days. Without a warrant the Portadown Orangemen would not have had the Order's authority to function and organise parades. In the end it was decided not to take such drastic action because the county feared that the move would exacerbate the growing factionalism within the Order and provoke a massive split.

Meanwhile Trimble had travelled from Belfast International Airport to Armagh to see Eames and the other church leaders. All four gathered at the Church of Ireland See House in Armagh at 2 pm to talk to Trimble and plan their strategy. Cardinal Daly recalls: 'We were being, in effect, asked to mediate and get an agreed settlement. That is why, in good faith, I agreed to take part. It was agreed to have more discussion to see how we could bring the Garvaghy Road and Orange people together, at least into the same building to try to have a face-to-face meeting but, failing that, to have bilateral meetings.' Trimble left to join the officers of Portadown District to discuss their expectation of a parade going ahead and the position they would adopt at the coming talks. Not for the last time, however, this proved to be a difficult, obstacle-ridden process. Although he was not an Orangeman, the local UVF leader Billy Wright and his henchmen were exercising a formidable influence over the crisis through-out Northern Ireland. English-born Wright, a greengrocer, was highly prominent among the crowds at Drumcree hill and through a trusted go-between and a mobile telephone had direct access to Harold Gracey and at least two other members of Portadown District. Indeed many of the senior Orange figures present at the Drumcree Bunker and visiting the area openly feared Wright and his uncompromising views, but they would not speak out against him. Trimble and others had tried to remonstrate with them about the violent elements running wild at Drumcree but were merely laughed at. A former colleague of Wright says: 'Drumcree was about a lot more than a walk down the Garvaghy Road. It was seen as an attack on the Unionist family and Protestant culture. Billy felt that the protest had to be supported because if it did not succeed there would be a knock-on effect for other parades throughout Northern Ireland. It was made clear to them that there could be no backing down. The parade was Portadown District's but there was a lot more at stake. It was a province-wide issue because it was an attack on the Protestant way of life.'

With Wright's sinister shadow thus hovering over their tortuous deliberations, the Reverend Warren Porter, an assistant grand master, chaired a meeting of Portadown and county officers in the church hall to discuss the talks invitation. After a heated debate, the Portadown officers said they would not go to the talks themselves. Instead it was agreed that Watson, his deputy Joe Campbell and Stephen McLaughlin, the county secretary, would go, providing that there was no face-to-face contact, that the delegations would be in separate rooms and that McKenna would not be involved in any way. They did not even want him on the factory premises.

In the light of Wright's undoubted capacity to destroy the initiative, for the second time in as many days Trimble overcame his reluctance to treat with a 'terrorist' and arranged, through an intermediary, to talk to Wright in the church hall. 'There were some people who did not like the idea of taking part in a process of this nature and I found it necessary to persuade Wright. It was clear to me that I needed to neutralise him because he was going around opposing the planned talks so I had a conversation with him about the way in which we were trying to resolve the issue in a conciliatory way,' says Trimble, who did seek an assurance from Wright (which was given) that he was not involved in the McGoldrick murder. At the end of their discussion Wright said he had doubts about the process. Within a very short time, Trimble's efforts were temporarily sidelined, as the Reverend Ian Paisley and the Reverend William McCrea arrived at Drumcree church hall with their own peace plan which, they said, had been agreed with the residents.

The architects of this plan were Ignatius Fox, an SDLP councillor, and Mervyn Carrick, the DUP mayor, who had a friendship transcending their opposing political standpoints ever since they had been to technical school together. The 'deal' was that members of Portadown District alone would be allowed to walk down the road, without music, while the residents staged a silent protest. In return the Order would not object to a parade by Nationalists in the town centre on St Patrick's Day, something that had often been talked about as a sign that it was their town centre too. Paisley was so confident of the plan's success that he had already phoned the SDLP leader, John Hume, to share the good news. Hume immediately contacted Brid Rodgers, who was already receiving angry telephone calls from a number of residents who accused her and the SDLP of working behind their backs to strike a deal with the Orange Order. Rodgers told Hume that the Fox-Carrick 'deal' had not been endorsed either by the Garvaghy Road residents or anyone else in the SDLP. Paisley's plan promptly collapsed, returning the spotlight to Trimble.

Wright's doubts about Portadown District participating turned into outright opposition when one of his sympathisers in the Order passed him an illicit photocopy of the draft agreement document faxed to Trimble by Eames. When he read it, he found it contained a paragraph that he had not been aware of: the deal being put by the church leaders to the carpet mills talks would provide for a reciprocal parade through Portadown by Nationalists on St Patrick's Day. Wright was furious and asked to see Trimble again. They met in the back room at the church hall. Apart from

Trimble and Wright, attendees included McCrea, Gracey and Alex Kerr, a renegade UDA commander who had defied that organisation and teamed up with Wright. Wright said he didn't want to see Irish 'tricolours in Portadown town centre' and told Trimble he did not think the carpet mills talks were the way forward.

At around 5 pm Eames, who had spent the day setting up the talks and making arrangements for food and other services and preparing the draft agreement, faxed McKenna and the Orange Order asking them to submit the names of three representatives each to take part in the carpet mills factory talks the next morning. It was the first time the two sides had decided to engage, but both parties had fundamentally opposing perceptions of the terms on which they would do so. The Order had no intention of meeting any residents, never mind McKenna, face to face. The residents firmly anticipated there would be eyeball-to-eyeball negotiations. They replied saying they would only participate in the talks if Cardinal Daly was co-chairman with Eames. They also wanted Father Brian Lennon and the Reverend David Shillingworth, a local Church of Ireland minister, to be appointed secretaries. Around the same time Eames also faxed out copies of a draft agreement, to provide a basis for negotiation, that had been prepared as a result of his soundings by phone and in person over the previous 24 hours. It read:

1. Members of the Portadown District who attend the service at Drumcree will return to their assembly point along the Garvaghy Road with the utmost dignity.
2. No triumphalism will be portrayed. Only Portadown Orange District will take part.
3. In recognition of the importance of civil and religious liberty, the cultural and relgious heritage of both traditions in Portadown should be afforded full recognition. Facilities would be afforded to religious events including church parades. Every encouragement should be given to the establishment of mutual respect and understanding.
4. No Orange parade should take place along the Garvaghy Road on 12 July in future.
5. That, for the future, the Secretary of State provide for a speedy consideration of the parades issue generally. This consideration to be underwritten by the four church leaders.

While this was being done, Cardinal Daly was travelling from Armagh to visit the Garvaghy Road and meet the leaders of the residents. He remembers waiting while McKenna finished talking to a group of people who were patrolling the Catholic area and was impressed that he instructed them to visit the few Protestant people living among them to give assurances about their safety. From the community centre, the Cardinal was then driven to the Upper Malone area of Belfast, where the churchmen had arranged to meet and continue their discussions at the home of the Reverend Edmund Mawhinney, then president of the Methodist church. They were joined by the Church of Ireland press officer and the clerk to the General Assembly of the Presbyterian Church. Cardinal Daly recalls becoming increasingly concerned about the messages coming and going by fax and telephone as they talked and consulted from 8 in the evening until 4 in the morning. 'The feeling grew on me as the night wore on that there was much more going on than the group were being told, that decisions were being taken elsewhere, that we were being used. Now by whom I don't know.' He remembers one particularly worrying item of information: that Paisley had met the prime minister and afterwards said: 'We've won.' Although he was not in a position to know it then, the shrewd Cardinal was right to be suspicious.

That same tense night, around midnight, Richard Sullivan, a reporter for the *Belfast Newsletter* (reputedly the oldest continually published newspaper in the world) was among the crowds outside the church when his mobile telephone rang. He made a rendezvous with his contact, who was nearby, and then met him. There would be a march down the road the next day, he was told. The decision had been made. As his highly-placed contact melted back into the crowd and the darkness, the reporter alerted his newsdesk in Belfast and then perched on the church steps to file his scoop. Meanwhile the editor decided to publish a special late edition and when the presses started to roll at 2 am the exclusive story was in headlines on the front page: 'Marchers ready to hit road today'. McKenna was up and about very early next morning to prepare for the talks. At 7 am he joined Father Stack and Joanna Tennyson at Iona, the Jesuit residence in Churchill Park, to prepare for the meeting which was scheduled to start at 8 am. Brid Rodgers briefly joined the discussion. McKenna told her they were going for direct talks with the Order but, having become aware of the *Newsletter* story, they left for the carpet factory with a considerable degree of suspicion that all was not as it seemed.

A short distance away, across the police lines, the three Orange Order delegates were also getting ready to go to the factory when Gracey approached Watson, who, with Bingham, had emerged as one of the only people in the Orange hierarchy prepared to make decisions and give leadership. Gracey said he had changed his mind overnight and that the meeting was off. Senior Orange colleagues suspect he was contacted by Wright and warned there could not be any deal that included a Nationalist parade through Portadown as suggested in the draft agreement. Bingham recalls, 'Harold met us and said he didn't think we should go. He had thought about it and decided the talks were a bad idea and he was calling them off. We told him he couldn't do that and locked him inside the church hall. Harold was furious, so we left Warren Porter and others with him to calm him down.' It was not an easy task, especially after he was shown a copy of the *Newsletter*. 'I've agreed to nothing,' he barked, but the Reverend Warren Porter, who had chaired the meeting at which they agreed to take part, looked at him sternly and boomed: 'Harold, you did agree to it and if you say you didn't I will expose you as a liar.' The incident illustrated the gulf that had opened up between the district and the county.

When the talks participants reached the factory, in separate groups, at about 8 am, they were greeted by Eames, Daly and a senior member of the factory management. Eames vividly remembers the end of the journey from his home in Armagh: 'I will never forget to my dying day the atmosphere. Portadown was seething. Rumours galore.' The Cardinal, who had gone to his family's home in south Belfast for a short rest before coming to Portadown, remembers a 'general air of anticipation that something awful was going to happen'. Both groups were taken to the rooms allocated for them close to the company boardroom, which had been set up as the nerve centre of the initiative. Eames first went to the Orange delegation and asked for their names. They reiterated the terms on which they were present: that there would be no face-to-face talks, above all not with McKenna. Daly was in with the residents. Eames then went to the residents and said there was a problem: the Order would not meet them face to face. McKenna insisted that he was told there would be direct dialogue. 'We expected to be sitting face to face with the Orange Order at 9 o'clock that morning. We believed that was what we had agreed to,' he insists. For his part Eames says: 'At no time, and I hope before God I'm right in this, did I say to the Garvaghy Road you will meet them face to face, but I said they will undertake on my behest to come to the carpet factory. We had the Garvaghy Road group in that room and I had the Orange in that room, and I sat down with them and said, "I'll need names and your allegiance, where is it you're from?" Now I got them written on a piece of paper, and I went down the corridor to the Garvaghy Road people and I said, in the room up the corridor are XYZ. Brendan immediately said to me, "there's none of them from Portadown District." I said, "Look at their addresses and look at their connection with Grand

Lodge. This is what the Orange have produced to represent them," and I said "I can't do anything but say those are the people that are there. I'll give you time to think about it," and I left them.' Outside he arranged for refreshment to be sent in to buy a bit more time, but such was the hatred in the air that some of the factory staff declined to serve it and there was even a threat of a walk-out and strike.

Both delegations were highly nervous and deeply suspicious. Eames recalls: 'I'll never forget the atmosphere of fear. I saw grown men jumping if the door opened or there was a sound. "What's that? Can you see what's that?" And how do you conduct negotiations with that? My only hope was to keep them in that factory as long as I could.' McKenna used his mobile phone to contact Coalition members on the Garvaghy Road and asked them to check if there was any police deployment that would suggest the parade was going to be forced down the road. Eames remembers the Orange delegation becoming very frightened after one of them received a mobile phone call reporting that Wright was among the crowd gathered outside the factory. 'They said to me, "Is there any point in this?" I said, "Please give me time." That's when we introduced sandwiches and coffee. I went back into the Garvaghy Road room, and I am absolutely explicit about this, and I said, "Now are we prepared to say to each other there's something we can talk about here, otherwise this thing's going to erupt on us." McKenna said to me, "I cannot go ahead with this because we assumed that there would be Portadown people in the other room. We have been misled." And I said to him, "Did I mislead you?" "No, but," he said, "we thought the Orange would know that they should be Portadown people." I went back to the Orange and I said to them, "Is there any way in which we can enlarge your delegations?" And they said they would talk about that, and I left them.'

Shortly after 10.30 am McKenna received a call to tell him there was massive police movement and it looked like the parade was going to go ahead. McKenna stormed out of the room and into the boardroom where the four church leaders were gathered. Waving his mobile phone in the air, he swore and accused Eames of bringing him to the factory under false pretences. McKenna believed the talks were set up by the Northern Ireland Office as a diversionary tactic to take him out of circulation while they prepared to force the march through. Eames recalls how he had just returned to the boardroom to talk to the Cardinal, the Presbyterian Moderator and the Methodist President, who were also there, because 'I had the problem that if I was going to get anything out of this, I would have to say it was a broad Church approach. I cannot swear to how it happened, but the door burst open and Brendan McKenna waved his mobile phone and his words were, "They're coming down the road, we have been sold down the river," and he said a word that I can't repeat, and disappeared out of the factory. When this all happened I said for heaven's sake check up with the RUC, is this happening or is this a ploy and one of my staff got the message to say, sorry, time has run out and we've decided to bring them down the hill.'

Daly, who does not remember McKenna bursting in, recalls: 'We were still hopeful that another basis could be found for dialogue and were still in discussion. Indeed we were just finalising our concluding statement saying that, although we had not succeeded in arriving at an agreed proposal, that nevertheless we were still persisting with our efforts, when I was called out to take a telephone call from the chief constable to tell me that the decision had been taken and that the Orange Order were to be allowed to have their march. I immediately said to him, "Chief Constable, you have made a disastrous decision. It will have disastrous consequences." He said it was a matter of saving lives, a matter of protecting the nationalist population, and so on and asked me to help keep the situation calm. I was very angry. I said to him, "Sir, for years I have always tried to keep the situation calm and will continue to do so. I don't need to be asked to do so but you have made my efforts to do that exceedingly more difficult." I was very angry and the feeling had grown on me as the night went on that we were being used. I had that feeling. I have it still. I've never found any reason to doubt that we were being used. Now by whom I don't know. But some kind of story was put about during the night that there was a deadline by which a decision had been taken and agreement, if agreement was possible, had to be achieved. It was said to be 8.30 in the morning. By then wheels would be set in motion and they could not then subsequently be reversed.'

By the time McKenna received his phone call, Watson and his team had already received their own alert and were on their way back to the church hall. Bingham had stayed in the Bunker at the church hall and was kept informed about the discussions by Watson by mobile phone. 'There was no possibility of a compromise on our key demand. We went down to get a resolution of the problem that would let us get a parade down the road. That was the only thing on our agenda. Archbishop Eames may have hoped we would agree to direct talks, but that was never a possibility,' says Watson. When they found out that McKenna was there Watson and the others were terrified that Portadown District would think they had deliberately ignored the pre-conditions that had been imposed, and they became very uneasy about remaining. One eyewitness told Cardinal Daly that they looked like very frightened men as they left.

Help was, however, at hand. At this point, while the two delegations were still inside the factory, a senior member of the Order received a telephone call from a senior government official to tell him the parade was finally going down the road. Watson was immediately informed and, taking his two colleagues with him, decided to slip away and head back to the church hall. On the way he received a mobile telephone call from Flanagan, who knew the talks had collapsed and who had been ordered to push the march through, asking if Watson would meet him urgently at the rectory. Flanagan, who had remained optimistic that the churchmen might get a deal, had been somewhat surprised to receive a call from Annesley telling him to go ahead and push the march through. 'I think he had some contact through which he learned that the church talks were off. I said I was concerned that if we change our original decision, that the parade should not proceed, in a way that suits the Orange Order's argument, unless it's pretty clear that they're at least equally responsible for the breakdown, we're going to be destroyed in our reputation. The question would be why we've actually done all this for four or five days and then changed it in respect of those who may be, at least, equally responsible for the failure to reach agreement. So I remember asking, when this message came through that the parade had to go down, who's responsible, who's walking away from this? It was, I think, utterly damaging'.

Watson and his companions travelled along the Garvaghy Road, past the crowd of residents who were calm because they still believed the parade was not coming down the road. On the way to Drumcree, Watson called a number of senior Orange officers, including Donaldson, and told them to join him at the rectory. When he arrived there Flanagan immediately asked how quickly they could get the parade under way. 'Half an hour,' they replied. Watson and the others then fanned out across the fields, shouting for the Portadown District members to form up quickly as the parade was taking place. Stung by the accusation that he had been too triumphalist a year earlier and anxious not to expose himself to it again, Trimble proved to be exceptionally sensitive as the parade formed up and the clearing-up rituals of the stand-off got underway. So, when he heard loudspeaker calls for three cheers for the St John Ambulance personnel, the ladies in the church hall kitchen, who had prepared the tea and salads, and others, he urgently sent an aide to halt them in case they were overheard on the Garvaghy Road and condemned.

By now a very angry McKenna was also on his way out of the factory and he became even more furious when a security man told him the Orange Order delegation had already left. When they were prevented from driving back along the Garvaghy Road by the heavy police presence, the negotiators abandoned their car and climbed over walls and fences until they got to the point along the road where a crowd was staging a sit-down protest. As soon as McKenna arrived he was approached by a senior police officer who told him: 'I'm only carrying out orders'. 'The Nazis in Germany used the same excuse,' replied McKenna as he took up a position among the protestors in the middle of the road, still hoping to prevent the passage of the Portadown District march then hastily being assembled outside the Drumcree parish church to complete its 'walk'.

The pressure, and although the police deny it there was clearly some applied at a political level from government, that now caused Annesley to reverse his original decision to ban the march from the Garvaghy Road had been mounting steadily throughout Wednesday at the same time as Eames was putting together his initiative. It is clear from the episodes involving the Northern Ireland Office officials and Flanagan that the government and police position appeared to have hardened considerably towards allowing a controlled march after an operations meeting with the GOC on the Wednesday, and, from the well-informed leak to the *Newsletter*, that the decision had been taken and communicated to at least some of the Orange hierarchy by late that night, while the four church leaders were still meeting.

There is no doubt, as Flanagan admits, that the authorities were not expecting the furious and sustained reaction that the decision to ban the march had unleashed among the Unionist population right across Northern Ireland. By the Wednesday morning the police were not only overstretched but exhausted. Indeed staff association representatives advised Annesley that police morale was close to breaking point and they were demanding greater protection for their wives and families because of the large number of attacks there had been on police homes. 'We had reached the point where we couldn't take any more,' recalls one officer. A senior army officer who was in Portadown at the time recalls how the police, as in 1995, had tried to minimise military visibility and involvement as much as possible for solid political reasons. Getting the troops off the streets remained one of the most tangible achievements of the peace process and the RUC was most reluctant to take what would have been seen as a backward step. 'But they are not as well-equipped to live and operate in the field as we are and by Tuesday night there were clear signs of fatigue and a lack of fresh resources to keep roads open and tackle the large crowds at Drumcree.' The army was, in fact, already preparing to take a far more pro-active role in the fast deteriorating situation, if the call came from the chief constable asking it to do so.

During the day the police had become more and more concerned about the appearance of a heavy excavator and a slurry tanker in the field beside the church, especially when they also received intelligence that the plan was to use the excavator to spearhead an assault on the barbed-wire cordon and police lines before using the tanker as a flame-thrower to spray police and soldiers with a mix of petrol and sugar. During the morning Trimble, who had gone for a walk and a chat with Gracey and Watson, became alarmed when he saw the excavator being fitted with heavy metal plates to make it bullet-proof. When he attempted to intervene he was warned to mind his own business and his face went red with rage when he was told what the slurry tankers were intended for. He stormed off down the hill and used his mobile phone to call the police and Downing Street to warn them. The matter was taken so seriously that later in the day, using one of the telephone numbers direct to the Bunker which had earlier been supplied to the RUC and Northern Ireland Office, Mayhew called and demanded to know if it was true that the slurry tanks were full of petrol and were to be used against the security forces. The RUC had a plan to send in a strike force of ten Land Rovers headed by the SAS-trained Headquarters Mobile Support Unit to seize the vehicles, but it was aborted when Trimble gave the RUC a personal assurance that they would not be used. Sources close to Wright now say the vehicles were never intended for the purpose feared and were merely being used to draw excess sewage from mobile toilets set up for the protestors, but, true or not, at that tense and crucial time the Order and the Loyalists kept the government guessing.

Every day of the crisis, the army commander in Northern Ireland, Lieutenant-General Sir Rupert Smith (a former commander of the Parachute Regiment who had seen active service in the Falklands, Gulf War and Bosnia) and other military chiefs flew into the police headquarters at Knock for meetings with Annesley and his senior commanders to review the situation. Their helicopters landed on the lawn outside the suite of offices and flat occupied by the chief constable, but, rather than walk round to the main door at the front of the building, the senior soldiers habitually climbed in through the window of an office close to the conference room on the ground floor. When Smith arrived that Wednesday for the daily meeting, the threat posed by the digger and tankers was top of a long police worry list, aggravating existing concerns that the crowds gathering every night, which were increasing in size to 50,000 and more, would make a determined assault on the police cordons, overrun them by sheer force of numbers and end up on the Garvaghy Road itself with incalculable consequences. Everyone gathering for that meeting knew that it would be the defining moment for the outcome of Drumcree Two, as it had been dubbed, and there was a realisation that the ban on the march would have to be fundamentally reconsidered. The police were also fearful of how they would cope with the traditional drunken revelry at the bonfires on the night of 11 July and the demands of the Twelfth itself, where the Ormeau Road was once again looming as an incendiary flashpoint. The situation was even more volatile, as Flanagan recalls, because 'we had specific intelligence that other random sectarian murders, like that of Mr McGoldrick, were planned but the intelligence wasn't precise enough for us to be in a position to prevent it or know who was going to be abducted or where they might be abducted and so on.' The full implications of this grim security picture were added up and tested as the police officers and the soldiers brought their own professional philosophies and perspectives to bear on the possible scenarios and outcomes. The central question was the march: could they sustain the effects of continuing the ban or should they back down and force it through again?

Flanagan, who had been on the ground in Portadown for most of the preceding days, sums up the terrible dilemma they faced: 'When it came to reviewing the original march decision on Wednesday, we were reaching a position where we were getting very fearful of how we would be stretched over the next few days because support for this right across the province certainly wasn't reducing. We estimated middle Ulster would say "we don't want any of this nonsense," and we estimated that by the middle of the week the protests would have ended and scaled down. A number of things happened and my main concern was the abduction and murder of Mr McGoldrick and we had reason to believe from various intelligence a lot more of that was planned by the LVF, although they weren't called that in those days as they were still part of the UVF. The intelligence was not precise enough to know when or where or exactly who. In other words, we were not in a position to stop it and that featured very strongly by the middle of the week when we began to ask could we cope because the tide was not turning against these people?

'All the options were discussed with the Army. Can we stop protesters getting to Portadown? Can we put a seal in and around Portadown to stop them gathering in major numbers on the hill? We came to the operational conclusion that what we would do is open a whole new series of fronts and, therefore, it was actually better to contain people on the hill at Drumcree. But the fear then was, what if there are such numbers that we are actually overrun? It was a real fear because we didn't have the physical measures in place. There was some barbed wire but certainly nothing like subsequent years. It was lines of Land Rovers basically. So in all the discussions the question was: what happens if the police are overrun here, physically overrun, and you have hordes of people storming towards Garvaghy Road? And that's when the language began to change, gradually becoming the language of a policing operation to the language of a military operation. The philosophy was, a police service can be defeated in these matters but an army can't. There was some talk of the Army withdrawing to a final line along the edge of the council housing estate and leaving the Garvaghy Road itself as a channel for people to flow through. Somebody said, do you think if they actually overrun us, were burning houses, if we'd expended every plastic baton round that we had, and that's not enough, do you think they're then going to line up in ranks of three and march in an orderly fashion. The answer was: I see no problem, I'd shoot them. And suddenly there was great horror. This can't happen. The police service, since it was created in 1822, with its number one priority the protection of life, must act in all circumstances to protect lives, whatever the damage to the reputation of that organisation.'

This was precisely the scenario that had been exercising the military minds for some days. The army planners had already devised a strategy for dealing with it and, in fact, had already put some of the necessary arrangements in place. At that point two further battalions of soldiers, including the First Battalion of the Parachute Regiment, were on their way to RAF Aldergrove and a reconnaissance party was already earmarked to hurry to Drumcree to assess the scene. They had been told to go in their distinctive maroon berets so that the 'yobbos' would see them. It must be understood that the army role in Northern Ireland was to support the police. Every patrol, every action was subject to police command and control. The GOC only deployed his troops when and how the chief constable decided. There could and would be no question of unilateral or freelance army action. So, within this operational framework, the army had quite properly prepared contingency plans, including an assessment of their capability and the means necessary to continue upholding the chief constable's ban on the march at the point where, either the police were unable to cope further on their own, or the situation escalated to the point where they could not contain it.

As the review of the situation proceeded that Wednesday, the GOC began to outline what the Army would be able to do if the chief constable, whose sole decision it still was under public order legislation, decided to continue the ban and requested much more pro-active army assistance in doing so and in ensuring the ultimate safety of Catholics in the Garvaghy Road by preventing any violent breakthrough. The army had already moved 6000 plastic batons rounds to Portadown, where at the time the police stockholding was 2000. A large quantity of CS gas was also in position – a means of riot control unused for more than twenty years because it all too easily blew back over the security forces and incapacitated them rather than the troublemakers. In the still summer air at Drumcree, however, the Army believed it might be more effective in breaking up the large crowds that had been assembling. The planning also provided for a number of fall-back lines of barbed wire entanglements to cope with any charge by large numbers of demonstrators.

The General coolly described, in line with conventional military logic, how the final line would be at the edge of the housing estates and that, if any rioters got that far and all else had failed, they would be shot. The Army had already prepared additional clarification of the 'yellow card' carried by every soldier in Northern Ireland outlining the circumstances in which they could legally open fire. Moreover, it had already inserted at least two concealed sniper teams with orders to monitor the excavator and slurry tankers and to shoot the operators dead if all other efforts to halt them failed. Some police officers claim that the army had even deployed a light anti-tank weapon to counter the threat but military sources deny this and say that armour-piercing rounds were already available to them and would have been an effective and more appropriate remedy if such circumstances had ever arisen. 'It was well within our capability to have contained the situation but it wouldn't have been a pretty sight,' said one senior soldier who was involved at the time.

The RUC's most senior officers, having worked closely with the Army for some thirty years, knew better than any other British police force that committing troops in such a situation would inevitably result in maximum and even lethal force being used. 'The proposition was unthinkable,' one said afterwards. 'We were looking at a possible "Bloody Sunday for Protestants",' a reference to the controversial events in Londonderry on 30 January 1972, when 1 Para shot dead fourteen unarmed civilians. Everyone in the conference room knew that the decision must now be changed, that a way must be found to get a march through quickly. Flanagan reiterates that 'a policing organisation always has as its number one priority the protection of life, so, in a position where holding to a decision is going to lead to the risk of much greater loss of life than changing it, then the police service, however badly its reputation might be damaged, has only one choice to make.'

Annesley therefore reversed his decision and gave the go-ahead to start planning to take a parade through on the Thursday morning, so that the situation would be calm by the time the bonfires were lit that evening. A senior man at the Northern Ireland Office remembers the police commanders looking 'tired and beaten' when they came to tell Mayhew of the decision. When he heard the Army's proffered solution recounted, the official was far from impressed and commented: 'Surely a battalion of paratroopers with pickaxe handles would have been more effective.' With the parade making ready to move, Annesley decided to go to Portadown. 'Over the preceding days he had been his usual self-confident and haughty self,' recalls one of his senior colleagues at the time. 'But when I saw him not long after the end of that chilling meeting, climbing out through the window beside his office, going off to Portadown in a helicopter because the roads were all blocked, he looked like the loneliest and saddest man on the planet.'

The RUC is adamant that the talks involving the two sides and the church leaders were not a ruse to enable the parade to take place. Flanagan recalls: 'There was still optimism that evening, that Wednesday evening. We thought there was going to be an agreement. However, by Thursday morning Annesley's view was that, with no sign of anything coming out of the church talks, the operational imperatives were that it's going to be difficult enough anyway so the longer we delay this the harder it's going to be.' Accordingly, as Eames was still wrestling with the preliminaries in the carpet factory, Annesley issued final orders for the stand-off to be lifted and for the Orange march to be quickly pushed through the Garvaghy Road. Watson shares Nationalist suspicions that the decision had been taken before they went to the carpet factory. 'Looking back now the talks didn't make sense. We were at the carpet mills at 9 am and I got a phone call from Ronnie Flanagan around 10.30 asking how quickly we could get the men assembled for the parade. It does make you wonder if we were only going through the motions.' Bingham could have walked in the parade but decided against. In terms of the agreement, he believed it should be restricted to members of the district. Instead, after days and nights with very little sleep apart from a nap in his car or on a chair, he decided to go home to bed. Before leaving he watched the parade set off with a feeling of relief rather than jubilation. He already knew they would have to endure it all again the following year. One member of the district, who had endured as much as Bingham for days and was fully entitled to parade, also missed it. Shattered after another sleepless night, he went off to his car to sleep and woke up to find the parade had gone without him.

The four church leaders went to Seagoe Rectory nearby to listen to the radio reports of what was happening. Eames got a call from Annesley. 'He said, "How are you?" I said, "I'm shattered, I'm tired, I'm disillusioned and I don't know what I'm going to do for the rest of the day." Annesley said, "That about covers me." I said, "You must have let them down the road," and I said, "You knew we were still trying." And he said, "All I can say to you is I apologise."' Those present remember the Cardinal sitting with coffee, hunched in thought and very deeply upset. 'I confess I was concerned to get to the Garvaghy Road as quickly as I could to see just what was going on there. I had great difficulty getting past the security cordons and then I got a very angry reception on the Garvaghy Road and this was not from any militant and certainly not from any Sinn Fein quarter. It was a total population which had been tricked and thought that I had been party to the trick played on them. People were banging on the side and windows of my car and telling me to get out of the area and never come back, that I was a traitor and I had let my whole community down, that they would never come back to mass or set foot in a Catholic church again and so on. The hostile crowd included people I knew well and people who were regular mass-goers and had no political affiliation with Sinn Fein or anything of that kind. It was quite clear that the whole population was enraged that the march had been allowed to come down, that the police behaved as they had done, and believed that I had been complicit in all this. I would say it was one of the most unpleasant experiences of my life, to have your own parishioners rejecting you. It was quite scary. I continued and went to the Jesuit house and met with Eamon Stack who was very shaken and very disturbed and very disappointed. There was a great air of apprehension but I told them how I felt, that I had been duped, just as the people felt that they had been duped, and that I felt it was a very bad day's work and that a very wrong and disastrous decision had been taken by the police and made the situation immeasurably worse. I made no secret of my feeling of having been tricked and used. I think that we were all, in good faith, trying to do our best to avert the kind of scenario which did in fact develop and we were, in good faith, all doing our very best to make sure that did not happen. I would still be convinced that a decision had been taken even while we were meeting in Belfast. We spent hours and hours fruitlessly there about something which had already been decided.'

Eames reflects: 'Our effort was not either by government or the Northern Ireland Office or by politicians. It was a church effort spear-headed by Cahal and myself. I had the hope that sometime during that day we might have reached a point where they might come together. I had no ground rules. I was praying my way through that morning. What do I do next? But don't forget, at that stage, nobody had tried to bring them together. We were actually the first in the field. I have to be honest and say if we were doing it again today we'd have people there with recorders making sure that nobody double-crossed. We were desperate in those days to get something going and I think if I were to live my life over again I'd still have tried it. But now with hindsight, probably I should have known in advance that they wouldn't have talked if there wasn't a Portadown person there. But the point is this, I had to say to the Orange Order, we want three representatives and we want three from the Garvaghy Road. If I had dictated to either side who was to be there, they'd have said get lost, or words to that effect, and I had to work with what I'd got.'

Annesley later travelled to Portadown to see the situation for himself. Speaking at the People's Park, he insisted there was no political interference in his decision and his original decision was right at the time. He went on to say that, faced with daily escalating violence and the prospect of thousands of Orangemen facing thousands of police and soldiers and the real risk of fatalities, he was not prepared to risk a single life in such circumstances and, therefore, after the best efforts of the four Church leaders failed to get an accommodation, he had no alternative but to take the decision to let the parade through.

The effect of his extraordinary about-turn on the Catholic community throughout Northern Ireland was compounded by the aggressive way the police cleared the road for the marchers. Catholic opinion was shocked by the forceful police action, which contrasted starkly with what was widely seen as their failure for days to take robust action against the Loyalist mobs. One observer was horrified when a police Land Rover halted beside him and the leader of the crew jumped out and shouted: 'Come on, let's get at the fuckers.' Brid Rodgers, who was visiting constituents at a housing estate in Lurgan, rushed back to the Garvaghy Road in time to see the march make its six-minute passage. 'That was one of the worst experiences of my life. The events of that day had the same impact on the Nationalist community as Bloody Sunday. People were traumatised by what happened. Even moderate Nationalists were outraged. For those who didn't already think so, that was the day the RUC became totally unacceptable.'

Cardinal Daly believes the comparison with Bloody Sunday is not exaggerated. 'It was one of a whole series of major blunders, misreading the situation – Bloody Sunday, internment – in which there was a strong, strong security element and in all cases they proved to be wrong. I don't think there's any way in which the decision could have been favourably received but the way in which it was executed made it still more unfavourably received. It had a devastating effect on the relationship between the RUC and the Catholic community. I have no doubt about that.' The next morning the front page headline of the *Irish News*, the paper which closely articulated the Catholic–Nationalist viewpoint, was simply 'Betrayed'. The residents are adamant that the talks were a smokescreen. 'We are convinced there was a pre-determined plan to get the parade down the road. There is no doubt about it, we were stitched up,' says McKenna.

The next day the issue came up during Northern Ireland questions in the House of Commons in London. The SDLP deputy leader, Seamus Mallon, expressed the anger of his party and supporters when he said: 'This is a government problem and the result rests with this government. The marches had not to do with who marched up what road, but whose writ runs in Northern Ireland. Your government was asked that question and you failed. The other question was asked: who polices Northern Ireland? Was it the legitimate police force or was it those thugs with sashes who once again imposed their will upon the whole of the north of Ireland?'

Later on 11 July, the day the march was forced through, while the impact of this decision and its violent implementation were still sinking in, further fatal damage was done to the RUC relationship with the Catholic community when the Ormeau Road was flooded with police and vehicles and the area sealed overnight so that sympathisers could not obstruct the route of the Orange march on the Twelfth. This march was being allowed because the Belfast Orangemen were again threatening to abandon their usual route and lay siege to the Ormeau Road. The decisions to permit the marches were bad enough in Catholic eyes, but the way they were enforced was worse. The result was to provoke further outbursts of serious disorder, mainly in the Catholic areas. The disturbances were at their worst in Londonderry, where the rioting was as prolonged and intense as anything seen in the early 1970s. For two consecutive nights the police were under sustained petrol-bomb attack in the city; each night, they estimated 2000 had been thrown. In a throwback to the height of the Troubles, seventeen people were injured when a vehicle-borne bomb exploded outside the Killyhevlin Hotel at Enniskillen causing such extensive structural damage that the premises had to be largely rebuilt. As the violence subsided on 16 July, its terrible extent and implications became clear. The police logged 8000 incidents and calculated that up to 24,000 petrol bombs had been thrown. They had fired 6000 plastic baton rounds, the most intensive use of the weapon since the week following the death of Bobby Sands in May 1981, when 4000 had been discharged. One man died in the disturbances, a Catholic crushed by a military vehicle in Londonderry, and 149 police officers and 192 civilians were injured; 39 police homes were attacked and 28 officers and their families forced to move permanently. As in 1985 and 1986 the personal allegiance of policemen and women was brought close to breaking point. Some officers were indeed members of the Orange Order and others had close family or relatives as members. During the stand-off there were people on both sides of that confrontation who were blood relatives,' one senior officer said, and not all RUC officers demonstrated the impartiality they should have. (During July and August six were suspended from duty and a seventh reported for taking part in Orange parades or protest demonstrations. Some subsequently left the force and others were dealt with by internal discipline.)

Annesley provided a much fuller explanation of the final course of events in a lengthy radio interview with Barry Cowan on BBC Radio Ulster on Sunday 14 July, exactly a week after the crisis had begun:

> *Annesley*: I will say that I accept that the rule of law has had a setback at Drumcree. The rule of law has had a setback. The rule of law has consistently had a setback. It's had setbacks in Dublin. It's had setbacks in England. It's had setbacks in France and in Germany. And there is one key golden public order rule and that is a number of people, if you get enough of them, can in the short term overrun a normal policing operation. Five thousand pickets at Hadfields in the steel strike. You can't do anything with them. The race disorders in Brixton and in St Paul's. The police had to withdraw initially. The British Embassy was burned down in Dublin, no criticism of my Garda colleagues, the resources were not there to deal with it. We have seen over and over again how French farmers can burn the autoroutes between Paris and Lyon and elsewhere. But it is a short-term issue and what must be a long-term acceptance is that if there is a rule of law, it must be accepted by the Orangemen the same as everybody else. Otherwise there is no long-term future for law and order in this province.
>
> *Cowan*: But it must be enforced by the RUC and that is what the RUC did not do at Drumcree. They backed off.
>
> *Annesley*: Ever since policing was formed, you police by consent. The consent to comply with the rule of law did not exist with the Portadown Orange Lodge. They were not encouraged to do so by constitutional politicians and they should have done. If there was another situation with those sort of numbers and they become uncontrollable, the police eventually are in a position, do they withdraw temporarily, or do they

find themselves in a position of the potential loss of life. Now unlike some of my colleagues, I do have direct experience of this. I was in charge in Trafalgar Square in 1981 when a fire brigade caused a crowd surge leading to two people trampled to death and hundreds of injuries. That was totally accidental but when a crowd begins to move, and I am talking about the same numbers, sixty to seventy thousand, they are not going to be stopped. And if I may come to the second decision, if you are finished with the first one.

Cowan: Can I just ask one thing before we get to that, Chief Constable: is it true you were advised by senior officers on the ground that the only way that that Orange procession could be stopped was with the use of live ammunition?

Annesley: No. There was no question of that occurring on the ground. I will say quite openly that I had a decision in my office with the general officer commanding and I made it clear in the course of that interview with him that there was no issue of using live rounds. You simply do not contemplate using live rounds on a public order crowd in the United Kingdom. It is not acceptable. It is not done. I would never have done it and I would not have risked one life if I had to trade that off against the potential overrun of the rule of law in the short term.

Cowan: When did you decide on the U-turn, if U-turn it was?

Annesley: Anybody can put what word they apply to it. Can I say this. I found it one of the most difficult decisions of my professional career. Looking at it now with hindsight I have to say that if I was facing the situation where I had half a dozen dead I would feel particularly different about it. I was faced with a serious and deteriorating public order situation, not only in Drumcree where we might have anticipated some protest but across the province. My resources were stretched. That's no secret. I expected large and growing crowds with significant hostile elements and in this I will say that the Portadown Orange Order had that site for the most part well behaved and well marshalled. But the gougers and the hoods got in as well and everybody knows that. I believe that there was the potential that other Orange Order parades would be diverted to that site. There had been an earlier attempt, I believe it was on the ninth, to breach the wire. That was repaired. We then became aware of the existence of a bulldozer, a slurry tanker with potential of JCBs to come. There had been a failure to get any accommodation between July last year and July this year between the two sides. Neither side would give an inch. The four church leaders despite their sterling efforts also failed and I was left in the position that if on the eleventh night, with a significant amount of alcohol consumed, other Orange marches were invited to come to Drumcree, the police would have faced a situation where a crowd of some sixty to seventy thousand would have approached and overrun that wire leaving only one alternative and that was to withdraw to attempt to protect the Garvaghy Road estate. If that had occurred and blood was up and alcohol was prominent, the potential accidentally or otherwise to hit the first Nationalist house which was probably three hundred yards away was obvious. And as I say I have personal experience of this done by accident not on purpose. And people have to remember, this was not a picnic. This was a potentially violent and disorderly crowd who were intent on making their protest and we did not and could not, even with three thousand policemen and soldiers, have contained that. That is why some papers have spoken about the question of live firearms. I have not and would not and never contemplated issuing the order to fire on a crowd in the United Kingdom. It had to be a back-off situation. And as I talk to you now even after the week of perhaps soul-searching and reflecting on all of this, I would not have traded one life for the Garvaghy Road. If the rule of law had to be turned back in the short term so be it. But that patch of road is not worth one human life.

The Police Authority calculated that the disturbances had cost the RUC well over £10 million. The housing authorities faced a £1 million bill to resettle 251 civilians driven from their homes, and public transport executives said it would cost £5 million to replace buses destroyed in the violence. Education authorities estimated damage to schools of at least £3 million and the roads service said that repairs would cost £1 million. Tourism, which had flourished during the summer of peace, was in ruins: hotels and boarding houses reported floods of cancellations. At the end of the year, announcing a £120 million boost to security spending, and knock-on cuts in other public expenditure allocations to cover it, Mayhew revealed that the cost of the summer disturbances exceeded £40 million – 'a grievous and wanton self-inflicted wound,' as he described it. Damage inflicted by sectarian arson attacks between July and September totalled £16.9 million, the equivalent of seven new primary schools, Mayhew pointed out. But what was incalculable was the damage done to the prospects for community stability and a lasting peace. The government's security and political policy lay in ruins. The disturbances had unleashed sectarian hatred that everyone hoped had been buried for good. The prospects for prosperity and inward investment evaporated as businesses, horrified by the destruction, pocketed their chequebooks and cancelled plans to provide jobs. Anglo-Irish relations plunged when prime minister

John Bruton accused the British government of reneging on its responsibility to protect all citizens and maintain the rule of law. As people talked openly of the violence being as bad as that of 1969, when the troops had to come in, the extent of the setback was summed up by a velvet-voiced US news correspondent who stepped from behind a burning vehicle in Londonderry and said to camera: 'Ulster is back to square one.'

Chapter Eight
Chernobyl

With the battle of Drumcree Two, Northern Ireland again navigated one of those decisive turning points which determine the course of events for years to come. Towards the end of 1996, Presbyterian Church leaders bitingly labelled the sectarian turbulence of the previous summer as 'Northern Ireland's Chernobyl' because it produced a meltdown in community relationships and widespread fallout. It was a particularly apt analogy. The deep bitterness stirred up on both sides would not abate and, indeed, would continue to flare up each year, further poisoning relationships in Portadown and inhibiting efforts for a final and lasting settlement of the political differences in Northern Ireland. A range of issues highlighted by the five-day crisis would prove to have profound and far-reaching consequences, especially for the RUC, the Church of Ireland and the Orange Order. The way parades were handled and policed would also substantially change.

When the immediate political implications began to be evaluated, Annesley was in the firing line and had to mount a robust defence of his actions, but his pending retirement, announced well before the crisis, insulated him from serious censure or pressure to resign immediately. The same Sunday morning as he gave his radio interview, the Cardinal pointedly returned to the Garvaghy Road where he coldly articulated the scale of the damage done to the RUC–Catholic relationship. Speaking at mass in St John the Baptist church, he accused the British government of an abdication of responsibility: 'When will the RUC, which many Unionists see as exclusively "their" police force, be seen by Nationalists as being equally concerned to safeguard their rights too and to respect their feelings too, so that Nationalists could some day call it "their" police force too? There is [. . .] a huge crisis of confidence in the police among the Nationalist community at large. In my own modest way I have tried for years to urge both the police and the Catholic public to work to build up mutual trust and confidence. For the present that confidence has been totally shattered. Restoration of confidence will require immense and prolonged efforts on the part of the RUC. Sadly, their whole process of confidence building has now to be built all over again, virtually from zero. That process must now be recommenced and it must be vigorously pursued and it should be conducted on the part of the RUC, as far as Nationalists are concerned, in a genuine spirit of humility, regret for what has happened and readiness for real change. Radical measures will be needed, both as regards the RUC and the Police Authority and the Police Complaints Commission, but changes are essential. Every society needs a police force in whose integrity and impartiality all political communities and all social strata can have confidence. Northern Ireland needs this more than most societies do.'

The mishandling of Drumcree imposed a terrible legacy on the RUC, exacerbated the longstanding problem of policing a divided society without full consent and co-operation and, at a single stroke, sundered 25 years of painful and increasingly tangible progress in transforming the relationship between the RUC and the Catholic minority community. In retrospect the Cardinal's words can be seen to have dealt the force a terminal body blow, although its full effect would take some time to be seen. A public opinion survey for the Police Authority, published in December 1996, underlined their accuracy: 82 per cent of Catholic respondents thought the RUC should be reformed, replaced or disbanded, compared to 70 per cent a year earlier. The proportion of Protestants supporting the same proposition had increased from 23 per cent to 32 per cent in the same period. It is now widely accepted that the replacement of the RUC by the Police Service of Northern Ireland in September 2001 and the raft of associated reforms flowing from the comprehensive report of the Independent Commission for Policing, chaired by Chris Patten and published in 1999, flow directly from the debacle of Drumcree 1996.

The Irish government, which was incandescent at the U-turn, got its chance to question the reasons and make its displeasure known when Annesley attended the Anglo-Irish conference meeting in London on 18 July. Echoing the account he gave in his BBC interview a few days earlier, he jointly blamed the Portadown Orange Lodge and the Garvaghy Road residents for what had happened, saying that over the preceding year they had failed to sort out the problem because of paramilitary manipulation on both sides: 'If you get two groups who will not give an inch then the RUC haven't got a magic wand,' he said. He turned the tables somewhat by referring to the powerlessness of the Irish police back in 1972 when they were unable to prevent an angry crowd from attacking and burning down the British Embassy in Dublin after Bloody Sunday. Annesley repeated that he was faced with a serious and deteriorating public order situation, not only in Drumcree but across the province.

Given that it was a potentially violent and disorderly crowd who were intent on making their protest, he said, the RUC could not have contained it even with 3000 policemen and soldiers. Again he asserted that he had not issued, would not issue and had never contemplated issuing the order to fire on a crowd in the United Kingdom. As he had earlier told the BBC: 'It had to be a back-off situation. If the rule of law had to be turned back in the short term, so be it. I made an honest, professional and proper decision with the entire support of my two deputy chief constables and the overwhelming number of my assistant chief constables. When we got to the position that it could not be sustained, I changed it.'

The previous day, making a statement about the crisis in the London House of Commons, Mayhew had announced two important initiatives arising from the Drumcree situation: a thorough independent review of parades and marches in Northern Ireland and a study about the use and effect of plastic baton rounds in public disorder situations. On 24 July 1996 he announced the terms of reference for the first project:

> To review, in the light of evidence received from any interested party and having regard to the particular experience of 1996, the current arrangements for handling public processions and open air public meetings and associated public order issues in Northern Ireland, including:
> - the adequacy of the current legal provisions, and in particular the adequacy of the statutory criteria used in making decisions on public processions and open air public meetings;
> - the powers and responsibilities of the Secretary of State, police and others;
> - the possible need for new machinery, both formal and informal, to play a part in determining whether and how certain public processions and open-air public meetings should take place;
> - the possible role for and composition of Codes of Practice for organisers of and participants in public processions and open-air public meetings and to make recommendations by the end of January 1997.

The names of the reviewers were announced soon afterwards. The chairman was to be Dr Peter North, QC, Vice Chancellor of Oxford University since 1993 and a distinguished lawyer and academic who had previously been Law Commissioner for England and Wales and chaired the Road Traffic Law Review. The other two members of the team were a complete surprise: Father Oliver Crilly and the Very Reverend Dr John

Dunlop, two distinguished Northern Ireland clergymen. Crilly was the parish priest of Melmount in Strabane, County Tyrone, but he was more widely experienced and high-powered than a simple small-town parish pastor, having served in a number of key church jobs including Director of the Catholic Communications Institute of Ireland, the executive arm of the Catholic Bishop's Commission for Communications, and as a member of the Irish Commission for Justice and Peace. In 1990 he was a member of a joint working party of the Commission and the Irish Council of Churches who visited all of Northern Ireland's prisons and produced an influential 'Report to the Churches'. He was also a frequent broadcaster in Irish and English, a member of the Western Education and Library Board and had recently visited Rwanda in the aftermath of the massacres and civil war and wrote a report for the Irish Catholic bishops. In 1995 Crilly took part in an inter-church speaking tour of the United States with Dunlop, who was now to be his colleague.

Dunlop's first ministry was at Fitzroy Avenue Presbyterian Church, Belfast, and he then served for ten years in Jamaica with the United Church of Jamaica and Grand Cayman until 1978 when he became minister of Rosemary Presbyterian Church in North Belfast. As Moderator of the General Assembly of the Presbyterian Church in Ireland (1992–93) he received the Cultural Traditions Award in recognition of his 'established and continuing contribution to the debate on cultural diversity within Northern Ireland'. There was some adverse comment about the narrow composition of the review team: North, an unknown outsider, and two clerics of decidedly broad outlook was not a combination designed to appeal to the loyal orders or those of a defensive disposition. The Northern Ireland Office view was that the two clerics knew as much as anyone about the parades and issues, had no obvious axe to grind and reflected the most basic community balance – Protestant and Catholic – which could not easily be boycotted. 'The more members, the more problems with balance and agenda and the longer it would take to get a report,' one official recalls.

With a tight deadline to meet, the small team got down to work promptly at the end of August, hosting a news conference to invite submissions and evidence and putting advertisements in the main newspapers. Letters were also sent to 130 interested parties and 15,000 leaflets were distributed. The group then went on a tour of the main parade flashpoints – a dozen of them including Portadown – and observed some parades at the tail end of that year's marching season. It is worth noting, as the reviewers eventually did, that despite the massive convulsion caused by Drumcree, there was disorder at only fifteen of the

2307 Loyalist parades in 1996 and none at any of the 218 Republican marches. Only 28 Loyalist and two Republican marches were re-routed or had conditions imposed. In addition another 527 'other' parades passed off in an entirely peaceful and orderly manner.

One of the first people the North team met was Ronnie Flanagan, widely expected to succeed the outgoing Annesley as chief constable (which he did at the beginning of November). Shortly before their meeting Flanagan had chanced to meet Lord (Gerry) Fitt, former leader of the SDLP, and two Conservative politicians on a flight to London. The two Conservatives were great admirers of Enoch Powell, the controversial British politician who had served for a time as Unionist MP for South Down, and enthused about how he brought his peerless powers of intellect and impeccable logic to bear on trying to solve the great problems of the day, like Northern Ireland. 'Logic. Logic,' spluttered Fitt, a lifelong socialist. 'Sure tell me what's the use of impeccable logic when you're dealing with two sets of illogical politicians in Northern Ireland.' Flanagan repeated the exchange as a good-natured warning to North that in deeply divided Northern Ireland he could not depend on conventional standards of goodwill, pragmatism or accommodation applying to his task.

Predictably enough, some submissions to North suggested that the so-called, but legally dubious, 'right to march' was pre-eminent, while others put the newer, and equally doubtful, proposition that a 'right for residents to withhold consent' for a parade to proceed should be paramount. It must therefore have been a source of some encouragement to the reviewers that by far the largest group of submissions argued that a way should be found to strike a balance between competing rights. At the end of November they sat down to sift the outcomes of their 93 meetings with 270 individuals and consider the 300 submissions and letters they had received, before drawing their final conclusions.

These were closely argued and articulated in a 250-page report with 43 recommendations, published in Belfast on 30 January 1997. As would be expected from such cultured and well-read scholars, their report is far from dry legalistic or bureaucratic reading. Among the varied and many references and sources it cites are the South African church leader Michael Cassidy, the Presbyterian historian Thomas Witherow, the Welsh Mabinogion and St Paul's Epistle to the Ephesians. It also uses quotes from the distinguished northern Irish poets John Hewitt and Seamus Heaney to underline points, and in a section entitled 'Giving a Lead' the authors themselves seek to define the parameters of the future. It 'does not just happen: people have to create it. The future that is created can depend on a shared vision, which can accommodate and celebrate diversity, on the will to persist in working for that vision in spite of difficulties and on the kind of trust that will permit us to take risks in yielding up some of our own control of situations in favour of tackling them together.' As well as its literary and philosophical nuggets and many dollops of common sense, the report also contains solid practical and legal recommendations designed to 'make easier the resolution of disputes relating to parades and protests.'

Picking up on the suggestion first made seventeen years earlier by the then chief constable Jack Hermon, its core suggestion was the creation of an independent Parades Commission with a comprehensive role. It should work for greater understanding at local level through education: finding ways to help people better understand their rights and responsibilities and improve their knowledge and understanding of each other's fears and perceptions of parades. By promoting and facilitating mediation it should seek to encourage the search for local accommodation to resolve disputes over contentious parades. Where all this fails, the envisaged Commission would consider, under statutory terms, consultation and a new Code of Conduct, what binding conditions should be imposed on contentious parades and issue a written determination to underpin their ruling. In a significant extension of the existing statutory criteria used to decide whether parades should go ahead, the reviewers proposed that 'the impact of the procession on relationships within the community' should also be taken into account. They suggested the need for new powers to control alcohol, frequently a contributory element to public disorder. So that there was time for proper consideration of all the relevant factors and mediation and consultation to take place, they recommended that the required advance notification period for a parade should be increased from seven to 21 days. (An opinion survey carried out for the reviewers revealed that four out of five people questioned actually favoured three months' notice.) In addition the reviewers believed a register of bands should be established, creating a framework to bring the rowdier 'blood and thunder' or 'Kick the Pope' ensembles under control. The freelance bands, which cost up to £30,000 to equip with uniforms and instruments, are simply hired by lodges to accompany them on parade. The reviewers comment: 'It is clear that, since the rights of neither group are absolute, our proposals for legislative and other changes must provide for reasonable proportionality in the balancing of those rights. In a democratic society this may mean that some people – potentially of any background or tradition – may have to put up with things that they would prefer did not happen.' In a section of the report entitled 'The Way Ahead', the authors make a passionate plea for good sense to prevail:

> Many people have said to us that Northern Ireland cannot afford a repeat this year of the events of 1996. We agree. Our report contains recommendations which we believe are in proportion to the problem, a situation where the vast majority of parades pass off peacefully, indeed enjoyably, and without offence; but where a very small minority have led to violent confrontation and where a further small minority, whilst on the whole peaceful, are nevertheless at best tolerated by one section of the community.
>
> Where thirty or even fifty contentious interfaces between marchers and local residents represent a major threat to peace and harmony in the community, that should not blind us to the other two and a half thousand situations where positive attitudes and good organisation by the Loyal Orders and the tolerance or support of local residents have ensured a peaceful outcome.
>
> We have analysed the rights and responsibilities which must be taken into account in resolving disputes over parades, recommended new structures, suggested new procedures for handling notices of parades, and proposed both guidelines and a code of conduct for those who parade and those who may protest.
>
> It is our view that the key to progress must lie with those individuals and groups who have a stake in the future of Northern Ireland, and must lie in their attitudes of tolerance and understanding, with behaviour to match.
>
> We recognise that, whatever new structures and processes are put in place, there may be those who will seek to challenge them at the outset. Nevertheless, we would hope that our approach would commend itself to most reasonable people in Northern Ireland, including those who organise parades, of whatever kind, as well as those who protest about them.
>
> We were given the very clear impression, from all the evidence available to us, that the great majority of people desire a peaceful and just resolution of these difficult issues. We hope therefore that most people will be prepared to accept what fair-minded people would accept as being reasonable solutions in local situations. We believe it is essential to encourage that constituency to be as broad as possible, and that those who would seek to object to constructive and reasonable proposals are positively influenced by the fair-minded majority.
>
> What other pointers are there for the way forward? Almost everyone

to whom we spoke stressed the importance, where there are contested parades, of arriving at local accommodation. Certainly, some individuals and groups saw different ways to that accommodation, and may have envisaged a different balancing of rights in that process. We do not wish to see a further drift towards an apartheid society. We believe that the future of Northern Ireland lies in consensus and interdependence. We take heart in this respect from the surveys which show that the great majority of the people of Northern Ireland still wish to live in mixed communities. One of the tragedies of the events of 1996 has been that, far from reinforcing the feeling of neighbourliness, there has been increased polarisation, and further moves towards apartheid both of mind and of location. Such a move towards intolerance can only be reversed through striving to understand one another and to reach local accommodation.

Since the difficulties lie in the areas of flawed communal relationships, neither the law nor our proposals can of themselves solve these underlying difficulties. The law is, however an important mechanism that provides a basic framework within which the competing and conflicting interests can be measured and reconciled. Our proposals represent one way of managing, and possibly resolving, one particularly complex area of conflict. They offer nothing more and nothing less than that. What is suggested and recommended provides an escape route from the repetition of last year's disasters. If our proposals facilitate this, and as people take advantage of the opportunities offered, they may generate a groundswell of movement towards accommodation. That is why we set store in our recommendations on building support for opportunities for conciliation and mediation at the local level. But all those steps will have only limited effect, if society, and by that we mean the people of Northern Ireland, shuns broad Christian and civic values.

Such a society would be built on mutual understanding, the celebration of diversity, a more secure sense of belonging and greater affirmation of self-worth. There would be no place for threatening disorder, abusing one's neighbours or committing criminal offences such as blocking roads. Marches and parades would no longer be seen as a pejorative and triumphal remembrance of victory by one side or the other, but a joyful recognition that together the community had created a better future.

As St. Paul put it to the Ephesians, "I urge you then – I who am a prisoner because I serve the Lord: live a life that measures up to the standards God set when he called you. Be always humble, gentle, and patient. Show your love by being tolerant with one another.

The government responded to the report later that day in the Commons when it was the subject of a lengthy statement by Mayhew. 'We recognise the report's description of the parades issue as a microcosm of the wider political problems of Northern Ireland and as one which has the capacity to polarise the community, and to engage levels of emotion and commitment which few other issues reach. Because of that the Government has a responsibility to take these issues forward as far as possible on a basis of widespread agreement within the community, so that whatever new arrangements are put in place may be recognised as fair and workable, and therefore acceptable,' he said.

Mayhew knew there was already a substantial head of steam building against the idea of a commission. For instance, four members of the Police Authority with Orange or Unionist affiliations had entered reservations about the suggestion in the body's own submission to North. He therefore opted to put this aspect of the report out for further consultation. He called it 'a precisely-focused and time-limited exercise to give public representatives and others who are directly concerned the opportunity to comment on an important matter of real concern to them and those whom they represent.' However, by the time that consultation period concluded at the end of March, all progress was stalled by the general election that would sweep Major and Mayhew from power and bring Tony Blair to Downing Street and Mo Mowlam to Stormont.

Meanwhile, with the likelihood of a Drumcree Three looming ever closer and the prospect of even dialogue between the parties still as elusive as it was when the carpet mills talks collapsed, the government decided immediately to establish a five-strong provisional Parades Commission, with voluntary mediation, conciliation and education roles as recommended in the report, to see if anything could be done ahead of the coming marching season. They also moved to prepare and publish the suggested Code of Conduct, covering parades, protests and open-air public meetings, and to put in place the registration scheme for bands, the extended period of notice for parades and tighter controls on alcohol. In line with the report, the government ruled out any requirement for parade organisers to be required to post bonds, provide proof of insurance cover or make a contribution to policing costs. 'The events of last summer cast a pall of fear across Northern Ireland. As the report states, an abyss of anarchy opened up,' said Mayhew. 'All people of good will must surely demand that there be no repetition. But no mechanisms and no procedures can be enough on their own. There needs to be within all who live in Northern Ireland the will and the personal determination that last year's terrible events shall never again occur.' As we shall see, that appeal, and the passionate plea from the North team, would once again be expensively ignored.

Some days after the statement in the House, Sir John Chilcott, the amiable Permanent Under Secretary at the Northern Ireland Office, who had been periodically involved in Northern Ireland Affairs ever since he had started his career in the 1960s when responsibility rested with the General Department of the Home Office in Whitehall, dialled a Leeds number. He was trying to contact Tyneside-born Alistair Graham, who, after many years living and working in London as General Secretary of the Civil and Public Services Association, had decided a year earlier to re-settle in the north prior to eventual retirement. Graham, who had then become chief executive of the Leeds Training and Enterprise Council, was out at lunch, and when he returned to the office his secretary asked him to return Chilcott's call. Although they knew each other slightly, Graham, who had no previous connections with Northern Ireland, was intrigued about why Chilcott wanted to speak to him. When he made contact, the senior civil servant quickly outlined the parades issue and explained the role of the envisaged parades commission. 'Would you consider chairing it?' he asked. Graham replied that he would, and a few days later Stephen Leach, from the Northern Ireland Office, flew over from Belfast to discuss the post further. The formal job offer came soon after that, when Graham was invited to meet Mayhew in his office overlooking Horse Guards Parade in London, a room once occupied by Winston Churchill. Mayhew was tired, but in good spirits, after a late night at the Commons pushing through some Northern Ireland business. After some preliminary discussion with the minister and officials, Mayhew turned to him and said: 'Well, Mr Graham, are you really prepared to take this ... em ... em ... chalice?' Although Graham instantly realised the word 'poison' had pointedly been left unsaid, he did not hesitate to say yes. He then signed a letter of appointment that had been prepared in advance. The Leeds TEC would release him two days a week as required and would receive his salary from the Northern Ireland Office in return.

Soon afterwards Graham made his first official visit to Northern Ireland, where he was introduced to the geographical complexities of marching routes in Portadown by Ronnie Flanagan. The chief constable unrolled the tribal maps of the town on the floor of his office and he and Graham got down on their knees to pore over them. Dr Peter Smyth, a civil servant from the Northern Ireland Office, then took him to Portadown to see the actual situation on the ground and was distinctly surprised when Graham asked him to park the car and walk the Garvaghy

Road. 'Ethnic maps with green and orange markings. It was like going to Kosovo or somewhere like that,' he said afterwards. His first encounter with an actual parade came on the Ormeau Road when he went along to see what happened when the police imposed a block. Later he attended others and listened in disbelief to clergymen and other speakers using the sort of language that he thought had been left behind in the seventeenth century. 'I was amused because I had recently bought a house in West Yorkshire, built in 1634, with the inscription "Fear God and honour the King" on the fireplace,' he said. By this time the other parades commissioners had been named: the Reverend Roy Magee, a Presbyterian minister, who had helped broker the loyalist ceasefire in 1994; Berna McIvor, an SDLP activist who worked closely with party leader John Hume; David Hewitt, a former rugby player and solicitor who was closely involved in reconciliation work through the Evangelistic Contribution on Northern Ireland and was previously Independent Assessor of Military Complaints procedures; and Frank Guckian, a Londonderry businessman who had also held a number of public appointments.

The British general election was held on 1 May and the following Saturday Mo Mowlam, the newly appointed secretary of state, flew into Belfast to take over from Mayhew. Their backgrounds and styles could hardly have been more different. Oxford-educated Mayhew was a towering, wealthy, ex-Royal Dragoon Guards officer and barrister, with a vice-regal aloofness and all the patronising airs and clipped mannerisms of the British upper classes. Self-made Mowlam, whose working-class upbringing was overshadowed by an alcoholic father, worked her way from the local comprehensive to Durham University and then the United States, where she both studied and taught, before coming home and entering British politics as MP for Redcar in 1987. Her common touch, irreverence, informality and unorthodoxy – it was said she once sent her male police bodyguards to obtain sanitary towels – and 'touchy-feely' style, regularly hugging and kissing people, struck a chord with the mass of ordinary people who felt she was one of them. As shadow Northern Ireland secretary Mowlam had visited Northern Ireland many times and made a point of winning friends on all sides, an asset she intended to use to good advantage when in power. Among many other things, she had therefore made a point of going frequently to Portadown and talking to both the residents and the local Orange Order.

Mowlam wasted no time in pointing to the parades issue as one of her first priorities. During the extraordinary hugging and kissing with passers-by that characterised her walk-about in Royal Avenue during the afternoon of her first day in Belfast, she said: 'I am determined to work with others to ease tensions arising from parades and marches, and to uphold the rule of law. We will implement the recommendations of the North Report with care and sensitivity. But as we approach the height of the marching season this year, I appeal to everyone with any influence to use it to defuse sectarian tensions and attitudes and find ways of balancing the legitimate rights of marchers and local residents.' Mowlam already firmly believed that accommodation between residents and marchers was the best way forward, and was determined to find a means to permit constructive dialogue with a view to avoiding a repeat of the crisis of July 1996. Events during her first weeks in office underlined just how dark a shadow the marching controversy had already cast over Northern Ireland and how its direct and indirect effects were hindering efforts to kick-start the peace process, which had been in growing disarray since the IRA had called off its ceasefire and carried out the bombings at Canary Wharf in London the previous January.

As Mowlam woke up in Hillsborough Castle the next morning, Sunday, the police were mounting a major security operation in Bellaghy in County Londonderry, after a Royal Black Institution parade to an annual church service was re-routed away from its customary passage along the main street. On their way to the church, and back again, the band and 200 marchers walked right up to the police cordon before turning on their heels in protest. The members of the Institution were far from pleased. Robert Overend, a nationally renowned breeder of pedigree pigs who was also a member of Grand Lodge, complained that after living his entire life in the village and 'making more of a contribution to getting it on the map than any other person, I'm now told I can't walk through it'. For their part, despite the peaceful outcome of the situation, some of the residents accused the police and Army of heavy-handedness. They complained that 'explosive sniffer' dogs had been brought in to search the village at 6.30 am and that the deployment of fifteen Land Rovers and 100 RUC officers amounted to an invasion. It was a timely reminder for Mowlam of the intractability of the marching issue and the unenviable role of the police in regulating it. The RUC was, as she had previously put it, 'the meat in the sandwich'.

A few days later, on 8 May, with the death of Robert Hamill, the force was thrust into a much more serious controversy, indeed one that would become a *cause célèbre* of major proportions when the focus switched back to the underlying sectarianism that Drumcree had once more propelled into the forefront of the entire life of Portadown. Hamill, a 25-year-old Catholic whose partner was pregnant with their third child, was returning home from a night out with three members of his family around

1.45 am on 27 April when they encountered a 30-strong crowd of Loyalists at the junction of Market and Thomas Streets in the town centre. What happened next is, and remains over four years later, a matter of fundamental dispute. Eyewitnesses claim that Hamill was set upon and violently beaten by the crowd. He later died from his injuries in the Royal Victoria Hospital, Belfast. The incident caused a local outcry, aggravated by a number of inconsistent press releases by the police, after it was alleged that four RUC officers sitting in a Land Rover nearby witnessed the incident and did not intervene. Six men were accused of murder but, after some witnesses withdrew statements, charges against five of them were withdrawn. There was conflicting evidence during the trial of the sixth man. Eyewitnesses said they had to go to the police vehicle and plead with the officers to get out, and police witnesses said they had been out on the street doing their best to handle the disturbance. Lord Justice McCollum reserved judgement on 25 February 1999 at the conclusion of the prosecution evidence when Paul Hobson, aged 21, from Portadown, who was accused of murder, did not call witnesses and declined to give evidence himself. Later the judge acquitted Hobson of murder but sentenced him to four years imprisonment for causing an affray. Flanagan had earlier called in the Independent Commission for Police Complaints to supervise the entire investigation of the incident. When it was later decided not to prosecute the officers concerned, the family and influential Nationalist politicians, as well as the Irish government, called for an independent investigation. As a result, the incident, which remains an open wound between the Catholic community and the RUC, is now, in 2001, being re-investigated by the new Police Ombudsman for Northern Ireland.

More bad news followed swiftly. During the evening of 9 May, an unarmed, off-duty police officer was murdered in a gay bar in downtown Belfast. Darren Bradshaw, aged 24, who had been formally warned by his superiors that he was compromising his personal security by frequenting the Parliament Bar, was drinking inside with a number of friends when at about 10 pm a red Toyota car pulled up outside. The vehicle had been stolen the night before and was fitted with false number plates. Two gunmen got out, one from the rear, the other from the passenger seat. One held up the bouncers at the door while the other entered the bar, singled out the policeman and shot him three times in the neck and body. The gunmen were then driven off in the car, which was later found burned out in a side street off the Falls Road. The dead officer was the first RUC terrorist casualty for some three years. Following that incident, on 12 May Sean Brown, a Catholic and prominent member of the GAA was abducted and murdered near Randalstown, County Antrim, by extreme Loyalists, bringing to an end a violent honeymoon for the new administration.

Mowlam did not allow the violence, which she vociferously condemned, to deter her. Barely a week after the election she secured parliamentary approval for two pieces of legislation arising directly from North. The Public Order (Amendment) (Northern Ireland) Order 1997 increased the period of notice required of parade organisers from seven to 21 days, and the Public Order (Prescribed Form) Regulations (Northern Ireland) 1997 introduced new controls on the carrying and consumption of alcohol and enabled the police to confiscate alcohol being consumed at a parade or in the possession of persons travelling to a parade. Mowlam said: 'These are small, but significant steps forward in line with the recommendations in the North Report earlier this year. I want to see people engage in frank and constructive dialogue, through intermediaries if necessary, to try and reach local agreement. That is the best way forward. Alongside the education and mediation work of the Parades Commission, I hope the notice Order will help by providing extra breathing space during which agreement can be sought.'

A week later, the promised priority for the parades issue was confirmed when it was given prominent mention in the reference to Northern Ireland during the Queen's Speech at the ceremonial opening of the new parliament: 'In Northern Ireland my Government will seek reconciliation and a political settlement which has broad support, working in co-operation with the Irish Government. They will work to build trust and confidence in Northern Ireland by bringing forward legislation to deal with terrorism and to reduce tension over parades and other measures to protect human rights, combat discrimination in the workplace, increase confidence in policing and foster economic development.' Elaborating on the speech, Mowlam said later, 'I am committed to doing everything I can to ensure that we do not witness a repeat of the appalling events of last year. As Archbishop Eames has said, history will not easily forgive anyone who seeks to bring about such a repetition. I am convinced that the best way of making progress is through dialogue leading to accommodation and agreement at local level. As the Queen's Speech indicates, the Government will take steps to establish a comprehensive and even-handed approach to encourage this. This year, I urge all who are working to achieve accommodation to redouble their efforts. They have the full support not only of the Government, but I am sure also of the vast majority of people throughout Northern Ireland. We will work with them to ensure that the rule of law is upheld.'

Apart from bringing forward legislation and encouraging the Parades Commission and others to seek a way of forestalling another round of Drumcree violence, Mowlam had renewed her own contacts. On 21 May, polling day for elections to the local councils, she headed out early to visit both the Garvaghy Road and the lower Ormeau parade flashpoints. While in Portadown she talked with the residents for nearly 90 minutes and met members of the Hamill family to hear their concerns. McKenna, who was bidding for a council seat for the first time, interrupted his last-minute campaigning to join the meetings. After earlier negotiations with Sinn Fein, the party agreed not to field candidates against the coalition, who would run two candidates on an anti-parades ticket. They were to be Joe Duffy and Joanna Tennyson, but Tennyson became ill and backed out, so McKenna was selected instead. When the votes were counted the Nationalist turnout of 2795 was up by more than 45 per cent on 1993. With 1493 first preference votes, the highest ever first preference Nationalist vote in the town, McKenna was comfortably elected to a seat on Craigavon Borough Council. Such a convincing electoral endorsement of the stand against unwelcome parades, which confirmed the results of earlier surveys in Portadown and flashpoints elsewhere carried out for the North team, greatly encouraged the residents' group. It gave them a voice on the council for the first time and dispelled, once and for all, the Order's claims that the group did not represent the views of the majority of people on the Garvaghy Road.

Meanwhile, in the aftermath of Drumcree 1996, the Orange Order was experiencing its own internal convulsions. Many moderate members of the Order were appalled by what had happened and exasperated by the way they had been backed into a cul-de-sac by Portadown District. While there was uncompromising sympathy and support for their call to continue marching the traditional Garvaghy Road route, the way that hardliners like Joel Patton and thugs like Wright had been allowed to hijack the protest had caused widespread unease. 'That's when many of us started to get very worried,' recalls one senior Orangeman. 'It was clear that the protest was being taken out of our hands and that more sinister elements had decided they would dictate what happened. Many of us privately said they should have talked to the residents face to face, but once the stand-off had started it became impossible because that would have been perceived as weakness.' Some specifically criticised Gracey for not doing more to discourage violence. 'I think that if Harold had taken a much stronger attitude as leader of the district that things could have been brought under control a lot sooner and that the violence would not have been as bad. He was the leader of the protest and people went to

Drumcree to support him,' one senior figure told us. Another who travelled there on the second day of the stand-off told us: 'I was met by a senior member of Portadown District who mentioned the violence that was raging across much of the province, adding that "a wee bit of trouble doesn't do any harm." I was sickened and left immediately and I have never set foot in Drumcree again.'

While there were many, often conflicting, views among members of the Order as they analysed the legacy of the summer, two main strands of thought seemed to represent a consensus: that Grand Lodge should be taking a much tougher line with Portadown District but that at the same time it ought to be putting far more pressure on the government by mobilising the entire membership in a concerted programme of action to assert its right to parade. Joel Patton said a campaign 'to wake the sleeping giant' would have reunited and rejuvenated the Order and he was critical that the Order was 'blowing the opportunity'. He was, however, still implacably opposed to showing any sign of weakness or pragmatism. He made it clear that he would rather not march than march under a deal. 'There is no dignity in marching with the permission of Nationalists,' he fumed. Support for Patton and his 'Spirit of Drumcree' group had steadily dwindled from the high point of the Ulster Hall rally but they remained a persistently sharp thorn in the Order's side with a hardcore allegiance of 500 and another 1000 they could rely on to come out to take part in protests. Their activities and criticisms were clearly foremost in the mind of the much denounced Grand Master, the Reverend Martin Smyth, who warned the Order of the danger of enemies within when he stepped down from the office in December 1996 after 24 years. Handing on what he described as an institution with a vibrant membership and a strong financial position, he commented: 'Like other tested and tried organisations, we are not without critics within and without the institution. While we should not ignore those without, it is still true the greatest danger comes from within.'

In the past the office of grand master had been one of the most coveted and prestigious positions in the Order and many distinguished figures had held it: a duke, four earls, a prime minister (of Northern Ireland), a senator, a privy councillor, four knights, a lieutenant-general, two colonels and a captain, one Reverend and one plain Mister. Five of them had also been MPs. This time, however, there was no queue to replace Smyth and it was left to the considerable political fixing talents of James Molyneaux, the Ulster Unionist leader and a leading light in the Order, to find a suitable candidate. The search was clearly problematic. Jeffrey Donaldson, Molyneaux's able young protégé who would soon succeed him as MP for Lagan Valley, was already assistant grand master but immediately ruled himself out of the running. The Reverend Brian Kennaway, who had been sickened by the violence he had seen associated with Drumcree, received a series of telephone calls from Molyneaux trying to persuade him to let his name go forward. Despite his repeated refusals, John McCrea, the grand secretary, visited him at his manse in Crumlin six days before Grand Lodge was due to meet on 11 December to elect the new leader. Kennaway had no hesitation in rejecting the overtures. He knew the summer violence had severely tarnished the image of the Order. Others, whose names were canvassed, included Fermanagh Orangeman Roy Kells, a former Lieutenant-Colonel in the Ulster Defence Regiment who had survived a number of IRA murder bids, and Lord Brookeborough, who had also served for a time in the regiment. His grandfather had been prime minister of Northern Ireland and a pillar of the Order and the Unionist party.

In the event, Grand Lodge unanimously appointed Robert Saulters to lead them. A 61-year-old accountant and an Orangeman for 44 years, he had first walked in a Twelfth procession as a twelve-year-old. Despite his simplistic hardline views, soft-spoken Saulters was what they call in Northern Ireland 'a decent ould spud'. His main interests were motor-cycles and cars and his principal recreation was watching soap operas on television. He was especially fond of the Australian soap 'Neighbours'. As would all too rapidly become clear, Saulters was supremely ill-equipped for the rough and tumble of cutting-edge sectarian politics, and lacked the verbal dexterity that was so essential in an age increasingly dominated by the insatiable demand of the electronic media for the all-encompassing, carefully crafted, 30-second soundbite. As County Grand Master of Belfast, he had been party to the unsuccessful Quaker initiative on the Ormeau Road in 1995 but had since gained some notoriety for publicly questioning, during a Twelfth speech, Tony Blair's fitness for high office because he had married a Catholic. Referring to what he called 'gutless men in Westminster', Saulters singled out Blair who, he said, had 'already sold his birthright by marrying a Romanist and serving communion in a Roman Catholic church'.

Saulters did not resile from his comments upon taking over the new, much higher profile position some months later, and, during an intro-ductory news conference, amplified his remarks by saying Blair had been 'disloyal to one's self, to one's religion' by marrying a Catholic. At the same time he displayed a long-overdue hint of pragmatism by saying the Order would talk with elected representatives of the Catholic community, but not 'Sinn Fein-IRA or self-appointed residents' groups.' Over the quiet winter months a number of local Orange Lodges stealthily engaged in talks within their own communities in a bid to sort out local problems locally. In some cases mediators became involved and in time they were encouraged to do so by the fledgling Parades Commission, acting in the pre-statutory but highly pro-active role it quickly adopted. Saulters appeared to be openly endorsing this approach in an interview with the *Belfast Telegraph* in mid-March when he said there was no harm in mediation and that he would not be heeding calls for him to resign over the issue. Earlier that month members of Mullinagoagh Loyal Orange Lodge 669, in Dromore, County Tyrone, had reached an accommodation with a local Nationalist group which would allow it to parade through the town on the coming Twelfth. Discussions were also taking place between Orangemen and Nationalists in other areas where there was substantial opposition to parades, including Newtownbutler in County Fermanagh. Word of this activity had already reached Patton, whose vociferous criticisms exasperated the inherently secretive Grand Lodge, not least because they were always made in public.

Patton's answer was to flex his muscles on 27 March by mobilising some 400 of his supporters and laying on eight buses to convey them to the Carnlea Orange Hall in Ballymena, where the Antrim County Grand Lodge was due to meet. They had been involved in negotiations, through the Mediation Network, about a contentious church parade through the village of Dunloy, and were due to report back to the members. The situation was particularly delicate because for weeks Catholics going to Saturday evening mass at Our Lady's Church in the Harryville area of Ballymena had been subjected to a barbaric picket, carried out by a noisy coalition of fanatics and hardliners, which frequently erupted into violence. Prominent among them was William McCaughey, a convicted killer known as 'the protestant boy', who had abused his position as a police officer to wake a Catholic shopkeeper in the middle of the night before shooting him dead. With some of the demonstrators openly wearing Orange sashes and flaunting their membership of the Order, the protest embarrassingly called into question the Order's frequent affirmation that it stood for civil and religious liberty for all.

Many moderate Orangemen deplored what was going on, and Kennaway and others encouraged Saulters to take part in one of the many counter-demonstrations mounted as a show of solidarity with the parishioners and priests, which he did. This civilised gesture, of course, further enraged Patton and those of a like mind who packed the hall and vented their feelings to Robert McIlroy, the county grand master, and his officers. They decided to abandon the meeting and were roughly jostled as they left the hall. Once they had departed, Patton took the floor and launched a strongly-worded attack on the mediation process and accused the county of working to strike a deal with the Nationalist residents of Dunloy. McIlroy in turn protested about the hijacking of the meeting and called on Grand Lodge in Belfast for action. 'Brother Patton is hell bent on doing his own thing outside the institution and I certainly think he should be taken to task,' he said. One of his closest supporters commented: 'These militants would rather fight their way down the street with two people behind them than march down with 32 and a bit of respect for their neighbours.'

Three days later Saulters launched an outspoken attack. He accused Patton of endangering efforts to avoid a repeat of the violent protests of the previous year. In an interview with the *Belfast Sunday Life* newspaper, he said: 'It is ironic that this thuggery should take place on the eve of Good Friday when our Lord was betrayed by Judas Iscariot. Strange that the leader of this so-called group's name begins with a J as well. He calls himself a born-again Christian. Some advertise that they are born again Christians, but never seem to learn the true message of Easter.' Saulters also said again that he was opposed to talking to Sinn Fein members, but not to mediation. 'The Drumcree parade is a matter for the local district. If the district is happy with the outcome of any mediation, then I will be happy.'

The real trouble at that time was that, while there was no shortage of mediators, there was no real engagement between the parties and little inclination for it on either side. The residents insisted there had to be face-to-face contact with Portadown District before they would even talk about the specifics of a parade. The local Orangemen were equally adamant that they would not talk about anything as long as the 'terrorist' Brendan McKenna was involved. Furthermore, they would not talk about the parade because they had no need to ask permission to walk what they quaintly referred to as 'the Queen's highway'. Although the two main protagonists would not engage unconditionally themselves, many others were engaged in thinking about ways to ease or solve the Drumcree problem.

The Ulster Society, a small think-tank which specialised in researching Orange and Unionist history, came up with the idea that when the Orange Order started to march from Drumcree parish church back into Portadown all those years ago the present line of the Garvaghy Road did not exist. This was based on an old hand-drawn map they had unearthed. Denis Watson and the Reverend William Bingham took the map to Flanagan with the suggestion that if the map was accurate a new road could be built well away from the Catholic housing along the modern Garvaghy Road down towards the Bann River. Watson and Bingham argued that if they could establish that then they could convince Number One District, because their whole argument was based on tradition. If a new route could actually be created they would take it, reasoned Flanagan, and he made approaches to Mayhew, the Department of the Environment and the Roads Service about the possibility. They were distinctly unenthusiastic about the concept of building a new road for a once-a-year march but did say that they would look very favourably at the construction of a cycle-way or footpath that could be used by the Orangemen on occasion. Outline approval was then given, the route was surveyed and contractors were even selected and put on standby. Given the gravity of the Drumcree situation, it was intended to have the job completed in weeks. The projected cost, at about £300,000, was nothing compared to the millions that another crisis would cost. The initiative came to nothing, however, when further research into old maps at the Public Record Office in Belfast provided no corroboration. Everything in the archives pointed to the line of the Garvaghy Road always being there.

Ronnie Flanagan, who had come to regard July as the worst month of his year, also tried hard to sell a compromise version of the 'Orange feet on the Garvaghy Road' scenario to senior Unionist and Order figures. He pointed out that if the parade came down from the church and wheeled right, rather than left along the disputed route, it could then proceed along another stretch of the 'Garvaghy' Road, past the front of the St John the Baptist church, and enable the Orangemen to claim they had indeed walked the Garvaghy Road. Using his by now well-thumbed set of maps, he promoted the idea during a meetings with a number of potentially influential people in his office at police headquarters. Martin Smyth arranged a meeting for him to try to sell it to the Order, but at the end of a very aggressive three-hour encounter in the House of Orange a senior member of Portadown District told him that even if they thought it was acceptable they could not agree to it because Loyalists would burn all their houses down. The delegate did not mention Billy Wright by name, but that was who he meant.

Inevitably the range of efforts to break the Drumcree impasse gave rise to a constant barrage of rumours, disinformation and hostile propaganda and it became increasingly difficult to discern the facts from fiction. Sometimes press statements, instead of clearing the air, often thickened it further by recounting and rebutting the merest slights, as with this typical missive from Portadown District on 14 January 1997:

This statement from the Officers of Portadown District LOL 1 is in response to items that have appeared in the media over the past weeks concerning the issue of the annual Orange church parade to Drumcree in July. In an article, which appeared in the *Portadown Times* of 10 January 1997, under the banner headline 'Council meets both sides in Drumcree parades dispute', a report was given stating that secret face-to-face talks had taken place between Craigavon Borough Council and the two sides in the Drumcree parade dispute. This item of information is factually incorrect. While a letter was received by the Portadown District Master from the Chief Executive of Craigavon Borough Council requesting a meeting, to date, no such meeting has taken place between any officers of the District Lodge with either the Chief Executive or the Council's Police Liaison Committee. During an interview with Brendan McKenna on the Talkback programme on Radio Ulster on Friday 3 January 1997 it was stated that letters had been sent to the District Lodge since July, on a monthly basis, detailing proposals concerning the parade route along Garvaghy Road. This item of information is untrue as no such letters from this person have been received. When interviewed on UTV Live on Friday 10 January it was also implied that objections were now being raised about the outward route to Drumcree as local residents had allegedly been subjected to abuse by Orangemen. This is untrue as over the years the Portadown Orangemen have shown themselves able to parade with dignity and their discipline and determination not to give offence, despite extreme provocation, has been a feature of the Orange Parades to and from Drumcree over the years with no breach by those on parade ever having been committed. Mr. McKenna also added that with regard to his group's contact with Craigavon Borough Council they had little faith in the actions of the Council due to their treatment of nationalists in the area in the past. The Officers of Portadown District Orange Lodge would like to repeat that over the years changes have occurred concerning parades in this area of town. While previously ten parades passed through this area these have now been reduced to one. No Orange or Royal Black parades now pass through Obins Street. Only a limited number of bands take part in the parade along Garvaghy Road. These bands are permitted to play hymn tunes only. Bands do not play when passing the Roman Catholic Chapel. It is viewed with regret by the Portadown District Orange Lodge that the Garvaghy Road Residents' Association have proved to be unable, by their intransigence, to accept these changes and to move forward. It would appear that they are unable to accommodate the fact that a culture other than their's [*sic*] exists and their sole intent and actions prove that they simply do not wish anyone who identifies themselves with a Unionist/British culture to have access through 'their' area. This is borne out by the recent press reports that identity cards are to be issued to Garvaghy residents during July 1997 creating in effect a no-go area. The Orange Order has always stood by the principle of Civil and Religious Liberty for all, as recently demonstrated by the presence of the Grand Master of Ireland, Brother Robert Saulters, in support of Roman Catholic worshippers at Harryville, Ballymena. We do not believe that a small self-appointed grouping can be allowed to prevent the lawful and free passage of worshippers returning from a church service. It remains the intention of Portadown District Orange Lodge to uphold its right to Civil and Religious Liberty.

As the two groups in Portadown continued to trade blows with each other at this mundane level, like two punch-drunk heavyweights ignoring the referee's order to stop fighting, more powerful figures continued to manoeuvre in the background to head off another crisis. In May, the SDLP leader John Hume announced in an agreed statement that he and Saulters would meet the Garvaghy Road Residents Coalition, including Brendan McKenna. However, after coming under pressure within his own organisation, Saulters was forced into a humiliating back-track and claimed there had been a 'misunderstanding' over the issue.

With the Grand Orange Lodge thus devoid of any cohesive policy, although they had established a Strategy Committee to devise one, and Portadown District as uncompromising as ever, in the run-up to Drumcree 1997 it increasingly fell to the Armagh County Grand Lodge to establish some credibility and support for the Orange cause. During the 1996 debacle, Bingham and Watson had developed a close friendship and an increasingly shared understanding of the problem. Both felt there had to be a far more pro-active approach and embarked on a crusade to educate people inside and outside the order by stimulating debate about the Drumcree situation and its implications. They also studied other areas in Northern Ireland where residents' groups had emerged, to test their belief that they were inter-linked and understand more about how they operated. They also became painfully aware that the world outside did not quite understand Orangeism and wondered why the police had to beat people off the road where they lived so that a procession of grown men, dressed in their best suits, sashes and bowler hats in the middle of the summer, could parade where they were not wanted. Bingham and Watson therefore concluded it was essential to put across more effectively the reasons why Drumcree was so important and what Orange tradition and culture was all about. They drew up plans for a public relations operation and compiled a list of influential figures who might come to their aid.

One of the first they contacted was Lord Cranborne, whose family, the Cecils, had been one of the powers behind the British throne for centuries. As leader of the House of Lords in the Major government, he was an avowed Unionist who had resigned from Margaret Thatcher's government in protest at the signing of the Anglo-Irish Agreement. He was also known to be virulently opposed to the ongoing peace process because he feared that any concessions to Nationalists or Republicans would ultimately serve to weaken the union. However, his long-term potential as a powerful ally was somewhat inhibited by the expected demise of the Major government. With this prospect in mind, they recognised the need to woo the Labour establishment which was never favourably disposed to the Orange Order or Unionism. The former shadow secretary of state, Kevin McNamara, was viewed as a bogeyman because of his sympathy for Nationalists, and they believed that Mo Mowlam, his successor, was similarly minded. Nevertheless they decided to do business with her if and when the opportunity arose.

In Orange eyes the United States was another unfriendly and interfering opponent, but again realpolitik dictated that contact was necessary. Bingham recalls: 'We realised Clinton was never going to make a statement backing our protest, which was a pity, because civil rights is at the core of the American constitution. The best we could hope for was that the US would adopt a neutral position on the issue.' So they developed a contact with Blair Hall, a senior diplomat working with Admiral William Crowe, then US ambassador in London, and soon came to realise there was a direct line to the White House. During their discussions, they asked to be consulted before Clinton made any statement, and that anything he said should be balanced. In due course, when the President came to comment on the parades problem, they were consulted and what he said was more informed and sensitive than they had ever dared hope. While some in Portadown District later complained about the activities of Bingham and Watson, everything of significance was reported back and they were meticulous in observing the protocol that it was their district, their service and their right to decide what they wanted to do. 'We felt that we were ambassadors on their behalf and could never commit ourselves to anything without the approval of Portadown District,' says Bingham.

However, despite their outreach mission, as they entered 1997 neither really believed that a deal was possible with McKenna. 'From our point of view it was a 99 per cent education process to try and convince people of the strength of our position so that opinion, when and where it mattered, would be in favour of a parade going down the road,' says Watson. In line with this twin strategy of winning support and increasing understanding for their case, Watson and Bingham conceived the idea of sending a letter to all the Nationalist residents in the Garvaghy Road area, signed by them on behalf of the County Armagh Grand Orange Lodge. They said the letter, which went out by post on 4 June, was 'a sincere and genuine attempt to deal with the many misconceptions concerning the walk'. It then set out a number of points:

- The service on the first Sunday in July is partly to remember those who died at the Battle of the Somme in 1916. We pay tribute to all those of both communities who died for the cause of peace and justice.
- The Orange Order is traditionally a parading organisation. We see our parade as an outward witness to our sincere belief in the Reformed Faith. For that reason, we see attacks on our parades as both a denial of civil liberties and an attack on our religion. For us, this is as distressing as the disgraceful protest – which we unreservedly condemn – outside Harryville chapel.
- In the interests of harmony, mutual respect and reconciliation the Orange Order has acknowledged objections raised by the nationalist community and has already implemented the following principles for the Drumcree church parade:
  a) The number of parades in the area has been reduced from ten to one in the past ten years.
  b) Only members of Portadown District parade.
  c) No bands take part which could be perceived as antagonistic to our nationalist neighbours.
  d) The Orangemen walk four abreast so that the walk will pass any one given point in less than five minutes.
  e) The Order marshals and disciplines its own members to ensure there will be no confrontation on our part. If this was reciprocated, then there would only be a need for a minimal police presence.
  f) The right to walk peacefully and in a dignified manner and the right to protest in a peaceful and dignified manner should not be denied to anyone.

[The letter concluded] It is the sincere hope of the Orange Order that the vast majority of the people of Portadown will work together in a new spirit of tolerance to defeat extremists who want confrontation this summer. As a matter of principle, we cannot be involved in talks with convicted terrorists because of what they have inflicted on our community.

Mo Mowlam immediately welcomed the letter as 'a sincere and genuine attempt to promote understanding. On my first day in Northern Ireland as Secretary of State, I appealed to everyone with any influence to use it to defuse sectarian tensions and attitudes and find ways of balancing the legitimate rights of marchers and local residents. During my recent round of meetings with local residents' groups and the Loyal Orders, I again stressed the importance of dialogue and local accommodations as the best way forward. I believe the letter from Mr Watson and Mr Bingham to the residents of Garvaghy Road is a very positive step and is welcomed.'

The Residents Coalition was unimpressed. They viewed the letter as a propaganda stunt and sent a most discouraging reply on 10 June, signed by Eamon Stack, the Jesuit priest and secretary:

We accept that, in an ideal society, everyone should enjoy the right to full freedom of expression of their political and civil beliefs. Those rights include freedom of assembly, freedom of movement, freedom of one's political, civil and religious beliefs. We also recognise and accept the reality that, due to the political conflict which has taken place on this island for many years and for the past three decades in particular, we live in an abnormal society. Events in Portadown in recent times are also significant:

1 The events of Drumcree 1995, the stand-off, the agreement and the subsequent triumphalism by the unionist politicians and the Orange Order itself;

2 The events of Drumcree 1996, the violence and the lawlessness, the death of Michael McGoldrick and the behaviour of the RUC on the Garvaghy Road on July 11th;

3 The recent murder of Robert Hamill by a gang on the main street of Portadown.

Therefore, while we are agreed to working towards a future situation whereby the rights of all can be respected and exercised freely and equally, we recognise that certain limitations and responsibilities need to be exercised in relation to particular rights and that due protection be given to the rights of political, religious and ethnic minorities. We suggest that both sides publicly apologise for any hurt, offence or injustice caused by the conflict of interest in relation to marches. The nationalist community recognises and accepts the right of the Orange Order to parade to Drumcree and defends their right to hold a religious service at that location. The Orange Order are [*sic*] asked to recognise this willingness by nationalists to secure the rights of Orangemen in relation to the parade to their church service at Drumcree. The Orange Order is asked to reciprocate this gesture by voluntarily re-routing their homeward parade away from Drumcree and Garvaghy Roads by returning to Carleton Street Orange hall by their outward route for an agreed period of time. Such a gesture by the Orange Order would be viewed as a demonstration of goodwill and sincere friendship towards the nationalist community in Portadown. Nationalists would recognise and accept such a gesture as not foreseeing a future where Orange parades, as a true expression of cultural diversity, would never be welcomed in nationalist areas of Portadown. Both sides will give an undertaking to embark upon a long-term process aimed at securing full equality of treatment in relation to the exercise of all rights for everyone, irrespective of their individual or communal political, civil and religious beliefs.

The letter went on to say that both sides would agree to take part in a long-term process to create 'a society based on justice and equality of treatment for all citizens in Portadown, in which every encouragement would be given to the establishment of mutual respect and understanding. After an agreed period of time, the question of Orange parades along Drumcree and Garvaghy Roads can be reviewed, by representatives of the nationalist community and Orangemen in Portadown, in light of any progress made.' Stack concluded the letter by declaring the coalition's readiness 'to meet with any Orangemen, any place and any time'.

Shortly before the exchange of letters, the RUC's unenviable position as 'piggy in the middle' of the parading issue was again tragically underlined. In the early hours of Sunday 1 June another off-duty police officer lost his life, this time by the hand of violent Loyalists. Late on the Saturday evening, Constable Greg Taylor, aged 41, married with three children and a policeman for 23 years, went into a crowded bar in Ballymoney, County Antrim, for a drink, along with a police colleague and a friend. The police officers were recognised by some of the hundred or so customers, who included Loyalists, and there was some angry jostling and jeering about the RUC's role in upholding a ban on a Loyalist parade in the nearby village of Dunloy. When the officers and their companion left the bar at about 2 am on the Sunday morning, a crowd was lying in wait for them outside. Taylor made a frantic call from his portable telephone to the local police station seeking help but none was available: there was only a single constable on duty and the nearest patrol car, with two officers on board, was eight miles away. The crowd closed in on Taylor and he was so savagely kicked and beaten that he died almost immediately. His two companions managed to escape the mob. Eight men went on trial for the murder and two were jailed for life. Another two, who denied murder but admitted manslaughter, were imprisoned for four years. The other four were acquitted.

Sixteen days later, the rising tension in Portadown was stoked even higher with the murder of two police officers in Lurgan. On the morning of Monday 16 June, Constable John Graham, aged 34, and 30-year-old Reserve Constable David Johnston were patrolling along Church Walk in Lurgan, a short distance from the town's police station, when they were both shot at close quarters. Eyewitnesses said the attackers approached, fired at the officers and then shot them again after they fell to the ground. The incident took place outside a doctor's surgery and medical staff immediately rushed to their assistance. 'We heard the shots from inside the surgery and we were at their sides within thirty seconds. But it was too late, they were already dead,' one of the doctors recalled. The cold-blooded double murder sent shock waves through the efforts to restore the IRA ceasefire and was widely condemned. At the White House in Washington the official spokesman pronounced President Bill Clinton's 'outrage'.

Mowlam had actually arrived in Belfast with a foreboding that it was already too late to head off another bad Drumcree. She believed the Conservatives had been far too amenable to the Unionists, whose support had often been necessary to keep their crumbling administration in power. She made the criticism that it was for this reason they had dragged their feet in implementing North with the vigour and speed the situation deserved. Indeed, she had harried them behind the scenes to get a move on. Furthermore, she feared not enough sustained work had been put in place after the previous year to bring the two sides into contact. 'If we hadn't attempted to douse the flames, we'd have been in real trouble but we hadn't all that much faith in being able to deal with it that year,' one of her closest advisers recalls. Despite these feelings, Mowlam started doing the rounds of the protagonists in the parades controversy, trying to breathe some life into the deadlock, but even her best down-to-earth, jolly-them-along efforts failed to initiate any progress. The Garvaghy

Road people were at ease with her informal ways, for instance going round a restaurant picking chips off people's plates, and did not blink when she breezed into the community centre one afternoon for a meeting and demanded a plate and fork to eat a Chinese takeaway which her driver had been sent to purchase. 'I'm starving,' she said, tucking into the food while they discussed their latest concerns. Although Mowlam was instinctively sympathetic to the residents' cause, she sometimes found the exchanges with them uncongenial. During one heated encounter, she suddenly pushed back her chair, walked round the room and seized a cigarette from a woman. She took two long, deep puffs from it before handing it back and completing a circuit round the other side of the table back to her own chair. Her aides were surprised, for she had given up smoking months earlier because of her brain illness.

The Orangemen, however, found her unpredictable, unorthodox conduct more disturbing. At one stage of her drive to crack the Drumcree problem, a senior civil servant rang Bingham one afternoon and asked if he and Watson would talk to the secretary of state at Hillsborough Castle that evening. When they arrived at the appointed time, both men were on their guard. Cranborne and other politicians had earlier warned them that as Drumcree grew closer and the stakes increased the government would attempt to soften them up with a charm offensive. They were shown into the breakfast room, where tea, coffee and cheese and crackers were served. Bingham, a Presbyterian minister with a whiff of manse austerity about him, who approaches government and royalty with respect and reverence, is not at ease in such surroundings. When invited to attend royal garden parties, he goes out of a desire to be respectful to the Queen, not because he enjoys them. So he was stunned when Mowlam suddenly kicked off her shoes, then took off her wig and pushed it under her chair. (At the time she had lost her natural hair as a result of recent treatment for a brain tumour.) The unease he already felt was compounded when Mowlam got into full oratorical flow, for her conversation was peppered with swear words. 'I don't know what her impression of Orangemen was, but if she had done any homework she would have known not to approach us the way she did. I think she thought she was dealing with two men who would feel at home at a working club in the north east of England with a pint of beer and a lot of bad talk. Her language was absolutely appalling. She could not put a sentence together without four-letter words and it just went from bad to worse. At one point I interrupted and said, "Secretary of State, I have respect for the office that you hold, but no respect for the language that you're using and I will find it difficult to sit here much longer if you don't stop using such language."' To his astonishment, she asked him: 'What do you do?' As Bingham was wearing a shirt and tie rather than his clerical collar, she was taken aback when he replied he was a minister and added: 'That is not the reason alone that I find your language offensive. As a Christian, whether a minister or not, as a common decent person I find it offensive.' He recalls: 'For us the meeting was over as soon as it started. It was clear that this was a person we could not do business with. We left feeling she was not capable of resolving anything.'

What was not yet fully apparent was how Mowlam's hands had been tied and her pragmatic instincts curbed by the responsibility of office. She had yet to come to terms with the need for even-handedness in dealing with the two parties to the conflict. In her heart she had long been on the side of the residents and unsympathetic to the majority community. Like many people from beyond Northern Ireland, especially the 'lasagne luvvies' and 'chardonnay comrades' who populated the new Labour movement, she found Unionism and Orangeism, with its obsession with the past and unyielding traditionalism, entirely illogical and out of step with a world, and especially a Europe, where fusion and integration were the political order of the day. She was also plainly less at ease with the grey, dour men of Unionism than their more amiable Nationalist and Republican counterparts who were far more accomplished politicians and more colourful and exciting personalities. She had also rapidly become disenchanted with the civil servants around her who became exasperated at having to go to her rescue when she failed to measure her words and behaviour in navigating the maze of nuances and sensitivities that had to be taken into account in every encounter in Northern Ireland, whether in talking to political leaders or giving radio and television interviews. As she had been able to do in opposition, she wanted to go out into the hard areas, call on the contacts she had made and sit on their sofas, sipping tea with her shoes off and her feet curled up beneath her, without the necessary discipline and claustrophobic umbrella of office, private secretaries, note-takers monitoring her every word, an armoured car and armed police bodyguards and escorts. 'You must have all these things,' a senior man had cautioned her. 'You are the secretary of state. You might be attacked or kidnapped and we need to prevent that.'

Despite what she knew was the hopelessness of the situation, Mowlam was also facing unpalatable security advice about Drumcree. With the prospect of an accommodation becoming more and more remote by the day, the minds of the mandarins and senior police officers were increasingly turning to the difficult choice they again faced: deciding whether or not to allow the parade, and the collateral cost of whatever was decided. The entire background and options were sketched out for her on 20 June by Stephen Leach, the associate director of policing and security, in what became known as the 'gameplan' document. (The document, which was widely distributed inside the Northern Ireland Office, was later leaked to a journalist and published in full.) It provides a rare insight into the way options are laid out and considered in such trying situations and shows that, while the chief constable is operationally independent and legally accountable, the reality is that he must act within the wider political context and take full account of the implications. As we have shown happened in 1996, the document also reveals how the government can manoeuvre in the background, providing political cover for operational police policy and seeking to manipulate 'influencers' to ensure its acceptability. The lengthy paper also shows how the government uses what it calls 'offsetting measures' to sweeten unwelcome outcomes. The thrust of the advice was that Mowlam should intervene by convening proximity talks between the parties at Hillsborough in a last ditch bid to head off another year of violent disorder. If they failed, then the 'least worst option' was a controlled march along the Garvaghy Road. A covering note attached to the minute by Steele says: 'This is the game plan which the Secretary of State requested. I am sure this is the only way open to us that has any chance of success.' Headed 'Drumcree: Intervention by Secretary of State', the document reads:

1. It now seems clear that no local accommodation will emerge to resolve the problem posed by the Drumcree church parade planned for 6th July. Although there have been one or two recent positive signs (for example, the possibility of informal contact between the GRRC and the Orange Order) there is rather stronger evidence of considerable hardening at grassroots level (not least on the loyalist side following the Lurgan murders). It is indicative that (as reported in Mr Crawford's note of 18th June) Trevor Reaney, the well-informed chief executive of Craigavon District Council has commented that although he was cautiously optimistic about the outcome at Drumcree before the Lurgan murders, he was now filled with 'insurmountable pessimism'.

2. It is therefore necessary to consider what action should be taken in the two weeks or so before Drumcree. We would recommend that (on the lines sketched out in my submission of 6th June) the Secretary of State should invite the two sides to proximity talks under her chairmanship in a final effort to achieve progress. We understand that the Secretary of State would favour holding such an exercise at

Hillsborough on Friday 27 and Saturday 28 June. It would be the logical culmination of the "listening meetings" and the further initiative involving the Secretary of State and John Steele announced on 15 June, and would build on the foundation of constructive relationships with both sides which have been achieved by those efforts.

3. Officials are working on the practical and logistical aspects of the initiative and further advice will be submitted as plans develop. The purpose of this note is to consider the tactical and policy challenges, and to suggest how they might be handled. It may be worth listing the main issues in question form.

What is the Government's objective?

4. The prime objective of the proximity negotiating exercise will be to achieve an accommodation between the two sides. Failing that, we would aim to gain agreement that protests against whatever decision is taken would be within the law, avoiding any physical challenge to the security forces or attempts to overbear them by summoning reinforcements; and we would also hope to gain a sense of what off-setting measures might be deployed to reduce the negative reaction and perceptions on whichever side was disappointed by the operational decision eventually made. A key objective would also be to demonstrate that – at what is widely perceived as a moment of crisis for the province – the government is playing a pro-active and imaginative role, and going the extra mile to find a solution (even if that effort eventually fails).

5. Those are the general objectives. But there is also a more specific one. While the Chief Constable has genuinely not made a decision, the consensus among the key players – the Secretary of State, the Minister of State, the Chief Constable, the GOC, Parades Commission Chairman – is that, if there is no local accommodation, a controlled parade on the Garvaghy Road is the least worst outcome. An underlying objective of the talks will therefore be to:

Identify the maximum concessions which the Orange Order are willing to make to strip out from the parade resonances which nationalists might find offensive;

To broker offsetting measures which might help to reconcile the GRRC to this outcome;

And to gain an undertaking from the residents that any protest they mount will be peaceful and restrained.

What activity before proximity talks?

6. While it will be important to maintain some momentum in the

days leading up to the proximity talks, the high level of exposure by the Secretary of State in recent days should probably be scaled down, to avoid the risk of dissipating the responsibility and authority of her position, which will probably need to be exploited to the full if the negotiations are to be successful. She should probably do no more than the meeting planned for Derry on 23 June, with Mr Steele taking on the remaining meetings next week.

How we do get the two sides to Hillsborough?

7. The two sides must clearly be given invitations sufficiently in advance of the proximity talks for them to make practical arrangements, but not so far ahead that they (particularly the GRRC) have time to devise plausible preconditions which might scupper the whole exercise. The scenario we would recommend is for the Secretary of State to write on, say, Wednesday 25 June, to the GRRC and the Orange Order inviting them to bring delegations (with the Orange Group including both the County Grand Lodge and Portadown District) to discussions at Hillsborough under the chairmanship of the Secretary of State on Friday 27 and Saturday 28 June.

To assuage Orange sensitivities the letter would spell out that these would be proximity talks, with each side dealing with the Secretary of State and her team, but not directly with each other. These invitations might then be delivered in person by Mr Steele or other officials who could explain the Secretary of State's intention in a little more detail and deal on the spot with any concerns which either side might have. Since the invitations will rapidly become public once they are handed over, we should pre-empt this by publicising the initiative ourselves, stressing that it is a proactive attempt to reach a fair local accommodation which no reasonable person should have any problem with. It will be important to brief key influencers in advance so that they can come in in support of the invitation: for example, Saulters and Trimble on the Orange side, and Hume, Brid Rogers [*sic*] and the Irish in respect of the GRRC. The two Archbishops and the two morning newspapers (who may well wish to continue their joint approach on parades) would also be important in helping to build up public expectation and momentum as the invitations are issued and the talks approach.

How should the negotiations be organised?

8. The logistics and physical arrangements for the talks could be quite important in helping to achieve a successful outcome. Separate

advice will be submitted on the detailed arrangements, but the main features will probably be – Secretary of State to chair the talks with support from an official team led by Mr Steele (with appropriate support staff also available at Hillsborough); Chief Constable and Parades Commission chairman to be present (or at least available to come to Hillsborough at short notice if required); GRRC and Orange Order each to have six representatives (although if they ask for more it will be politic to agree); Complete separation between GRRC base and Orange base, with no chance of inadvertent meetings. (It may be that a condition of the invitation to the GRRC is that Brendan McKenna will not seek to confront the Orange men in person.); Food, drink, etc. available as appropriate; Appropriate press handling facilities.

What is the government's negotiating stance?

9. A key challenge in these negotiations will be to induce the two sides to start thinking about what compromise they are willing to accept, rather than whether they will compromise at all. Since we know that the compromise is likely to focus around a controlled march on the Garvaghy Road with offsetting measures, the way in which we play this reality in will be particularly important. It would clearly be wrong for the government to disclose an early fixed position; a bald statement that a march will almost definitely be going down the road, and the only issue for discussion is the modalities of that event, would probably cause the residents to become more obdurate while taking the pressure off the Orange Order. On the other hand, negotiations in a vacuum, with no steer at all being given to the participants about what the likely outcome is on the balance of probabilities, might not sufficiently focus minds on the practicalities. It may be possible to set the negotiations in a realistic framework (and therefore remove grounds for subsequent accusations of bad faith) by making the following points:

- The Chief Constable has genuinely not reached a decision.
- If a reliable local accommodation could be reached, then he would happily accept that and do his best to support it – e.g. through light policing if that was operationally justifiable.
- One clearly possible outcome is for a controlled march on the Garvaghy Road. The Secretary of State proposes that the negotiations should address that as the base case for discussion, with the task of considering how it could be made tolerable to the residents through the specific arrangements for such a march and possible offsetting measures.

Other options – e.g. a ban on the march, with compensating

measures for the Orangemen – would not be excluded from the nego-tiations, provided they were judged to offer the prospect of a realistic outcome. At the end of the day, the Chief Constable would make his decision informed by the outcome of the negotiations and the flexibility shown on each side.

10. The precise details of the government's negotiation brief would be for further consideration and refinement; but something on the lines of the above might with luck establish, in practice if not explicitly, that all sides are in the territory of finding the lowest common denominator for getting some Orange feet on the Garvaghy Road. It will be important to establish the atmosphere that, while the Secretary of State recognises the rights of both the residents and the marchers, both of those rights must in the end accommodate themselves to her over-riding responsibility, as the executive authority in the province, to ensure along with the police that good government and the rule of law are maintained. She will support a reasonable compromise, but will not hesitate publicly to expose unreasonable positions for what they are – and allow public opinion to judge. Establishing the idea that the government means business and is capable of mobilising a significant range of public opinion in support of its position could be an important factor in persuading McKenna (and Sinn Fein) that it is time to play for the draw.

How could the parade be adjusted to make it more acceptable to residents?

11. The arrangements for the parade currently being proposed by the Orange Order are:

• Only Portadown District members parade (probably around 1200 in total);
• No "offensive" bands taking part – only accordion bands playing hymn music common to both traditions;
• Marchers walk four abreast so that the parade will pass any given point in less than five minutes;
• Parade well marshalled and disciplined; no triumphalism or confrontation (and therefore only minimal police presence needed if residents reciprocate).

12. Against this background, the main menu of possible adjustments to the march to make it more acceptable to the residents could include:

   i. Numbers: some, perhaps sizeable reduction?
   ii. Bands: no bands or music at all.
   iii. Time: change time of church service and parades to reduce

further any disruption to residents – e.g. earlier in the morning.

iv. Direction: reverse direction so that outward leg is on the Garvaghy Road in the early morning.

v. Regalia: remove regalia (swords, flags, banners) which residents claim to find threatening.

vi. Incorporate visible sign of respect for Catholic tradition in parade: e.g. if parade is indeed partly in memory of those who died at the Somme, specifically commemorate Catholic combatants – the 16th Irish Division – as well.

vii. Package deal: e.g. Newsletter/Irish News idea that next year's march voluntarily foregone. Probably unacceptable to Orange Order – but might they be pushed to agree that form of next year's parade would be subject to discussion with the residents – perhaps to include McKenna if he were specifically to acknowledge his terrorist past and disclaim any present influence by Sinn Fein?

What offsetting measures are possible?

13. Possible counter-balancing measures which might help reconcile the residents (or, failing them, wider nationalist opinion) to the parade could include:

i. "Equality of cultural recognition" – if the root cause of the residents' opposition to the parade is retaliation for the fact that they feel excluded from Portadown town centre, then support for a nationalist parade/festival at an appropriately symbolic location in Portadown might be an effective counterweight. Support might include some resources and other practical measures (perhaps, channelled through a body such as the Community Relations Council?) as well as a firm general statement that the nationalist community in Portadown has the right to expect generosity and tolerance in the town which they share with their Protestant neighbours. The residents may well be able to suggest other concrete ways in which parity of esteem for nationalists in Portadown could be demonstrated.

ii. Task force to examine community relations in Portadown: Central Secretariat are working up proposals for a task force bringing together the relevant public bodies and a small number of local figures prominent in the community relations field, which would aim to identify measures to improve community relations in Portadown, to promote such measures and to manage an agreed coordinated scheme. Further advice on this (including the public expenditure implications, which we would aim to contain within the existing budgets of the bodies concerned, though probably with some skewing towards the Portadown area), will be submitted.

iii. Tougher approach to band parades: Band parades (which the Drumcree parade, of course, is not) are a manifestation of the marching season which is criticised not only by nationalists but also by many unionists, on the grounds of offensive sectarian behaviour and disproportionate disruption to the life of the community. The last government undertook in principle that a registration scheme for bands would be introduced. It is however proving extremely difficult to devise a registration scheme which would be of practical value and would not be vulnerable to attack under the ECHR. But when the new parades legislation is enacted, the Commission will have sweeping powers over band parades as over all other types of procession. Subject to discussion with the Commission and the RUC, it should be possible to provide a strong form of words for the Secretary of State to use indicating a much tougher regime for band parades in the future.

iv. Continuing access to Ministers: Esteem and recognition are clearly important to the GRRC. Some undertaking that the HMG would continue communication with them after this year's parade – continuing the very valuable confidence-building symbolism established by the Secretary of State's promise to let them know herself what the Chief Constable's decision is could well be valuable.

What external influences can we bring to bear?

14. It will be of the highest importance to maximise public, media and political support for the concept of proximity negotiations and, even more importantly, the decision which is eventually announced. If we can shift the terms of the debate towards a general perception that what is on offer is reasonable and should be accepted, then it is far more likely that the GRRC will decide to cut a deal. Key influencers here will be the Irish and (to a lesser extent) US government, the SDLP (particularly John Hume and Brid Rogers [*sic*]), Archbishop Brady, and the Newsletter/Irish News (if they can maintain their joint approach). On the other side, Trimble and Archbishop Eames will have a role to play. There will be a need to keep very close to these key influencers as the proximity talks progress, to ensure that they can indeed support the

outcome and that this message is passed to the GRRC. Careful coordination will be required; and (if the Secretary of State is content) a more detailed game-plan will be submitted in due course.

15. The general media presentation of these developments will also of course be very important. The strategy will need to include very timely guidance telegrams to overseas posts, as well as detailed briefing of the foreign and domestic press in Northern Ireland, taking up the Secretary of State's idea that an information pack on the parades issue should be made available.

What should happen in the final days?

16. The outcome of the proximity negotiations will have a critical bearing on the timing of the Chief Constable's decision and its announcement. Ideally, it would be possible to announce the decision early, and accompany it with light or no policing on the Garvaghy Road, on the basis of an understanding with the residents. But if we cannot secure a reliable agreement with them that they will not occupy the road, the Chief Constable will clearly have to make the operational judgments he thinks appropriate.

Conclusion

17. If the Secretary of State is content with the broad approach sketched in here, we shall work up and submit a more detailed gameplan next week, including:- draft letters of invitation for the Secretary of State to send to the GRRC and the Orange Order;- detailed practical arrangements for the Hillsborough talks;- a negotiating brief to guide the government side at the talks, and- a handling plan covering arrangements for the media and the other significant players.

Signed: S.J. Leach.

In the mean time, Flanagan had come up with another idea that was not in the paper. During his own discussions with Orange leaders, they had disclosed that some of the people who lived in the Garvaghy area had replied privately to the Bingham–Watson letter. 'I said, you've got some responses and you've actually got some credit for it publicly because people are saying this is a step forward. Why don't you take that on via a video conference? If video conferencing, as a technique, has been created to help people who are geographically distant, why can't you use it for people who are philosophically distant? Why don't you sit in your Orange Hall and the residents sit in their community centre. As the advertisement says: it's good to talk.' The chief constable suggested that a wealthy organisation, like British Telecom, might even be prepared to sponsor such an exercise. 'The Orange Order were within an ace of accepting it. Whether the residents would have accepted it I don't know. I never tested it. But the Orange Order I think were within an ace of accepting it as a possibility until it was overtaken by the talks at Hillsborough.' With every other option virtually closed down, the government finally committed itself to the proximity talks, but for the first time the Drumcree issue was elevated to one that required open prime ministerial attention. On 25 June, speaking in the House of Commons, Tony Blair announced that invitations would be issued for talks at Hillsborough Castle to encourage a local accommodation at Drumcree. 'Nobody will be forced to talk face-to-face with those they do not wish to,' he said. 'I appeal to all concerned to accept this invitation to talks. Accommodation need not be a dirty word where human lives may be at stake.'

Over the next 48 hours, there was frantic activity to prepare for the encounter. Rooms were assigned for the use of the two delegations and routes mapped out so that they would not come into contact, arriving or leaving, when using the washrooms, taking a walk in the manicured gardens or having a meal. No detail was overlooked. The Hillsborough staff knew from bitter experience that even the most innocuous oversight could cause great offence to the micro-sensitivities always paraded on such fraught occasions. Once a Unionist dignitary had walked away from a secretary of state's dinner table in high dudgeon. He was convinced that the vegetables, peas, potatoes and carrots, had been deliberately chosen to insult him because they matched the green, white and orange of the Irish tricolour. Similarly, portraits of royal ancestors, on loan from the Queen's art collection, had to be stripped from the room to be used by the residents.

Although there was a growing sense of crisis and fear gathering, and travel agents reported that every seat to holiday destinations for the Drumcree fortnight had been sold out for months, hopes of a settlement had still not been exhausted as the parties gathered at Hillsborough on Friday 27 June at 9.30 am. As they arrived, the Northern Ireland Office issued an upbeat statement by Mowlam: 'I very much welcome the fact that these discussions are taking place today, and I am grateful to the representatives of both the Garvaghy Road Residents' Coalition and the Orange Order for agreeing to attend. My objective for these talks, which I know is shared by the other participants, is to find an honourable and principled accommodation on this difficult issue. No one will benefit from a re-run of last year's appalling events. For my part I am determined to leave no stone unturned to prevent this, and today's discussions build on the round of meetings I have held in recent weeks with all the various groups. These "proximity" talks represent a genuine attempt, in good faith, to find a way through a complex and highly emotive problem: I have no predetermined outcome in mind, and no hidden agenda.'

The reality was very different and the talks got off to an inauspicious start. The Order's representatives were not enthusiastic about being there at all and had slipped in by a side gate to avoid having to run the gauntlet of reporters and cameras at the main gate. They had only turned up because they knew it would look bad, and could count against them, if they stayed away. In another sign of unease, they would not allow the residents to be given their names for 'security reasons'. Despite Mowlam's statement talking up the significance and importance of the discussions, she was not there, having gone to visit a school in Lurgan. The two delegations, Alistair Graham of the Parades Commission, the Chief Constable and others thus spent a fruitless morning in their separate cocoons, drinking coffee and watching television. From time to time, as the news programmes crossed live to Hillsborough, both delegations watched incredulously as journalists standing outside the ornate gates of the royal palace reported that talks were under way. When Mowlam did arrive at noon with Jonathan Powell, the prime minister's chief of staff, she spent a few minutes 'going over old ground' with both the Order and the residents. Each simply restated their position then they broke for lunch. As they dined, both delegations were again amused to hear the news bulletins reporting that talks had been under way for some three hours when they had actually lasted for no more than ten fruitless minutes. By early afternoon it was clear that neither delegation would move and the day's only decision was taken – that they should all go home. Everybody left feeling it had been a waste of time. One of the first things the residents had asked was whether the Orange delegation was bound by Grand Lodge policy, which forbade face-to-face talks with them. 'When Mo came back and said that policy was unchanged, it was clear the meeting was a waste of time,' recalls McKenna. 'We were there to negotiate with them.'

Mowlam put a bold face on the failure in another statement early that evening: 'I am grateful to those who agreed to attend today. These discussions formed part of our continuing effort to find a principled and honourable resolution to the difficult problem we face in Portadown. While we have not reached a resolution today, there are a number of areas which I want to consider further. I shall do this and be in touch again with both sides early next week. We must all continue to play our part in the search for a reasonable local accommodation.'

Mowlam did not give up and, with her officials, continued to try and find some way out of the confrontational position that was hardening by the hour. The Orange Order was the principal focus of her interest and she was more inclined to get it to back down than to ask the residents to do so. Robert McCartney, the flamboyant former barrister turned independent Unionist MP for prosperous North Down, injected some new thinking into what had been a completely sterile debate by suggesting that the Order should be given permission to walk the Garvaghy Road and then gain the moral high ground by voluntarily declining to do so. Mowlam invited Bingham and Watson in again and pleaded with them to ask the Order's representatives to end the protest unilaterally. They told her they would not because they knew the plea would be rejected. Mowlam punched her fists into the air in frustration and exclaimed: 'If they won't listen to you who will they listen to?' Bingham replied, 'Secretary of State, if King Billy himself came back from the dead with that suggestion, they wouldn't even listen to him.' When the two leaders reported this back to Gracey he replied caustically: 'I hear so much talk about the moral high ground, I'm getting dizzy.'

Although she had that day authorised the army to bring in two battalions of soldiers as precautionary reinforcement for the police, Mowlam directed the move be unpublicised so that it would not prejudice her now eleventh-hour efforts to head off a violent eruption. Apart from her own cajoling of the main protagonists, she was also having to take account of high-level political lobbying. Trimble says it would be 'overstating' it to suggest he threatened to pull his party out of the simultaneous political talks being chaired by the former US Senator George Mitchell if the march did not get the go-ahead, but his recollection of events and discussions at the time is that they concentrated on the kind of limitations that could be placed on a parade, such as the numbers involved and whether there should be any music. While Mowlam was repeatedly telling McKenna that no decision had been taken, Trimble says the discussions he had were entirely about the nature of the parade. 'As far as I was concerned it was not going to be blocked. All of the talks I had concerned the modalities for the parade.' Donaldson agrees. He says the real battle was fought behind the scenes with himself, Trimble and Molyneaux exerting political pressure and exhorting the government to permit the parade. 'I warned him it would be impossible to participate in the political process if the parade was blocked again. Looking at the situation realistically, it was not going to be tenable for discussions to take place against the backdrop of a stand-off and all the implications that would have flowed from that. There was no way any progress could have been made politically in that situation. I would be surprised if David did not make that position very clear to the government.'

On the Friday morning before the parade the Order hosted a breakfast to make its case to journalists. There was much amusement when it was noticed that jars of 'Prince William of Orange' marmalade had been provided to accompany the toast. The gesture, and the issue of passes, was the first effort of its kind by the Order to win friends in the media and protect them from the attentions of the more extreme of their members who had harassed and even assaulted journalists, photographers and camera operators during earlier Drumcrees. That evening, at the beginning of the Drumcree weekend, before departing from Stormont Castle, Mowlam came out to the front steps and went on television and radio to call on the Orangemen 'to listen to the voice of reason'. But she was not slipping off for an early night. Instead, accompanied by the security minister Adam Ingram, a Glasgow MP who had been an Orange member as a boy, and John Steele, she was heading to historic Brownlow House in Lurgan, the world headquarters of the Royal Black Institution, the senior of the Loyal Orders, for an 11 pm meeting to make a last-ditch personal appeal to Portadown District. Lord Molyneaux, the former Unionist leader and a senior Orangeman, was also present. In line with her short statement from the steps at Stormont earlier that evening, Mowlam's over-arching priority remained to persuade them to back away from the march in the interests of the wider community. She was listened to politely by the several hundred Orangemen, all clad in their bright sashes, but then, one after another, they rose to their feet and told her it was not on, that they would not consider such an approach. They reminded her of the compromises they had offered in the conduct of the parade to take direct account of the residents' criticisms. At one point she had to agree that no comparable concessions had been made by the residents. There was general respect for her outstanding courage in going there, into the lion's den, as it were, but there was criticism afterwards that she had offered the Order financial support to promote itself as a major cultural organisation. 'That was viewed as very naïve, very insulting, in thinking we could be bought off. At times we thought she was on a different planet,' one hardliner said afterwards. In her armoured police limousine, speeding back along the M1 motorway to Hillsborough with Ingram, Mowlam was said to be near despair.

With all possibilities of compromise now at an end, Flanagan moved to centre stage and early on the Saturday morning Mowlam returned to her office at Stormont Castle to await contact from him. That morning he had called in his chief officers' group to decide what should be done about the march. One late idea for an 'anti-clockwise' march, up the Garvaghy Road to a very early church service with a return along the customary outward route, was still on the table but finding little favour. The possibility of conducting the march under cover of darkness had also been explored, as had the feasibility of a choreographed confrontation: the Orange march marking time at the mouth of the Garvaghy Road while the residents protested peacefully before stepping aside to let it past while they stood with their backs turned. The police chiefs were told that there was still no sign of any compromise and, after some discussion, a consensus emerged for the 'least worst option' – a controlled march. Meanwhile, as the drive for compromise continued, a final decision was left on hold. Flanagan's operational planners had come down in favour of the controlled march after weighing up the various options. They concluded that the RUC, with the limited army reinforcements available to them (the Army's international overstretch problem remained), could not contain the province-wide disruption and violence which would flow from another stand-off at Drumcree and a ban on the march along the Garvaghy Road.

One potentially helpful development had been the earlier removal of Billy Wright from the scene. His apparent immunity came to an end in 1997 when a Protestant woman neighbour in Portadown, infuriated that her son had been viciously beaten by the UVF, identified two of the assailants to the police. Wright sent a message that she'd be 'a body bag job' if she didn't withdraw her statements and, next day, drove up in his flashy red sports car to reinforce the threat in person. The woman courageously refused to back down, and additionally agreed to testify against him. As a result, in March 1997, Wright was jailed for eight years for threatening to kill her. The judge said that Wright was a sinister man whose evidence of his innocence was impossibe to believe. The woman witness was resettled in England with a new identity for her safety. At the time of his imprisonment, Wright was facing a UVF death sentence for his opposition to the ceasefire and died violently soon afterwards. It was, though, imprisoned members of the extreme Republican group the INLA who murdered him inside the Maze prison the following 27 December. Wright was buried in Portadown with his Drumcree siege medal pinned to his breast.

Despite Wright's absence, Special Branch gleaned from its sources in the Protestant community that there were still elements in the Order, and Loyalist paramilitaries, actively planning for far more serious disruption. In particular, they intended to put large numbers of women and children at road blocks because it would be far more difficult for the police to physically remove them. The police had learned lessons from the events of 1996, but they were all too painfully aware that, in the final analysis, the threat of force of numbers breaking through at Drumcree would again put them back in the unenviable position of a year earlier. If the Order decided to stretch them by staging a second-stand off elsewhere, the dilemma would double. The need to commit the army to stop them would be no more acceptable this time. For this deeply pragmatic reason, and most certainly not out of any sympathy or support for the Orange Order, the overwhelming advice to Flanagan was in favour of pushing the march through, and containing the resultant Nationalist anger, which they predicted would last for some 72 hours.

'I've never known such apprehension in the RUC in twenty-seven years' service,' said a senior RUC officer that morning while mentally bracing himself to cope with the potentially catastrophic consequences of the coming Twelfth of July period. 'There have been many sleepless nights and there is a growing sense of dread.' Throughout that tense Saturday convoys of Land Rovers from all over Northern Ireland converged on Mahon Road barracks, where a massive logistical operation to support and feed them had again been put in place. Mowlam and Flanagan officially kept all their options open: 'Hoping for peace, preparing for war,' the senior policeman put it. 'If there had been a last-minute breakthrough, we would simply have pulled everyone back.' In reality this was one of the options turning over in Flanagan's mind, but for very strong political, tactical and operational reasons it was prudent not to say so until the very last moment. The RUC were therefore happy to keep both sides guessing and keep the inestimable advantage of surprise for themselves, although they became increasingly apprehensive that, in so doing, they were vulnerable to judicial review and an adverse finding for failing to give either side the chance to challenge the decision.

However, an entirely different strategy had been forming in Mowlam's mind, one that she understood was shared by Flanagan and the RUC: imposing an outright ban on the entire Drumcree church parade, an action she would approve if Flanagan decided to ask for it, as the public order legislation obliged him to do although he could order the march to be halted or re-routed himself. During her talks with both sides she had promised to let them know in advance what would be happening. Indeed she badly wanted to do so and during the day enquired repeatedly if the police had taken a decision so that she could contact them. The idea horrified her officials and the police and she had to be very firmly discouraged, which greatly distressed her. Indeed she was only dissuaded from going to Portadown herself when it was pointed out that it would be necessary to deploy a large number of police and troops to ensure her safety. To observe her own legal duties in respect of the request for a ban she was anticipating, Mowlam had convened the Public Order Consultative Committee of the Police Authority who came to Stormont to see her at 8 pm, the first and only time it ever met in 27 years. After speaking with them, Mowlam was expecting to announce the ban, but with no formal word from the police there was no business to transact. 'She was very serious and concerned,' said one of those at the 90-minute meeting. 'It was clear that no decision had then been taken.' The judgement was entirely accurate. Shortly afterwards, she rang Alistair Graham, who was dining with a friend in his house close to Strangford Lough in the rolling County Down countryside. 'What the fuck's Ronnie doing?' she asked. Graham was unable to enlighten her.

If they had been asked to bet that Saturday evening, the residents would have said the parade was not coming through. On the Friday they had established a Greenham Common-style 'women's peace camp' at the side of the road and found lodgings with families in the area for many of the influx of 'international observers' they had invited. Throughout the next day, the Saturday that was the eve of the march, Rosemary Nelson, the group's solicitor, tried on numerous occasions to get in touch with Mowlam at Stormont to find out what was happening. She failed to make contact, but shortly after 5 pm the secretary of state called McKenna to say she did not know. Brid Rodgers also thought there would be no parade. 'I felt the mistakes of the previous two years could not be repeated and we were reasonably confident that the Orangemen would not be allowed to go down the road unless there was agreement. Shortly before midnight I left Portadown and went home to Lurgan. I was exhausted but before going to bed I used a direct line to contact John Steele, who was still in the control room in Stormont, and he assured me that no decision had been taken. He dismissed claims by the residents that the large-scale deployment of police and troops in the area was a signal that the parade was to be forced through. He told me that since it was now clear there would be no accommodation, a meeting to take a decision was about to take place.'

By that time, Bingham and Watson and other senior officers were already in the church hall discussing strategy and opening up the 'command bunker'. They expected a re-run of 1996, with the parade being banned but then allowed down the road after a few days, and had come prepared. Watson had a tent, clothes, food and a laptop computer piled into his car, while Bingham had also packed up for a lengthy stay before leaving his manse in Pomeroy.

Not long after midnight, a large convoy of heavy military transports trundled up to the bridge by the churchyard and soldiers began to erect layers of razor wire entanglements in the fields adjacent to the church. To the watching Orangemen these were the necessary preparations for the parade being halted again, the outcome they were expecting. However, a few hours later, as the work was being completed, Watson's mobile phone rang. The caller was a senior RUC officer. During very guarded exchanges, he told Watson not to misinterpret what he was seeing. From the conversation, Watson deduced the parade would now take place.

The sudden military deployment caused some apprehension among the residents of the Garvaghy Road, who had teams of people out on the streets watching carefully for any activity. They had also set up an early-warning system using alarm sirens attached to lamp posts, the centrepiece of which was a large air-raid siren 'liberated' by local Republicans from an army base on the Whiterock Road in west Belfast soon after troops had been moved out. The sirens were not sounded, however, and when the spotters reported back what the army were doing many of the wary residents actually went home to bed, believing this signalled that the parade was to be blocked.

The preliminary operation was not a calculated deception, although it did serve to keep all Flanagan's options open. By putting the physical obstacles in place in advance, if any sort of change, such as a mass blockade on the Garvaghy Road, had required him to hold the parade back then he would have been able to do so. In reality though, the senior RUC officer's call was the correct signal. At about the same time as it was being made, Flanagan, who had only just decided that the march was to go ahead provided the road could be held open, was at Stormont House telling Mowlam he was not going to ask for the ban she was expecting. Instead he had used his operational discretion under the law to go for a controlled march. During the day, he told her, he had received 'deeply worrying' intelligence information that had led him to that conclusion. Mowlam knew she was powerless to overrule him and grudgingly indicated her support for the decision, but after Flanagan left, according to officials who were present, she was livid.

Soon after this late-night meeting ended in Belfast, back in Portadown a friend called McKenna on his mobile phone to warn him that large numbers of police and troops were on the move from Mahon and heading for the Garvaghy area. This time McKenna gave the order for the alarms to be sounded. As people began to emerge from their homes, McKenna and two others got into a car to go on a scouting mission but had gone no distance before they were met by dozens of police Land Rovers travelling three abreast towards them. Rushing back to the Garvaghy Road, they encountered an army checkpoint on Ballyoran Hill. McKenna feared that if they were stopped and recognised they would not be allowed back into the area, so the driver mounted the pavement and screeched past the startled soldiers. When the car reached the Garvaghy Road, McKenna leapt out and shouted that the parade was definitely going to be forced through. At that point the sirens sprang into life for the second time. At about the same time, the SDLP press officer Conal McDevitt telephoned Brid Rodgers to say she should go to Portadown immediately because the police were on the move. She got up, dressed and drove to the Garvaghy Road. Soon afterwards, about 3.30 am, in a deployment aimed at taking and holding the road clear for the march, a strong police and army force virtually invaded the housing estates along the road. Long convoys of vehicles swept in and up to 1500 police and soldiers began sealing off streets with cordons to stop residents moving out and forming large crowds. The operation was not without its surreal moments. As police baton-charged a 300-strong crowd, including McKenna and Joe Duffy, to clear them from the junction of Garvaghy and Ashgrove Roads, a Welsh choir entertaining protestors at the nearby peace camp continued to sing the civil rights anthem 'We shall overcome'. Some petrol bombs and stones were thrown at the police during this phase of the operation.

By dawn the Garvaghy Road was clear, quiet and under the full control of the police and Army who also enforced strict movement controls. It was the one flaw in the carefully-planned operation. The police planners had taken no account of the fact that the several thousand Catholic residents would be going along the road to mass during the morning and had failed to see the massive propaganda opportunity on offer: the irony of such heavy-handed force being used to deny Catholics their right to worship in the name of protecting that of the Orangemen. The two Jesuits and other local priests quickly appreciated the situation and, after hundreds of people complained that they couldn't get to mass, plans were made to set up an altar and say mass in the middle of the road. For a time, the police and army tried to prevent it and then to insist that males of combatant age, sixteen years and over, would not be allowed to attend, but they were soon embarrassed into backing down. The subsequent images of mass being said against the backdrop of British Army Saxon armoured vehicles once again underlined the surreal absurdity of the entire Drumcree situation.

After a tense morning, the Orange parade was eventually forced through around 1 pm. It took about six minutes to pass. A short time previously, when it was given the go-ahead to proceed from the church,

Portadown District rejected advice from Bingham and Watson not to march. They wanted the district to accept that they had won the fight to have their right to walk restored, but not exercise it, thus gaining the moral high ground and defusing the situation. The district wouldn't have it. There was a noisy protest as the march took place. Residents banged bin lids and shouted abuse and also unfurled a banner that read 'Mo-Mayhew – No Change'. As soon as the parade had cleared the contested section of the route, the security forces swiftly withdrew, but rioting had already developed and 40 plastic baton rounds were fired.

The decision outraged Catholics throughout Northern Ireland, and for the third successive year the church parade caused a major communal convulsion and serious violence. Nearby at Lurgan a train was burned. Over the next four days, 60 RUC officers and 56 civilians were injured and 117 arrests were made. The security forces fired 2500 plastic baton rounds in answer to 402 hijackings, the throwing of 1506 petrol bombs and another 815 attacks on them. The Northern Ireland Ambulance Service responded to 500 emergency calls. As ever the graffiti writers summed it up: 'New Labour, same old shite, Dr Mo must go.' That Sunday evening a young Protestant bandsman on his way to a church service was halted at an illegal roadblock by Catholic youths who ordered him out of his car. When they discovered his accordion and uniform in the boot of the car, they made him put on the uniform and walk up and down the street while they stoned him.

Flanagan conducted a news conference at Mahon Barracks early on the Sunday morning to explain his decision: 'I am not interested in Orangeism, I am not interested in parades, I am interested in doing my very best to preserve the peace as far as is humanly possible.' He condemned the paramilitary influences on both sides and said there was no doubt that they wanted to use this issue as an excuse for violence. 'The intense feelings of people on both sides of the debate surrounding the Drumcree issue have been manipulated by evil people who want to use the issue as an excuse to wreak outright violence. I was left, during Saturday, with a simple stark choice in terms of balancing two evils, each evil bound to bring about serious violence. I had to make a decision in terms of which of these evils would be likely to bring about less violence. In those circumstances I made the decision that the parade as proposed should proceed. I apologise to the people of the Garvaghy Road for the gross inconvenience that this has caused. I've taken the decision most reluctantly to ensure that the people of the Garvaghy Road, amongst other outcomes of this decision, are not surrounded for days on end. I want to subject them to the minimum of inconvenience. I had to take a course of

Drumcree church at night.

Robert Saulters,
Grand Master of the Grand Orange
Lodge of Ireland.

Harold Gracey,
District Master of Portadown District
Loyal Orange Lodge No 1.

The Reverend William Bingham,
County Grand Chaplain of Armagh.

Denis Watson MLA,
County Grand Master of Armagh.

Priests celebrate mass on the Garvaghy Road.

The RUC clear a Catholic crowd from the Garvaghy Road
to enable an Orange parade to pass.

Harold Gracey, leader of the Portadown Orangemen,
addresses his members outside Drumcree church.

Brid Rodgers MLA.

Brendan McKenna, chairman of the
Garvaghy Road Residents Coalition.

His Eminence Cardinal Cahal Daly,
former Catholic Archbishop of Armagh
and Primate of All Ireland.

Constable Frank O'Reilly of the Royal
Ulster Constabulary, murdered by
Loyalists in 1998.

Loyalist terrorist Billy Wright at Drumcree church.

David Trimble MP, the Ulster Unionist Party leader, passes through the police lines at Drumcree.

Sir Alistair Graham,
Chairman of the Parades Commission.

Brian Currin,
mediator in the Drumcree conflict.

Sir Ronnie Flanagan,
Chief Constable of the
Royal Ulster Constabulary.

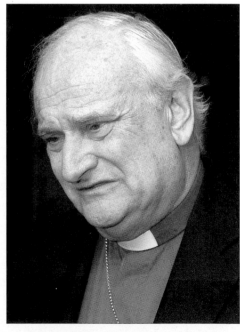

The Most Reverend Dr Robin Eames,
Church of Ireland Archbishop of
Armagh.

Soldiers erecting barbed-wire lines at Drumcree.

Army Crowd Control Obstacles (CCOs) at Drumcree Bridge.

action that would result in less violence. I'm talking about serious violence. I'm talking about a risk of loss of life. I was left with a stark choice: how much life was liable to be lost and that loss of life was liable to be in the Catholic community.'

Although her language was measured, Mowlam's unhappiness at the outcome was all too evident from her statement that morning: 'This is a sad day for all of us. Many will be angered by what has occurred but I appeal to them and to all with influence in their communities to exercise restraint. Northern Ireland has seen far too many tragedies. Peace and the preservation of life in the end matters most of all. The right to peaceful assembly – the right to march – is a basic right. But all rights carry responsibilities. They should be exercised with respect for the rights and freedoms of others. In this case a decision, which is for the Chief Constable to make, has had to be taken to preserve public safety. I fully support the action the Chief Constable has had to take but at the same time this is an outcome that I regret and that neither he nor I wanted. What we and the vast majority of people in Northern Ireland wanted was a sensible accommodation. I have done my utmost to achieve that as has the Chief Constable. But where there is intransigence on both sides that becomes impossible. And that is what I have met.' In words that deeply angered the Orange Order, and would come to be yet another obstacle in solving Drumcree, she said: 'I know many in the Nationalist community will be angered by this decision. It has been dictated by circumstances. I would have preferred it otherwise. Nevertheless I appeal to all in the Nationalist community to understand that overall public safety across Northern Ireland has to be the Chief Constable's main concern. Your voice is not ignored. I understand your feelings and I will address them in legislating on this issue. I am only sorry that option was not open to me this summer.'

Mowlam added that the way ahead for the future 'is a new arrangement designed to ensure that the pain of these events can be put behind us for good.' In private she was less diplomatic. One of her aides recalls: 'I remember feeling hopeless at the time because there was nothing we could do. We were looking at the situation where we were basically being told that the people who were threatening to use the most force had to be given their way, had to be entitled to do what they wanted to do, because the legislation was structured so that that's the way you had to make the choices. She was very angry about it. She was very angry that it had been left like that, because the whole point of introducing the Parades Commission was to change that structure so that the law, instead of being based upon "might is right" which is what it was, was actually based upon making rational decisions upon other criteria, broader interests.' For her own part Mowlam vowed that in making decisions on future parades, 'it wasn't all going to come down to a decision about who waved the bigger stick' with the police alone deciding the outcome.

Although the Drumcree parade was over, the subsequent violence, political fallout and deeply worrying police intelligence about an even more serious situation developing over the coming Twelfth, still had to be coped with. The week after Drumcree started badly for Mowlam. The top secret 'gameplan' document was leaked – an investigation never identi- fied the culprit – and was heavily misinterpreted, especially by some Nationalists who claimed it showed there had been a plan to force the march through all along. Much of this wrong analysis reflected the deep hostility Mowlam had aroused in so many quarters. She defended herself vigorously in a statement on 8 July: 'The document was an initial con- sideration by officials containing assessments and opinions of how the proximity talks should be approached. Neither I nor the Minister of State endorsed this document at the time or later. I insisted that the full range of options should be kept under review. In the event I explored a wide range of options at the proximity talks, with no preconceived agenda and treating both sides completely even-handedly. I worked until the last possible moment along with others to achieve a peaceful accommodation. As the document said, the Chief Constable had genuinely not taken the decision, and he did not do so until the night before the march. All feasible options were genuinely under consideration until the very last moment.'

Despite the firestorm of disorder now raging on the streets and the personal criticism that engulfed her, Mowlam did not flinch. In a series of interviews she robustly dismissed the leak, which had clearly been intended to damage her, and refused to give up on her mission for compromise. Instead she set out on a new round of talks to head off further dangerous confrontations threatened for the end of the week, when the main Twelfth marches were due. She had talks with Flanagan about the threat and met members of G7, a coalition of business, professional and trade union leaders who had come together to discuss ways to ease the economic damage of what had become the perennial Drumcree crisis. In a bid to defuse tension rapidly, she was now looking to the Order for a major gesture in response to the Sunday march going ahead. 'When I see members of the Orange Order, I will expect to see some willingness and understanding of the events of this weekend reflected in their words and actions during the days ahead. There can and should be no triumphalism. We will continue to work to resolve disputes during the rest of this week, but I can only do it if the people involved on both sides are willing.' On Wednesday, after dealing with angry representations about the Drumcree decision from the SDLP, she returned to London to face questions in the House of Commons. A sombre and sympathetic house refused to lynch her.

The next morning, as she was briefing the Cabinet in London, Flanagan and two of his most senior officers, Assistant Chief Constables Bill Stewart and Darryl Beaney, responsible for policing Belfast and Londonderry respectively, were on their way to the House of Orange, in Belfast's Dublin Road. There the grim-faced policemen spelled out the consequences of further Orange intransigence in graphic detail, then left without saying anything to the reporters waiting outside. Inside the leaders of Grand Lodge were left pondering what Flanagan later described as a 'very frank' security assessment. There were three problematic marches, in the light of the reaction to Drumcree, and the police intelligence: Armagh; Londonderry and, again, the Ormeau Road. The police had information that an IRA sniper attack was planned on the march at Armagh as it passed through the Shambles. The Orangemen quickly realised that going ahead with the marches would be untenable, but they had to get the local groups to agree and they were concerned about how to announce the decision. It was finally agreed that Donaldson, who was on the way back from Westminster, would do so in an interview already planned for the BBC's *Newsnight* programme that evening. The news was quickly communicated to Flanagan, who kept it to himself in case something went wrong. That evening he was out and about in the tense city and watched a tricky parade in the Donegall Pass area before going to the station there to watch the programme. The plan was that Donaldson would make the dramatic announcement and at that point a series of faxes would go out to news organisations from the House of Orange, who had a team of members standing by for the job.

To Flanagan's great surprise, the programme ended without the announcement being made. He quickly phoned the House of Orange to ask Grand Secretary John McCrea what had happened. It was good news, he was told. The march at Newry had just been called off as well and they were retyping the statement. Molyneaux, also concerned and angry, telephoned to tell McCrea to get the news out without further delay. Thus, when it finally came late on the Thursday, the tranquilising breakthrough, unprecedented in the long and tumultuous history of triumphalist marching in Northern Ireland, was a victory for the single-minded patience and persistence with which Mowlam and Flanagan had relentlessly pursued their goal for the 65 days since she had arrived at

Stormont: securing a balanced accommodation and minimising violence and the threat to life and property.

As the news spread, the RUC and the majority of the community in Northern Ireland shared in a collective sigh of relief. 'It's the first time I can remember when cool judgement has overcome tribal passion,' one senior officer said with evident relief. As she welcomed their initiative in an early Friday morning interview on BBC Radio 4's *Today* programme, the slight tremble of emotion in Mowlam's voice was understandable. The Order, however, feels it never got sufficient credit or payback for the gesture and that it was bounced into it by dire warnings from Flanagan. Watson now says: 'I am not totally convinced that the situation was as bad as it was painted at the time. I think Ronnie Flanagan may have overstated the situation in an attempt to force those lodges to re-route the parade.' Looking back, many in the Order are deeply suspicious that Flanagan exaggerated the security situation because of fears that the security forces could not have coped with the Nationalist and Republican backlash if there had been any more contentious parades. Despite the callous sectarian murder of Bernadette Martin, an eighteen-year-old Catholic girl, in her Protestant boyfriend's home at Aghalee not far from Portadown, and all that had happened in previous days, the IRA finally succumbed to the months of sustained private political pressure and reinstated its ceasefire, ordering another cessation of military operations from midnight on 20 July. The decision reinstated bold new hopes for the peace process but there was still not the slightest sign of the confrontation at Drumcree being permanently resolved.

Chapter Nine

The Settling Day

Ever since his appointment to the Parades Commission, Alistair Graham had spent a considerable proportion of his time in Northern Ireland either in Portadown or dealing with aspects of the Drumcree situation. With other commission members, he went to Carleton Street on the morning of the 1997 parade and walked beside the Orangemen along the route to the church. On the way he spotted a deeply antagonistic sentiment displayed on a poster board in a garden: 'There are no nationalist areas of Portadown, only areas under temporary occupation.'

For Graham, that brutal sentence summed up the core issue of the Drumcree battle: equality. Many Protestants did not see the Catholic citizens of Portadown as equals, but merely as residing there under temporary sufferance. This was also evident in his meetings with the residents, whose immediate demand was for face-to-face dialogue as a signal that they were being treated as equals, but whose long-term vision was for a virtual town within a town, where the people of the Garvaghy Road could live, work, shop and relax without having to go into the 'hostile' town centre less than a mile away. The divisions in the town were so deep that a shopping centre development straddling the interface zone had to construct two entrances. Similarly, when the commission wanted to hold a public meeting in the town in line with their desire to be open and transparent about their work, they found they had to hold two: the residents would not come to the Town Hall, which they regarded as a Protestant, not a neutral venue.

Graham and the entire commission attended the first meeting. The Town Hall was packed and tense and for over an hour they faced very aggressive questions and endured a barrage of sustained abuse. At that point, after Richard Buchanan, the commission's secretary, suggested ending the meeting, a woman at the back of the hall stood up and foolhardily announced that she was from the Garvaghy Road. There was a hushed silence and a host of hostile eyes turned on her, making it very clear she was not welcome. She said she wanted to put a different view to those that had been aired in the previous hour – she was a Protestant, a member of the Women's Coalition. Sensing the aggression and anger in the crowd, Graham moved quickly to have her escorted from the hall because he feared for her safety. When the Commission members met the Residents Coalition in the community centre there was a far more relaxed, even jolly atmosphere but Graham felt it had clearly been choreographed and the questions stage-managed. He was still coming to terms with the extensive lexicon of nuance and sensitivity that permeates life and language in Northern Ireland, and there were audible gasps and murmurs from many of the audience when he referred to 'Londonderry' rather than 'Derry'.

After the trials and tribulations of the summer, Graham's commission was set to move to centre stage. Mo Mowlam wasted no time in bringing forward legislation to fully implement the North report, give the Parades Commission statutory powers beyond education and conciliation and relieve the RUC of its conflicting responsibility to rule on whether a parade could take place and then to implement the decision. A bill was published on 17 October 1997, to begin its passage through parliament in time to become law in advance of the 1998 marching season and the likelihood of what was already being described with dread as Drumcree Four. Mowlam said the Government's approach to the parades issues was based on rights and responsibilities: 'We are convinced the way forward is a policy based both on the right to free assembly, which includes the right to march and the right to protest against marches, peacefully and within the law, and responsibilities. In a democratic society we all have the responsibility to express our rights in a way which respects the rights and freedom of others.'

The bill also provided for the secretary of state to take powers to extend the remit of the Parades Commission to cover expressions of cultural identity other than parades. Mowlam said: 'We have also looked at claims that establishing a Parades Commission focuses too narrowly on a method of expressing cultural identity which, in practice, is undertaken particularly by one side of the community. We understand these concerns. The problems of fear and intimidation as a result of aggressive manifestations of community identity are not only found in the parades context.' The commission's further role, she envisaged, would be to keep the situation under review and make recommendations to Government about the law and practice surrounding public manifestations of cultural identity, from wherever they might come, which might damage relationships within the community – but not to include sporting events. This new provision would not come into effect straight away: 'I have put this provision on the face of the Bill because I believe it is important to ensure that parades are not the only facet of cultural identity which could receive attention. However, the Commission will initially have a great deal to do to establish how it will take forward its new responsibilities. I will therefore not bring this further remit into operation immediately. But I will keep it under close review and hope that it will be possible to activate the provision within a matter of months.'

Ten days later, the commission published drafts of three new statutory documents for public consultation: a Code of Conduct, setting standards of behaviour for participants in parades, and the Guidelines and Procedural Rules the commission intended to use when making decisions on parades once the Public Processions Bill was in force. It was also signalled that the commission planned to express a preliminary view on the pattern of parades in contentious areas across Northern Ireland in advance of the coming 1998 marching season.

Mowlam's formula did not meet with the unanimous approval she had expected. Widening the remit beyond parades found little favour with Graham and his fellow commissioners, who objected very strongly. 'Dealing with the issue of parades was going to be difficult enough without becoming involved in disputes about where kerbstones could be painted red, white and blue or on which lamp posts the Irish tricolour could fly,' said Graham. This dimension had been added to the legislation to help sweeten it for the Unionists and the Order. Immediately after Drumcree 1996 the Northern Ireland Forum for Political Dialogue, established in parallel to the ongoing inter-party and inter-government talks chaired by former US Senator George Mitchell, had set up a standing committee to study Public Order issues. During a series of subsequent hearings, which were boycotted by the Nationalist community and the residents' groups, the committee received 34 written submissions and took fifteen hours of oral evidence before producing a report in June 1997, virtually on the eve of Drumcree and while Mowlam's officials were still consulting about and drafting the parades legislation. In the absence of any independent or Nationalist input (the SDLP withdrew from the Forum as a protest about the 1996 Drumcree decision), it provided a sharply focused view of how the Loyal Orders and the Unionist community saw the way ahead on an issue that was increasingly central to their civic and community well-being.

Most significantly, the committee utterly rejected the concept of an independent Parades Commission and recommended that the RUC should retain responsibility for regulating marches under the Public Order legislation and for ensuring that the law was enforced equitably and fairly. The committee also said that traditional parades should be given protection under the public order legislation and called on the Government to address the 'flaws' contained in it 'so that the law will recognise the fundamental right of peaceful assembly and procession by all legal organisations not supporting terrorism, and not reward those resorting to the greatest threat of violence, which it does at present'. In a further swipe at the proposal that the Parades Commission should have a remit to promote mediation and conciliation, the committee doubted that a body can be both a mediator and adjudicator. It conceded, 'there may be a role for mediation but firmly believe[d] that procedures which relate to mediation must be kept quite separate from those relating to decision-making.' It concluded that the final decision regarding the routing of parades must remain with the RUC as it believed 'decisions which could ultimately affect the stability of a community should remain with the body which has the expertise to deal with such matters.'

The Forum report crystallised the opposition to a Parades Commission which had progressively hardened in the majority community ever since the publication of the North report. There was a strong view that, as marching was overwhelmingly a feature of Orange culture, this was simply a single-edged instrument to undermine it. As we have seen, from the Unionist perspective, the GAA, with its commitment to Nationalist values and exclusion of the security forces from membership, was an insidious manifestation of Nationalist culture. Why should it not be subject to the same sort of statutory scrutiny and control, they asked. Indeed, during their preliminary talks with Mowlam in September, before the legislation was finalised, Denis Watson and William Bingham had made this point and wrung from Mowlam an undertaking that the new body would be not a Parades Commission but a Cultural Commission with the much broader remit she subsequently outlined. 'We felt it was being targeted against Protestant culture as it did not look at aspects of Nationalist culture that Protestants would find offensive,' says Bingham. The two Orangemen were still seething about the tone of Mowlam's comments after the 1997 parade, especially when she apologised to the residents for what had happened and said it would not be allowed to be repeated.

Following the end of the 1996 stand-off, David Trimble's relations with Bingham and Watson had significantly cooled. They did not meet him, partly because they felt too much had gone on behind the scenes that year which they knew nothing about, and because they blamed him for consenting to the inclusion of 'an independent review' of parades as one of the points in the draft document prepared by Eames for the abortive carpet mills talks in 1996. This, they believed, provided the justification for the creation of the North review. Despite their differences, Trimble shared their hostility to what was now taking legislative shape. At a meeting with Adam Ingram, the security minister, he tossed the proposals angrily on the table and exclaimed they were 'anti-Orange'. An Order delegation, made up of Watson, Bingham, John McCrea, George Patton and Grand Master Robert Saulters, also expressed outrage and accused Mowlam of breaking her word. Shortly afterwards, Mowlam contacted Bingham and Watson and asked them back to a meeting in her office in Castle Buildings. (Stormont Castle had been vacated to enable a three-year refurbishment programme to begin). When they arrived, she was pacing the room, drinking tea and eating a biscuit. She apologised and said she had not been able to keep her word. Bingham said angrily that they would have no further contact with her. In the end, taking account of the Commission's strong objections, Mowlam's concept of widening its role beyond parades into territory just as dangerously mined was quietly abandoned. In so doing, the government ensured that the Loyal Orders would not engage with the more powerful Commission and that it would become a growing focus for discontent and hostility. Indeed Graham would become a significant hate-figure for them and encounter much personal abuse and hostility. Not long afterwards, while having a meal at the Crawfordsburn Inn near Bangor, where he often stayed, a drunk marched up to his table and bellowed 'How dare you enjoy yourself when people are dying at Drumcree!' On another occasion at the Inn, he was just about to tuck into a raspberry pudding when a civil servant came into the restaurant and told him he had to leave immediately because the police had intelligence that Loyalist paramilitaries were hot on his trail. He was moved to a 'safe' house in Bangor fitted with alarms, bullet-proof glass and so on, but he found the security trappings claustrophobic, and only stayed for one night before moving to another hotel.

The Public Processions (Northern Ireland) Act 1998 finally became law on 16 February 1998, having completed its journey through parliament and been given the Royal Assent. Mowlam commended the act to everyone, pointing out that, in coming to a determination on contested parades, the commission would be able to take into account not only the existing public order-related factors, but also the new factor recommended by the North Report, that of the wider impact of the parade on relationships within the community. She said: 'Under North's pro-posals, the Parades Commission would be able to balance all the different considerations. The internationally recognised right to march. The legiti-mate expectation of local residents not to feel intimidated in their own neighbourhoods. The danger of serious public disorder.' But there was now implacable opposition to it among the Loyal Orders and Unionist community. They would abide by the requirement to give 28 days' written notice of their parades, up from the 21 days suggested by North, but beyond that they would refuse to treat with the commission or its members.

With the new legislation coming into force, the membership of the commission also changed. Graham remained as chairman and Roy Magee, David Hewitt and Frank Guckian as members. Out went Berna McIvor, at her own request. In came Glenn Barr, Chief Executive of the Maydown Ebrington Group and a former member of the Fair Employment Agency and Community Relations Council who was involved in cross-community work in Londonderry. Barr was, however, best known as one of the leaders of the Loyalist general strike in 1974 which brought down the groundbreaking power-sharing executive. Others appointed were: Tommy Cheevers, a member of the Apprentice Boys of Derry for some twelve years and Director of the Greater Shankill Partnership, Director of Ballysillan Community Initiative, and a member of the Steering Group of North Belfast Interface Group; Roseanne McCormick, a barrister who was a member of the Police Authority for Northern Ireland from 1991 to 1997; and Aiden Canavan, a senior partner in a Belfast law firm who was president of the Law Society in 1995 and had participated in several community development projects in west Belfast. The tenure of Barr and Cheevers was short-lived. Both resigned after a month and were replaced by Billy Martin, a farmer active in the Ulster Farmers Union and President in 1985/86, who had also been a member of the Police Authority from 1991 to 1997, and Dr Barbara Irwin, a senior lecturer, who worked with both Catholic and Protestant school children in the area of Education for Mutual Understanding. In announcing the appointments Mowlam stressed the independence of the commission and said: 'The Government has given the Commission no "steer" as to its preferred outcome for this year's marching season. The only outcome we seek is a peaceful one, that those who wish to parade, as well as those who wish to protest against parades, will conduct themselves in a way which respects the rule of law and which does not lead to disruption and violence.' They were visionary, well-meaning words but they would all too soon have to be publicly eaten.

The creation of the commission was largely overshadowed by the successful outcome of the Mitchell talks on Good Friday, 10 April, when the Belfast Agreement was concluded after a marathon 33-hour final negotiating session. The talks, which had begun almost two years earlier in June 1996, produced the Belfast Agreement, which provided for the most fundamental redefinition of the British–Irish situation since partition in 1922. The comprehensive terms provided for a new north-south constitutional relationship, guaranteeing partition as long as the Unionists wanted it, and put in place new mechanisms for day-to-day co-operation on a range of common issues such as tourism, transport, energy and so on. It also provided for a series of reforms to policing, justice and prisons among many other areas, and created new bodies for joint activity by Britain, Ireland and the off-shore Channel Islands and Isle of Man. But the hard-won deal had to be put to a referendum, north and south of the border, for final approval by all the people of Ireland. There was little doubt that the people of the Irish Republic would enthusiastically endorse it in great numbers, but the political stakes in the north were far greater, for the Protestant population was closely divided on its merits and a vociferous 'No' campaign had swiftly emerged. Blair and Mowlam were so deeply troubled by the distinct possibility that a majority would oppose the agreement that they pulled out every personal stop to make sure of winning the referendum, scheduled for 22 May.

As ever at momentous moments in Northern Ireland, the vexed question of parades threatened to compromise the 'Yes' campaign and caused the prime minister himself to intervene to save it. The problem arose after Trimble learned that the Parades Commission was planning to publish its preliminary view of the coming marching season. Its intention was to condition public thinking and put down markers about how it would be using its legal powers for the first time. The commission was also keen to demonstrate that it would be taking a balanced view about contentious marches, allowing some and halting others, to counter Orange suspicions that its only role was to ban them. What alarmed Trimble, though, was information that the commission was going to signal the Drumcree church parade was to be banned. Trimble was in a highly vulnerable position. Although he demonstrated considerable personal courage and a new political maturity during the Mitchell talks, and his own party was some two to one in favour of the Agreement, the broader Unionist community was more narrowly divided and ensuring a convincing 'Yes' vote was still a close call. With Paisley, as ever, crying 'Ulster Says No', and given his tangential involvement at Drumcree over the years, any suggestion that the march was to be halted would be seized on and exploited to bolster the 'No' vote. In addition to opposition from significant sections of his own party, Trimble was also under serious pressure from the Orange Order. A few days earlier, on 15 April, 130 members of the Grand Orange Lodge held a five-hour meeting at the West Belfast Orange Hall on the Shankill Road. After discussing the forthcoming marching season they decided not to endorse the agreement because of reservations about police reform, the early release of terrorist prisoners and other matters. Joel Patton, the Spirit of Drumcree leader, said he was 'absolutely disgusted' that the Order did not reject the Agreement outright and again accused its hierarchy of 'a lack of leadership'. Trimble decided to call Alistair Graham to find out what was going to happen.

Graham had just returned from a five-day, 25-meeting swing through a range of interested groups in the United States, explaining the new legislation and parades regime, and arrangements had already been made to make public the preliminary view document at a news conference on Thursday April 23 in the Commission offices on the twelfth floor of Windsor House, Belfast's tallest building. On the morning of the previous day, Graham had just arrived in his office in Leeds and was sipping a cup of coffee while reading through the morning papers when his secretary called to say Trimble was on the line. Even by his own volatile standards the Ulster Unionist leader was in furious form, and launched a tirade of criticism saying such an announcement would destroy him and seriously undermine the campaign for a 'Yes' vote in the coming referendum. Graham quietly explained that they had a formal commitment to issue the preliminary view and were legally bound to it by their procedural rules which had been approved by parliament. In those circumstances, Graham said, he could not do anything, and the conversation ended on angry terms.

An hour later, Graham's phone rang again. This time it was the prime minister, Tony Blair. The two men knew each other from the days when Blair was employment spokesman for the Labour Party and Graham was a leading light in the Industrial Society. Blair spelled out the political dangers of publishing a document containing views about Drumcree at such a sensitive time. Graham was sympathetic. While solving parading problems and defending the independence of the commission from government were important issues, he recognised that getting a convincing vote in favour of the Good Friday Agreement was more immediately important. However, Graham explained, arrangements for making the announcement were well advanced. That afternoon he was due to fly to Belfast for a dinner with the editors of the main newspapers in Northern Ireland, the *Belfast Telegraph*, *Irish News* and *Belfast Newsletter*, and notification had already been given of the press conference the following morning when the report was scheduled to be published. Blair appeared surprised. Graham then went on to say the only remedy would be for Blair to send him a letter, which could be made public, formally requesting an urgent meeting of the commission to consider deferring the preliminary view until after the referendum. He said he would be very surprised if the other commission members would not be sympathetic to such a request. Blair was reluctant to send anything in writing that would be published because it would indicate that he had interfered with the role of an independent body. Mowlam had earlier stressed that the commission was independent and the government had given it no 'steer' for the marching season, yet that is what was now taking place.

Graham insisted on the need for a letter; that was the only way he could consider the request for a delay. 'The critical point was that it had to be a formal request that could be published. My judgement was that, providing it could all be above board in a transparent, public fashion, given the importance of having a public debate about the Good Friday Agreement and a strong vote in the referendum, this was a perfectly legitimate request from a prime minister who had been at the heart of the negotiations on the agreement. What I was not prepared to do, and what I think the prime minister would have preferred, was to unilaterally decide to postpone publication.' At the end of the call, Blair said he would need to consult his advisers. Some time later, around lunchtime, Jonathan Powell, Blair's chief of staff, called and said he was faxing a proposed draft for the letter. Almost immediately the fax in Graham's office clicked into life and the proposed letter rolled off the machine.

I understand that the Independent Parades Commission is about to make public its preliminary view about this summer's parades. These decisions are of course entirely for you and the Commission, and I have no desire to intervene in them in any way. I am, however, concerned that people in Northern Ireland are currently focused on the recent political agreement, and the highly emotive issues it raises on either side, with a view to the forthcoming referendum. This is a difficult and sensitive time for both communities and their political representatives. I have therefore come to the view that it would be preferable to avoid overloading the political system by putting your preliminary view in the public domain now. The recent agreement also creates a new context in which parades can be considered, with a better chance of local accommodations. There may be more goodwill if the commitment to peace is clearly there on both sides in the wake of a successful referendum. In these circumstances, I wonder if there is not a strong case for allowing more time for discussion, in order to see whether there is a better chance of building cross-community support for whatever view you make public. This is clearly very important for the future credibility and effectiveness of the Commission, to which I attach enormous importance. My request to you is therefore that you should reconsider publication of your preliminary view. I stress again that the content of this view is entirely for the Commission to decide, and that I am not in any way trying to override your statutory rights and powers. My concern is simply to ensure that the broader political situation, at an already volatile time, is kept fully in mind.

Graham immediately called Downing Street to say the wording was acceptable and confirmed that he would recommend the commission to postpone the announcement. He then rang each of the commission members, calling them to a special meeting that evening and set off for Leeds–Bradford airport to catch the 4 pm flight to Belfast. The commissioners gathered at Windsor House in the early evening and quickly accepted the prime minister's plea. A number of them were already concerned about the possible impact of the announcement on the political process. The postponement was than announced. Graham reflects: 'I think it was the right thing to do, although we did pay a price because some people argued that, as an independent body, we should not have been open to political intervention. But I think there is a significant difference between us doing it quietly, with a strong suggestion that there had been political intervention, and the way it was done, which was all transparent and above board. What we did was say, yes, there was political intervention, these are the terms that were put to us and this is the basis for our decision.'

In a sign of some turbulence within the commission, Glenn Barr, the former UDA leader, and Tommy Cheevers, spokesman for the Apprentice Boys on the Ormeau Road, announced the very next day that they were resigning. There was inevitably speculation, which he vigorously denied, that Barr was going because he opposed the likely indication that the Drumcree march was to be banned. Both refused to specify precisely why they were going but stated they had no difficulties with the Commission and called for all sections of the community to lend it the support it undeniably deserves.

In the event the Belfast Agreement was comfortably approved. Four out of five voters in Northern Ireland, the highest turnout ever, voted in favour by a margin of 676,966 (71.1 per cent) to 74,879 (28.9 per cent). In the Irish Republic, a simultaneous referendum on the agreement and on changes to articles 2 and 3 of the Constitution, removing the territorial claim over Northern Ireland, prompted a 56 per cent turnout and overwhelming approval by 1,442,583 (94.4 per cent) of voters. 'No' votes totalled 85,174 (5.6 per cent). With one poll out of the way, attention quickly turned to the election of members to the new Assembly to sit at Stormont. After voting took place on 25 June, Trimble's Ulster Unionists won 28 seats, becoming the largest party. The SDLP won 24; the DUP 20; Sinn Fein eighteen; Alliance six; the United Kingdom Unionist Party (UKUP) five; the Progressive Unionist Party (PUP) two; three anti-Agreement Unionists were elected and two members of the Northern Ireland Women's Coalition. However, Trimble's position remained a highly vulnerable one. Apart from the DUP, UKUP and the three 'No' members, a considerable number of his own Assembly members were also opposed to or doubtful about the merits of the Agreement. The last votes were counted at 6 pm on Saturday 27 June and the Assembly was due to hold its inaugural meeting the following Wednesday, 1 July.

On the Monday, the commission, in line with its legal obligation to give five working days' notice, published its formal determination banning the 1998 Drumcree church parade from returning along the Garvaghy Road the following Sunday, 5 July, and outlining the reasons why. The lengthy determination stated:

> The following is the decision of the Parades Commission in relation to the Portadown District LOL No 1 due to take place on July 5 1998. Section 8 (1) of the Public Processions (Northern Ireland) Act 1998 provides that: The Commission may issue a determination in respect of a proposed public procession imposing on the persons organising or taking part in it such conditions as the Commission considers necessary.
>
> We have noted the details provided on the Form 11/1 dated April 1 1998 about the parade proposed by Portadown District LOL No 1 in Portadown on July 5 1998.
>
> We have considered the need to issue a determination as outlined above, against the factors described in our Guidelines document.
>
> Decision
> The Commission's determination is that the proposed July 5 1998 Portadown District LOL No 1 parade is prohibited from entering that part of the notified parade route between the junction of High Street and Woodhouse Street and the junction of Obins Street and Charles Street, or any part of that route.

The parade shall process from its point of departure at Carleton Street into Church Street, Market Street, and High Street to the West Street and into Charles Street. It shall then process along Charles Street to the Dungannon Road–Moy Road roundabout, along the Dungannon Road to the Rector's Turn, Drumcree Road to Drumcree Church.

The parade is also prohibited from proceeding beyond Drumcree Parish Church, Drumcree Road, or entering that part of the notified route which includes the entire length of the Garvaghy Road including Parkmount and Victoria Terrace.

In addition, the following conditions are imposed on the proposed Portadown District LOL No 1 on July 5 1998:

When the procession is in progress there are no undue stoppages or delays.

The organisers shall arrange for the presence of an adequate number of stewards to ensure that all parade participants act in an orderly manner.

The organisers shall ensure that only the four notified bands, namely Edgarstown Accordion Band, Pride of the Birches Band, Star of David Accordion Band and Mavemacullen Accordion Band, shall accompany the procession.

The organisers shall ensure that the procession returns from Drumcree Parish Church following the outward route in compliance with the conditions outlined above, or disperses after the church service at Drumcree Parish Church.

The organisers shall ensure that these conditions are brought to the attention of all participants at the assembly point.

The organisers shall ensure that all directions by police in relation to the parade are promptly obeyed.

Unlike the other locations on which we have expressed a broad view on parades, we are not considering the whole range of Loyal Order parades in the Portadown area, but rather one highly significant parade: the annual July Drumcree Church parade.

We use the term 'significant' advisedly: the sheer scale of the conflict surrounding the dispute over the return route from Drumcree Church along the Garvaghy Road in previous years and the depth of emotion it provoked was the primary motivation for the Government to set up the North Review Team, on whose recommendations the Parades Commission was established.

We have heard references throughout the many locations of our evidence-gathering to the importance of this parade in terms of its impact on disputes in other areas.

We have also heard that the 1996 stand-off at Drumcree was the event which spawned antagonism towards loyalist parades in many locations throughout Northern Ireland.

Given the historic pattern of disputes over parades in Portadown, the significance of the area in relation to the genesis of Orangeism and the erosion of elements of traditional routes as a result of past disputes over parades, its status at the pinnacle of a hierarchy of contentious locations is hardly surprising.

This is further exacerbated by divisions within the town itself, where the nationalist residents of the housing estates along the Garvaghy Road suffer from considerable social deprivation.

Their clear perception is that they do not enjoy equal status with their Protestant counterparts. As our earlier analysis of the evidence suggests, recent experience of the parade itself (its numbers, the manner in which it has been conducted and its duration) is not the main source of antagonism towards it. Rather, it is the context in which it occurs that generates resentment. This is characterised by the apparent assumption that it should take place without any reference to or recognition of the feelings of the local nationalist community. In Portadown, there is deep resentment between the two communities. That resentment seems to us to have deeper roots in much wider issues. Such issues include the apparent disparity between the socioeconomic status of Protestants and Catholics in the area; and relate to events, such as the bombing of Portadown town centre in 1993, the murders of taxi driver Michael McGoldrick in 1996, and of Robert Hamill in Portadown town centre last year, and of two policemen in Lurgan last June, all of which have exacerbated tensions between the communities; and to the manner of the apparent triumphalist display by Unionist politicians which negated the benefits of the agreement brokered in 1995.

The murder of Billy Wright in December 1997 and subsequent retaliatory murders, the bombing of Portadown town centre on February 23, 1998, and the murder of Adrian Lamph can only have further deepened divisions. Those deepened divisions were clearly evident in the conflict surrounding the Junior Orange Order parade along a small part of the Garvaghy Road earlier this year.

All of this militates against the creation of a climate for conciliation and is certainly not a scenario in which we would envisage the prospect of any form of accommodation between the people concerned in the short term. This leaves us with the invidious task of making a decision which does not hinge purely on the factors of threat of disorder and serious disruption as did those decisions taken in the past. More significantly, it turns on the extent of the impact of allowing a parade to return or, alternatively, preventing it from returning along the Garvaghy Road on what is already the most hostile of community relationships.

Clearly, while both parties maintain their current stance, either course of action will result in a downturn in relationships which we fear might be manifested in physical violence. In reaching our decision, we have focused on what we describe in our Guidelines document as the 'Broader Context'. In particular we refer to: 'Where there has been a year on year history of conflict surrounding the parade, the Commission will take into account the demonstrable impact of decisions taken regarding that parade in previous years, not only on the immediate community but on the wider Northern Ireland community.'

We do not underestimate the impact on the Protestant community, particularly in Portadown, of a decision which would effectively prevent the parade from proceeding back along its traditional route down the Garvaghy Road. The strength of feeling within that community and the wider Protestant community was patently clear in the 1995 and 1996 standoffs. An accommodation was achieved in 1995 albeit that it was, in the eyes of nationalists, subsequently undermined by what took place immediately afterwards. Those events, and the circumstances in which the parades have taken place in the two successive years have thrown all sections of the community in Northern Ireland into turmoil and have left no individual untouched. Given the absence of any positive movement towards accommodation, we cannot see at this stage how a parade could proceed again this year down the Garvaghy Road without having a serious adverse impact on community relationships, both locally and more widely across Northern Ireland. We stress that we have not reached this decision lightly and that it does not imply an erosion of the rights of Orangemen in Portadown. It is taken in anticipation of the cumulative adverse effect on the nationalist community, both in Portadown and across Northern Ireland as a whole, of successive parades proceeding in the fact of such total opposition.

We would also want to stress that our decision relates to 1998 alone. There are many elements of the Drumcree church parade which are not at odds with most of the factors in our Guidelines. For example, it is a church parade, it has been demonstrated that it can take place in an orderly fashion, and the Garvaghy Road is an arterial route. However, we see the need to break the cycle in 1998. The opportunity provided by such a break should be seized by political, community and religious leaders to demonstrate greater responsibility and to make strident efforts to bridge the chasm between both sides of the community, so laying the foundations for a more tolerant atmosphere in the future.

Although they were not detailed in the determination, there had, in fact, been many attempts to bridge the chasm. The Commission had its own mediators at work and the church leaders, despite having their fingers burned so badly in 1996, were still highly active. Archbishop Eames flicks through the pages of his diary listing meetings with the chief constable, the Parades Commission, Secretary of State, church colleagues and so on. 'There's hardly a week passes in the year that there isn't at least some aspect of Drumcree on my desk.' It also brings him a heavy postbag, not all of it flattering. ' "Dear Mr Eames". As soon as I get a "Mr Eames" letter, I know what's coming.' Politicians on all sides were also active and there had been some unpublicised, surprising get-togethers and initiatives designed to break the deadlock ever since the events of 1996. In November that year, for instance, while emotions were still running high, Graham Montgomery, a cerebral grammar school teacher, who was a member of the Order's education committee, attended a conference about marching, one of a series funded by the Craigavon Council which were held in the community centre in the Garvaghy Road area. In a wide ranging and passionate address he explained the history of the Order, what it stood for and why it felt so strongly about the current situation that had developed, and concluded: 'Orangemen do not wish to encourage fear and tension, we do not want to alienate, we do not want to entrench sectarianism in an already deeply divided society. You and I have to share this town, this county, this country and indeed Orangeism is an island phenomenon. We have to share this island. Life is short and sacred and precious and it doesn't and should not be squandered in conflict. The parades can be used as an open window of opportunity for the future or they can become a slammed door, closing us in with the past and all its mysteries. The mistakes of the past must be the lessons for the future not merely its grievances. Have we the courage to rise to the challenge? I used the word "we". Have we the courage to rise to the challenge, have we the confidence in our own tradition and the tolerance for the traditions for others to create for ourselves and our descendants a fairer, more just society than the one we had delivered to us? We reject the ghetto system, we fear the day when culture will be confined to an area where it is completely acceptable, where it can be completely understood. We reject and we fear the development of a system of cultural apartheid in this country. Protestants keep out, Catholics keep out, no one would suggest that race relations in South Africa are stronger today because they had a system of racial apartheid, and the challenge to us is to ask ourselves, will community relations in this country be stronger if we have cultural apartheid? Orangemen stand resolved not to fail in the challenge of the future, we have a culture to share a society to build and to improve. We trust that we will not be left to stand alone.'

After the speech Montgomery was very warmly applauded, and when the conference ended he talked informally to McKenna and other members of the audience and residents' groups over tea and coffee. He had been nervous about accepting the invitation in the first place but far more about the possible reaction from hardline Loyalists than the residents. As going into direct contact with the residents in what was considered to be enemy territory was such a huge personal risk, he had prepared the ground carefully. Portadown District had been told what was happening, and on the morning of the conference Denis Watson arrived at his house and spent an hour going through Montgomery's speech with him. Watson told him he fully supported what he was doing and suggested some alterations to the speech. As far as Montgomery was concerned, while he was speaking in a personal capacity, he was indirectly conveying a message from the county and district. The risk backfired on him. Soon afterwards, he was dismayed to read newspaper reports that he had engaged in a face-to-face meeting with McKenna on behalf of Portadown District, which then tried to distance itself, saying it had not approved his participation.

Montgomery now feels that someone who attended the conference tried to use him to damage the Order. His conversation with McKenna after the speech was purely polite and personal, observing the niceties. The fallout from the episode, however, served to discourage Orange liberals like Montgomery from making any further forays onto the middle ground. It made it all the more difficult to puncture the uncompromising environment which inhibited, and would continue to inhibit, all efforts to bring about the dialogue between the two sides in Portadown which was the essential prerequisite to a solution. Watson and Bingham themselves refused to be deterred by the impenetrable internal politics of Carleton Street, where the confusing machinations of the Portadown 'politburo' over who was in and who was out, and what was policy and what was not, by comparison conferred on the 'Kremlinology' of the Cold War period the status of an exact science. Some months later, in March 1997,

Bingham and Watson visited Brid Rodgers' house in Lurgan for a discussion with her and Sean McKavanagh, an SDLP member of Craigavon Council. The encounter produced nothing of lasting substance but, in the longer term, may have contributed a measure of mutual understanding which could ultimately assist in permanent resolution of the conflict.

Throughout 1997, and into 1998, as any initiatives for compromise either foundered or were crushed, Joel Patton and his men continued to harry the leadership of the Order at every opportunity. When the Belfast Agreement was finalised, Patton thought his call to arms had finally come. With the Orange Order and the Unionist community convulsed by it, he saw his radical group and tactics as being at the cutting edge of the protests to bring the Agreement to a swift end. He believed Unionists should refuse to take their seats in the Assembly if the Drumcree parade was stopped. 'We offered the perfect vehicle to stop the Agreement,' he says. 'Tens of thousands of people were supporting the protest anyway, so why not channel the anger and frustration into campaign against the agreement? I voted against the agreement because it was a betrayal of my interests and many others felt the same way. It made perfect sense to us to combine the two issues.' Talks were held with members of the Ulster Unionist Party, the DUP, UK Unionists and other anti-Agreement parties, but Patton found there was no appetite for a militant pan-Unionist front or the rough-house tactics he still favoured to win a lasting victory at Drumcree. Nevertheless he issued another battle-cry for Orangemen to take to the streets on 29 June, after the commission announced that the parade was not going to be allowed down the Garvaghy Road. 'I'm not talking about a token protest. It has to be forceful and it has to be a widespread protest.' Away from the battlefield Patton's stand was costing him dear. Turnover in his market garden business near Dungannon had dropped by half because of a boycott by Catholic and other customers, including Orange members, opposed to his political activities. Earlier in April 1997, his wife, eight months pregnant with their fourth child, was roused by noises in the early hours of one morning. When she went to investigate, she found that flammable liquid had been poured through the letter box of their home but that, fortunately, it had failed to ignite.

Although they did not share his militancy, Patton was far from alone in being dismayed by the Commission decision blocking the homeward route for 1998. Among the most disappointed was Denis Watson, who had defied the advice of his friend Bingham and put himself up for election as an Assembly candidate for the Ulster Unionists, winning a seat in the Upper Bann constituency. He had called on Trimble to delay taking Assembly seats or transacting any business until the commission's decision was reversed, but he was overruled. However, when the Assembly convened on 1 July, after the members were enrolled and other formalities completed, Watson got the chance to make his maiden speech and have his say at the end of an adjournment debate on the topic:

Here is what a resident wrote to the *Portadown Times* on 12 July last [1997]: "When I recall the violence of the past few years I ask myself what has been achieved? Has our community in the Garvaghy Road gained anything? Have we shown people of a different faith that we wish them to continue living in our community without fear?" This is the kind of response we have been getting from people on the road. What has changed since 6 July last year? The Orange Institution made a magnanimous gesture, wrong-footing Sinn Fein-IRA, on 10 July when it re-routed four parades. What recognition did it get? Everybody talked about the moral high ground, but the Government imposed draconian legislation on us. It should not be forgotten that five weeks ago some 160 petrol bombs and six shrapnel bombs were used against junior Orangemen – boys aged between six and eleven peacefully celebrating their culture. And within the last few weeks another sixteen crates of milk bottles have been found. It will hardly surprise anyone to hear that they were not going to be refilled with milk. It seems that some residents of the Garvaghy Road are determined to cause trouble come what may.

As the County Grand Master of Armagh, who four weeks ago had no intention of being involved in politics, I want to say that people should make no mistake about the Portadown brethren. They are prepared to stand one day, 31 days, 365 days, or as long as it takes for their basic civil and religious liberty to be upheld. There were ten parades on that road, nine of which have been given up voluntarily. We have only one parade now, and the brethren are not prepared to be suppressed any further. What is happening is wrong. Orangemen feel that the only cry coming from the road is that there will be no Orange feet on it. Contrary to what some people have been telling Members, work went on behind the scenes last year and this year. Indeed, it continues. I am one of those who travelled to the carpet mills in 1996. One of the things on offer then was recognition of rights of both communities, including the right to hold St Patrick's Day parades. But the Nationalist people of the road did not want to know.

I repeat that accommodation, not segregation, is the way forward. In this era of tolerance and mutual respect I appeal to the residents of Garvaghy Road to show tolerance. Members who have influence in the Nationalist community should use it wisely. Finally, I appeal to the Government to overturn this iniquitous decision.

Trimble, who had earlier been elected first minister designate at that inaugural meeting of the Assembly, had already begun exerting his own pressure to have the determination overturned. He believed there was a good case for convincing the government of the merits of a parade in 1998 because of the contrast between 1996 and 1997. The violence that followed the latter parade, which took place without a stand-off developing, was only a fraction of the violence that had engulfed Northern Ireland the previous year, when the parade had originally been halted. 'It seemed to me that anyone looking at the situation rationally would compare the two years and come to the conclusion that 1997 was the better outcome,' he recalls. On the day the commission announced that the parade was not to be allowed down the Garvaghy Road, Trimble sent an open letter to the Garvaghy Road Residents Coalition. In it he compared the residents' 'distaste' for the march to the early release of paramilitary prisoners, an issue which had caused widespread dismay among his own supporters and Unionists as a whole. He wrote: 'You too, must do your bit in delivering peace. That now requires you to indicate that you will not oppose by physical means the return to central Portadown of the local Orangemen by the Garvaghy Road after their church service at Drumcree church. You know that the church service and the freedom to process on the main highway are important parts of the culture, identity and ethos of the Ulster British people, and respect for such rights is central to the agreement. You may say that this is distasteful to you. But making peace has required many of us to accept things which are distasteful, such as the early release of convicted prisoners.'

Apart from the role he hoped it might immediately play in getting consent for a march, the letter was doubly significant because Trimble had, unwittingly or not, raised the stakes by openly linking the outcome of the Drumcree confrontation to that of the wider political process, a link that would endure and bedevil the situation for years ahead. Up to that point the official line from the government, the police, the Commission and others had been that Drumcree was a parochial difficulty needing to be resolved by local accommodation. Now Drumcree was to join the long litany of grievances spawned by the Belfast Agreement. In his reply to Trimble, McKenna invited the MP to meet the coalition. He said: 'We, like all those others who voted for peace, wish to see that peace delivered.

However, like ourselves, you also have a responsibility in ensuring a peaceful and non-confrontational marching season. We therefore again extend the invitation for you to meet with us.'

Emboldened by the way Blair had been prepared to use his prime ministerial clout against Alistair Graham earlier in the year, Trimble had followed up his letter to McKenna with another approach to Downing Street. During a telephone conversation with Blair he asked him to put pressure on Sinn Fein to use its influence to persuade Brendan McKenna and the residents to agree to a parade. Trimble continued: 'The prime minister told me that Gerry Adams had said the atmosphere would improve if the Orange Order entered direct dialogue with the residents. The clear implication of what Downing Street told me was that if I could get people to talk directly to the residents, Adams would reciprocate by getting agreement for a parade.' Trimble swiftly delegated Graham Montgomery, who had spoken at the conference in the Drumcree community centre, and David Thompson, who although not an Orange member was a confidant of Trimble's and a senior party figure, to represent him at a meeting with McKenna and other coalition members, which was hastily arranged for Friday 3 July, some 48 hours in advance of the annual parade, at the Parochial House in Obins Street.

While the two Orange delegates arrived at the agreed time, they had to wait over an hour for the residents to show. When they did, a proposition was put forward for a parade on the following Sunday to be immediately followed the next day by the inaugural meeting of a civic forum where local social and economic issues could be handled by the entire spectrum of local community leaders working together. The idea had originally come from Bingham, who had already canvassed its feasibility with Trimble and the British government. Montgomery recalls: 'It was obvious to us that this frightened the Garvaghy Road Residents Coalition and after a lot of talking McKenna said that there was no way they could guarantee there would be no violence at such meetings, because of past hurt and so on.' The encounter ended inconclusively and the two Orangemen travelled back to Belfast to report to Trimble at the party headquarters in Glengall Street. During these discussions a fax arrived from the Irish government, who, in the surge of effort to make the Belfast Agreement stick, had their own people on the ground in Portadown encouraging the residents to find a compromise. The fax contained nothing new. 'In reality it was our own offer faxed back to us as a starting point,' says Montgomery. The Orange/Unionist discussions later reconvened in Trimble's office at Stormont, where Watson and Bingham were also present. Some senior Nationalist politicians came in. 'To my surprise the atmosphere was good between them all, although there was tension about the parade,' Montgomery recalls. 'We reported what we had done and then were informed by phone that there were representatives from Dublin on the way up to see the residents.'

After these meetings, during which neither side had really moved from its well-established position, Trimble contacted Downing Street again to say there had been contact and they must now push for the promised response from Adams. Trimble recalls: 'There was no response. That was the first time, but certainly not the only time, when we realised that the word of Gerry Adams doesn't really mean very much.' What Trimble singularly failed to understand was that a march was not in the gift of either Adams or McKenna. As Ignatius Fox and others had found in 1996, any deal would have to be a community decision.

Earlier in the week, on 29 June, the residents' leaders had gathered in Drumcree community centre to wait for the determination from the Parades Commission, which was to be delivered to them by courier. As McKenna and Donna Griffin, a coalition member, were still reading it in one room, a loud cheer went up from another room where residents listening to the radio heard Alistair Graham announcing the decision on a news bulletin. They were delighted but wary. After their experiences of the three previous years, nothing was taken for granted, so they decided against dismantling a communications room they had set up in the centre, containing a computer, telephones, fax machine, television and radio. Fearful that the decision could still be reversed by the police or government, they also continued to make arrangements to accommodate more than 80 international observers, from the United States, Canada and South Africa as well as the Irish Republic. They stayed in the homes of local people, some of whom also had advance 'reservations' from visiting journalists.

Trimble's initiative was based on the view, widely held in Orange and Unionist circles, that the residents' groups in different localities were one and the same body, all controlled and manipulated by the hidden hand of Adams and the IRA. No matter how often Unionists and the Orange Order repeated what Adams had said at the Athboy conference to convince themselves that the opposition to their marches was merely an IRA post-ceasefire tactic, it would not change the uncomfortable political reality: however much they wanted to manipulate the groups and exploit the issue, Sinn Fein-IRA was only one element within the Catholic community opposed to contentious marches. As Cardinal Daly confirmed about the events of 1996, the opposition was not confined to those of a Republican disposition. Churchmen like himself and other Catholic leaders and politicians, who had courageously condemned the IRA's violent excesses over the years and had little sympathy for Sinn Fein, wanted an end to unwelcome parades. The episode also illustrated the limits of Sinn Fein's influence on McKenna, despite his IRA past. Republicans see him as a very stubborn and strong-willed person. 'He is very determined. If he does not want to be moved you will not move him. He will ask for advice and talk about issues, but he is his own person and does not like being told what to do,' says one senior figure. (At this time, McKenna became the subject of a whispering campaign suggesting that he had, in fact, gone over to the emerging dissident Republican cause opposed to the Belfast Agreement, and a well-placed Loyalist politician became aware of a serious threat to McKenna's life from mainstream Loyalist terrorists. He received assurances that the rumours were untrue and made sure this was made known to McKenna's potential killers. A year later the government, grudgingly it must be said, admitted McKenna to the Key Person Protection Scheme, which provides appropriate security measures at public expense to people considered by the police to be at risk.)

However, where Trimble's reasoning was more seriously flawed was in his calculation that, as in 1997, a controlled march was, in Flanagan's earlier description, 'the least worst option' because it would cause less violence. With the Labour government committed to a more structured and democratic way to resolve the problem, through the various means open to the newly created Parades Commission, the 'who can wave the bigger stick' argument was never going to succeed. 'From that point on it was clear there was never going to be a march again. It was going to be difficult. It would take time but it had to be done. Things had irrevocably changed after the Agreement,' one senior British source recalls.

This very point was underlined by Blair himself, who was sufficiently concerned by the gravity of the crisis, to fly to Belfast on the Thursday in yet another eleventh-hour bid to break the enduring impasse. Although it was not fully evident at that time, Blair was at loggerheads with Mowlam because she was resisting a move back to London as minister of health. A major reason for the transfer was that while Mowlam was hailed as a heroine by the people on the streets, her credibility with many influential political and community leaders had been heavily impaired. Her relations with many of her own officials and those from Downing Street, whom she openly disdained, were so bad that she had been effectively bypassed in the final crucial stages of the Good Friday negotiations. The lines she had, in opposition, so carefully cultivated to both sides in the parades dispute had been severed. The residents never forgave her for failing to

keep her promise to come back and tell them what was going to happen
when the march was forced through the previous year. Since then there
had been only one conversation with McKenna, an unusually
acrimonious public exchange live on *Talk Back*, the current affairs
programme on BBC Radio Ulster. Sitting in the community centre two
weeks after the parade, McKenna heard Mowlam being interviewed. The
producers at Broadcasting House in Belfast could not believe their luck
when McKenna rang and said he wanted to talk to the Secretary of State.
In the fiery exchange that followed, he accused her of breaking her word
to the residents. When the programme went off air, a furious Mowlam
accused the producers of setting her up and stormed out.

Mowlam's relations with Watson and Bingham were no better. After
the commission's determination met with such a hostile reaction,
Mowlam called Bingham and Watson to another meeting. Despite the bad
taste left by their earlier encounters, which totally discredited her in their
eyes, they agreed to go. It proved to be another fruitless encounter and
they told her there was no point in any further contact. Despite this, she
later called Bingham at home in his manse in Pomeroy. When he refused
to speak to her, she called back again later that evening and reminded him
that she was the secretary of state. Unimpressed, Bingham again declined
to talk to her and warned he would complain to Downing Street if she
called again. A short time later she did ring again and Bingham
immediately called Jonathan Powell and said that he was being harassed.
He never heard from Mowlam again.

As the prime minister's chief of staff, Powell, a high-flying diplomat
whose elder brother Charles had performed a similar role for Margaret
Thatcher when she was prime minister, was now set to play a central role
as Blair's designated envoy in trying to settle the Drumcree dispute. He
travelled to Belfast with Blair, and was at a meeting in Stormont soon
after their arrival when Blair urged Gerry Adams and Martin McGuinness
of Sinn Fein to try to persuade the residents to allow the parade 'in the
interests of the wider community', a subtle reworking of Trimble's
analysis of the violence. Speaking after the meeting, Gerry Adams, the
Sinn Fein president, alluded to the pressure that had been applied. He
said: 'This can only be done by direct dialogue between those who wish
to march into that area and the people who live there. None of this
nonsense about representation, or who is involved or anything, is at all of
any substance. If the Orange want to go down Garvaghy Road they are
compelled to go and talk to the people of that area. Secondly, I want to
stress that once again I and Sinn Fein will play no part in pressurising the
people of Garvaghy. This is an issue of equality. It is of crucial

importance especially in this new era that those people have a sense of their worth. They are ratepayers, they are taxpayers and every democrat has to uphold their rights.' Dara O'Hagan, the newly elected Assembly member, who was at the meeting, recalls: 'Our position was very clear. We were not going to make any deal on this because it was not up to us, it was up to the community. It is absolutely vital that this is resolved by the local community. Any deal made behind their backs is not going to last so there wouldn't be any point in doing that.'

The previous night, Loyalists had launched a wave of ten arson attacks, destroying or damaging ten Catholic churches. When he heard what had happened, the prime minister decided to visit one of the scenes to show his sympathy. At St James's church in Crumlin, he said, 'This is the past in Northern Ireland and we are trying to give people a future.' At the end of a long day, during which he refused to interfere with the commission's decision, there was still no breakthrough. Even the intervention of President Clinton, who spoke to the various leaders by telephone during a visit to Hong Kong, failed to help and another round of confrontation became inevitable.

The next evening, hundreds of residents attended a public meeting in St Mary's Hall in Obins Street. It had been called to seek endorsement for a negotiating position drawn up by the Coalition leaders and to reassure people there would be no deal without their agreement. Dara O'Hagan and Brid Rodgers were both asked to attend to answer questions directly. There were some angry comments from people in the packed hall, but the audience accepted the assurances that no deal would be done behind their backs. More importantly, they also endorsed five proposals the coalition wanted to put on the table for discussion if and when talks were convened by the government or any other party, and if there was engagement with the Order. These proposals were:

> 1: Nationalists would not now or in the future interfere with the Orange Order's right to parade along Corcrain and the Dungannon roads to Drumcree or to hold its service at Drumcree. (The outward route from Carleton Street to the church).
> 2: That the Orange Order should go to Drumcree and attend the service and either return to Carleton Street via the alternative route or disperse.
> 3: That we would acknowledge such a move by the Orange Order as a reciprocation of the gesture we had made in 1995 when a march did get down the road.
> 4a: A forum should be established, on an all-inclusive basis, involving all interested parties, including both governments, to discuss and seek

an agreed resolution of problems such as future arrangements for marches, measures to reduce sectarian tension and improve community relations in the town, and reduce the marginalisation and exclusion of the town's Catholic community and provide equality of access to employment to an educational facility in the town centre and equality of access and provision of commercial and other social activities.

4b: Direct dialogue will take place as soon as possible between all parties concerned on an all-inclusive basis. That this direct dialogue will be on the basis of seeking a resolution to all the social political and economic difficulties in Portadown within a five year time frame.

5: If all the above things are to happen, then the Garvaghy Road Resident's Coalition would encourage the community to explore the possibility of an Orange presence on the Garvaghy Road in the future.

Speaking afterwards, McKenna said the coalition would be prepared to consider a parade the following year if the Order were to call off the protest and accept that there would not be a parade in 1998. The Orange Order promptly dismissed the proposals as a stunt and rejected them, but they were to be of lasting significance and would form the bedrock of the residents' position in all future negotiations. The inclusion of social and economic issues in the 'shopping list' reflected their high priority for the residents, who regarded the town centre, where all major amenities were located, as hostile Loyalist territory.

At the same time that evening as the residents were holding their meeting, more soldiers were flying and sailing into Northern Ireland. A long convoy of armoured Saxons, packed with troops and their equipment, had earlier come off the Liverpool ferry and travelled from Belfast to Mahon Barracks. Heavy military engineering equipment and vehicles had also been shipped in and formed up in convoys at Mahon and Massereene Barracks in Antrim. In the preceding weeks thousands of RUC officers had been put through rigorous public order training. At the Sprucefield complex outside Belfast, in highly realistic training sessions, they had learned how to cope with petrol bombs thrown by the instructors, how to use riot shields to protect themselves and how to fire plastic baton rounds to new stricter guidelines. New techniques had been taught to lift protestors from roadways, using a number of pressure points on the body to prevent people from resisting and struggling. Also based on the lessons learned from earlier Drumcrees, many of the Mobile Support Units had been equipped with state-of-the-art flameproof overalls, footwear and balaclavas and orders were placed to have every officer better protected as soon as possible.

This time the police and Army were determined that if they were ordered to hold the march they would do so effectively and not have to back down after a few days because of collateral violence in Portadown and elsewhere. Over the winter, they had made detailed preparations. Because of concerns about the durability of the bridge below the church, the halting point where the annual confrontations had become focused, army engineers had made a covert visit to survey it and take measurements. Over the winter months it had been quietly rebuilt and strengthened to their detailed specifications by contractors. At their Antrim barracks the same soldiers, from 25 Engineer Regiment, whose main roles are force protection, search, construction and demolition operations for the Army in Northern Ireland, were improvising Crowd Control Obstacles, pieces of equipment to slot onto the bridge. With the Army's love of acronyms, they were swiftly called CCOs. Using two international standard freight containers, loaded with heavy concrete blocks, the aim was to use two transporters to drop the strong obstacles, designed to withstand crowd surges and prevent any repetition of the plans to use an excavator or slurry tanker to break through on the bridge and attack the security forces.

As a result of their experience of three previous Drumcrees, and the thorough debriefings that had taken place afterwards, police and army contingency planning had become ever more detailed. Each year the Army started in March, and the RUC in May, to muster the necessary personnel and ordering in equipment and supplies. This included contacting the hospitals, ambulance and fire service to put complementary arrangements in place for dealing with large-scale casualties. It is so thorough that different routes, hospitals and entrances are detailed for security force and civilian casualties to prevent clashes at the hospitals. The main focus is on the local Craigavon hospital and secondarily on the Musgrave military wing in Belfast which has facilities to receive casualties by helicopter. Keeping main and access roads, designated 'white routes', open also forms part of the plan and police and army personnel are earmarked for key points like the roundabouts at Corcrain and the footbridge at Edgarstown, where protestors have stood on the bridge and thrown stones at passing traffic. At Drumcree itself, detailed drawings and maps are prepared showing where the fortifications are to be placed and the position each MSU and army unit is to hold. Each year a number of trees and large shrubs have been trimmed or removed to provide unobstructed views. The 1998 plans included instructions for MSUs to bring a supply of plastic rubbish bags with them, to avoid littering the fields where they were posted, and advised that ear-plugs would be available for units sleeping at Mahon Barracks. The previous year there had been complaints that people could not sleep when on stand-down because of the incessant noise from the military helicopters coming and going on an almost constant basis. In even more attention to detail, the camp supermarket had been ordered to open on a flexible basis and to ensure that there were extra supplies of Sunday newspapers for the huge influx of personnel.

Earlier in the week, the Orange Order had pledged to march the 'traditional' route despite the ruling from the Parades Commission. If the march was halted, it said, the Order would stand its ground for as long as it would take to complete it. On 2 July, the day before Blair arrived, the Grand Orange Lodge of Ireland issued an open letter to the people of Northern Ireland setting out its view of the situation:

> Dear Fellow Citizens. I am sure, in common with members of the Orange Institution, you are concerned about events over the coming days in respect of traditional Orange parades. In order to assist understanding of our historic culture and noble traditions we wish to outline certain facts which are relevant to the situation. The disputed parades occur along main arterial roads which are shared by all communities. All are traditional routes, none have been concocted or organised to cause offence. We are not engaged in coat trailing or triumphalism. We simply want to celebrate our culture and identity peacefully and with dignity. We recognise that along with the right to parade comes responsibility, which we have exercised by talking to residents' groups, local politicians, clergy from all denominations and other interested parties. We have taken on board the fears and concerns of the many people we have spoken to. This has resulted in the restricted playing of music and the improved marshalling of our parades. However, in all conscience we cannot talk to those groups influenced by republican terrorists whose purpose is to deny our civil rights. The Orange Institution also does not talk to the Parades Commission, because it is a discredited Government quango whose remit and actions are clearly in violation of democracy, justice and human rights. Traditional Loyal Order parades are attacked as part of the republican strategy to remove the British presence from Northern Ireland. All things British are being opposed on three fronts: military, political and cultural, the latter being the excuse to invest time and effort into planning and creating unnecessary opposition to traditional Orange parades. The restricting of loyal order parades along main roads creates cultural apartheid, where one community has a veto on

another community's expression of identity and heritage. Banning and rerouting Orange Parades from shared roads and village main streets will only lead to further segregation of our respective communities. This is not the way to build a future where there is mutual respect and tolerance. Ethnic segregation is morally wrong. It did not work in South Africa and the United States. It must not be allowed to work in Northern Ireland. In a democratic, divided society accommodation is the only way to build a future where people of differing traditions can peacefully co-exist. Toleration needs to be the approach when matters of tradition and heritage are expressed. While much of gaelic and nationalist culture is politicised, the unionist community does not go out of its way to be offended or to be obstructive. We may not identify with gaelic and nationalist culture, but we do not attempt to censure it. All we ask for is the same in return for our Protestant heritage and unionist identity. We would especially appeal to all free-thinking people in the nationalist community to consider the parading issue carefully. Are your views asked on toleration and mutual respect? Have you thought about the time it takes a parade to pass along these so called contentious routes, and the changes which parades organisers have made? Or are your views based on bigotry and an anti-British mindset in which there is no place for those from the unionist tradition? What we celebrate through our traditional parades is civil and religious liberty for all; not just for Protestants, not just for dissenters. But civil rights for all, regardless of race, creed, denomination, or gender, and special privileges for none.

[The letter ended as follows] 'NOTICE: We would respectfully request that prayers for peace and toleration take place in every Church this coming Sunday and would advise those who wish to join members of the Orange Institution in prayer that selected Orange Halls will be open this Saturday (4th July) for a time of meditation. Please contact local Orange Order officials for details.

With people like Archbishop Eames and others still making frantic efforts to head off Drumcree Four, in the early hours of Saturday 4 July, in support of the legally binding decision from the Parades Commission, 25 Engineering Regiment were at the forefront when one of the biggest security operations for years moved off the start line and swung into action. The CCOs were placed on the stone walled bridge and surrounded with razor wire and sheeting to make them secure. Closed-circuit televisions were concealed so that the police operations room back at Mahon could keep a close eye on the road leading up to the church.

Through the fields on either side the Army ploughed a strip of grass into soil, widened a small stream into a moat fourteen feet wide and constructed thousands of yards of parallel razor wire entanglements to hold back the anticipated crowds. Their plans to flood the moat were however scaled down when they found that draining water from Portadown's mains nearby reduced pressure in the taps elsewhere in the town to a trickle. As the confrontation went on, they solved the problem by using helicopters under-slung with large buckets to ferry large amounts of water from nearby Lough Neagh.

Jonathan Powell, who had stayed behind at Hillsborough, was again talking to McKenna and his team during the day, but without much hope of winning any concession. During the day Denis Watson went out to Drumcree to see what was evolving and was shocked by the extent of the fortifications. He had been to France the previous year to take part in a remembrance service at the site of the Battle of the Somme, and had visited the interpretative centre in Conlig, County Down, which recreates the conditions of the battle. 'It was like stepping back in time on to a First World War battlefield. I couldn't believe what I saw,' he remembers. That Saturday, as the Reverend Pickering worked on his sermon for the next day in his book-lined study in the Rectory, he watched from his window in disbelief and dismay as the Army dug the trenches and erected the wire fencing. He wrote: 'I never thought I would see the like of what I see at Drumcree this morning. And to think that the barbed wire fence is a symbol, as it is, of Northern Ireland, makes me very sad. It is a symbol of the divisions in our country. To think how these divisions have been present for nearly 30 years is quite depressing.'

As Drumcree Sunday dawned yet again there was dread and apprehension in the air all over Northern Ireland, not just in Portadown, where hundreds of police and soldiers had spent the night deployed along what was already being called the 'Maginot line'. From early morning, in now well-practised rituals on both sides, even greater numbers of the police and Army moved into their positions soon after first light and by breakfast time the Orangemen and their supporters began to gather outside the Orange Hall in Carleton Street. The buzz of thousands of conversations was counterpointed by the arrival of the accordion bands who would accompany the main march. Before the Orangemen left for Drumcree, a prayer service was conducted by a lay pastor. Speaking though a loudhailer, he asked the Lord to ensure that the country might rise from the ashes, that He would be with the Brethren as they went out to Drumcree and on their return, that He would keep each one of them safe and that nothing would be done that would dishonour the Lord's name 'for it is in Your precious name that we ask it all.' Harold Gracey then appeared at a first-floor window of the building, peering over a window-box of colourful summer flowers, and announced they would soon be going out to Drumcree and 'can I say we will be staying as long as it takes.' He was followed by another clergyman calling for the blessing of the Lord on the march and the brethren.

In time-honoured tradition the parade moved off soon after 10.30 on its outward route, accompanied by an escort of photographers and camera crews. There were some youths in the ranks, with fashionably close-cropped hair, but the vast majority of the marchers were middle-aged or older men. The only women on parade were in the bands. The outward procession was uneventful, as was the service. During the opening hymn, a colour party marched up the centre aisle of the church and presented two rolled flags to the Rector. He took them and laid them against the walls. A ruddy-faced man with spectacles, clad in a suit and Orange sash, then spiritedly sang a highly appropriate solo: 'I do not know what lies ahead'. Later Pickering delivered his prepared sermon before the service concluded with the singing of the national anthem. Afterwards the leaders of Portadown District formed up outside the church, smoothed down their Sunday-best suits, donned their bowlers and white gloves, draped their tightly rolled umbrellas over their forearms and hoisted their swords and standards. At the command 'quick march' there were was a loud burst of applause, and to the pace of a drumbeat they set off to march the short distance down the hill to where the army had positioned the CCOs to halt them.

It was just short of 1 pm when they reached that point and stopped. As an accordion band played softly, one of the Orangemen called: 'Would the senior officer in control please present himself at the barrier.' Harold Gracey, bemused and nervously licking his lips, paced from side to side, looking for some sign of movement. 'Brethren, it doesn't appear as if there's a senior officer about,' he said before turning round away from the barrier to address his Orange colleagues and the cameras. 'I want to say to Her Majesty's government this is a total disgrace, stopping British subjects from walking the Queen's highway with barbed wire and whatever. I can assure Her Majesty's government, and especially the Secretary of State, that we will be staying here until such times as we are allowed our legitimate right to walk our roads. We are taxpayers, British subjects and loyal to the Crown and we'll be here until such time as we can walk our road into Portadown.' At the command 'about turn' the marching party wheeled round and retraced its steps back up the road to the church, where they were addressed by Grand Master Robert Saulters.

The fourth successive confrontation at Drumcree had begun but on that balmy summer Sunday, nobody knew that this time it was going to last for more than 1000 days. Jeffrey Donaldson, one of the leading opponents of the Belfast Agreement, says: 'The nature of the protest changed after the Agreement and referendum. Drumcree became not just symbolic of a stand for Protestant civil rights but a stand, also, against the ideals under-pinning the agreement, including the participation of Sinn Fein-IRA in government. It was regarded by many Orangemen as the last stand. That made it very difficult for David Trimble as the local MP and first minister in a government that included Republicans. While he was still strongly supportive of Portadown district, he came to symbolise much of what supporters of the protest opposed.'

Trimble's emissary, Montgomery, shared the opprobrium. He had missed the opening events because he was taking part in a radio discussion in Belfast at the same time, putting the Order's case. When he reached the hill at Drumcree, he was quickly surrounded by a group of about 40 very hostile people, some wearing Orange sashes. Prominent among them was Joel Patton, who told him he was 'as welcome as Gerry Adams' and said for his own safety that he should leave the hill. Montgomery recalls: 'He accused me of treachery for partaking in the conference the year before, which had been supported by LOL 1, and claimed that it was because of me that they were not down the road. From behind me a few men tried to grab me but couldn't reach – there were two friends in the way. I was then abused for being a Trimble man and pro-Agreement. Patton told me in front of the whole group that they were going to bring Ulster to its knees to get the parade down the road, then there would be no agreement left and what would I be doing then. I told him I would be doing what I had been doing that morning, defending the rights of LOL 1 to parade along the road as it had always done. At this point things looked ugly so I made to leave the hill. The three of us walked up the hill being followed and shouted at by those people. I was put into the back of a car and driven home.' (Patton's threat proved to be as empty as his commitment. A few weeks later, the *Sunday World* published a photograph of him enjoying a dip in the sea in Ibiza, while Portadown District were continuing the stand-off. Patton accused the Northern Ireland Office and MI5 of leaking the photograph to discredit him.)

Once again Orange supporters set up tents and catering facilities in the fields by Drumcree church and settled down for what they felt might be a long stay. Once more, too, protests and serious rioting erupted there, spread throughout Northern Ireland and continued overnight. This time the security forces were not so vulnerable. One of the factors taken into account in the design and alignment of the 'Maginot line' had been to create some distance between themselves and the protestors. This also served to prevent individual police officers being identified and singled out for abuse and intimidation as they had been in 1996. Flanagan recalls watching one demonstrator try to breach the lines. 'I remember a young soldier standing there with me and watching this boy weaving his way along. It took him about half an hour. The soldier, who was a plastic baton round gunner, kept saying, should we not shoot, he's coming across. I said, hold on, that's the whole purpose of these things. When we want to arrest him, he's knackered by the time he reaches us.'

Within the first 48 hours of the protest the RUC had recorded 384 acts of public disorder, including a blast bomb attack on the home of a policeman and multiple hijackings, arson attacks, lootings and shootings. By 6 am on 7 July the number of incidents exceeded 1000 and by the time a delegation of Orange leaders flew out to London to meet the prime minister, on 9 July, 1681 had been logged: 50 police officers had been injured; 501 attacks on the security forces had taken place including fourteen shootings and 29 blast bombings; there had been 509 petrol bombings; 154 hijackings; 317 vehicles damaged, and 86 houses and 114 other buildings attacked. Many police families had also been attacked and forced to flee their homes. The chief constable said, 'We had all hoped that the scenes which we witnessed these last nights had been consigned to the past. There are legitimate ways for people to protest. The RUC, along with all reasonable people, would like to see this done in a peaceful and lawful way. There are some people with malevolent and sinister purposes who may seek to hijack such protests. That is what we must guard against and that's what we must all work together to avoid.' In private to the Orange leaders, Flanagan's warning had been in even starker terms: 'I met the Portadown District officers the previous week in my office and I told them that, however honourable their intentions were in terms of peaceful protests, that we had very good intelligence that people of an evil disposition were waiting to hijack their protests. And I said people will die before this week's out. "Oh no, we'll rigidly control these protests, they'll all be peaceful," I was told. I said it won't happen, it will slide out of your control, once you embark on this you'll lose control of it very quickly.' Events at the hill were already proving his point, as Vincent Kearney reported for the *Sunday Times*:

> It was like a scene from *Apocalypse Now*. Arc lights swept the fields around Drumcree, silhouetting bowler-hatted men against billowing

smoke. Helicopters hovered low. The bangs of blast bombs and plastic bullets competed with the messages blaring from a Tannoy and music from the Orange flute bands. The Orangemen had come to commemorate the Battle of the Somme; at times it seemed they had remained to re-enact it. They said they would not give in to the threat of nationalist violence, and they were defending their religious and civil liberties. In the process they threw every conceivable missile at the police and Army lines – ball bearings, rocks and smoke and petrol bombs. On Friday night, masked loyalist paramilitaries fired shots from a rifle and a handgun.

Nigel, smartly dressed and thirtysomething, looks like an accountant or a lawyer out for a picnic. He surveys the security forces and dials a number on his mobile phone. 'Get here quickly,' he says, 'and bring some planks and mattresses to help cross the ditch and wire. Steal some farm gates if you have to.' The message was being relayed to other Orangemen about to make their way to the fields around Drumcree Church for the nightly escalation in hostilities.

Further along the line, Alan was on his phone too. Solidly built and wearing a sash, his attire was more suitable for the task in hand: walking boots, jeans and raincoat, and an Ulster flag draped across his shoulders. 'We need spades and shovels to fill in this ditch. Also bring ropes and chains to tear the wire down,' he shouted into the phone. On the other side of the trench, a man in his forties, who unlike other ringleaders went unmasked, walked along the lines of barbed wire and calmly gave instructions to men and boys armed with wire-cutters and grappling hooks. While the middle-class Orangemen plotted mayhem, others, bellies spilling over their jeans and muscular arms bearing loyalist paramilitary tattoos, hurled missiles at the RUC and shouted 'No surrender'. Masked loyalist paramilitaries hurled blast bombs at the police. Others set off fireworks, aimed at the lines of police and soldiers, while teenagers used catapults to fire ball bearings and jagged stones.

'We're not going to be stopped by a crowd of Fenian bastards,' one Orangeman yells at the police, huddled behind rows of barbed wire. 'This is our country and they won't stop us walking our roads. You should be ashamed of yourself protecting that nationalist scum. They've tried to kill you for thirty years.' Every so often, the crowd sings a rousing chorus of the Orange Order anthem 'The Sash', followed by a rendition of 'The Billy Boys', which includes the line: 'We're up to our necks in Fenian blood.'

Up on the hillside, like a Greek chorus, thousands of loyalist spectators munch crisps and burgers and enjoy the scenes below. Some are horrified by the violence. Most cheer every move by the loyalist protesters. There is applause and laughter when fireworks hit police officers or soldiers, and shouts of approval when blast bombs explode. One of the devices left three RUC officers injured. "Get into the bastards," screamed one man, wearing a sash over a Glasgow Rangers jersey. His son, who looked no more than nine, waved his Ulster flag and cheered.

A woman in her late thirties, with a badge declaring 'No Compromise, No Surrender' on her jumper, urged others to follow those trying to breach the police lines. 'It's time to end this softly-softly nonsense,' she said. 'It's time to get stuck in.' Joan, a woman in her fifties who travelled 40 miles to Drumcree, said: 'I think it is going to take violence to get us down that road. It will come to people being shot and the Protestant people are prepared for that. If it is the only way we will get down that road, then so be it.' The so-called stormtroopers arrived to find much more formidable barriers in their path. The trench was three times wider and much deeper, and thousands of metres of barbed wire had been added to the fences. They responded by bringing in an industrial cutting machine which they held triumphantly aloft and shouted: 'We're coming over, you bastards.' The police used a megaphone to warn that they would open fire with plastic baton rounds if any attempt was made to get through their barriers.

Paul, a factory worker, shook his head in despair as the police fired plastic bullets in a bid to drive the crowd back. 'It is sad that it has come to this, but this is a fight the Orange Order has to win. We cannot walk away from it,' he said. 'This is more than a row about walking down a road. It is about the civil and religious liberties of Protestants. If we lose those we are left with nothing. We have made a stand and have to win, whatever it takes.' There were fewer protesters but their bitterness was undiminished.

One large woman, three children standing beside her, singled out two female RUC officers with binoculars. 'We're going to get you, you bitches,' she shouted at the officers 50 yards away. 'Then we're coming for your children. We know who you are and we know where you live. The days of living in our community are gone, you are not wanted.' Turning to her friend, who was also accompanied by children, she urged her to join in the verbal onslaught. 'It really gets to them, especially the women, when you get personal,' she said. Then she led the way: 'You're nothing but groundsheets for the men. That's all you're good for; you're just there to keep them happy.'

Although the police lines are positioned at least 50 yards away from the Orange protesters to prevent officers being singled out and threatened as they were in the 1996 stand-off, dozens of protesters carry binoculars and have succeeded in identifying a few of the RUC. 'It is ridiculous,' said Robert, an Orangeman for more than 40 years. 'I cannot believe what I am seeing – Protestants fighting the British Army. Gerry Adams must be delighted. I have been here every day and will come for as long as my Portadown brethren want me to, but those people should stay away. They are doing the work of the IRA.' The ringleaders remained undeterred, continuing to taunt police and planning for the next instalment of their nightly battle. 'You won't stop us on Monday,' shouted one masked man, catapult in hand. "Then we'll kill you and the Fenian bastards behind you.'

Minutes before the four Orangemen boarded the plane at Aldergrove, Flanagan phoned Bingham and said he had heard there was a possibility of a deal to end the dispute. Bingham replied there would be no deal: 'The only item on our agenda is a march down the road.' This thought was uppermost in the minds of the Grand Orange Lodge delegation as they filed into 10 Downing Street through the famous front door and were shown upstairs to the first-floor meeting room, past the portraits of Blair's predecessors, many of whom were considered arch-traitors to the Orange cause: Gladstone, the champion of Home Rule; Heath, who had taken away the Stormont government; Thatcher, who had given them the Anglo-Irish Agreement and started the secret peace talks with the IRA. Ever since the Parades Commission determination, some ten days earlier, the government had taken the uncompromising line that it was legally binding and that they would not interfere with the decision of an independent body. However, like Trimble, they believed that having interfered in a highly political fashion before, to halt the preliminary view document, Blair could be persuaded to do so again. Bingham says: 'We went there to try to get the prime minister to put the parade down the road. There was no question of any agreement at that stage because it was too late. We had a very frank discussion. It was a very bad meeting. We told the prime minister we would not accept a decision to ban the parade because we felt that was a denial of our basic civil rights.' During the fruitless exchanges Blair repeatedly insisted he would not try to overturn the commission's decision, while the Order delegates contrasted that with his earlier interference. The only way for a parade to go through would be with the agreement of the residents and getting that would entail talking to them, the prime minister insisted.

At the end of the meeting, Alistair Campbell, Blair's official spokesman, anxious to put a positive gloss on the proceedings, suggested that the government and the Orange Order should issue a joint press statement about the talks. Bingham said they would not agree because it had been a terrible meeting. Campbell even so produced a draft which he felt would be acceptable, describing the meeting as an open and frank discussion that had been constructive. The Order objected to the use of the word 'constructive', so the government put out its own statement. After the meeting the Orange delegation linked up with a number of Unionist MPs to hold a news conference but it was not the outcome of their meeting that dominated it. Unknown to them, while they had been in Downing Street, David McNarry, a Newtownards councillor who was a member of the Grand Lodge parades strategy committee, had given a radio interview to the BBC in Belfast, warning that the Orange Order would bring Northern Ireland to a standstill if the parade continued to be banned: 'If Her Majesty's Government is quite prepared to say these people who are suffering at Drumcree, who are staying out at night, who are there because they firmly believe in their civil and religious liberties, if they are to be treated so scantily, then I've got to say that we can, if we wish, put our minds to paralyse this country in a matter of hours.' Even before the Orange leaders in London learned of the remarks, there had been a highly critical reaction. Brid Rodgers said: 'Mr McNarry's remarks clarify and confirm the view that I have been expressing all week. The clear intention of this protest is to challenge the authority of the state. The language used by Mr McNarry was clearly a threat and a bullying tactic. Made as it was before the Orange Order's meeting with the British Prime Minister, it was clearly an attempt to bully and blackmail him and the people of Northern Ireland. We've seen five days of bullying of both communities.' In actual fact, the Orange delegation was furious because McNarry's threat became the focus of the press conference, with reporters asking if the Order planned to make Northern Ireland ungovernable. The delegation reaffirmed their support for the right of Portadown District to walk the Garvaghy Road, but stressed the need for 'peaceful and legal protest'.

They returned to Northern Ireland that evening and travelled back to Drumcree, where the scene was still like a mediaeval battlefield and where, like many other places, the protest was far from peaceful and legal. Bingham, Watson and Donaldson went out to the graveyard at the back of the church and watched in dismay. Bingham turned to them and said: 'This is the beginning of the end.' He believed the Order's position had been seriously compromised by the violence and had been urging it to adopt the ethos of Martin Luther King and opt for peaceful non-violent protest, believing the government would have found that more difficult to resist. 'The reason we were able to bring such large numbers to Drumcree in 1996 was because people believed they were going to a peaceful protest. The vast majority of Orangemen are law-abiding and have no time for violence of any kind. They were horrified by what happened in 1998. The violence had serious implications because many people stopped coming to the field and walked away from the protest. Our strength had always been the support of middle Ulster, of ordinary decent Orangemen and their families. We knew that that would end if there was serious violence at Drumcree or an attack on the police. As we stood in the graveyard that night I believed we were witnessing the demise of the protest.' Alarmed by the escalating violence, Bingham prepared a statement for Harold Gracey to read to the crowd. To his astonishment, Gracey said he would not read it unless a paragraph condemning the violence of some of the protestors was removed. Bingham said he would not remove it and the statement was never made. Recalling a meeting in the House of Orange the next day, at which the deteriorating situation was discussed, Bingham says: 'I remember distinctly saying that if we did not get control of the situation, sooner or later we would be burying a family killed because they had driven into a tree across a road or something similar. At that stage I said clearly that no protest would be worth the lives of a family and the district officers agreed fully with that.'

Beyond the confines of the Garvaghy Road, Nationalists were also deeply concerned at the violence, lawlessness and intractability of the situation. Within the SDLP there was a desire to calm the crisis, lest it fatally destabilise the ongoing efforts to implement the provisions of the Belfast Agreement, the immediate aim being to get the planned inter-party administration into power at Stormont. Seamus Mallon, deputy leader of the SDLP, who was deputy first minister designate, had there-fore been working closely with Trimble to try and secure some move-ment. On 7 July, standing beside him at a news conference in Stormont, he said: 'What we are trying to do is to get an accommodation that will allow both sections of the community to be able to proceed and live their lives without fear and without the terrible type of tension that we have now. This will certainly involve compromise and they should follow the example of the political process which has now advanced on the basis of honourable compromise. The idea of a win-win situation for any section is simply a very hollow victory. The real strength of purpose would lie with those who make compromise.'

It was a subtle call for the residents to take the moral high ground, but it set alarm bells ringing and raised deep suspicions on the Garvaghy Road where it was feared Mallon was signalling a deal taking shape to push through a march. The fact that he was standing shoulder to shoulder with Trimble, who was held in such low regard by his Catholic constituents, compounded their doubts. When Brid Rodgers heard that Mallon intended to come down the next day to see the residents she had deep reservations. She had spent the last few days reassuring them there would be no repetition of the previous three years. Speaking on the Garvaghy Road on Drumcree Sunday, July 5, she said, 'I absolutely understand why people are nervous because of the events of Drumcree 1996. But I would appeal for people to keep calm. I have been assured by the highest levels of both governments that the decision will be upheld.' More than that, she knew the residents would react strongly to any suggestion of a deal that had not been endorsed by them. She had earlier conveyed this message strongly from her home in Lurgan when Powell set up a conference call from Downing Street with Bingham, who was in his manse in Pomeroy. Powell expressed the government's concern about the continuing violence and implored the SDLP and Bingham to use their influence to bring about a settlement. Rodgers told him the only way the problem could be resolved was for the Order to talk directly to the residents, including Brendan McKenna. Bingham said that was out of the question. The Orange Order would have nothing to do with a convicted terrorist, a man they compared to Hitler.

Before travelling to Portadown, Mallon signalled to close colleagues that, despite their reservations and advice, he still intended asking the residents if there was any possibility that they could agree to a parade in the interests of the wider community. The meeting took place on 8 July in the Jesuit house in Churchill Park and it was not long underway when Mallon, who was accompanied by Rodgers and Alex Attwood, realised there was no appetite for compromise. Being a shrewd politician who understood his community, he knew not to push the matter. However, he had been spotted arriving and his presence fuelled rumours that he was indeed there to do a dirty deal. A crowd gathered and he suffered an unjustified tirade of abuse when leaving. Mallon was visibly shocked by the anger. McKenna now confirms that neither Mallon or Sinn Fein put pressure on the coalition to agree to a parade to improve the political atmosphere. 'Seamus came down to ask us if there was any chance of a resolution, but he did not pressurise us to let the parade down the road. There had been a lot of talk about us being put under pressure by the SDLP, Sinn Fein and the Irish government, but the reality is that we were not.'

While Mallon was pursuing his initiative, a far more unconventional, even bizarre, effort was going on to break the ever more costly stalemate. At its heart was Sean O'Callaghan, a former IRA terrorist who had become a double agent, betraying IRA operations to the British and Irish security forces. While in prison serving a total of 539 years for his crimes, the cold-blooded murder of a police officer in a public house and the killing of a female UDR soldier in a mortar attack, O'Callaghan had become something of a pundit, a position he exploited on his release. He came into his own with the terrorist ceasefires of 1994, warning in his writings and interviews that the cessation was only a short-term tactical ploy, and ever since had been adopted as an expert witness by the *Daily Telegraph* newspaper and right-wing Conservatives in Britain, all vigorously opposed to the Irish peace process. Under their auspices, O'Callaghan had been introduced to some Unionists and had been the star speaker at a well attended, multi-factional think-in hosted by Lord Cranborne, which was held at his historic family seat near Hatfield in Hertfordshire over two days in November 1997. Among those present were Paisley, Trimble and McCartney. The Orange Order was represented by Saulters, Watson, Bingham, Kennaway, Montgomery, Dr Warren Porter and Henry Reid.

During that violent week, O'Callaghan urged the Order to walk away from the Drumcree protest, warning them they were walking into a carefully laid IRA trap. Staging stand-offs was playing into the hands of the IRA, who wanted the police to be under fire from the Loyalist community as part of their campaign to have the force disbanded. Bingham recalls: 'His analysis was that the IRA would be delighted if Protestants turned against the state and started to oppose the security forces because that would prove their argument that the state was ungovernable.' The contact with the double murderer O'Callaghan was all the more remarkable given the Order's consistent refusal to meet Brendan McKenna because of his terrorist conviction. Bingham, however, defends the decision to meet O'Callaghan: 'As far as we were concerned he was public enemy number one for the IRA. We wanted to get an insight into the thinking of the Republican movement on the parades issue and could think of no-one better to provide that analysis. As far as we were concerned this was a war and this was someone who had turned against our enemy.'

Ruth Dudley Edwards, a Dublin-born academic, newspaper columnist and author who was researching and writing a sympathetic history of the Orange Order, also crossed paths with O'Callaghan during their travels in Northern Ireland that summer. Making common cause with the Unionists and Orangemen, they became involved in an extraordinary push to persuade Tony Blair to deliver a speech praising the Orange Order for its defence of civil liberties at the height of the Drumcree crisis that week. Some of the text was drafted during a six-hour brainstorming session at a house in Belfast on 9 July. Also present was Professor Paul Bew, a senior academic at Queen's University, Belfast, Chris McGimpsey, an Orangeman and prominent member of the Ulster Unionist party, and Liam Kennedy, another Queen's academic. McGimpsey said afterwards: 'We believed it would be helpful if Blair would give a speech giving some confidence and a bit of solace to the Unionist community in general and the Orangemen in particular.' Others dropped into the house during the course of the day to help articulate a series of points to be included in the suggested speech by Blair. Another of those involved said the initiative was taken in a context where it was assumed the rule of law would prevail. 'There was a need to find a form of words that would de-escalate the situation and soften the blow for the Unionist and Orange community,' the source said. Among the passages written for Blair was: 'While the loyal institutions have often during their history been involved in sectarian conflict, they have also been a force for stability and community cohesiveness. And nobody could doubt their commitment to their country.' The draft and rationale for the speech was passed through Powell, who was in Belfast, to Downing Street that evening, where it was overruled by other advisers who feared it would only encourage Orange intransigence. While a speech expressing such pro-Orange sentiments might have had the desired effect in mollifying Unionist opinion, it would undoubtedly have inflamed Nationalists who still feared that the Orange Order would cause the British government to back down through weight of numbers, as it did in 1996, and force the march along Garvaghy Road.

Seeing how far the situation had deteriorated through Wednesday and Thursday, with violence on an unremitting scale and increasing numbers gathering at Drumcree, the Dublin and London governments became even more anxious to stimulate the prospect of dialogue. Hope soared late on Thursday when Portadown District softened slightly for the first time and indicated they might be prepared to meet the residents, provided they did not have to meet McKenna. It was an encouraging shift in that it demonstrated some flexibility. By Friday, Powell had pulled together all the background information from the other peace-broking efforts, completed his own groundwork and was ready to move. During the day he contacted the Orange Order and the residents with the offer of an immediate new round of proximity talks at an agreed venue. The two sides need not meet but would sit in separate rooms, while two facilitators shuttled between them under his co-ordination. The Orange Order objected to Brendan McAllister, a former probation officer who runs the Northern Ireland Mediation Network, on grounds that 'he was too close to the Parades Commission'. During the day Powell recruited Peter Quinn, a high-powered businessman who was also a former president of the GAA as one of the facilitators. The other, the Reverend Roy Magee, first heard he was being asked to act in phone calls from the Northern Ireland Office that Friday afternoon and again at tea time, but at 11.30 pm he had still not received final details from Powell, who himself was still labouring to complete the arrangements from the base he established in a room on the first floor of Hillsborough Castle, near the flat used by the secretary of state.

Powell had hoped to get his talks going first thing on the Saturday, but wrangling over the venue and then procedures delayed their progress. Hillsborough had been ruled out by McKenna, as had another location in Armagh because of its proximity to a Loyalist housing estate. British officials came to dread the way the residents had learned to elevate mundane things such as car parking, security, adequate food and refreshments into preconditions, and then, when they thought everything had been agreed, would produce another couple of dozen procedural issues. Finally, it was agreed the talks would take place in the Palace Demesne in Armagh, an eighteenth-century, three-storey spacious house in its own grounds on the fringe of the town, which had once been the home of the Archbishops of Armagh and was now the headquarters of the district council. True to form, though, the start time had to be put back until all the residents' preliminary demands had been satisfied.

While this aspect was being settled the Orangemen, who had met early to discuss their position over breakfast in a convenient restaurant, were left to drink endless cups of tea and coffee, waiting for Powell to call them by mobile and confirm the starting time, a delay that did nothing to improve their humour at the outset of what were already extremely fraught talks. 'It was all a stalling process," says David Burrows, the deputy district master of Portadown. 'We were only there to talk about one thing, a parade, and McKenna knew that, but he always exaggerates grievances to bolster his argument, brings in other issues, constantly erects obstacles and prevaricates to make things more complicated. He regularly went off at a tangent with a tirade about the fact that Catholics in Portadown had been discriminated against for generations. We kept being told that the parade was offensive, but they never spelt out exactly what they meant. I think that's because the real objections are to the Orange Order and Protestants and not the parade down the Garvaghy

Road'. It was after lunchtime before the parties finally established themselves, the Orange off the main hall, in a high-ceilinged room lined with portraits of the mayors, and the residents in a modern room overlooking the garden. Powell took over the chief executive's office on the first floor while other officials, including an Irish diplomat whose presence was not overtly mentioned by anyone, camped in different offices. David Trimble's own chief of staff, David Campbell, was also there as an observer.

The residents raised some more points about the agenda before Powell played the card he had been keeping up his sleeve: money. For the first time the government recognised the wider parameters of the dispute, that the march was only a symptom of much deeper alienation on the part of the Catholics of Portadown. What was now being offered was a comprehensive long-term package to regenerate Portadown, not a quick trade-off to get a march through and then for everyone to go away and hold their breath for another year. The government recognised that while for the Catholics of Portadown the issue was equality, the package must be a balanced one that took similar account of Protestant pride and principle. The amount that was on offer to both sides, for projects to regenerate the town and build a new sense of shared civic pride by demonstrating their rich cultural heritage and diversity, was as much as £15 million. The money would come from the government's contingency vote, not the Northern Ireland budget, so there would not have to be corresponding cuts in other areas to pay for it. The offer was thereafter referred to as 'the McCusker package', after Tony McCusker, the Portadown-born civil servant, who had been one of the government's frontmen in the efforts to solve Drumcree. 'It was not an enormously significant sum given what we spend on security at Drumcree, so it was good value for money,' said one of the officials concerned. The talks ended inconclusively late that evening but there was still some hope for both sides agreed to meet again within days.

On the other side of Armagh that evening, in the modern See house beside the Cathedral, Archbishop Eames was reflecting on what, from any perspective, had been an awful week. By 6 o'clock that morning, 11 July, with no sign of the violence abating at Drumcree or anywhere else after five days, the police had logged 1957 incidents. At Drumcree 64 policemen and women had been injured in a constant hail of ball bearings fired from catapults, thunderflashes, fireworks and petrol bombs. Shots had also been fired, and from all over Northern Ireland the RUC reports being filed back to headquarters in Belfast painted a bleak picture. Police families having to flee their homes after intimidation or attack; Catholics and Protestants clashing violently on the streets; hijackings and assaults in many areas; roads being blockaded; looting and burning on an extensive scale. During the week the Catholic village of Dunloy had been 'besieged' for a period by over 1000 County Antrim Orangemen, with all access routes blocked and its members holding 'positions'. The coldly factual reports contained no mention of the human factors at work, the anger and hatred, the pain and hurt, the fear.

With the bonfires due to be lit that evening and the Twelfth marches still to come, Eames, like many others, feared what might happen on what Paisley had ominously predicted would be 'the settling day'. He put his feelings into words and issued a statement: 'Once more Northern Ireland has been plunged into confrontation, anger, despair and fear. Once more the outside world looks on with disbelief. In our streets and homes fear reigns. Our security forces again are placed in impossible situations. Angry words and threats fill the air. Our economy, our tourist industry and our employment prospects have taken a step backwards. At this late hour I appeal to everyone to draw back, give us space and recognise that unless there is some solution to the impasse we will face a disaster in which every one of us will be the loser.' Like Flanagan and Bingham, who had already expressed similar forebodings, he did not know how grimly prophetic his words would turn out to be.

Chapter Ten
About turn

Not long before 4.30 am on 12 July 1998, Garfield Gilmour, a 24-year-old farm machinery salesman, drove two men into the Carnany Park housing estate at Ballymoney in north Antrim. The car passed the still smouldering embers of the eleventh-night bonfire and stopped nearby. Gilmour let the passengers out of the car and waited. When they returned, he drove off at speed.

During the brief time they had been out of the car, the two men had swiftly ignited a petrol bomb and thrown it against the window of a house. Within seconds the flames were spreading rapidly inwards and upwards through the broken window in the two-storey dwelling. As furniture and other items caught fire, intensifying the flames and heat, poisonous fumes further thickened the choking smoke. With the blaze already raging out of control, Christine Quinn, a Catholic, her Protestant boyfriend Raymond Craig, and Christina Archibald, who had been staying the night, were woken by the screams of Christine's three sons, Richard, aged ten, Mark, aged nine, and Jason, aged eight. (The eldest brother, thirteen-year-old Lee, was staying with his grandmother). They jumped from their beds and tried to get to the children's bedroom, but were driven back by the flames. Their ears filled with the sound of the boys' desperate screams and cries for help, they jumped through a window to safety. Craig immediately climbed onto a porch roof and smashed a window in another vain attempt to reach the boys, but could not. Blood stains later visible on the charred walls testified to his brave efforts. Neighbours, woken by the commotion, tried to help but they were also defeated and forced back by the intense heat. Others watched the inferno in horror. One woman told how she heard Richard shouting that his feet were burning and he couldn't get out. Another said: 'All you could see was one of the wee ones, Richard, upstairs. I tried to get up twice but I couldn't, the heat and smoke were that bad. I shouted and he said "I'm in a corner." Another neighbour told the boy to go to the front of the house to the stairs. 'That's when he shouted from the corner he couldn't find the stairs, then the whole stairs went up in flames. It was a nightmare.'

Firefighters and the police arrived on the scene within seven minutes but by then it was too late. Neighbours watched in stunned silence as the charred bodies of the three young boys were taken from the house. Very quickly the experienced fire officers ruled out any accidental cause for the blaze and pointed to its origin by the broken window where the lit petrol bomb had landed. The police at the scene established equally quickly that the likely motive was sectarian and that the attack was far from random. The Quinns were Catholics, and had returned to Ballymoney, settling in the mainly Protestant estate, only six days earlier after living in England for two years. They had fled there after the boys' father, John Dillon, was ordered out of the area by the UVF. (Another member of the family was later intimidated.) When the parents separated, Christine and her four sons returned. It soon emerged that five Catholic families living on the estate, where the kerbstones and lamp posts were painted red, white and blue, and dozens of Union Jacks and other Loyalist flags had been erected, had received death threats shortly before the attack: UVF Christmas cards with the warning 'get out now' and a letter containing a 9mm bullet. Earlier in the week, Loyalists had set up an illegal roadblock at the entrance to the estate in support of the protest at Drumcree, and petrol bombs had been thrown at police. It was precisely the atrocity that everyone had feared would be the inevitable consequence of the hatred and fury unleashed by the deadlock at Drumcree.

Ronnie Flanagan, who had been out and about in troubled Portadown and Belfast overnight, had only been asleep for 90 minutes in his flat at police headquarters when the duty inspector in the control room at the opposite end of the complex rang him to report the three murders, which were already being treated as sectarian. The chief constable went to his office and waited for more detailed information to come through. He was already weighing up the implications for the continuing stand-off at Drumcree, where the Portadown District had again applied for, and been refused, permission to walk the Garvaghy Road later that morning. The hundreds of Twelfth parades scheduled for the next day added to his concerns, especially the one due to pass along the volatile Ormeau Road early in the morning. (When the Twelfth falls on a Sunday, the parades move to the following Monday.) At about 6 am he lifted the phone on his desk and called the Orange grand master, Bobby Saulters, who was horrified by what he was told. The two men agreed to meet at Musgrave Street police station in central Belfast later in the day to discuss the much more serious crisis that had now developed.

As news of the tragedy spread that morning, a wave of shock and revulsion rippled through the entire community. For many people, hearing of the deaths of the Quinn brothers was a chilling moment which they would never forget. In a community consumed for days by its ancient hatreds and deep divisions, the deaths had a sobering effect, like a sharp slap on the cheek. In an early morning radio interview, Flanagan said it was 'a very black morning, quite the blackest I remember for some time'. Over in his Yorkshire home for the weekend, Alistair Graham was deeply worried that the Drumcree decision had contributed to the three tragic deaths. Archbishop Eames, who had so profoundly feared just such a tragedy, moved quickly to express his 'horror, disgust, anger and sorrow'. Speaking on the BBC television programme *Breakfast with Frost*, he said Northern Ireland was on the verge of disaster 'unless we all pull back. The attack is one more disastrous consequence of the madness that is gripping us; one more disaster following on the hatred and the sectarianism we are trying to live with and trying to overcome. At the end of the day is anything worth a human life?' Later the Archbishop, who had been subjected to increasing criticism especially from Church of Ireland members south of the border, issued a more trenchant condemnation of the Drumcree protest and the situation that now existed: 'I now believe the time has come. They have made their point. They should leave the entire Drumcree area. They should return to their homes, and they should allow those who are negotiating a solution to this space to get on with the job. The Church of Ireland is not going to condone the violence, it is not going to condone the confrontation and, as far as I am concerned, I totally distance the Church of Ireland from what is going on. It is time to say that what is happening at Drumcree is wrong. What is being done in the name of Protestantism is wrong.'

From Downing Street, prime minister Tony Blair described what had happened as an 'absolutely heartbreaking act of barbarism'. Mo Mowlam asked people to 'think twice before they exit their front doors' and urged Orangemen not to treat the stand-off at Drumcree as their 'last stand. If they make this the last stand and things get worse and worse, then only the people of Northern Ireland will suffer.' In an extremely rare foray into Northern Ireland politics, the home secretary, Jack Straw, called on Orange leaders to 'reflect on the abyss of the alternative' if they continued their protest at Drumcree. Similar sympathy and frustration was expressed on all sides. The Reverend Robert Coulter, a Presbyterian minister who had recently been elected as an Ulster Unionist assembly member for the north Antrim area, spoke eloquently for many when he said: 'We are burning our children on the altar of our hatred. This is the harvest of inflammatory speeches and intransigence on both sides. We have used up all our words of condemnation.' The chief constable said, 'I know how important marching is to people. I know how important opposing marches is to other people. But, surely, against the backdrop of last night's events there are things more important than that. I would ask those residents to take stock. I would ask the Orange Institution to take stock. I think the loss of the lives of three children, while they slept in their beds, for me, changes everything. I would ask people to take stock of their positions.'

One person who was profoundly doing so was William Bingham, who had returned to his manse in Pomeroy in the early hours of that Sunday, having spent most of the previous day and night at Drumcree. He got up shortly before 7 am, turned on the radio and was shocked when he heard of the deaths, especially as he had been sickened by the violence he had seen at Drumcree on preceding nights. Hungry for more information, he turned on the television where he saw an interview with Flanagan, whom, Bingham noted, did not use the word 'Drumcree' in association with the attack but linked it by inference. 'He very clearly linked it to Drumcree, by using the words "protest" and "murder" in the way he did, he was clearly identifying the attack with the protest at Drumcree.' If it was indeed linked to Drumcree and the Order, Bingham wanted to dis-associate himself from it, but first he wanted to be certain. He tried calling Watson, but he had already left after being phoned at home by Saulters, who had summoned an emergency meeting of senior officers in the House of Orange after his call from Flanagan. Bingham was also receiving calls from journalists. 'The message was coming through loud and clear from the media that the attack was linked to the protest at Drumcree and I had nothing, no indication from the institution that it was otherwise. I was left in position that it looked very likely that the incident was connected to the institution and certainly the words of the chief constable gave that impression and had to be taken seriously because I knew that he would have access to intelligence information. It left me with absolutely no alternative but to come out and say it was wrong and that no road was worth the life of children.'

Under pressure to do interviews, Bingham, who strictly observes the Sabbath and does not give interviews, said he would say something after the twelve o'clock service and, even more uncharacteristically, agreed to a request to allow the cameras to film his sermon believing, naïvely, that it would help dispel many of the myths about the Order: 'I thought it would let people see what Orangeism is really about, that it is a religious organisation and a family occasion with young people singing, reading, saying prayers and so on.' Bingham, who has two congregations, then departed to conduct a service at Sandholes in Cookstown. When he got back to Pomeroy, the church was packed with Orangemen in sashes, as it was the annual Orange service for the Pomeroy District, and the media had arrived in force, with a number of television crews waiting for him.

For his sermon that morning, Bingham decided to preach from Micah 6:viii. In a moving, emotional and sombre tone, he told his hushed congregation: 'Brethren and sisters, members of the congregation, when I was a young lad growing up, something like the age of our Juniors here this morning, the one day that I most looked forward to in the year was the Twelfth of July. It was a day of fun when you could walk, parade, enjoy the bands and meet with friends. I looked forward to it as the best day in the year as I grew up in Markethill. Today is the Twelfth of July, and this morning I have wept, and I am not ashamed to say that I wept, as I heard of the loss of three little boys burned to death in Ballymoney. Every decent Orangeman cannot but feel for that family today and be absolutely revolted at what has happened and, to make it even worse, perhaps those that did it would say that they did it for the cause of Orangeism, in the name of Orangeism and for the sake of a parade at Drumcree. Whatever reason this was done they could never say they did it for Orangeism because it is exactly the opposite to what Orangeism stands for. It is anathema to Orangeism and it ought to be so and will be declared to be so, I hope, in every Orange service that is taking place throughout our land today. On Thursday, having visited the Prime Minister, in a television interview I said that "no road is worth a life" let alone the lives of three innocent little boys. I believe wholeheartedly in the principles of Orangeism. I believe in civil and religious liberties for everyone, I believe in the right of Orangemen to walk the streets of this province, that's a principle that we have stood for, that's a principle that we uphold and seek to have upheld today. But I have to say this, that after last night's atrocious act a fifteen-minute walk down Garvaghy Road by the Orange Order would be a very hollow victory because it would be in the shadow of three coffins of little boys who wouldn't even know what the Orange Order is about. As I stood at Drumcree this week I asked myself this question, "Brethren, where are we going, and where are we allowing ourselves to be led?" The throwing of blast bombs at the RUC, is that Orangeism? If it is, I will have no part in it. The verbal attacks on people just because they think differently than we do, is that Orangeism? If it is, I will have no part in it. The violence that we have seen, if that is Orangeism, then many of us here want no part in it. You and I know it's not Orangeism.

'Out of respect for what has happened it is my belief that two things need to be done. First, that the residents' groups that would try to prevent people like us going our traditional routes should stand down. They were never interested in accommodation, no one here knows that better than myself. They are committed to taking out us out of their areas and ultimately ensuring that there is no Orange culture to express. Secondly, I believe the Orange Order needs to call off its protests because we can't control them. Drumcree is rapidly getting out of our hands, we have to back off from that. Yes, we can have a peace camp there for as long as it takes for men's rights to be established. But more bloodshed in our land, I ask you, do you think it would be worth it?'

Despite what he had said, Bingham still harboured some unease about the apparent linkage to the Order and Drumcree and was troubled by the growing wave of allegations that the incident was related to drugs or a family feud. Several people who had heard reports of his sermon called to suggest these motives. Anxious to get first-hand information, he phoned Ronnie Flanagan at RUC headquarters around 2.30 that afternoon 'I told the chief constable what I had been hearing and asked him to clarify the position. He said police were absolutely certain and totally convinced that it had been a sectarian attack, and not drugs-related. When I pressed on whether there was a direct link to Drumcree, he was more evasive, much more cautious. The difference was very clear to me. Earlier in the day he had used the words "murder" and "protest" in the same sentence in a way that was clearly aimed at suggesting the attack was directly connected to Drumcree. When I spoke to him later the same day he did not do that.'

Bingham is still smarting from the sharp criticism he attracted within Orange circles and remains blindly convinced that the police and Northern Ireland Office deliberately misled the public about the circumstances of the attack to discredit the Orange Order. 'What was amazing was how quickly the chief constable blamed the institution. Usually when there is a murder the police take a while to say anything definite about it and during the first few hours the police say it is too early to be able to say what might have happened. That didn't happen with the Quinn murders. Ronnie Flanagan came out immediately and said, this is not protest, this is murder. That was very clearly linking the murders to the protest and he was very wrong to do that. In the subsequent trial the judge stated that the murder had been committed by the UVF and that the murder was sectarian. The UVF had been carrying out sectarian murders for thirty years. But the judge did not make any direct link to the situation at Drumcree. I was very angry because Flanagan's statement on the morning of the murders set the tone for the whole day and the weeks to come. There is no doubt that what was a terrible tragedy for the Quinn family was a gift to the Northern Ireland Office and the police and they used it against the institution. The fact that Orangemen are now labelled with being members of an organisation that murdered three children is a terrible indictment and has caused a lot of anger. I think it is beholden on the chief constable to make clear that he was wrong.'

'No, that's nonsense. It was clearly sectarian,' recalls Flanagan. 'Although the family is mixed, it would have been a clearly identified Catholic household and if you get a house petrol bombed on the eleventh night, coming in that week of sectarian attacks, hijackings, attempted road-blocking, gun and bomb attacks on police officers on duty, and bomb attacks on the homes of police officers and widespread intimidation of their families, it was undoubtedly a sectarian attack. I never said that the Orange Order were responsible for it. I never thought for a second that the Orange Order would condone it and there was certainly no question of exploiting that. I think people judged for themselves whether they wanted to continue to support this protest What I said is exactly what happened. Sadly the evidence of that could not be more plain for all to see.'

Watson heard Bingham's cry from the heart on his car radio as he was driving along the M1 to Portadown after attending Saulters' Grand Lodge meeting in Belfast. He was surprised Bingham had gone public without consulting Grand Lodge, and at his apparent linking of the murders to the protest, although he had been despatched to Portadown District to suggest that it might be prudent to call off or suspend the protest because of the tragic turn of events. When he got there, he found the district's anger towards Bingham at boiling point, because they felt he had betrayed them, and Watson himself was sharply rebuffed for suggesting that tactics could be changed. Saulters and others who arrived from Belfast a short time later sensed the hostile mood and decided not to call for an end to the protest, as they had intended, again letting the Portadown tail wag the Orange dog.

After a week of confrontation and frustration, the district was in a defiant mood. Their myopic horizon only extended as far as the nearby Garvaghy Road and they could not understand why they should have to call off their protest because of something that had happened in seemingly far-away Ballymoney. Their paranoia, however, knew no bounds. Some Orangemen claimed the murder was the result of dirty tricks by British military intelligence. David Jones, the Portadown District press officer, even claimed the murders had been the result of collusion between the police and Loyalist paramilitaries as part of a government plot to undermine the Order. 'We condemn those murders but we do feel, unfortunately, that certain individuals have attempted to use these murders in their own way to achieve their political ends,' said Jones, who had grown up in a flat in Carleton Street Orange Hall, where his father was caretaker. Gracey, the district master, said: 'There was tragic death in Ballymoney and everyone abhors that. They gave it out as a sectarian murder but there's some doubt about that. The true facts will come out before long, and when they do come out we will be asking for an apology from the chief constable and everyone else.'

By this time, anonymous callers were hard at work ringing newsrooms in Belfast, distancing the Order and the Drumcree protest from the incident and offering all sorts of explanations for the attack on the Quinns. In a hard-hitting statement, Trimble rebutted them all: 'There is no doubt in my mind that the house was petrol bombed in the context of a spate of sectarian threats in that area. To suggest anything else is quite despicable. The only way the Portadown brethren can clearly distance themselves from these murders and show the world that they repudiate them is now to leave the hill at Drumcree parish church and return home. I know they have tried to conduct their protest peacefully, but those responsible for the murders have used those protests as an excuse for an appalling week of barbarity.'

'Portadown District felt they were being blamed in the wrong,' Watson recalls. 'While the rest of the world, and many of their brethren, were urging them to call off the protest, they were more determined than ever that it would continue. They made it very clear that they were not going to back down.' The international opprobrium was, however, unprecedented. The murders provoked outrage throughout the world, expressed in newspapers and on radio and television stations in the US, Australia, Hong Kong, Japan and Europe. Bill Clinton sent a personal message from the White House: 'Dear Mrs Quinn: On behalf of all Americans, Hillary and I want to convey to you our deepest condolences. I know that it is impossible to make sense of this senseless act or to soothe with words the loss of your sons but I want you to know that peace-loving people everywhere, here in America and around the world, mourn your loss and share your grief.' Ken Bates, the chairman of Chelsea Football Club, who was born a Protestant but later converted to Catholicism, offered a £100,000 reward to anyone who helped police catch the killers. He said: 'You can debate forever the rights and wrongs of Nationalism and Ulster Loyalism. But after what happened with these three kids – they could have been my grandchildren – I decided it was time for someone to stand up.' (The money never had to be paid. On 29 October 1999 Garfield Gilmour, the driver, received three life sentences for the murders.

Sentencing him, Lord Justice McCollum said it was 'a UVF attack with a clear inference that its motive was sectarian. The accused proved a resourceful liar at times in the course of his interviews and I am sure he has not disclosed his full involvement in the events of that morning.' On 5 June 2000 the murder conviction was overturned on appeal, and nine days later Gilmour was sentenced to fourteen years for the manslaughter of the three brothers. Two other men, named in court as the actual petrol bombers, have never been convicted.)

Flanagan met the Orange leaders at Musgrave Street later that Sunday as arranged, but, taking a hardline cue from Portadown, they declined to scale down or abandon any of the hundreds of parades the next day. Flanagan and ACC Bill Stewart, who was in command of the Belfast area, then swiftly ordered a large force of police and army to move into the Ormeau area during the afternoon to secure it for the Orange Order march due early the next morning. The operation, which was to continue overnight, was designed to contain the area so that protestors could not gather and block the march, aggravating an already difficult operation. It had been given the go-ahead a week earlier by the Parades Commission after an emotional heart-searching session which Alistair Graham recalls as the toughest moment of his time in Northern Ireland. It took place in his office in Windsor House, where worry was expressed about the ability of the police and Army to cope with a second stand-off after all the violence that had flowed from the decision to halt the Drumcree march. While the protestors at rural Drumcree gathered in fields, the lower Ormeau was in the heart of the turbulent city, surrounded by densely populated Catholic and Protestant areas and within touching distance of localities that had been sectarian flashpoints for generations. Flanagan arrived and gave his assessment of the situation, painting such a gloomy picture that Graham was in no doubt that the Ormeau parade had to go ahead. He argued that there had to be a balancing act, a trade-off. When it became clear that the balance of the argument was for a parade to take place, Roseanne McCormick broke down in tears, and Aiden Canavan looked visibly upset. Neither believed a parade was justified. Soon Billy Martin was also in tears. Just as the meeting was drawing to a close, his mobile phone rang. It was his wife, calling to say someone had contacted their isolated hilltop farmhouse, near Greyabbey on the Ards peninsula, to say their pedigree cattle-breeding business would be destroyed unless he resigned from the commission. Pickets had already been at the gate of his farm for days, but Martin and his family bravely defied the regular threats and he continued to serve.

The Parades Commission's pragmatic decision to allowing parade on the Ormeau Road was then tested through the courts, by judicial review and appeal, and upheld. However, not long after the start of the police operation to hold the road open, Flanagan, who had gone to a meeting at Stormont, got a call from Gerard Rice, the frontman for the Ormeau residents. After some negotiation, Flanagan accepted assurances that there would be no attempt to halt the march next morning and rang Stewart to ask him to scale down the security operation. The next morning, after being delayed by bomb scares close to the Ballynafeigh Orange Hall, which proved to be hoaxes, the Orange march passed along the disputed section of the Ormeau Road, silent and restrained except for a single drumbeat setting the pace. True to their word, the residents' protest was peaceful. They displayed black flags in mourning for the Quinn boys and released a cloud of black balloons as the parade passed. Later at Drumcree, Portadown District staged a march from the church to the block on the bridge, where the officers again pledged to stay at the church for as long it took to complete their walk back to the Orange Hall. The only serious clash of the day occurred between Orangemen at an Orange demonstration.

The catalyst for the clash was the former IRA terrorist Sean O'Callaghan, who turned up at the Pomeroy demonstration with Ruth Dudley Edwards. On the way down the village street that morning Bingham, who was due to speak from the platform, thought he caught a glimpse of O'Callaghan but could not believe he would have had the audacity to turn up at such an event. Bingham was still slightly apprehensive about the overall situation, especially as his outspoken sermon had dominated the overnight news coverage. He was reassured though by the large number of calls he had received, many from Orangemen, endorsing what he had said. Later, when he arrived at the field, outside the village, where the demonstration was to take place, he received more support, although some Orangemen were highly critical of his comments.

The Spirit of Drumcree leader, Joel Patton, who was also due at the demonstration, was far from pleased at what Bingham had said the previous day, but his displeasure turned to fury after he received a phone call telling him that Bingham had not only invited O'Callaghan to Pomeroy but had entertained him at the manse. Soon afterwards, as they paraded through the village, Patton and some of his supporters spotted O'Callaghan and Dudley Edwards. Walter Millar, a deputy district master, broke ranks from the parade and chased the former IRA man, waving his rolled umbrella angrily above his head. Out at the field, there was an air of tense expectancy as the parade, with Patton in the ranks, arrived. Patton had let it be known to some journalists that he was going to challenge Bingham, who had also been warned by a member of Patton's district lodge that 'there's going to be trouble today.'

At the end of Bingham's address, which was purely religious and did not contain any mention of Drumcree, Patton moved forward and shouted 'traitor'. There was an eerie silence and some Orangemen told Patton to keep quiet and leave the field. He refused and continued to shout at the minister before scuffles started and Orangemen started assualting each other with their umbrellas. Bingham initially sat with his eyes fixed firmly on the floor before hurriedly leaving the platform to stop the situation deteriorating further. Patton recalls: 'There was a terrible atmosphere when we arrived at the field. We had been blamed for the terrible murders of three young children and people felt very bad and very let down. I was so angry that I had to say something so when William Bingham finished his sermon I shouted that because of him we would go down in history as murderers of children and that what he had done would allow people to demonise the order throughout the world. In the eyes of the world he had made the institution as bad as the Ku Klux Klan. Looking back on it I'm not sure that I was getting my message across. It may not have been the best way to do it, but I was so incensed I had to say something.'

Bingham reflects: 'I think Joel Patton had a right to be angry that O'Callaghan was there, but he was no more or less angry than I was. He had been misinformed and told that O'Callaghan had been at my home and that was not true. Sean O'Callaghan has never been through the door of my home and never will be. He would not be welcome. Indeed I could not believe that he was there. As far as I was concerned the last place Sean O'Callaghan should have been was Pomeroy. He had no right to come to an Orange event as he had been part of an organisation that had been involved in a campaign against Protestants.'

That night, Bingham did a live interview for the BBC's *Newsnight* programme, in which he made it clear that he believed Portadown District should maintain the protest until they got down the road and suggested they should set up a 'Greenham Common'-type peace camp, as he had said in his sermon. Later other Orange Order chaplains issued a statement backing him. 'Brother Bingham rightly emphasised that no road is worth a life and we entirely support this sentiment. Those who vilify him are rejecting the clear teaching of the Word of God.'

That evening and the next, many of the vilifiers were still in violent action at Drumcree and elsewhere. An estimated 5000 Loyalists joined a protest organised before the Ballymoney attack – a fraction of the size of the crowd expected – and heard Paisley reject suggestions that the murders had been connected to the protest. 'There is a lot of dancing on these young fellows' graves. I was told that the Orangemen of Drumcree were responsible for the hellish murder of three young children. Nothing could be further from the truth.' With typical bluster, he then urged the Portadown Orangemen to continue the protest: 'There can be no weakening and there can be no giving up. Should it take until Christmas we shall be here. We must not fall by the wayside, we have to keep going.' Not long afterwards police fired plastic bullets as trouble again erupted at Drumcree, but the confrontation was much less intense than before the murders. Over the next few days the police reported a marked drop in tension and in the number of acts of public disorder taking place throughout Northern Ireland as the protest crumbled.

Meanwhile the Bishop of Down and Connor, Dr Patrick Walsh, told hundreds of mourners packed into Our Lady and St Patrick's Church in Ballymoney, where three white coffins with plates bearing the names of each of the Quinn boys lay before the altar, that responsibility for the killings lay with those who had incited violence as well as those who carried it out. He said: 'For all too long the airwaves, the printed page, have been saturated with noises, strident, harsh, discordant voices, carrying words of hatred, of incitement, of recrimination, words not found in the vocabulary of Christianity. The weapons of hate-filled words inevitably fuel weapons of murderous destruction – indeed how true are the words of the psalm, "Their teeth are slings and arrows, their tongues sharpened words."' One of the mourners was David Trimble, who was later criticised by many Orangemen who believed his attendance breached the rules of the Order, which forbade attendance at any Catholic service.

By now the violence had considerably subsided everywhere, after 2201 acts of public disorder had been recorded by the police during the preceding ten days. The police and Army had come under attack 615 times and 76 officers and soldiers had been injured; 144 houses and 165 buildings had been attacked and damaged; 645 vehicles had been hijacked and destroyed, and there had been 632 incidents involving petrol bombs. Churches and Orange halls were among the premises attacked. Constable Jason McBride, one of the police officers injured in a blast bomb attack at Drumcree, had sustained injuries in an IRA mortar attack at Lisnaskea five years earlier. 'There is a certain irony in being blown up by both sides,' he commented. At 6.30 am on 15 July the RUC moved out beyond the 'Maginot line' for the first time and began a search operation in the fields at Drumcree. A number of weapons were uncovered including a home-made machine gun, ammunition, explosive devices, material for making blast bombs and petrol bombs, and crossbows with home-made explosive arrows.

During the search the Orange Order members were excluded from the area. On behalf of Portadown District, Jones advanced the almost incredible theory that Republicans could have been responsible for the haul. He said: 'Some of it could have actually been placed there by Nationalists to be picked up at later times, we don't know because we don't know the full level that is there at the moment or any tests that have been carried out.' Violent Republicans had not been idle, however. At the height of the crisis, breakaway groups opposed to Sinn Fein's support for the Belfast Agreement attempted to create further havoc by carrying out a major attack. A 1400lb bomb and firing mechanism was discovered just off the Moy–Armagh road after a telephone warning and was defused by army bomb disposal experts after a 48-hour operation. Later on the day of the search, Bingham, his wife Janice and their two children went off on holiday to the south of France, where they had been during the first stand-off. He was sickened by all that had happened and needed time to think. He decided not to phone home during the family break.

A few days later, on 21 July, with the worst clearly over for the time being, the Army moved in and dismantled the massive fortifications that had been erected and strengthened. Portadown District vowed they would keep a presence on the hill at Drumcee for 'as long as it took to get down the road'. Their position was more formally articulated on the home page of the website that had been established as one of the sinews of their propaganda campaign:

> 'This stand is for basic human and civil rights as enshrined in the United Nations charter on Human Rights. This stand is not about domination, in fact it is quite the opposite – a stand against the Fascist tactics used by the IRA. This principled and honourable stand is not just about being allowed to walk along the Garvaghy Road but is also about the future of our beloved Northern Ireland. A future in which all citizens are allowed basic human rights such as freedom of religion and assembly. A future in which we and our children are free to practice the Reformed Faith. A future where we can maintain our cherished position as equal citizens of the United Kingdom and indeed the world without the fear of sectarian intimidation and hatred. A future based on tolerance, a future based on accommodation not segregation, a future based on "Civil and Religious Liberty" for all. Here we stand – We can do no other.'

The police also maintained a small presence in the area to ensure the Parades Commission's decision was observed. This stalemate, with periodic ups and downs, would prove to be long-lasting. Although Jonathan Powell's proximity talks at Armagh had ended inconclusively the previous Saturday, both parties had agreed to meet again a week later at the same venue. When at last they had got into their stride, the tortuous process of negotiating at arm's-length continued. It was the job of the facilitators to act as guarantors to both sides, sitting in on the alternate exchanges between Powell and the two groups to ensure that each received an accurate account of the opposite position. Quinn acted for the residents and Magee performed a similar function for the Order. The residents put forward the points agreed at the earlier public meeting in St Mary's Hall. The Orange Order's position was that it would agree to a civic forum and to discussing the parades issue, mediated by a chairman, but ending the protest at Drumcree was conditional on an immediate parade that year and the issue of future parades being addressed to their satisfaction. Despite the size of the financial package on the table, the two parties continued to squabble. The Orange delegates rejected the residents' proposal for the money to be split 50-50 to benefit the town. They wanted a 70 per cent allocation to reflect the Protestant–Catholic population ratio. There was similar disagreement over the role and composition of the proposed civic forum, the broad-based body designed to channel the funding into the town and stimulate a new sense of shared ownership and pride.

After a day spent going back and forwards, with stocktaking sessions in between, sufficient engagement had been created for the parties to agree to meet for a third time on the following Tuesday. At one point during the negotiations, Powell judged he had nudged the two sides close enough to get an interim deal. He telephoned the influential Sinn Fein leader, Martin McGuinness, in the hope that pressure from him might tilt McKenna and the residents enough to clinch it. The call backfired badly. When McGuinness contacted McKenna, he was told bluntly it was none of his business. One of those present said McKenna went 'ballistic' and refused to listen.

Unknown to the Orange delegation, however, Powell had earlier dealt McKenna a winning hand, on Downing Street notepaper. During the tortuous preliminaries, the residents, aware that senior members of the Order had been briefing journalists that the government supported a parade, asked Powell for a guarantee that the Parade Commission's determination would remain in force if there was no agreement at the talks. Powell assured them the prime minister had made it clear that the government would uphold the rule of law and the ruling would stand, a position then confirmed in writing. In seeking to reassure McKenna, Powell had also removed any incentive for agreement. The residents knew that if they did not get enough by way of concessions from the Orange Order side, the status quo would prevail and the parade would remain banned. By early Tuesday evening all momentum had gone out of the talks and Powell was forced to conclude they were going nowhere. As at Hillsborough the previous year, the delegations were spending much of their time watching television and talking to each other in their own rooms. At 7.05 pm Powell went to see the residents and summed up the Order's position. When he was told there was no possibility of them agreeing to a parade, he said there was no point in continuing.

Despite the fact that the gap between the two sides had not narrowed in the interim, Powell contacted both sides again later that year and a further round of proximity talks was set up, this time in an office building at Nutts Corner, the original Belfast civil airport, which had since become an industrial park and open air market. The encounter took place on 12 December and only underlined the fact that neither side had moved a millimetre. Powell flew back to Downing Street to tell the prime minister they would have to find a new way to try and break the impasse and start again.

By that time, events on the ground had taken a serious turn for the worse and were still deteriorating. While it was not even indirectly attributable to Drumcree, the Omagh bombing on 15 August, in which 29 people died when a car bomb planted by an IRA breakaway faction exploded without warning, caused common revulsion. Unionists and Protestants rightly called into question the credibility of the ceasefires and the durability of the peace process when some Republicans were still prepared to engage in such mindless violence. The Nationalist and Catholic community was appalled by the bombing and the death toll, the worst single atrocity in Northern Ireland in the entire three decades of violence, and unambiguously disowned and condemned it. However, in a display of breathtaking bigotry, the Orange Order later called Trimble, and a senior party figure, Denis Rogan, to account for apparently breaching the tenets of their membership by attending the funerals of some of the Catholic victims of the atrocity.

When the major confrontation on the hill at Drumcree crumbled in mid-July, Gracey had pledged he would stay on the hill until the march got through. Portadown District put a caravan in place to ease the vigil, and members and supporters maintained a presence, sometimes a handful of

them, at other times a couple of hundred. Every week they handed in an
'11/1 form', as it was known, to an officer of sergeant rank or above at
Portadown police station, giving formal 28-day notice of parades,
including one each Sunday from the church to the Orange Hall via the
Garvaghy Road. The RUC passed the form to the Parades Commission,
which the Orangemen refused to recognise. The commission considered
each application and confirmed the restriction on the route, and a Sunday
ritual soon developed whereby the police would block the bridge with
Land Rovers at lunchtime and accept a protest letter from Gracey. In all
the district held 130 marches and demonstrations in Portadown between
July and Christmas 1998.

More militant elements continued to add a violent dimension to the
situation with inevitably violent consequences. During the Saturday
afternoon of 5 September a Loyalist crowd, which at one point numbered
700, staged a demonstration in the town centre. Carrying placards
proclaiming 'No Taigs Here', they jostled and shouted abuse at Catholics.
Dozens of families out for an afternoon at the shops, many with children,
fled in terror. One woman, in the town centre with her two young sons,
recalls: 'They were like animals. The hatred was in their eyes. Women
with children as young as mine were calling us Fenian bastards.' Shortly
before 5 pm, in broad daylight, a Catholic-owned business was gutted in
a petrol-bomb attack and others were damaged by thugs openly carrying
baseball bats, chains and crowbars. The RUC became engaged in a series
of running battles as they tried to calm the situation. During a confrontation at Corcrain Road, someone taking cover among a crowd of protesters
hurled a small section of metal pipe packed with explosives, ammunition
and shotgun pellets towards a line of police officers. It landed close to the
feet of Constable Frank O'Reilly and he took the full force of the blast. It
shattered his riot shield and blew the visor off his helmet, peppering his
face and body with shrapnel. A colleague standing beside him suffered
serious leg injuries. Some of the crowd cheered as the officers were taken
to hospital.

There it was discovered that 30-year-old O'Reilly, born a Catholic,
who only hours earlier had smilingly said goodbye to his Protestant wife
and three children before setting off for work, had lost an eye, had
shrapnel embedded in his skull and was fighting for his life. Although the
doctors gave him little chance of surviving, he was rushed from
Craigavon Hospital to the Royal Victoria Hospital in Belfast for
specialist surgery. Ronnie Flanagan remembers going to the hospital to
meet O'Reilly's parents and wife, while the gravely injured officer was
in the operating theatre. 'I was speaking to his wife who had just given

birth a short time before and the new-born child was with her. Also seeing his mum and dad. I remember going down to the wee Chapel in the Royal to see them. They were praying for Frankie but sadly he didn't pull through. These are the things you remember. The real cost.' After serving as a policeman for eight years and fighting for life for five weeks, O'Reilly died on 6 October, the 301st RUC casualty of the conflict.

O'Reilly's death provided a poignant reminder of how all the parties to the Northern Ireland conflict are so closely interlocked despite their deep divisions. One of the people who witnessed the fatal blast was Brid Rodgers. She was in the Catholic Craigwell Avenue enclave, which O'Reilly and the other police officers were shielding from Loyalist attack. She was angry when she heard a police officer had been injured, and later bitterly regretted that he had died. In a bold gesture for an SDLP figurehead, given the party's highly conditional attitude to the police, she visited the family home to sympathise privately and, in a more public show of solidarity, attended the funeral. The attack also caused great distress within the Orange Order, which could not dissemble, as many members had done over the death of the young Quinn boys, about its association with the Drumcree protest. Denis Watson was at home when a senior RUC officer phoned to tell him what had happened and that O'Reilly's injuries were so severe he was not expected to live. A former member of the RUC part-time reserve, Watson felt angry and ashamed: 'I have always said that if there was any protest organised in support of the brethren at Portadown, they must take some responsibility for what happens. As the protest that night had been organised to show support for the Orangemen at Drumcree there was no doubt that it was linked. As a former policeman, I felt sick.' The dead officer was married to a relative of William Bingham's wife. From his bedside they telephoned and asked him to pray. 'I couldn't believe that so-called Loyalists would do such a thing, attack and kill a member of the police. It was contrary to everything the Orange Order stands for. That was the last straw for many people who decided they would be having nothing more to do with the protest.'

When O'Reilly died, Bingham telephoned Watson and said he was going to the funeral because he believed the institution should be represented. Watson said he would go too. They issued a joint statement condemning the murder and then attended the funeral, where they sympathised with his widow, Janet. Watson recalls: 'That was one of the most uncomfortable afternoons in my life. William and I wanted to be there and felt we should be there, but we could sense the anger of many of the mourners who were in the police and believed the Orange Order was responsible for the death of their colleague.' The death also had a deep impact in Jeffrey Donaldson's household. As a former solider in the Ulster Defence Regiment, the young MP knew how hard a death in action hit inside the security forces. His own wife, Eleanor, was also deeply concerned. She and O'Reilly's wife had studied together. Donaldson denounced those responsible, saying they had brought disgrace upon the name of Loyalism. 'It was a complete contradiction for anyone who described themselves as a Loyalist to murder a servant of the Crown. The murder did enormous damage to the cause of Portadown District. It dramatically reduced the level of support from middle Ulster Protestants who, whilst being sympathetic to the cause of the Portadown Orangemen, felt there were sinister elements outside the Orange Order, including anti-RUC elements, who were trying to exploit the protest. The attack had happened during a protest organised to support the stand-off so it was much more clearly linked to the situation at Drumcree than the tragic murders of the Quinn children'.

For Melvyn Hamilton, who had played a key role in the negotiations to secure a parade in 1995, the killing of a member of his own church congregation was the last straw. Although born a Catholic, since his marriage, Frankie O'Reilly had regularly attended Waringstown Presbyterian Church with his wife. 'I did not know him personally, but I was an elder in the church, and his murder had a deep impact. I was outraged that people who called themselves Loyalists and claimed to support the Orange Order would attack members of the security forces.' Already deeply troubled by the Quinn murders and the Order's denial of responsibility, he decided it was time to leave after nearly 30 years of membership. He wrote to his lodge secretary and resigned. 'How could I explain to Mrs O'Reilly what had happened? It was a disgrace that the Order was allowing itself to be used as a conduit for evil people. I could not believe that after bearing the brunt of violence from the enemies of the state for thirty years, the police were now being attacked by the people who claimed to support them.'

Hamilton still upholds the right of the Portadown Orangemen to walk the Garvaghy Road, but believes they must also consider the rights of the residents: 'I do not think the Bible contains an absolute right for anything. In exercising your right you have to be a witness and understand where other people are coming from.' As events over the winter of 1998/99 would vividly demonstrate, such enlightened thinking was all still too rare, not only within the Order but among all involved in the intractable impasse over Drumcree. Ever since Trimble had linked it to the implementation of the Belfast Agreement, and since the prime minister had intervened in its negotiations, the stand-off was no longer a little local difficulty. It was now inextricably linked to the wider political process, which was also in utter gridlock with equally little prospect of any breakthrough. By the autumn of 1998, after four years of confrontation, the longstanding tribal divisions in Portadown were running deeper than ever. In a place where everyone and everything is colour-coded orange or green, there was no middle ground. Even trouble-hardened police who had worked in other sectarian flashpoints were shocked by the level of bigotry. One said: 'It is a different planet. The hate is much more entrenched than anywhere else and seems to be getting worse'.

Local Loyalists regarded themselves as the most loyal and ruthless. Local Orangemen felt superior to the rest of their brethren. As the direct descendants of the founding fathers of the Order, they regarded themselves as the truest defenders of the Protestant faith and heritage. Anyone who disagreed with them was a traitor. They had increasingly come to believe that if they lost the battle for the Garvaghy Road, they were finished, and with them the Orange culture and tradition. Their public enemy number one was McKenna, the spokesman for the Garvaghy Road Residents Coalition, who they firmly believed was a Sinn Fein puppet working to the IRA's agenda. 'He is not trying to protect Nationalists, he is trying to destroy the Orange Order,' said one Orangeman. 'He has been sent to this town to do a job and is doing it very well – bringing it to its knees.' The entire Catholic population was viewed as a threat and treated as enemies. 'Those Fenian bastards have no right to be in this town. They've tried to destroy it for the past 30 years and now they want to own it,' said one Protestant man.

Such extremism was far from the monopoly of Loyalists. Portadown Nationalists, surrounded by Protestants and outnumbered three to one, felt under siege and were equally uncompromising. The murder of Robert Hamill was constantly cited as an example of all that was wrong in the town. One Orangeman parading to Drumcree church in July had turned to the Nationalists looking on from Garvaghy Road and laughed as he stamped the ground, mimicking the way Hamill was killed. One Nationalist resident said: 'Loyalists have been murdering and threatening Catholics in this town for decades. We are sick of being pushed around and they can't take it because this time they haven't got their way. They should have been taken on a long time ago.' The tension and constant trouble in the town centre had a devastating economic effect. Turnover was down by 50 per cent in some shops. Many were struggling to keep going and others were at breaking point. Some people even boycotted shops owned by 'the other sort'. 'This is a bitter hole and I don't think I can take much more,' one businessman said. Another commented: 'What used to be one of the busiest shopping towns outside of Belfast is quickly becoming a ghost town.'

Around this time, a four-page document entitled 'Drumcree Winter initiative' was prepared by the Strategy Committee of the Grand Orange Lodge and marked 'Secret – Orange Eyes Only' at the top and bottom of each page. Its purpose was 'to map out a scenario whereby movement can be made in respect of concluding the July parade and providing a framework in which future parading issues can be addressed. It is an integral part of this initiative that the process is carried out within a four week time frame, thus there should be no undue delay in its implementation.' It then set out a number of phases of the plan:

> Step 1: A meeting to take place which will include the Institution, Archbishop Eames, Archbishop Brady and a Roman Catholic priest from the Garvaghy parish [...] prior to 13 November 1998. Note: Should this meeting become public knowledge before the process is complete, a carefully worded statement signed by District/County/ Grand Masters, should provide the cover required. The sensitivities of the institutions must be recognised and those attending must not be leading figures/office bearers of the residents association. The purpose of the meeting includes demonstrating our willingness to dialogue (not negotiate) with interested parties.
>
> Step 2: A parade of Portadown Orangemen, plus friends, to take place in London on 14 November 1998 to 10 Downing Street (possibly to hand in petition). Followed by a meeting with the Prime Minister. Finance is available for this trip. Wider demands need to be presented to the PM.
>
> Step 3: Portadown, County Armagh and GOLI agree to issue a joint statement on 19 November 1998 that all public protests will be suspended. The presence at Drumcree will remain. Note: The purpose of such protests as articulated previously was to highlight the ongoing dispute. The process itself will generate such publicity. The protests can begin again if the process is derailed although setbacks and a longer time frame than envisaged must be allowed for. While there are protests outside the control of the Institution, it must be made clear and forcibly that such are not welcome by the Brethren of Portadown District during this period. This move by the Institution should be welcomed with minimum detraction by interested parties, such statements need to be canvassed in advance.
>
> Step 4: The parade takes place on 29 November 1998 from Drumcree

Parish Church to Carlton [*sic*] Street Orange Hall.

Step 5: The Prime Minister creates a Civic Initiative to address equity in cultural accommodation.

Step 6: The Institution agree to play an active role in such an initiative.

It is hoped out of same may emerge a blueprint for local bodies, which could amicably address local contentious issues in a conciliatory rather than confrontational context.

While there was a conciliatory tone and evidence of some movement in the document, the initiative it outlined would never work, for it also contained the following: 'Proviso – The steps outlined will only be entered into when the following guarantees are forthcoming via accredited conduits from the Prime Minister. To be received by 6 November 1998. (I) Objections to the completion of the parade will be withdrawn. (II) Permission to complete the parade in a dignified manner will be granted. Note: The content or make up of the Initiative will not be negotiating chips in accommodating the parade. Such matters will be clarified after the parade has occurred.' Given the residents' unyielding insistence that a parade could not be a pre-condition, and that the most recent proximity talks had foundered on this very point, the Orange strategy was inevitably stillborn. The document set out a number of further objectives which compounded this likelihood. It wanted the Parades Commission suspended until a review of the legislation had taken place, demanded an assurance from the Chief Constable that the parade would be allowed to be completed in a dignified manner and called for the 'demonising of the Institution' over 'the tragic deaths of the Quinn brothers and Constable O'Reilly' to be 'halted and refuted'. In conclusion the document noted: 'At present the Institution has to continually defend its position or respond to negative criticism, the Garvaghy Road Residents are off the hook with regard to justifying their position. This process will highlight the inconsistencies and interagency [*sic*] of that position.'

Shortly before Christmas 1998, after Jonathan Powell's fruitless trip to the Nutts Corner talks, the prime minister decided to support another high-powered initiative in an attempt to help Trimble and and head off Drumcree Five in 1999. Its genesis lay in some earlier work by Alistair Graham. Given the sensitivity and complexity of the mediation task, Graham had been frustrated by the lack of a professional negotiator and believed the participation of an experienced mediator was essential if the dispute was to be resolved. In late 1998, in an atmosphere of general despair after yet another violent marching season with no sign of a solution, Graham went to see his friend Campbell Christie, the general secretary of the Scottish TUC in Glasgow, and asked his advice. Christie put forward the name of Frank Blair, the head of the Advisory Conciliation and Arbitration Service in Scotland, whose expertise was in bringing parties to disputes together and helping them find a solution. Graham passed the name to security minister, Adam Ingram; it was fed into the government discussions about a new Drumcree-broker, and Blair was approached and agreed.

As part of the preparation for this phase of the resolution process, an Orange delegation went to Downing Street on 23 November to see the prime minister, Tony Blair. When McKenna heard about it he too insisted on a meeting with the prime minister before agreeing to participate. It was about this time that Frank Blair made his first contact with the two sides, holding separate meetings because the Order would still not agree to direct talks. For the first time in the arm's-length negotiating process, Frank Blair introduced a formal structure: the parties first had discussions with him to air their views, in what were lengthy, sometimes heated brainstorming sessions. They were then asked to draw up detailed position papers, setting out their agenda, concerns and desires. By forcing each side to articulate its position and commit it to writing, he intended to identify what common ground existed between them and calculate their bottom lines. He was also plotting to draw them to the point where the inevitable next step would be direct dialogue to resolve the outstanding issues.

The indirect exchanges dragged on through the early months of 1999 without any signs of flexibility or compromise on either side, the deadlock exacerbated in March by another violent murder. The victim was Rosemary Nelson, legal adviser to the residents and the solicitor acting for the family of Robert Hamill. That morning she had just driven away from her home in Lurgan when an under-car booby-trap bomb placed by Loyalists exploded, killing her instantly. There were immediate accusations of RUC collusion in the killing and calls for a murder investigation entirely independent of the RUC. Over the course of a violent moment Nelson was instantly transformed from a campaigning small-town solicitor into an international crusader for human rights and her brutal killing was set to become one of the enduring controversies of the troubles. At the time of her death she had, in fact, been embroiled with the RUC and the Independent Commission for Police Complaints (ICPC) in a decidedly tangled dispute about the investigation into a series of formal complaints alleging that police officers had threatened Nelson would be killed. She had first emerged as a controversial figure in the summer of 1997 after one of her clients was acquitted of the murder of a former member of the Ulster Defence Regiment. Shortly afterwards she again represented the same man when he was charged with the close-quarters murder of two community police officers in Lurgan, and she was instrumental in having the charges dropped. During the same period she was also closely involved in the Drumcree situation as the legal adviser to the Garvaghy Road Residents Coalition. Arising from these events, the series of official complaints was made for formal investigation.

In a country town comparable to Lurgan anywhere beyond Northern Ireland, Rosemary Nelson would have been preoccupied with buying and selling farms and houses, making wills and settling estates and representing clients who have fallen foul of the law in many minor ways. But she found herself in a cauldron of political turmoil, civil disorder and sectarian hatred with clients and a stock-in-trade of an altogether more serious nature. Her work took her well beyond the confines of the local courthouse. A few weeks before her death she had accompanied a delegation from the Garvaghy Road to Downing Streeet and she regularly received visitors from all over the world inquiring into the events she was handling. Such was the partisan nature of the community she served that the traditional neutrality of the legal profession had evaporated: she worked for one side and was hated by the other. Hardline Loyalists, to whom she had become as much a hate figure as another murdered solicitor, Pat Finucane, sought to justify her murder and smear her reputation by spreading malicious untruths about her. She had been having an affair with one of her clients, a notorious Armagh Republican, they said. Others claimed that her slight facial scars were the result of surgery to repair injuries caused by a premature explosion while she was making bombs for the IRA. They were actually the result of a botched operation to remove an unsightly 'port-wine stain' birthmark.

The murder was a particularly bitter blow for Brendan McKenna. The two had known each other since childhood, attended the same primary school and played together; Rosemary Magee, as she was born, was a year older. McKenna and Brid Rodgers were in the United States at the time of the murder and flew back early to attend the funeral. 'It was devastating,' he recalls. 'A lot of the residents regarded Rosemary as a friend as well as their solicitor and her murder had a very traumatic impact. It made people very angry and that got deeper because of the disgraceful way the Orange Order behaved.' The night before the funeral, coincidentally St Patrick's night, the Orange Order held a 'stew night', with a number of noisy bands playing party tunes, in Corcrain Orange

Hall, the first time they had ever held such an event. Nearby on the Garvaghy Road, several cars and a bus were burned out, petrol bombs were thrown and police fired seventeen plastic bullets during the disturbances. The RUC later admitted that one of its officers struck McKenna on the eye.

The killing amplified concerns that were already on the table about the safety of the residents' leaders from the increasingly violent threats and intimidation coming from extreme Loyalist quarters. McKenna had raised the issue of Nelson's personal safety during the talks in Armagh when he gave Powell copies of Loyalist leaflets being circulated in Portadown. One branded McKenna 'the man with no future', and another accused Nelson of being a former bomber, a lie that was repeated after her murder. It also listed the address and phone number of her office. An official from the Northern Ireland Office had visited McKenna a couple of days later and said he and Duffy might qualify for inclusion on the Key Persons Protection Scheme because they were elected representatives, but that Nelson and others were not eligible, and the RUC had said there was no reason to believe she was in immediate danger. McKenna says he raised the matter with Powell again and received assurances that it would be dealt with. McKenna recalls: 'We said we were very worried because Rosemary was a high-profile person because of her work for the coalition and she was an easy target. It was ridiculous for the RUC to say she was not under immediate threat. Jonathan Powell wrote to us saying he was surprised that Rosemary would not be eligible and promised to do something about it.' One senior British official involved in the effort to resolve the dispute said: 'There was a very noticeable change in the attitude of the residents after Nelson's murder. They became much more hardline and blamed the Orangemen for what happened because they believed she had been killed because of her involvement in the dispute.'

Whatever the hardening of their position, McKenna was not deterred from soon afterwards taking a bold step: meeting David Trimble. On 29 April, Alistair Graham said that the commission had not decided whether the Drumcree parade would be given the go-ahead or blocked again come July, and warned that time was running out to find a resolution which would avert another crisis. He called on all sides to engage and work together as quickly as possible to avoid another decision being imposed on them. Throughout Frank Blair's process, David Trimble had been working in the background to keep the Drumcree issue in play as one of the outstanding factors in the overall political process and the efforts to trigger the final stages of the Belfast Agreement. He used his influence to open doors for Portadown District, to persuade them of the importance he attached to the protest and the priority he still assigned to it himself. The district was divided. Some were supportive and content to work quietly with him; others were unimpressed and labelled him 'the absentee MP' because he now rationed his visits to Portadown and his constituency to avoid having to face ostracism for his support of the Agreement. When he took the bold step of meeting the Pope during a visit to the Vatican during a two-day conference of Nobel Peace Laureates (he had been jointly recognised with John Hume in 1998) diehard Orangemen shuddered. David Jones, the Portadown District press officer, said what many of them felt: 'It's ironic to think he can go and meet the Pope but he can't come near his own constituency without an armed guard. People here no longer feel he represents them or Loyalism in any way. I think people would be only too glad if he went over and stayed with the Pope.'

In April, Trimble wrote to all elected representatives in the area, Assembly members and councillors, asking them to take part in discussions about the dispute, which at that time had lasted for just over 300 days. McKenna was now, of course, an elected representative and included on the invitation list. He accepted. As far as he was concerned, it was a response to four years of requests from the residents for a meeting with their local MP. The encounter took place on 4 May in the Craigavon Civic Centre. Trimble hoped that a meeting with McKenna would have two positive outcomes. By acting as proxy for the Portadown District, he thought the residents' demands for direct contact could be neutralised, and by drawing McKenna into discussions he hoped to begin the process of engagement that the Parades Commission required in order to even consider the prospect of a parade that year. Trimble was wrong on both counts. The residents continued to demand direct contact with Portadown District.

Trimble's hand, in seeking to present a united front from the Orange side, was also considerably weakened when both the Mayor of Craigavon, Mervyn Carrick, and Denis Watson announced they would not be attending the meeting. Watson said: 'I will not be attending a meeting convened by the MP for Upper Bann, who has sat back for nine months and done absolutely nothing about Drumcree. He has not done anything for his Unionist constituents in Portadown, who are in the front line of this dispute. I will also not be sitting down with people who are representatives of Sinn Fein-IRA. As far as I am concerned the ACAS negotiating work of Frank Blair is the only operation in town.' Despite being accused, in all but name, of using Drumcree for his own political gain, Trimble intensified his deal-making efforts, holding a series of meetings with Portadown District officers, the majority in an Orange Hall in Moira, well away from prying eyes who kept an eye on the comings and goings at Carleton Street. Contemporaneously he also met McKenna, Joe Duffy and other Garvaghy residents at Stormont.

All this activity, against the backdrop of inter-party talks there and summits in London and Dublin, with prime ministerial involvement, to push forward the provisions of the Belfast Agreement, aroused deep suspicion among the people in the Garvaghy Road. Their strong feelings were evident when over 800 of them packed into St Mary's Hall in Obins Street on the evening of Monday 17 May to discuss widespread reports that Sinn Fein and the SDLP were preparing to agree a political settlement that would include a financial package for the area in return for a parade. Their fears had been fuelled by the recent talks between Trimble and local elected representatives. McKenna's own position was that a further parade would be possible as part of an agreed settlement, but it could not simply be in return for money. The Orange Order would have formally to recognise Nationalists as equal citizens of the town. Speaking afterwards, McKenna said, 'There have been absolutely no proposals put to us about a deal, and it is clear from the response at tonight's meeting that the issue of the Garvaghy Road is not negotiable.' Contrary to the continuing Orange claim that the Coalition was a puppet of Sinn Fein, a government official who attended the meeting as an observer reported that many of the grass-roots speakers had expressed distrust of both Republicans and the SDLP.

With another Drumcree looming and no sign of a settlement taking shape, Archbishop Eames was facing yet another period of Calvary. Over the preceding couple of years his role in the Drumcree crisis had fundamentally changed. Instead of being an 'honest broker', trying to assist the two main parties towards a mutually agreed solution, he had been forced into a firefight to prevent his entire church being torn apart. The modern Church of Ireland, with some 350,000 adherents, is one of the 37 independent provinces of the world-wide Anglican Communion. It is an all-Ireland, cross-border body, fully independent of state or political control in either jurisdiction. It is organised into two provinces, Armagh and Dublin, each headed by an archbishop. Robin Eames, the Archbishop of Armagh and Primate of All Ireland and Metropolitan, is the most senior of the two archbishops and ten bishops who run the dioceses through which the church operates. The overall policy-making body is the General Synod, the church's parliament, which consists of two-thirds laity and one-third clergy. Its members come from the diocesan synods who are, in turn, elected by the parishes. In each parish, power resides with the locally elected select vestries, who appoint the Rector and oversee the way the church is run. So, unlike the authoritarian Catholic church, where the laity are excluded from any formal role in governance, a bishop's power is unquestioned and parish priests largely dictate the rules to their congregations, the Church of Ireland operates in a more democratic fashion. The relationship of a bishop to his clergy is that of a pastoral 'Father in God'.

With the annual Sunday Orange service at Drumcree parish church such a central focus of the turbulence, it was inevitable that the church would not escape the effects of the convulsion. Orange influence in the church in the north is considerable. About a quarter of the 1500 clergy are members, some holding senior chaplain positions in the Order, although some Orange sources put the figure at only 75. With most local select vestries having a substantial representation of Orange members, the Institution's influence reaches up through the Diocesan to the General Synod. Except for the border counties of the Irish Republic, there is little interest in the Orange Order in the Irish Republic, where Protestants, including the Church of Ireland, are a minority in a state which, though increasingly secular, is still heavily influenced by Catholic standards and sensitivities. For instance, the national broadcaster, RTE, still precedes its 6 pm television news bulletin with the Angelus bells.

Concern about the way the church was caught up in the Drumcree conflict steadily escalated among southern Anglicans as confrontation succeeded confrontation. It came to be shared by many of the northerners, reflecting the fact that many Orange brethren from the other denominations had been appalled by the scenes of violence associated with Drumcree and had distanced themselves from it or, in many cases, resigned. A pressure group, which called itself Catalyst, emerged within the church in late 1996 calling for the organisation to act to protect its image and reputation. After the events of 1997 its voice became more strident. Following what it called 'a fourth scandal surrounding Drumcree church', Catalyst wrote to all clergy in the Church of Ireland, north and south, asking them to sign an open letter requesting the rector and select vestry of Drumcree not to invite the Portadown Orangemen to participate in the morning service the following year. On 30 September, having been signed by 162 Church of Ireland clergy and laity, including Dr Walton Empey, the Archbishop of Dublin, the second most senior figure in the church, it was sent to Drumcree parish.

Soon afterwards, the matter was considered by the Reverend John Pickering and the select vestry and rejected in ringing tones. On 12 October, Pickering said: 'It must be stressed that nobody can be denied the right to attend a service to worship Almighty God. I want to state clearly that I will never deny the right of worship to any person, including any member of the Orange Order. Let there be no doubt that Morning Prayer will be held on the Sunday before 12 July every year as it is held every Sunday.' Archbishop Eames, who feared the situation could fatally divide his church between opposing factions in the north and even north-south, decided to steer a middle course. Eight days later, in an address to his diocesan synod in Armagh, with Pickering looking on, Eames said the Portadown Orangemen would have to honour three pledges before being welcome at Drumcree church the following July. He called on Portadown District to pledge to avoid any action before or after the service which would diminish the sanctity of worship at Drumcree parish church, to obey the law of the land before and after the church service, regardless of the Parades Commission's decision on whether the parade could return via the Garvaghy Road, and to show respect for the integrity of the church and avoid the use of church property in civil protest.

Immediately afterwards, outside the meeting, Pickering defiantly said: 'The service at Drumcree goes ahead as it does every Sunday in our church'. The Archbishop's pledges were also swiftly rejected. David Jones, the press officer for the district, said: 'We will not be able to honour the pledges. One of them is to obey the law but regrettably, because of the situation which has developed, we don't accept the authority of the Parades Commission. So regrettably that's one particular law we cannot accept. Our protest still goes on.' In a radio interview ten days later, Jones made a much more personal attack on Eames, accusing him of acting 'against the principles of the reformed faith' by trying to ban the Orangemen from Drumcree. Denis Watson, the county grand master, who had earlier said that Orangemen would have no problem accepting the pledges, accused Jones of breaching protocol and immediately suspended him from the Order, but as a result of severe pressure from many in Portadown District the suspension was rescinded the following day.

There the matter simmered uneasily over the winter, but the scale of the rift that was now threatened within the church became evident in May when the General Synod convened in the Royal Hospital at Kilmainham in Dublin. There Eames again warned the Portadown lodges that they would not be welcomed at Drumcree unless they resolved the dispute or pledged to obey the three conditions he set out in October. A motion calling on the rector and select vestry to withdraw their invitation to the Portadown Orangemen to attend the July service if they did not promise to adhere to the three pledges of good behaviour was passed by a majority of 363 to 67, discrediting claims that opposition to the service was mainly from the Republic. Archdeacon Alan Harper, who proposed the motion, said: 'The actions and attitudes of those congregating outside the church after public worship have made a mockery of the worship itself, have damaged seriously the Church of Ireland in the eyes of the world, have compromised its mission and witness and have scandalised very many of its members. Such a situation is intolerable. An act of worship must not be perverted by using it as an occasion for acts of violence, verbal or physical.'

Pickering was unmoved. He pointed out that the vote did not change the situation because the synod did not make law, a view confirmed in an official church policy statement explaining a motion passed at Synod 'is not about permitting or prohibiting, rather it is an attempt to convey an expression of the mind of the General Synod and has moral but not binding authority'. The Catalyst group accused the Bishops of abdicating responsibility and failing to give leadership. They pointed to the work of a sub-committee on sectarianism which had recommended new church legislation giving bishops the power to 'determine that a particular service should not take place because it might be attended by specified scandalous circumstances', but the bishops rejected the proposal and it was not put to a vote. Given the large majority in favour of withdrawing the invitation to Drumcree, Catalyst believed Eames would easily have secured support for the additional powers.

By June 1999, with Drumcree Five fast approaching, and the possibility of Frank Blair engineering the right circumstances for direct dialogue as elusive as ever, both sides grew impatient and asked him to set out his own proposition for a way forward. He agreed to draw up a paper that would be put to both sides during proximity talks at the Interpoint Centre in Belfast which would be held over two days in the first week of June. The key element in the document was the proposals for the church parade that summer and in the years ahead. In a draft headed 'to be used as a discussion vehicle', with some conditional sections in square brackets, Blair listed the inward and outward routes, street by street, providing for a return march along the traditional Garvaghy Road route that year but not in the following year or thereafter. Instead his proposal was to 'establish a [field] commemorating Orange Culture', somewhere in the neighbourhood of Drumcree church, during the year June 1999 to June 2000, to and from which the Portadown District would march. The 2000 march would, he envisaged, be a ceremonial one to inaugurate what a later part of his document described, in square brackets, as a Commemorative Field and Cultural Heritage Centre.

Frank Blair's proposal was seen as the first stage of a five-year plan, taking up the £15 million 'McCusker package' that was still on the table, earmarked to improve infrastructure and social conditions in the town. Some of it would be used to build the heritage centre or memorial, which could have been in the form of a building or a museum, according to unformed ideas which emerged during the months of brainstorming. There had also been, for instance, discussions about rates rebates for Orange halls and greater recognition of Orange and Protestant culture. At the end of the first day of the talks, despite his feelings about the Nelson murder, McKenna was reasonably happy with the Blair formula and the other residents, unsure about it, were coming round. Another sectarian murder, however, soured the atmosphere. In the early hours of Saturday 5 June, the second day of the Interpoint proximity talks, Loyalist attackers hurled a brick through the window of a house in the Corcrain estate, and then followed it with a blast bomb. Elizabeth O'Neill, a 59-year-old Protestant married to a Catholic, tried to throw the device back outside but it exploded in her hand, killing her instantly. The Coalition members only agreed to go back to the talks after much heart-searching debate. If they had known fully what was going on in the Orange constituency, they would probably have been more outraged still.

When Blair's formula was shown to them it was immediately rebuffed. Nigel Dawson, the district secretary, a hardline traditionalist who worked for Craigavon Council and whose duties including acting as mace bearer, flicked through the outline proposal when it was presented by facilitators. He did not even read to the end. When he realised it did not provide for an immediate parade he pushed it aside and said there was no basis for agreement. 'It was exactly what the residents had been asking for,' recalls David Burrows. 'We were being asked to agree to have one more parade and then no more in return for money. It was an attempt to bribe us. It seemed like Blair had completely ignored everything we had said. We just told him the whole exercise had been a complete waste of time.' Such dismissive behaviour was typical of Dawson and the majority of Orange leaders, who were only interested in getting a parade, lacked negotiating skills and saw every document or proposal in black and white terms, failing to understand the necessity to read the implications between the lines, an essential skill in any mediation process.

David Campbell, Trimble's chief of staff, immediately telephoned Downing Street to tell Powell the Blair initiative was dead. A short time later, Powell received a similar call from William Bingham. He was not directly involved in the talks but had been faxed a copy of the document by Watson. Bingham says: 'It was unbelievable, absolutely incredible. It

contained everything the residents wanted and nothing that we wanted.'
The next day, Sunday 6 June, the Order held its now weekly protest
parade at Drumcree and Gracey, who had just returned from a two-week
holiday in Rhodes, recited a two-page statement denouncing the ACAS
negotiator as 'anti-Orange' and making it clear that Portadown District
could see no point in further talks.

By this time the peace process too was in utter gridlock. Two major
initiatives, each presided over by the British prime minister, at
Hillsborough Castle just before Easter and at Downing Street in May, had
both failed to persuade either Sinn Fein or the Unionists to take the next
steps, unilaterally or together, in triggering the transfer of power to
Belfast and the full implementation of the Agreement. All sides were
lining up to settle for a review by the original peace-broker, George
Mitchell, which would last until September. On 15 June Tony Blair flew
yet again to Northern Ireland for more political talks and meetings to try
to kick-start both the peace and the Drumcree processes.

That day, Powell and the prime minister met an Orange delegation in
the secretary of state's office at Stormont in a bid to persuade them to re-
engage with the ACAS negotiator. They were expecting a hard time from
the Order but not the bad-tempered eruption that so suddenly took place.
At one stage during what both sides remember was a tense meeting,
Richard Monteith, who had been appointed as legal adviser to the district,
stood up and angrily threw Frank Blair's proposal on the table in front of
the prime minister. Other members of the delegation watched in amaze-
ment as Monteith shouted at Blair, and at Powell who stood up and
shouted back. Then the prime minister raised his voice, pointed at
Monteith and told him sternly and coldly that he would not be
intimidated. The solicitor was then persuaded to sit down.

The incident marked Monteith's emergence as a key figure in the crisis,
but he was a man with a chequered history. That same month, the Lurgan
solicitor, who was deputy district master of an Orange lodge there, was one
of ten men found guilty of obstructing traffic during the Drumcree protests
in the town on 9 July the previous year. It later emerged that eight of the
ten were members of the Order. Another of those convicted was Philip
Black, who had acted as election agent for Denis Watson in the recent
Assembly elections. Monteith and Black were fined £150 each for causing
a tree to be on the roadway and £150 for obstructing traffic. Craigavon
Magistrates Court heard how soldiers, hiding in undergrowth, had seen
four cars containing ten men pulling into a lay-by. They got out and pulled
a tree, which had been cut down two days earlier, across the road. They
were challenged by the soldiers and ran off but were caught a short distance

away. (Later a motorist crashed into the tree. His car was damaged but he escaped with minor injuries.) After his Stormont outburst Monteith apologised to his colleagues, explaining that it had been triggered by an aversion to Jonathan Powell's pointing a finger to emphasise his conversation. The outcome of the meeting with the prime minister was negative. The Order refused to re-engage with Frank Blair, a message they conveyed in person at their final meeting with him in Belfast 48 hours later.

Despite these setbacks, Powell had not given up on making progress and the morning of Saturday 26 June found him back in Northern Ireland on another unpublicised mission, with yet another formula on the table. It drew elements from all the previous rounds of talks but contained some interesting new ones that had their origins in the direct contacts between Trimble and the residents. Expectations about making it stick were so high that the prime minister was on stand-by to fly over and witness a signing ceremony which would obviate the need for the Parades Commission to issue a determination, due 48 hours later on Monday. The formula was based on two documents, one from Trimble, the other prepared by the residents. Their six-point document stated:

1. Portadown District LOL 1 agrees to meet and engage directly with the GRRC. Such talks are not conditional and have no pre-determined outcome, except that both parties give a written undertaking stating all options are open for discussion and debate. An explanatory note should accompany this undertaking stating, that for the GRRC, this means exploration of the possibility of an Orange march, and for Portadown District, the exploration of the possibility of no march. The Frank Blair discussion paper should form the agenda for such talks.

2. Portadown District, the Grand Orange Lodge of Ireland and all other associated and support groupings recognise and acknowledge the damage which 11 months and three weeks of continuous demonstrations, marches, rallies, etc., have caused, and announce an immediate, guaranteed and permanent ending to all such activities. Such a guaranteed and permanent ending must allow the creation of a breathing space and goodwill period of several months to be established in order to determine the bona fides of such an announcement.

3. An agreed Portadown Community Forum is established and will meet as soon as possible.

4. The annual Drumcree march, after having obtained the consent of at least 66% of the residents of the Catholic community in Portadown, may possibly proceed to or from Drumcree, on a date to be specified and agreed upon.

5. A proper and meaningful socio-economic initiative for Portadown is announced and is to be effectively implemented, targeting those areas of greatest need in compliance with TSN (Targeting Social Need) and other requirements, including the provisions of the Northern Ireland Act 1998. Structures that operate elsewhere be examined to establish their appropriateness to the Portadown situation, taking into account methods of best practice, etc.

6. In addition to working together in the (yet to be agreed) structures of the Forum, all parties commit themselves to working genuinely and constructively in an agreed format to improve community relations in Portadown, to understand each other's positions, and to reach consent and agreement on all future marches to or from Drumcree.

The most important developments were the willingness of Portadown District to meet the residents directly for unconditional talks with no predetermined outcome, and the proposal for any march along the Garvaghy Road to proceed only after the residents had held a poll and at least 66 per cent approved.

Powell started his work in the Drumcree community centre, discussing the issues with Brendan McKenna and Peter Quinn, the facilitator for the nationalists. During their exchanges, Powell commented how difficult it was to get to grips with the situation when he didn't know the local geography. Quinn immediately suggested a trip to Drumcree hill to let Powell see the situation on the ground for himself, and asked McKenna to accompany them. The leader of the Garvaghy Road residents, hated by the Orangemen, feared that he might be recognised and shifted nervously in his seat when they arrived at the hallowed ground and parked. Quinn pointed out to Powell the various landmarks and indicated where the army fortifications would be placed again the following week if the dispute was not resolved. After dropping McKenna back at the community centre, Quinn drove Powell to Craigavon Civic Centre, the offices of the local council, which were normally closed at weekends but had been opened specially after a request from the Northern Ireland Office. Powell wanted somewhere easily accessible but discreet for his round of highly sensitive preliminary talks, which unlike the other initiatives were not publicised.

Early in the afternoon, Gerry Kelly, the hardbitten Sinn Fein negotiator and IRA veteran whose terrorist exploits included the planting of car bombs in London in 1973 and escaping from the Maze prison with 37 other prisoners in 1983, arrived by car and slipped quickly through the doors to meet him. Others present were Quinn, Roy Magee and senior civil servants. Although Powell's attempt to use Martin McGuinness to pressurise McKenna had backfired, Powell was again hoping Sinn Fein would use its muscle to persuade McKenna to compromise on a formula in the interests of the wider peace process. Kelly refused, insisting that only the coalition could decide whether to accept anything and ruling out any interference by his party. The next morning, Sunday, David Trimble and his chief of staff, David Campbell, arrived at the council offices to meet Powell and the facilitators. Powell told them he still had hopes for a deal. Shortly before lunch, Powell, Quinn and Magee drove back to Castle Buildings at Stormont, where a more formal round of negotiations had been scheduled. Trimble was accompanied by David Campbell, Richard Monteith, David McNarry and Graham Montgomery, while Denis Watson, David Burrows and other senior county and district officers were in a room nearby to be briefed on developments and give their endorsement to a deal.

Trimble believed a deal was possible because a parallel proposal, which he had persuaded Portadown District to endorse at a special meeting the previous Thursday, would give McKenna his key demands: direct contact with Portadown District, a financial package to improve the area, a civic forum to discuss economic and social issues in the town, and an end to all protests. While endorsing the proposal, the district had made it clear that it would not negotiate directly with McKenna and had appointed Trimble and the rest of his team to act on its behalf. A senior member of the Order recalls: 'Many of the senior officers believed there was a strong possibility of a parade if they talked. They wanted off the hill and knew their support was haemorrhaging badly because the wrong elements had come in, dozens of new members who never darkened a church door and were only attracted by an opportunity for confrontation. There was a concern that the influence of those people was growing and that the chances of a deal would fall the longer the protest went on.'

As far as Trimble was concerned that Sunday, it was only a matter of dotting 'i's and crossing 't's. David Kerr, one of Trimble's closest aides and his press officer, was telephoned at home in Fermanagh, where he was having dinner with his family, and summoned to Stormont to prepare for a press conference. Other party apparatchiks, such as Ray Hayden and John Laird, were also called and asked to come and help. Trimble recalls: 'We went into those talks with a high expectation that they were going to succeed.' He remarked to colleagues on the way in: 'If this works I'm opening champagne tonight.'

When McKenna came into the room with his large delegation, he embarked on what had now become one of his classic diversionary ploys.

Adopting a very aggressive posture, he refused to get into negotiations until Trimble clarified in what capacity he was at the talks: as First minister, as MP for Upper Bann, or as a representative of the Orange Order. When Trimble said he had been mandated to speak on behalf of Portadown District, McKenna asked if everyone around the table would reaffirm their commitment to the Belfast agreement. In support he tabled an eight-point document stating that the Agreement 'and the Northern Ireland Act which followed must form the blueprint for any resolution in Portadown.' There followed eight rights ranging from the right to freely choose a place of residence to the right of women to full and equal political participation, all of which, McKenna said, must be respected. Angry and incredulous, Trimble pointed out that as he was one of the key figures responsible for bringing the Agreement about and was one of its signatories, his own commitment could not be in doubt. However, he had to admit that Portadown district had declared its opposition to the deal. McKenna then changed tack again and rejected the proposal from Trimble. It was very closely in line with the residents' draft, but fatally differed in that it provided for everything to flow after a march along the Garvaghy Road had taken place. McKenna said they could not facilitate a parade in circumstances where it was a precondition. When Trimble angrily suggested that McKenna had given clear indications that he would endorse such a proposal, the Coalition asked for an adjournment, saying they would rejoin the talks in an hour. They never returned.

Attention swiftly moved to Windsor House in downtown Belfast, where that afternoon the Parades Commission was meeting to consider the application for the Drumcree march along the contested Garvaghy Road route. Portadown District was convinced that McKenna had no intention of negotiating and was engaged in a deliberate stalling exercise because he knew the commission was in session. Burrows says: 'The problem is that Brendan McKenna knew he could sit back and do nothing. After the decision in 1998, he knew the commission was probably going to rule in his favour. There was no incentive for him to talk to try to resolve it.'

Outraged by McKenna's behaviour and virtual walk-out, an angry Trimble left Stormont around midnight and travelled to Windsor House, where Alistair Graham and the other commission members were still meeting. He asked them to delay their decision to allow more time for discussions and urged them to take into account McKenna's rejection of the deal and rule in favour of the Order. Powell also travelled to meet the commissioners and asked them to delay the announcement. Having acceded to Tony Blair's pressure the previous year, Graham was adamant that he would do nothing to place another question mark over the commission's independence, but he agreed to delay the announcement by 24 hours only after the meeting degenerated into a shouting match. 'I have never in all my life encountered such sustained hostility as I did in that meeting,' recalls Trimble. Next day the commission, in its second major Drumcree determination, ruled in favour of the residents.

Graham recalled, in his ruling, that a year earlier he had expressed the hope not to be issuing a determination on this Drumcree parade: 'In 1998 we explained that we were breaking the cycle which had seen successive parades forced down the Garvaghy Road. A breathing space was needed and we urged all those involved to demonstrate greater responsibility in moving forward whatever processes were necessary to resolve the problem. Instead we have all watched, with growing frustration and disappointment, the way in which the Portadown District has used that available time. They, like the rest of the Orange Order have refused to meet with or to recognise the Parades Commission. They have applied week after week to complete last year's parade while doing nothing to change the circumstances which led to our ruling. They have held other parades and marches adding to a collective pressure to change the Commission's decision through a series of support parades, demonstrations and protests, some of which have degenerated into sectarian disorder and violence.'

Graham went on to spell out the 'serious impact which this ongoing failure to resolve the situation is having on the commercial, social and economic life of Portadown. Public disorder on a frightening scale. Sectarian hatred spilling over into violence, even tragic deaths. Families traumatised on both sides. Businesses which are just about hanging on by their fingertips. Commercial rents have dropped through the floor – ever fewer want to rent space in the city centre. Continuing parades and protests deter shoppers and casual visitors. These activities put jobs at risk. Jobs of Catholics – jobs of Protestants – jobs of everyone.' Continuing his scathing attack, he turned to 'the often-repeated accusation that the Commission is somehow out to destroy Orange Culture and Heritage by banning marches. I have said from the day I was appointed that this is a Parades Commission, not a No Parades Commission. It is our job to try to find ways to facilitate parades whilst balancing the rights to which I have referred. And if you look at the results, I would say that we have done just that. Over 4500 parades have been notified to the Commission since the first of July last year. We have looked in detail at 259 of these, and in turn have imposed route conditions on only 141 parades. 141 out of 4500. And when I tell you that over a third, 55 to be precise, of that 141 were for Portadown No 1 District, I do not believe that accusations of anti-Orangeism really stand up. Nor can we accept that the Commission, through its decision last year has contributed to heightened tensions or to worsening community relationships. The difficulties over the Drumcree church parade are a symbol of a fractured community, and it is the failure of all sections of that community to come together to find solutions that leaves the Commission no option but to arbitrate.'

Expressing regret that the high-powered efforts of recent days had not led to a resolution of the dispute, Graham welcomed the recent proposals, which were tabled during the failed face-to-face talks. Noting that while their positions had moved closer together, the absence of local accommodation, and the late hour at which the discussions had been brokered, had contributed to their failure, he went on to say that there was still no evidence that sufficient steps had been taken to demonstrate a substantive and sustained process of engagement on the part of Portadown District LOL No 1 and the Garvaghy Road residents. 'The Commission reiterates its view that such substantive and sustained engagement is required to stabilise and restore community relations in Portadown.' He then gave the Commission ruling that the return parade was prohibited from proceeding beyond Drumcree parish church or Drumcree Road, or entering that part of the notified route which included the entire length of the Garvaghy Road, including Parkmount and Victoria Terrace. 'The return parade shall, therefore, retrace the outward route as detailed above, or alternatively parade participants shall disperse no later than 2.30 pm from Drumcree parish church.'

Meanwhile, Tony Blair had flown into Northern Ireland and travelled to Stormont for a series of talks with political leaders, intensifying his efforts to secure agreement to devolve power to a new inter-party administration. While this was his main objective and preoccupation, he also made time in his packed itinerary for the Drumcree protagonists, seeing again members of Portadown District and the residents of the Garvaghy Road. McKenna also consulted the Irish prime minister, Bertie Ahern, who had joined the political talks. Both sides were equally uncompromising because they shared a deep concern that their sacred traditions, in terms of Portadown, would be swept aside in the wider interest of revitalising the peace process and the Belfast Agreement.

To bolster his own politically vulnerable position in the wider political context, Trimble's priority remained the prize of a Drumcree deal which he felt had been so narrowly swept from under his nose. Insisting that the matter had to be resolved, he persuaded the prime minister to meet an

Orange delegation which included Harold Gracey, David Burrows, Nigel Dawson, Denis Watson, David McNarry and Richard Monteith. The Orange delegation was actually shunted into a waiting room while Blair and Ahern held simultaneous meetings with Gracey and McKenna in a desperate bid to secure a last-minute compromise. What exactly transpired at that subsequent meeting between Blair and the Orange delegation would become the subject of enduring conflict, but for the time being, although they maintained a hard line in public, the Orangemen went away from the prime minister reasonably content that he had taken up their concerns and would soon deliver.

With tension rising in the community and the security forces now gearing up for another confrontation, Trimble tried to gain the moral high ground on 29 June by releasing details of his proposals in an attempt to increase public disapproval of the residents and Parades Commission. Trimble said he had publicised the terms to enable 'people to know how close we came and how reasonable the Portadown District proposals were'. He added: 'People also need to know how unfair the Parades Commission determination was. They said they wanted a degree of accommodation and dialogue. That happened and it wasn't recognised.' At the same time Trimble's chief of staff, David Campbell, sent a confidential memo to him and Jonathan Powell. It stated that Portadown Distract had indicated that if the parade was not allowed to take place on July 4, it would refuse to enter any further discussions and hold nightly protests for the next two years.

In the run-up to Drumcree 1999, the police in Portadown had been coping with an upsurge in sectarian tension and a potentially troublesome parade in their area virtually every night. Again they had planned a massive security operation with an enhanced and improved 'Maginot line' which, it was generally agreed, had been a successful innovation a year earlier. This time the ploughed and boggy field, a moat and the much-photographed lines of razor wire were the work of 33 Field Squadron Royal Engineers. Among the innovations they had incorporated in the CCO this time was a gate which could be opened for a senior RUC officer to receive a protest letter from the leaders of the halted parade. The layers of defence across the fields were to provide protection for the RUC and to make sure that peaceful protesters were not endangered. 'We put in a twenty-metre ploughed zone on the far bank, an enhanced, deepened and widened ditch and a single concertina of barbed wire on the home bank. This was another statement of intent, spelling out that this was the point of no return. We had signs saying that. The razor wire was a last line of defence. The unit worked very hard and it paid off,' said Major Guy Jackson. 'The barricade looks horrible but it's effective, and all credit to my guys'.

With the imminent incorporation of the European Convention on Human Rights into British law and tighter restrictions imposed on the use of plastic baton rounds, the RUC faced new legal hurdles in keeping the peace at Drumcree within the law. One of the requirements was to maintain a graduated and proportionate response to any disorder. The previous year, while soldiers were topping up the moat, they had turned a hose on some troublemakers preparing to bombard them with stones. The dispersing effect of the water jet was noted by the police and raised during the comprehensive debriefing that followed each Drumcree. At the time, the force was working with the Belgian police on a project to train police in South Africa for public order work and the idea of borrowing two water cannon vehicles from them for the 1999 marching season was taken to Flanagan and approved. As a result two RUC crews travelled to Belgium for training and drove the lumbering navy-painted vehicles back to Belfast in time for Drumcree Sunday. 'The principal aim of our operation and tactics is to make it virtually impossible for violent demonstrators to come "nose to nose" with the police and to protect us from injury by blast or pipe bombs,' said one senior officer. Following the death of Constable O'Reilly, officers undergoing public order training had been given a stark lecture about the danger of such weapons and how to deal with them.

Again there was an equally major logistical operation to back up the 3500 soldiers, and the similar number of police who would be deployed, most from Mahon Barracks. There the army had mustered 100 tents and 800 camp beds and tables, a daily ration of 4000 litres of petrol and 1000 litres of diesel and a bank of portable latrines and 500 bales of toilet rolls. The cookhouse and a field kitchen, with a team of ten chefs, ordered in 2500 kilos of steaks, 2236 kilos of pork chops, 52,000 rashers of bacon, 36,000 sausages, 9000 eggs, 500 loaves of bread, 10,000 bread rolls for packed meals, hundreds of gallons of milk, 240 kilos of pears, apples and bananas and 1000 oranges.

The evening before the march, Flanagan visited the barracks to talk to his officers and oversee final preparations. He said: 'I have a duty to protect the safety of my officers and the entire community. We are therefore preparing for the worst and hoping for the best. I am sure common sense will prevail.' The Orange Order in Portadown had backed the police in taking increased security measures. While Harold Gracey, the district master, publicly criticised the preparations, the lodge contacted local police a month earlier and indicated it would support such measures. Watson said: 'We have learned our lessons this year. The image of the Orange institution has suffered enough in recent years and we do not want any further damage.'

While Flanagan was at Mahon barracks, a couple of miles away, on the night before the parade, Pickering paid a visit to Gracey's caravan at the church, where he was meeting Watson, Burrows and a number of other senior county and district officers. Pickering, who had been at the forefront of the controversy within the Church of Ireland throughout the year, reminded them of the three pledges requested by Eames and suggested that they should hand in a letter of protest to the police when the parade was stopped and then ask people to go to the field at the back of his rectory, well away from police lines. After the service the next morning, that is precisely what happened. In an operation carefully choreographed in a series of mobile telephone calls between district officers and the police officers at the CCO on the bridge, the parade formed up after the service and walked to the barrier, where Superintendent Mervyn Waddell came out through the specially-fitted door to accept their letter of protest about the parade being halted. Then, to general surprise, the marchers did an about turn and returned to the church, where they were asked to disperse and go home. The majority did. The Order had also taken a deliberate decision not to provide food or any catering facilities to discourage people staying on, a move which defused tension and ensured peaceful protests. That night, although the massive security operation stayed in place and there was some very minor trouble, the atmosphere at Drumcree hill was more relaxed than at any time since the stand-offs had begun. It was a welcome relief for the police and soldiers on duty at the lines. During the evening, some of them were even able to accept an invitation to a family barbecue in one of the houses marooned within the operational area. The Army added to the party spirit by deploying two pipers to entertain them.

Fears that Loyalists, still discontented by the failure to get a march along the Garvaghy Road, would open a second front by creating a 'new Drumcree' in the warren of streets around the Ormeau Road in Belfast were defused when the Parades Commission pragmatically co-operated in allowing the main demonstration in Belfast to be held at the nearby Ormeau Park, across the river Lagan. So, despite the real fears of another major community convulsion, Drumcree and the Twelfth of July period passed off far more peacefully in 1999 than the RUC had dared hope. The security statistics for the period from 4 to 13 July underline the dramatic change in the situation. Public order incidents were down from 614 to 43;

arrests from 266 to 49; petrol bombings from 625 to seventeen; hijackings from 178 to four; and criminal damage to homes, buildings and vehicles from 761 incidents to 70. Only 25 RUC officers were injured, compared to 76 the year before, and one plastic baton round was fired in contrast to the previous year's 823. The water cannon were deployed but not used, and were shipped back to Belgium at the end of August.

The respite, while welcome, was just that. In the week between Drumcree Sunday and the Twelfth, relations between the Orange Order and the government had seriously deteriorated again when a delegation met the prime minister in Downing Street on July 8. Proceedings got off to an encouraging start. As soon as the prime minister came into the White Room, overlooking the Downing Street garden and Horse Guards Parade, the first priority was for the Orangemen to be photographed with him. Gracey, however, was not enthusiastic and refused. When they settled down to talk, relations swiftly plummeted when they were told there was no guarantee of a parade in Portadown that year. To the prime minister's bewilderment, during the exchanges about parades, one of the delegates persistently tried to turn the conversation to the plight of the pig farming industry. The Orangemen, who had smiled for the cameras on arrival at Downing Street, were grim-faced and angry when they left. As far as they were concerned, Tony Blair had betrayed them.

The Orange Order insists that, at the previous meeting in Belfast, just before Drumcree, the prime minister gave a clear, unequivocal undertaking that he would guarantee a parade along the Garvaghy Road at a later date if they ensured there was no violence and appealed for calm when the parade was again halted, in line with the Parades Commission determination, the following Drumcree Sunday, 4 July. Downing Street insists that the prime minister never gave a specific guarantee. They put it down to 'a clash of cultures' with the prime minister saying he wanted to get the march down the road, was going to try to find a way to get the march down the road and couldn't see why it shouldn't be done, particularly because it would help in resolving a bigger political problem at that time. In their view they failed because, in the end, they couldn't get the residents to sign up. An official recalls: 'Gracey took that very literally as meaning that he would get the march down the road, which is a different sort of thing. The prime minister was describing what he wanted to try and achieve. He did not realise that Gracey would have taken him quite so literally and, indeed, he didn't take it quite so literally until after we failed to deliver it, when it suddenly became holy writ.'

The Order still insists they were given a specific guarantee and even cite dates that were mentioned by Blair at that meeting: Sunday July 11, or others in August or September. Some within the Order believe Gracey misinterpreted what the prime minister said, but others insist his interpretation was accurate. In fact, they say Blair identified three possible alternative dates for the return parade from the church to be completed. David Burrows recalls: 'We were led to believe that the parade was going to go down the road if we kept the protest peaceful. That is why Harold asked people to leave the field. It wasn't just Harold who thought that was what Tony Blair said. We all did. Our attitude was that he was the prime minister and the most powerful person in the country, so, if he promised to get a parade down the road, we believed him. Looking back now I think we were betrayed by him.' Watson feels equally let down: 'They walked to the police lines and then walked away, but never received any recognition for that. After all the talk about taking the moral high ground, the district did it and then found that nobody seemed to notice.' Trimble gives Blair the benefit of the doubt. He believes that Blair, having persuaded the Parades Commission to delay its announcement in 1998, had failed to grasp that he had no power to override its decision. 'I don't think the government at that stage fully appreciated the consequences of the existence of the commission. I don't think the prime minister misled them. I don't think he realised that the government had no power over the issue.'

Throughout these tense weeks, Graham and the other Parades Commission members, had become more and more uneasy about Trimble's back-door access to Downing Street, which, they believed, undermined not only their credibility and effectiveness but also their legal standing. During often acrimonious encounters at the House of Commons, Trimble maintained relentless pressure on Graham to have the commission permit a parade. The suggestion that the prime minister had made a direct arrangement with Portadown District to let them march aggravated their anxieties, which reached breaking point at the end of July when a flurry of Sunday newspaper reports, undoubtedly the result of briefings by Unionist politicians, suggested that the government was preparing to abolish the body as part of deal to settle Drumcree. Graham phoned Downing Street the next day, Monday 21 July, and asked if there was any basis for the reports. Powell responded by letter 24 hours later: 'Dear Alistair, you told me yesterday that there had been a number of stories in the press in Northern Ireland suggesting I had proposed the abolition of the Parades Commission as part of the negotiations on Drumcree. As I told you, this is entirely untrue. We issued a denial to the press yesterday. The future of the commission has not been, nor will be, part of the agenda for these discussions and, as you know, the prime minister continues to have complete confidence in the work of the Parades Commission.' At the end of the month, the day before he departed for a family holiday in Tuscany, Blair invited the Commission over to Chequers, his official country residence in Buckinghamshire. He reassured them in person but also signalled that it would be desirable for a march along the Garvaghy Road 'in the right circumstances'.

Whatever the actual truth of the matter, ignorance or calculated political deception by the prime minister or misunderstanding by the Orange Order, the reality remained, after the 1999 marching season, that a solution to the Drumcree problem still had to be found. The problem was clearly still preying heavily on the prime minister's mind, even while he was on holiday. A few weeks later he took time to call McKenna to persuade him to take part in another negotiation. That autumn, the government launched another round of talks. Their principal imperative in doing so was now abundantly clear: to help Trimble, whose anti-Agreement opponents within his bitterly and almost equally divided party were gaining ever more ground and posing a serious threat to his very leadership. The British judgement was now deeply concerned that Trimble would be unable to deliver a compromise on the Agreement if a parade did not take place. Drumcree and the Northern Ireland peace process had now become inextricably entangled. Brian Kennaway says the nature of the protest changed dramatically in 1998 as it was seized on by anti-agreement Unionists as a means of attacking Trimble. 'They portrayed the blocking of the parade as evidence that Unionists were being sold out and Trimble needed a parade to show the contrary. The shift was discernible. After the referendum Drumcree became an anti-Trimble, anti-Agreement protest and that alienated many people inside the order who had voted for the Agreement. While Grand Lodge voted and came out against the Agreement, the reality is that the institution was deeply divided, just as the wider Unionist community was divided, but those who supported the Agreement increasingly felt that they were not wanted.'

With such an urgent political imperative, this time the government kept the effort in-house, under the control of two junior ministers at the Northern Ireland Office, Adam Ingram and George Howarth. They took the chair when a series of proximity talks got under way on 24 September. The venue was Stormont House, an elegant red-brick mansion, once the residence of the Speaker of the Northern Ireland parliament but which had since been converted into a complex of meeting and dining rooms for the Northern Ireland Office ministers and officials, some of whom also lived in small suites on the upper floors when they were in Belfast. Ingram had come to Northern Ireland as Mo Mowlam's deputy and had stayed on to assist Peter Mandelson who replaced her in 1999. He was seen as a semi-abrasive 'Glasgow Jimmy' figure and the residents distrusted him from the outset because of his boyhood links with the Orange Order and a fear that, as security minister, he would be too heavily influenced by the police. George Howarth, a Liverpool MP and recent arrival, was an unknown quantity in Belfast who kept a low profile.

Given his past experience of McKenna's methods, Trimble tried to forestall any of his now customary procedural wrangling by producing a mandate, signed earlier that day by Harold Gracey, which stated: 'This is to confirm that Rt Hon David Trimble MP, Richard Monteith, David McNarry and David Campbell are the political and legal representatives of Portadown District LOL No 1 and have authority to represent the views of the said district in talks to resolve the Drumcree impasse, subject to any proposals for agreement being brought back to Portadown District LOL No 1 for consideration and approval.' To Trimble's fury, McKenna was still not satisfied. Minutes from the meeting record that he complained that the statement did not say the four people named had authority to represent the views of the district, or the power or authority to engage or negotiate.

For its part, the Order, which was still sore about the prime minister's perceived betrayal and which felt it had not been given sufficient credit for already participating in a series of similar talks, proposed that the Parades Commission should send independent observers to monitor the talks and report back. The Commission agreed, but when the observers arrived the Coalition representatives, McKenna, Joe Duffy, Donna Griffin and the solicitor Patricia Drinan, who had taken over from Rosemary Nelson as the legal representative, refused to agree to them being admitted and they were sent away. The talks finally collapsed on 1 December after a head-to-head between McKenna and Ingram, whom the residents accused of being biased in favour of the Orangemen and determined to allow them down the Garvaghy Road. In a terse statement issued afterwards, Ingram said the talks had ended because the residents 'no longer accept me or any other government minister as the chair of these or any future discussions. I therefore have to say that it has not been possible at this stage to reach agreement on the complex and sensitive issues involved in the Drumcree situation.'

The Ingram talks were doomed from the start. In yet another twist, McKenna took to arguing that as the British government was part of the problem, it should not be adjudicating. He said the initiative ended because the government ignored repeated calls by the Coalition for a 'neutral third party' to chair the meetings. It was more than just a negotiating ploy, for McKenna well knew that just such a party was already in the wings, waiting for a cue to move to centre stage.

Meanwhile in the cold and dark early hours of a December morning, with getaway cars close by, nine foolhardy Orangemen, wearing their sashes, led by one carrying a Union flag, staged a march along the Garvaghy Road. An accomplice video-taped the escapade. The residents dismissed it as an early Christmas pantomime, but it annoyed most people in the Order, especially Portadown District, who saw it as a cheap stunt that made their uphill task all the more difficult.

Chapter Eleven

The cancer of Drumcree

While millions throughout the world marked the start of the new millennium at midnight on 31 December 1999 with spectacular firework displays, lavish parties and rivers of champagne, Portadown District's celebration was notably more modest. Sixty-four-year-old Harold Gracey and his family attended the traditional watch-night service in Drumcree parish church, watched a fifteen-minute firework display along with a couple of hundred of the brethren and their families, and then participated in a feast of hot soup, tea, sausage rolls and sandwiches. They all expressed the hope that the new year of 2000 would see an end to the vigil at Drumcree. Afterwards Gracey returned to his caravan by the church to continue the protest which had begun in July 1998 and which, he said, would last until they won permission to complete the march along the Garvaghy Road. Within a couple of weeks, however, the leader of the Orange Order in Portadown appeared to have broken his pledge to maintain a permanent protest on the hill.

Apart from a holiday in Rhodes the previous May and a week when he mourned the death of his mother, Gracey maintained he had been constantly in residence in the caravan, which was equipped with power, heat, a television and a telephone, but a survey of activity at the caravan over two weeks in January found no sign of life. Vincent Kearney, for the *Sunday Times*, visited at random times on ten days after 17 January, calling in the morning, afternoon and evening. The earliest call was at 7.15 am and the latest 1.30 am. On all occasions the caravan was empty, and there was rarely anyone in the vicinity of the church. Shortly before 11 o'clock on the morning of one of these visits, David Jones, press officer for the Portadown lodge, was telephoned and asked if Gracey was still at the caravan. Jones said he was still there, but almost simultaneously a *Sunday Times* photographer pictured Gracey putting out the wheelie bin at his home. On the gate of the modest bungalow his wife Ingrid had tied a large orange ribbon, which she insisted would not be removed until her husband came home.

The episode demonstrated what many senior Orangemen, including members of Gracey's own district lodge, had begun to admit: the protest had degenerated into farce and disarray. A confidential document submitted by David McNarry from the Grand Lodge strategy committee to Trimble's Stormont office on 22 February commented: 'It is likely that politics will for the time being overshadow any government focus on the parades issue,' and warned that 'we cannot allow a prolonged drift to set in.' There were no new ideas, only a series of issues raised and questions posed that could have been formulated at any time in the years of deadlock. The hub of the issue was among them: 'A coherent strategy has to be established. Talk or not to PC [Parades Commission]?'

McNarry, who ran a tile supply company and was a Unionist councillor in Newtownards, was one of the most visible members of Grand Lodge but often steered an erratic individual policy course. About this time, in apparent defiance of the Order's non-recognition and boycott of the Parades Commission, he had unsuccessfully applied to join it. The restructured Commission was, in fact, announced on 16 February. Alistair Graham, who had recently been knighted and was standing down, was replaced as chairman by Tony Holland, the Principal Ombudsman with the Personal Investment Authority Ombudsman Bureau in London. A former senior partner in a firm of Plymouth solicitors, where he worked for 35 years, he was a past president of the Law Society for England and Wales and a former Chairman of the Executive Board of JUSTICE, the British Section of the International Commission of Jurists. Billy Martin remained a commissioner, and Roy Magee, who had served from March to December 1997, was re-appointed. The new members were John Cousins, Permanent Secretary of the Students' Union at Queen's University, Belfast, Peter Osborne, a senior consultant in economic and community development, Sir John Pringle, a retired High Court judge and former Recorder of Belfast, and Peter Quinn, managing director of a consultancy company specialising in economic analysis and strategic planning who, with Roy Magee, had been a facilitator in the Drumcree talks in 1998 and 1999. (The residents had earlier mounted an unsuccessful legal challenge to the composition of the commission, claiming it had too many Protestants and not enough women.)

At the same time, the secretary of state, Peter Mandelson, published the findings of a review initiated on 8 October 1999 into the work of the Parades Commission 'within the existing framework of law and structures'. The review concluded that the commission had achieved many of its objectives in encouraging local agreement wherever possible and had contributed greatly to the improved atmosphere in the past two marching seasons. It mapped how more could be achieved by way of mediation and education – more media activity, better exploitation of the internet and a CD-ROM pack for schools – and how acceptance of the commission's decisions could be further improved if the reasoning behind them were set out in more detail in published determinations. Most significantly, however, it signalled that the implementation of the Human Rights Act in respect of decisions on contested parades, to enable either side to rely on any of its European Convention rights when challenging in court decisions by the commission or secretary of state under the Public Processions Act, would be carried out in time for the coming marching season: a rushed commitment, which was quietly dropped soon afterwards.

Before departing his post, Graham's frustration with Downing Street became public when he accused the prime minister of hampering efforts to find a resolution to the Drumcree dispute. He said Blair's willingness to meet the Orange Order and the residents had encouraged them to ignore the commission and undermined efforts to promote direct engagement. Graham believed the various government initiatives had failed because Downing Street shared David Trimble's view and approached Drumcree in the context of the peace process, not as a separate issue that had to be resolved at a local level. He called on Blair and Mandelson to tell both sides they would not meet them again until they held face-to-face talks. 'There is no doubt that problems were caused because of misconceptions between Downing Street and the Orange Order. The Order had unreal expectations about what Downing Street could deliver and seemed to forget that legal responsibility for parades rests with the independent Parades Commission and not the prime minister. The Order held to the hope that the prime minister could somehow deliver a parade when he was not in a position to do so. It was firmly our view that this is a local problem that must be dealt with at a local level and pressure should have been applied on both sides to resolve it themselves. The Order did appoint intermediaries to meet with us after their talks with Tony Blair, but that was not a satisfactory alternative because we never got to meet the actual leaders of Portadown District, so were dealing with the issue second hand. I believe that the prime minister and the secretary of state should not only encourage both sides to have discussions with the new commission, but should also encourage discussions at the most local level, and that would be face-to-face talks. The government should only become re-involved if those talks are tried and fail.'

While Graham was critical of Downing Street for interfering too much, he was also privately frustrated with the lack of interest in the issue from some politicians, particularly John Hume, leader of the SDLP. As the leader of the largest Nationalist party and one of the architects of the peace process, Graham believed Hume carried enormous moral and political authority and that he could have applied considerable pressure on McKenna, as he did on the main parade protest group in Derry, to be more amenable to compromise. Instead, he told colleagues, he was dismayed that the SDLP seemed to have opted simply to parrot McKenna. Graham's assessment of the negative effect of government intervention was supported in a report drawn up for the Commission by Brendan McAllister, director of the Mediation Network for Northern Ireland, which had attempted to assist both sides to reach an agreement ever since the first stand-off in 1995. The report was submitted to Graham in January 2000 and was then passed on to Tony Holland, the new chairman. Copies were also sent to Downing Street and Mandelson. McAllister was also sharply critical of government initiatives to resolve the dispute, which he said lacked direction and a clearly defined agenda: 'In what other dangerous situations would this be permitted in our modern times? For example, how many people would knowingly board a plane without confidence in the pilot, without knowing the plane would take them where they wanted to go, without confidence that the plane was designed to carry its load and that there were safety procedures in the event of a fault?' His view was that the government initiatives were 'cobbled together very quickly at the eleventh hour in a time of crisis when both sides would find it most difficult to engage with each other.' What he wanted to see was a more carefully constructed and sustained initiative rather than another attempt at a 'quick fix'.

In their discussions with Unionist politicians and with Orangemen who met the commission as elected councillors and representatives of the business community, Graham consistently pointed to the example of Derry, a predominantly Catholic city, where the Apprentice Boys could parade, while the Loyal Orders could not parade in Portadown, a predominantly Protestant town. The crucial difference was that the Apprentice Boys had engaged in face-to-face talks with the local residents' group, despite the fact that it was led by Donncha MacNiallais, one of the triumvirate of ex-prisoners, along with McKenna and Rice, whom the Orange Order had convinced themselves were the public face of a centrally-controlled IRA strategy. Giving evidence to the House of Commons Northern Ireland Affairs Committee at Stormont on 9 February 2001, MacNiallais said: 'Part of the reason why the Nationalists in Derry do not have the same sense of outrage about Apprentice Boys' marches through Derry is that the Nationalists do not feel unequal within the City of Derry. Whatever about the political inequalities Nationalists do not feel that they are second-class citizens within the City of Derry. That is in stark contrast to the situation in Portadown where Nationalists do feel they are treated like second-class citizens. The Orange Order need to update. Why do they exist? Do they exist to march down the Garvaghy Road or do they exist to uphold Protestant values and cultural values? If that is what they are about, if that is all it is about, the Protestant values and culture, the Orange Order should take a leaf out of the Apprentice Boys' book and look back to why they were formed and start to deal with the issue.'

The new Parades Commission cut no immediate ice with the Orange or Unionist community, where strident, hardline, anti-Agreement voices remained dominant. Infighting at the highest level of the Order was intensifying. Robert Saulters fell foul of them for meeting Mary McAleese, the Irish president, and Bertie Ahern, the prime minister, during a visit to Dublin. The Grand Master kept news of the engagements to himself to avoid being forced into yet another humiliating public climb-down. A year earlier, after publicly stating that 'face-to-face talks with Nationalist residents were inevitable' and that he would ask Grand Lodge to reconsider its policy, he was told there would be calls for his resignation at the next meeting if he did not backtrack. Despite the fact that he had given newspaper interviews and repeated his view before an audience of 3000 at an Orange rally in Ballymena, he did so. The ultimatum came at a meeting of the order's ten-member strategy committee, established by Saulters himself to devise plans for dealing with bans on contentious parades, when it met in the House of Orange in Belfast the next night. Saulters was told there had been an angry reaction to his comments from Orangemen throughout Northern Ireland who opposed it, and other Orangemen asked if the proposal for talks was worth resigning over. One senior Orangeman recalls: 'It was made clear to Bobby that his position would have been untenable if he had made a proposal that was rejected by a huge margin. It would have been very difficult for him to continue. Given that choice, there wasn't really a choice at all.' He was then presented with a text headed 'Press release by Robert Saulters' and told to put his name to it. It talked about 'confusion' over what he had said. Saulters became such a prisoner of the hardliners that he even refused to reply to a personal letter from the Parades Commission seeking to initiate dialogue and accused them of trying to drive a wedge between him and his Grand Lodge colleagues.

However, a year on, in June 2000, the issue was again back on the Grand Lodge agenda after Lodges in County Armagh, including Portadown District, voted by a three to one majority to change their policy and enter talks with the Parades Commission. With the new human rights-based legal regime now coming into general effect, lawyers for both the residents and the Loyal Orders had been poring over the implications of its Articles and case law to see if and how it could assist their respective causes. The Armagh motion was eventually passed after an impassioned plea by Richard Monteith, at meetings in March and May, that the policy change was necessary if the Order was to have any chance of mounting a successful legal challenge to the commission's rulings. They had to show that they had exhausted all avenues of action open to them to have any chance of being granted leave to seek a judicial review or to bring the new human rights elements into play before the courts. To widespread surprise, not least among the members of Portadown District, David Burrows, the deputy district master, spoke in favour of the policy change. Denis Watson remained silent.

The potential breakthrough was defeated by two to one when the proposal was put to the 160-strong Grand Lodge which discussed it for two hours at a meeting in Limavady on 14 June. Although Harold Gracey called for the policy change to be supported, the leadership remained silent. Watson did not speak at this meeting and abstained from supporting or voting on the issue, arguing that as county grand master it was his job to represent all his members, but privately he indicated to many Orangemen that he was opposed to the policy change. Liberals within the Order, and some of the conservative elements who supported the right of the Orangemen to walk the road but opposed the nature of the protest, were outraged at Watson's behaviour and accused him of failing to show leadership. Despite his highly pragmatic work in the early years of the protest, when he had once memorably declared that he would 'meet the Pope if I thought it would help resolve the situation', Watson had become steadily more hardline. His views changed after the Agreement, which he opposed, and his election to the Assembly. Brian Kennaway, who had worked alongside Watson during the first two years of the protest, was highly critical that he was not prepared openly to endorse the move by Portadown District. 'I think it was a dereliction of duty. What the Orange Order needed in a situation like that was someone to stand up and show leadership, to tell Grand Lodge that they had no option but to talk to the Parades Commission because it is a legally constituted body. Denis didn't want to do that because he didn't want to offend people who disagreed with that position. As county grand master he had a duty to argue in favour of a proposal that was put forward by his own county.' Monteith also attacked Watson the next time the county officers met, accusing him of betraying his members by failing to support them. Watson in turn accused Monteith and Trimble of playing politics with the protest for their own political advantage. He called them 'headlights men' trying to exploit the issue and take the spotlight. Some of his critics took to referring to Watson as 'forty shades of Orange' because of his desire to be all things to all men.

There was another damaging internal clash the same month when Saulters made critical comments about Portadown District. Before storming out of the private meeting, Gracey angrily reminded him that under the Order's rules, districts make their own decisions. Instead of getting a consensus on policy and tactics, however, Grand Lodge again backed down and assured Gracey that he had total control of the protest. All this infighting between the districts, counties and Grand Lodge and among the liberals and hardliners exploded into open confrontation on 15 June, when eight members of the Education Committee resigned: the convenor Brian Kennaway, the chairman, Arnold Hatch, Cecil Kilpatrick, the Order's archivist, and Richard Whitten, Graham Montgomery, Henry Reid, Warren Loane and Dr David Richardson.

This damaging debacle owed its origins to tensions generated after the Spirit of Drumcree rally at the Ulster Hall in 1995. It was the Education Committee who first sounded alarm bells about the group and its potentially damaging activities in a hard-hitting report. After a series of roughhouse incidents involving Joel Patton and his henchmen, animosity between the group and the committee reached a head on 12 September 1997, when Kennaway and other members of the Education Committee, including Hatch and Montgomery, were in the House of Orange preparing for a meeting with Alistair Graham. Patton had been tipped off in advance about the encounter and was furious. As far as he was concerned, the Commission was the hammer the government intended using to smash the Order, and the committee was anyway far too liberal. While Kennaway and his colleagues, who were operating as the Education Committee rather than representatives of the Order, were talking, around 50 Spirit of Drumcree members, including the towering figure of David Tweed, the former all-Ireland rugby international who had joined his team mates in standing for the Irish national anthem, 'The Soldiers' Song', when he turned out for the national team, burst into the Orange headquarters on Dublin Road and blocked the doors of the room where the committee was meeting. By the time the protest ended and the committee reached Windsor House, Graham was leaving for the airport. Kennaway spotted him leaving as he drove into the car park and they agreed to go back to his office for a 30-minute discussion.

Following the incident, the Education Committee attempted to have Patton and a number of other senior Spirit of Drumcree members suspended or expelled from the Order by bringing charges against them. One alleged a breach of rule 23, which stipulates that Orangemen should not wear their collarettes except at lodge meetings or parades. The blockaders had worn their sashes. The second charge alleged that the demonstrators had 'endangered the honour and dignity of the institution', a breach of rule 17. Patton decided it was time for drastic action. Outraged at the decision to re-route four parades in contentious areas the previous July, disillusioned by what he regarded as an abdication of responsibility by Grand Lodge and infuriated by the Education Committee and its charges against him, he planned a more defiant act of disruption: thwarting a meeting of the Grand Lodge. At 4.30 pm on 9 December, six Spirit of Drumcree members went to the House of Orange and asked George Patton, the executive secretary, for the keys to the building, saying they wanted to have a meeting and photocopy documents and would be staying late. After being given the keys, one of them went to a phone and called Patton, who was waiting anxiously at his home in Dungannon. 'The building is taken. It's ours,' he was told.

The take-over of the House of Orange, which was intended to be the most audacious challenge to the authority of Grand Lodge in the institution's history, had begun. It was the result of weeks of secret planning. With the building and its formal meeting room, festooned with Orange insignia and memorabilia, secured, the advance party began ringing around to tell other members to come quickly to Dublin Road to reinforce them. Patton travelled to Belfast with Walter Millar, his deputy, and his eldest son, Jonathan. When he left a few hours later, around 50 of his members were in occupation and bedding down for the night. Patton went home and phoned other members of the group throughout Northern Ireland to tell them to go to the building next day. Meanwhile the protestors inside faxed newsrooms in Belfast informing them of the occupation. Patton's main aim was to stop the Grand Lodge meeting and prevent the increasingly hapless Saulters from being re-elected Grand Master. The next morning, members of Grand Lodge arriving for the meeting were turned away. Patton was given a hero's welcome by over 100 more of his supporters who had gathered outside the building. Inside, posters had been put on walls, declaring 'End the betrayal now!', 'Stop selling out to Sinn Fein', and 'Saulters and Co must go'. Waxing ever more lyrical for the cameras, Patton made it clear that the question of re-routing parades was the key issue: 'The Orangemen of this country do not give Robert Saulters their consent. He betrayed them by forgoing parades down the Ormeau Road, in Londonderry, Newry and in Armagh.' The protest turned out to be futile. As the Grand Lodge delegates were turned away they were quickly re-routed to West Belfast Orange Hall in the Loyalist heartland of Shankill Road, where Saulters was re-elected unopposed.

However, in early 1998, within months of the House of Orange occupation, liberals within the Order were astonished when they learned that Saulters, the man who had branded Patton a Judas, had held a series of secret meetings with him. The meetings were organised by long-serving Grand Lodge member John McCrea, one of the two deputy assistant grand masters, who, Patton says, understood their aims. In all there were five meetings, three of which took place in the House of Orange, with the Grand Lodge delegation including Saulters, McCrea and George Patton, while the Spirit group was represented by Joel Patton, William Biggar, William Smyth and David Dowey, the self-proclaimed bigot. Meanwhile Patton had again mobilised crowds of supporters to travel to Orange halls, where disciplinary hearings were to be heard, and pack the meetings. The first was, ironically, fixed for Carleton Street Orange Hall. Around 200 Spirit of Drumcree members turned up. When they started heckling, Denis Watson, the county grand secretary, angrily banged the table and ordered them to leave but was eventually forced to abandon the meeting. On another occasion, Patton and another member were scheduled to face trial in Newtownsville Orange Hall, a ramshackle tin construction near Sixmilecross in County Tyrone. Again he organised a protest, and while the proceedings were going on inside dozens of his supporters surrounded the building and rocked it from side to side before forcing the door and going inside. That meeting also had to be abandoned.

After the incident at the 1998 Twelfth rally in Pomeroy, when he attacked the Reverend William Bingham in the aftermath of the death of the Quinn boys, Patton was called to account by the Order. In August, he got a letter instructing him to attend a meeting of the Tyrone County Grand Lodge in Clogher, followed by another from Armagh, signed by Denis Watson and all the districts in the county, including Portadown. This time, it was much more serious. He was to face charges of bringing the Order into disrepute and conduct unbecoming an Orangeman: 'rolled umbrellas at twelve paces,' as one eyewitness described it. True to form, Patton and his deputy Walter Millar, who was also charged, refused to attend the first two disciplinary hearings in Omagh. Eventually, in November, they went to face the music. At a packed meeting, chaired by Tom Reid, the county master of Tyrone, Patton (boldly wearing his district master collarette) and Millar heard the evidence outlined against them and put their own case. They were then shown to a side room to wait while a vote was taken. On the way, they were offered a deal: apologise for what they had done and they would be treated leniently. They refused and were both expelled. Although they could reapply to join after three years, they said they had no intention of ever doing so.

Many supported them. Patton's 150-year old lodge, Dungannon Hold Fast, 1620 (after the Pilgrim Fathers), handed in its warrant and disbanded. At a Spirit of Drumcree meeting in Cloughfern Orange Hall in County Antrim, 150 members pledged to campaign to have them reinstated. Within a few months the group announced that it was changing its name to the Orange Reform Movement. Its statement said the name was being changed because a bad press had distorted the nature of the organisation. It claimed 1000 members, and its mission statement said: 'The overall objective of the Spirit of Drumcree was, and still is the reform of the Orange Order to make it more democratic and its officers more accountable to the membership. Our original principles remain: (1) No voluntary re-routing of parades; (2) No talking to residents groups which are fronts for Sinn Fein/IRA; (3) One Orangeman one vote; (4) An accountable and democratic Grand Lodge and Orange Order.' With its puppet master gone, the movement disintegrated, but its hardline influence continued in the highest reaches of the Order. In line with its earlier demands, Grand Lodge conceded reforms in the way its members were chosen, and as a result a significant number of Patton's supporters gained a major foothold in the Order's policy-making circle. In another concession to them in 1998, Grand Lodge also ordered an investigation into the activities of the 'suspect' Education Committee, setting up a special committee to 'consider' its 'Constitution and Remit' without giving any reasons. When the Committee eventually reported, the Education Committee was not given a copy of the report, and, after they protested, it was only made available to them by appointment and only to be read within the House of Orange. 'We were treated like felons and when we did get to read it, it was peppered with falsehoods, half-truths and unfortunate innuendo,' says Brian Kennaway.

In a statement on 14 June, following the mass resignation, the 'Education Committee Eight' said: 'The Grand Lodge Officers have behaved in a way which has stood the principle of brotherhood on its head by instigating an "investigation" behind the backs of the Committee. To make matters worse they withheld the full Report which was the result of that investigation. Such behaviour is, in our opinion, both unbrotherly and unchristian, and therefore, as we had no other option open to us, we have, with regret, resigned.' This was an important and significant development, for it drove out of the Order a group of able people who recognised the need for it to change to remain relevant and who had a vision of what needed to be done. 'There is no doubt that the Grand Lodge officers wanted to make peace with the Spirit of Drumcree and were willing to sacrifice us to do that. Instead of tackling the extreme elements within the Order they targeted us. The Order is in crisis and the only ones who won't acknowledge it are its leaders. They are not living in the real world and are failing to offer any leadership to a very beleaguered Protestant community,' says Kennaway. The fact that such fundamental differences in the secret world of Orangeism were being aired so publicly was a measure of just how deeply and damagingly the Order had been sundered. Its internal turmoil, and the damage done to its cause by its unchanging policies, became all too evident when yet another stand-off, Drumcree Six, developed in early July, but it would be another year before the full extent of its intellectual atrophy became apparent.

The overture for the year's ritual was a low-key one. Having paraded at least once a week throughout the year, Portadown Orangemen filed the 11/1 forms for an almost continuous sequence of parades, many along the Garvaghy Road, in the run-up to the main parade. The Parades Commission approved them but continued the prohibition on any traversing of the disputed route. In a clear bid to heighten tension, Portadown District also announced there would be a Drumcree church parade on the Sunday before the main parade, this year on 9 July. Only about 500 turned up for a first march to the hill on Saturday 29 June and the advance march on 2 July was halted without trouble. The police even dared hope that, as in 1999, they might get through the coming tense days without having to activate the full extent of the massive security and military operation they had conceived and enhanced year by year as the crisis developed. When the Parades Commission chairman, Tony Holland, delivered the determination for the main parade, again excluding it from Garvaghy Road, at a news conference in Belfast on 3 July, the Grand Lodge and Portadown District were both soundly rebuked. Holland said 'the ongoing resolution of Grand Lodge not to permit members of the order to have any formal contact with the commission just does not help their case.' Of Portadown District, he remarked, 'their approach has too often been categorised by protest and implicit threats of violence.'

In line with its new policy of spelling out in detail the reasons for reaching a decision, the Commission said it has 'consistently taken the view that the freedom to parade is an important one which should only be constrained for compelling reasons. It is disturbing generally that the organisers of parades and those who oppose them often fail to acknowledge, let alone address, the genuine concerns of the other side.

That can be best demonstrated by showing respect. The simplest, and most direct way of showing respect is a willingness at least to speak to those who are most affected. And we continue to give due weight to evidence of real attempts, by either side, to address the legitimate concerns of others and a readiness to do something about them when it is within their power to do so. We don't have much evidence of any such efforts by Portadown District. Their approach has too often been categorised by protest and implicit threats of violence. They cannot escape all the responsibility for creating the circumstances in which rioting, assaults and other unlawful acts took place in 1996 and 1998. Support parades and rallies in Portadown and elsewhere have continued to provide a constant stimulus for tension and a worsening of relationships in the area. Among the results have been a climate of fear and intimidation in the Nationalist areas of Portadown, together with real stress.

'The Parades Commission has tried, time and time again, to alert the Orange Order that this strategy was unacceptable, even counter-productive. It has acted against the possibility of securing a local agreement over the Drumcree parade. We recognise that there have been moves, unfortunately unsuccessful, by some in the Order to permit some dialogue with the Parades Commission. Our very first action when we were appointed in February was to write to Grand Lodge and we are still waiting for a reply or acknowledgement. Dialogue with us would help so long as it was not a short term tactic for a quick result only. It could not however be a substitute for real engagement between Portadown District and the Garvaghy Road residents. The decision we issue today cannot – in the light of all of this – come as a surprise.'

The Order was not only unsurprised but seemed to be spoiling for a renewed fight. Brendan McKenna and seven others were arrested on 1 July after they protested at the erection of an Orange arch provocatively located at the entrance to the Garvaghy area. During the preceding week the residents had tried to mount legal proceedings to prevent the Orange Order erecting the arch, but when the Order applied to the Department of the Environment for a permit, and produced public liability insurance cover and a structural engineer's certificate in accordance with new regulations about arches, they were unable to do so. As the Orangemen finally arrived to erect the arch there was a protest and the police moved in, although those arrested were released soon afterwards.

When the first parade was stopped on 2 July, Gracey made a highly inflammatory speech: 'This battle is not just about Drumcree. This is about the Orange Order. It is about the Protestant people. They used to be on their knees, now they are on their bellies. If they don't get up off their bellies before it is too late this country will be gone. I say to Tony Blair today, last year you may have duped us. You'll not dupe us this year.' Saulters had already written to all 1350 Orange lodges in Northern Ireland, calling on them to support the stand at Drumcree with sustained province-wide protests, aimed at bringing the country to a standstill. Like moths to a flame, a growing number of protestors were attracted to Drumcree hill by these clarion calls, but they were not what one police officer described as the 'salt of the earth, decent Orangemen'. Instead they were some of the most sinister elements of violent Loyalism who would hijack the long-running protest, orchestrate street disorder on a grand scale, stage several gun-firing propaganda stunts and plunge Northern Ireland into a two-week convulsion of fear and disorder.

At the centre of this ugly manifestation of Loyalism was Johnny 'Mad Dog' Adair, a notorious Belfast-based terrorist responsible for the deaths of more than twenty Catholics, who was greeted like a hero when he arrived in the field outside Drumcree Church on 4 July with a large entourage of heavily-muscled escorts and supporters. All, including Adair's German shepherd dog, Rebel, were wearing white T-shirts emblazoned with the words 'UFF – Simply the Best'. Jailed for sixteen years for directing terrorism in 1995, Adair had no scruples about benefiting from the early release scheme under the peace-building terms of the Belfast Agreement, which he opposed in the terms: 'Shove your dove'. The Orange Order appeared oblivious to his dominating presence. In reality many were deeply frightened of him and his intimidating posse but others were prepared to hide quietly behind him in the belief it would assist their cause. So there were no attempts to ask him to leave the field, no statements distancing the Order from him, and no speeches from Gracey or any other brethren disowning the culture of sectarian violence and flamboyant criminality he represented. Instead there were cheers and loud applause as he made a triumphant progress through the crowd to the front of the CCO across the bridge. Later, as Adair looked on, masked members of the Loyalist Volunteer Force, the organisation founded by his violent soulmate Billy Wright, staged a 'show of strength' in a Loyalist housing estate in the town, reading a statement in support of the Orangemen and firing a volley of shots into the air. The incident was a clear indication that the two Loyalist groups were closely co-operating to exploit Drumcree for their own dubious ends.

Adair's manipulative manoeuvrings quickly became a vital element in propelling the entire Orange Order into one of the most serious public displays of division, disarray and disapproval in its history. As the violence progressively escalated all over Northern Ireland in the first week of protest, the RUC gradually stepped up the stages of its operation in response to the worsening situation on the streets. The two water cannon, again borrowed from the Belgian police, which were shipped to Belfast immediately after the Euro2000 football tournament ended on Sunday 3 July, were used at Drumcree on the Tuesday night, although only in light spray mode rather than with the forceful jets that are capable of knocking people off their feet. When it was brought to be refilled at the nearest hydrant, in a garden at Ballyoran, a Nationalist crowd gathered and offered encouragement to the crew to do the job quickly and get back to soaking Orangemen. The same night soldiers went out on the streets of Belfast for the first time in two years. A couple of nights later the water cannon was used to disperse protesters trying to close the vital corridor between Belfast and the ferry port at Larne.

But again some of the worst violence, night after night, took place at Drumcree. One balmy evening Chief Superintendent Cyril Donnan, the local head of the police, and a colleague were walking through the fields wearing shirt and tie instead of uniform and body armour, talking to officers on front-line duty. Suddenly an object was thrown at a line of officers taking cover behind riot shields, which landed close by. Donnan thought it was a firework and walked on, but an army bomb disposal officer later brought the remains of the object to him. It was a blast bomb of the type which had earlier killed Constable O'Reilly and, without their body armour, Donnan and his colleague would have been seriously injured or killed if it had gone off. Other new weapons used against the police were steel catapults, used to fire three to four-inch lengths of steel. The 'Drumcree golf society' also made its debut that year. A number of masked men appeared on the hill and used their clubs to strike golf balls long distances across the various layers of defences at the police. One night in the darkness a young female reporter from Downtown Radio thought for an awful moment she had been shot in the buttocks until police told her it was a golf ball, not a bullet, that had hit her.

As the week went by, without any sign of the situation easing, the Chief Constable was forced to call on the Army to erect the CCOs at Drumcree Bridge in advance of the main parade. These obstacles consisted of the two adapted freight containers that had been used the previous year, this time covered with armoured steel plate and topped with even thicker entanglements of razor wire to stop people trying to climb over them. By dawn on the Saturday morning a massive moat, earth fortifications and ploughed strip had again been completed along the fields between Drumcree and Garvaghy Road. Behind it lay miles of coiled razor wire entanglements to keep rioters and marchers at bay.

During the week, as widespread violence was going on in their name, the Portadown Orangemen had been working on a response to the Parades Commission determination encouraging them to engage with the residents and seek a mutual agreement. The offer of a parade, in such circumstances, was reinforced in a newspaper article by Tony Holland, the commission's chairman, who was facing his first marching season. A conciliatory response, in the name of Harold Gracey, was prepared and submitted to the Parades Commission as part of the last-minute push for the coming march on Sunday 9 to be allowed, on the promise that it would be followed by the talks about the crisis that everyone now agreed were essential. However, while it was being considered on the Friday morning, Gracey, who was now coming under pressure to condemn the growing violence on the streets, agreed to give two separate interviews. In the first, with a Downtown Radio reporter, recorded at 12.30 pm in his caravan, he said he wouldn't be disapproving of anything because nobody else condemned violence. 'Do you realise what you're saying? Are you sure you want to say that?' asked the incredulous reporter. Gracey nodded. He said much the same to a BBC television reporter who caught up with him a very short time later. When the Parades Commission heard his outbursts being broadcast soon afterwards, which were entirely at odds with the fine words in the document they were considering, it was concluded that Gracey had almost certainly not written and, most probably, had not even read what was submitted under his signature. The decision to block the march was thus confirmed. Next day his Orange Order front man, the incorrigibly disingenuous David Jones, claimed that Gracey had been taken unaware by the media.

Archbishop Eames had again watched the week's events with mounting horror. On 4 July he issued a statement appealing 'to everyone to exercise genuine restraint in word and action. I am well aware of the depth of feeling at this time and I urge everyone to act within the law and to think carefully of the consequences of their actions.' Above all he was concerned to avoid the Church of Ireland becoming embroiled in more controversy, so he also reminded Portadown District that 'the freedom to attend public worship is a fundamental right of any democracy but it is also a freedom of privilege and responsibility. Last July the Orange Order in Portadown acted with responsibility and within the law following their attendance at the service in Drumcree Parish Church. I appeal to them to act in a similar manner next Sunday when they are afforded such a privilege by a parish church. The responsibility of the rector and select vestry at Drumcree is great and I appeal for the utmost respect to be shown towards church property and the sanctity of public worship of

Almighty God'. In a bid to protect the church and enable them to keep the fields around it closed to demonstrators, the security forces had used one of the provisions of emergency legislation to take temporary possession of the glebeland adjacent to the church, land which is vested in the Representative Body of the Church of Ireland.

By the eve of the parade, however, Eames was so appalled he issued another statement. 'I see nothing of Jesus Christ in the nightly actions on Drumcree hill or on the roads and streets of Northern Ireland night by night,' he said. 'I see nothing of what decent law-abiding members of the Order hold dear in the words of those who call for further protest across the Province. Many such members have expressed to me their disgust at what they see in Drumcree. On Sunday the Portadown District plans to attend morning service at Drumcree Parish Church. I speak as plainly as I can. I do not consider violent protest is in any way appropriate before or after attendance at the worship of Almighty God. I do not consider the integrity of worship is enhanced by bitterness or attacks on the police before or after divine service. Much of what I have heard and witnessed lately compels me to repeat the three guidelines and conditions enunciated by the General Synod of the Church of Ireland in relation to Sunday's service: respect for the sanctity of worship, respect for church property and obedience to the law. I request an immediate, clear and unequivocal response from the leadership of the Portadown District to these points together with an equally clear call for all violence to cease immediately.'

By that evening a Church of Ireland spokesman said that Archbishop Eames had received a response from Portadown District which included this undertaking: 'At the conclusion of the Service, the District Master and Officers only will lead the District Lodge down to the bridge where a protest letter will be delivered to the officer in charge. Following an address by the District Master, the Parade will dismiss.' What the Archbishop had not been told was that same Saturday afternoon, fearful that their protest was not gathering enough momentum, the Portadown Orangemen, bypassed the Armagh County Grand Lodge and the Grand Lodge of Ireland in Belfast and issued a call for a province-wide protest on Monday 10 July. Gracey continued to send out an uncompromising and ambiguous message. At the CCO the next day, after the march had been stopped for the second Sunday, he told the crowds to get out onto the streets: 'The poll tax was brought down by street protests. Continue.' The Orangemen made great play that the local RUC superintendent was not there to receive their protest letter for first time in 104 Sundays. They did not admit that he was absent only because they had told him two weeks earlier that they could not guarantee his safety if he came though the barricade.

Against the background of a week of violence on a scale not seen since 1996, there was great apprehension about what would happen on Monday in answer to the Order's call for a complete shutdown of the country in the afternoon. Shops and offices in Belfast closed at lunchtime and sent staff home. Even the civil service was allowed to leave early, despite the contradictory signal that sent about the government's supposedly hostile attitude to the protest. By 2.30 pm the main roads out of Belfast were as busy as any rush hour, and by 3.30 the city centre was deserted. One shop owner said the closure was 'not consent for Drumcree but sheer intimidation'. Frank Caddy, the city traders' spokesman, described the call to protest as tantamount to an order to close. Although the violence subsided as the week wore on, the damage had been done: not only to the unyielding Portadown Orangemen, but to the very fabric and honour of the Order itself. Its leaders had vacillated about condemning violence, issued ambiguous and contradictory statements, refused to distance themselves from the likes of Adair and appeared to act like rabbits in a car's headlights. The depth of the internal split came into the open on Thursday night when Saulters, on television, called for an end to all protest. At the same moment, Jones was already on Downtown Radio calling for more protests. At one point some 200 people gathered outside the County Down home of the chief constable.

Again the Orange Order moved its main Belfast demonstration to the Ormeau Park to underline its protest about Drumcree and also about the continued refusal to let it march the Catholic stretch of the Ormeau Road. Some leading Orangemen used their Twelfth speeches to condemn the violence. Speaking in Ballinderry, County Antrim, Lord Molyneaux, the former Ulster Unionist leader who played a key role in persuading the government to reverse its ban on a parade in 1995, told more than 6000 Orangemen: 'Our resolution pledging loyalty to the Queen commits us to supporting the servants of the Crown. It is intolerable that some of our countrymen are launching vicious attacks on the police and the Army.' Jeffrey Donaldson also hit out at those responsible for the violence, accusing Loyalist paramilitaries of 'flaunting their aggression and engaging in displays of naked intimidation. The Order stands for higher ideals than this and must, at every opportunity, condemn the illegal activities of the paramilitaries and of all who engage in violence. There can be no room for equivocation lest the Orange Order's reputation is dishonoured by some kind of moral ambivalence.' Within Grand Lodge, equivocation and ambivalence were the order of the day. The RUC's public order statistics for the period from 1 to 13 July quantified how much physical damage had been done: 330 attacks on security forces, including thirteen shootings in which 88 RUC officers and six soldiers were injured; 313 petrol bombings; 99 cases of criminal damage to homes, 86 incidents of criminal damage to other buildings and 417 incidents of criminal damage to vehicles; and 105 hijackings. By 3 am on Friday 14 July, the chief constable judged the situation had calmed enough to send in the Army to remove the fortifications from around Drumcree, a task it completed in seven hours.

At the height of the turmoil, on 7 July, the London *Times* had reflected the stupidity of the Orange tactics in a leader entitled 'Mad dogs and Ulstermen':

> As matters stand, Orangemen, whether by accident or by design, have become the tool of the darker forces of loyalism. They must understand that there is no prospect that the Parades Commission will permit them to conduct the march as they would wish, or that ministers will overrule this under the threat of violence. If they keep on the present path of conflict, then unsavoury elements are certain to exploit it. It is not enough to ask protesters to act in a peaceful fashion in such circumstances. Drumcree is a sea of petrol and the Orange Order is handing out matchboxes. The sole manner in which the Orangemen can escape the "Mad Dogs" of Unionism barking at their heels is to march away from the Garvaghy Road and back towards the mainstream.

There are few signs that the Order is planning to do so. It blames all its troubles on the British–Irish political process and the Parades Commission and refuses to consider its role and relevance in this day and age or to re-assess what it should stand for other than marching. Drumcree has had a far more debilitating impact on the Orange Order than it admits or, more probably, even fully realises. While some new, younger members have been attracted by its increased militancy, many of the traditionalists and liberals have either left or reduced their involvement. That in turn has enabled more hardline elements to gain senior positions and influence policy-making accordingly. This will ultimately have serious consequences for the Protestant community, where many still look to the Loyal Orders for leadership and direction and regard them as a political and cultural touchstone. Without bold and imaginative leadership their sense of persecution will only increase and they will feel more and more betrayed as joint British and Irish oversight of the governance of Northern Ireland consolidates and expands in the years ahead.

In its heyday in the early decades of the twentieth century the institution was all-powerful, with an estimated 100,000 members and considerable powers of patronage. Membership was almost a prerequisite for achieving high political office or good positions in both the public and private sector. By 1972, when the Reverend Martin Smyth took over as Grand Master, membership stood at around 60,000. When he stepped down in 1997, after three Drumcrees, it was 43,000, and by the spring of 2001 it stood at 38,000, a fall of more than 1000 a year. The Order still boldly maintains that its membership is 'around 60,000 to 70,000' as Saulters recently told the Northern Ireland Affairs Committee of the House of Commons.

Even the Order's long-standing influence within the Ulster Unionist Party, the source of its patronage, is now under threat, with David Trimble pressing ahead with radical plans to transform the party structure. Under the proposals, the Order will no longer be able to send 120 delegates to vote at meetings of the 860-strong Ulster Unionist Council, the party's ruling body which elects the leader and makes decisions on policy. A majority of the Orange delegates opposed the Good Friday Agreement and voted against Trimble in a number of key votes such as the decision to enter government with Sinn Fein, which the Order's leadership opposed. Melvyn Hamilton believes the Order has changed beyond recognition: 'In addition to becoming more and more political, it has also lost its credibility and influence.'

Meanwhile the battle for its soul goes on. David Trimble says: 'I would not say the Order has been damaged beyond repair. It is too big an institution to be damaged beyond repair by an issue such as Drumcree. I think it has been more damaged by anti-Agreement politicians who have exploited the situation. Without their attempts to exploit the situation I think the Drumcree issue could have been resolved. There is a perception that some people do not want to resolve this issue and would rather keep it alive, no matter what damage it will do to Orangeism, because they hope it will somehow help them destroy the Agreement.'

Joel Patton believes Drumcree will be the breaking of the Orange Order. 'They had no option but to play the Orange card, but they played it in the wrong way and it has been trumped. It has been beaten but Grand Lodge haven't accepted that yet, and the people in Portadown haven't accepted that. This is not about walking down a road. It is right of people to have their freedom, the right to express their identity and culture in the way they want to. It is about the civil and religious liberties of Protestants. They can't walk away because if they do there won't be a next year. People must realise that Portadown is not just another parade, it is *the* parade, it epitomises every parade that the Orange Order has. If they lose in Portadown, they'll never stand on any other parade issue. They would be finished.' While many Orangemen oppose the tactics used by Portadown District and abhor the violence that has accompanied the protest, the majority still support their right to march. Denis Watson says: 'The vast majority of Orangemen are still one hundred per cent behind Portadown District's right to walk the road. Where the disagreement comes is on the strategy.'

Among the many people who had visited Drumcree and the Garvaghy Road, during the violent events of July 2000, was the latest person who had been called in to assist them back into the mainstream, Brian Currin. The South African lawyer, who had international experience of mediation and political transformation, had first come to local prominence soon after the signing of the Belfast Agreement two years earlier, when in July 1998 he was appointed the joint chairman of the Sentence Review Commission, the body established to manage the early release of what were called 'politically motivated prisoners'. Currin, who specialises in human and civil rights issues, was at the forefront of efforts to promote socio-political transformation in his native country and played a leading role in the campaigns to abolish the death penalty, release politically motivated prisoners, identify members of the security forces involved in third force death squad activities and establish a Truth and Reconciliation Commission. On the basis of this work he was invited to other countries and areas engaged in political transformation, such as Sri Lanka, the Middle East and Rwanda. Currin first came to Northern Ireland in 1995 to participate in an international conference exploring the issue of the early release of politically motivated prisoners, and following a number of subsequent visits was asked by Mo Mowlam to become joint chairman of the Sentence Review Commission. While carrying out this task he came into contact with a number of people in the Northern Ireland community, including some concerned with the prolonged Drumcree crisis.

Invited to address the British–Irish Association, an exclusive discussion group of politicians and academics which meets annually in Oxford and Cambridge alternately and is known as 'toffs against terror', Currin unwittingly sowed the seeds of his own involvement in the Drumcree saga by making a scholarly speech entitled 'Negotiation: A conflict resolution process'. Dissecting his subject with all the precision of a forensic pathologist, Currin thoroughly analysed its meaning and dimensions, all the way from its Latin roots to its role in concluding the

Belfast Agreement, which he described as a remarkable achievement. Pointing to why its implementation had been so difficult and prolonged, he ventured the opinion that 'the Agreement fudged the most difficult issues by means of ambiguities and by avoiding detail, and that the chickens are now coming home to roost,' but he added that 'in order to reach an agreement in April 1998, ambiguity on priorities and aspects of implementation [was] necessary.' The way out of the impasse, he said was to keep going. 'You've got an in-principle agreement. Don't throw that away simply because you are not able to meet implementation deadlines. It is the responsibility of the collective leadership that supported the Good Friday Agreement to negotiate and navigate your way through implementation. To do that you have to create mutual understanding, respect and trust, not only amongst yourselves, but also amongst your constituents. If that takes time, so be it.' He continued, 'Those of you who are Latin scholars will know the source of the word "negotiate". It is composed of the Latin roots *neg,* "not", and *otium,* "joy" or "leisure". It came into the English language exactly four hundred years ago in 1599. It described a process, which was not meant to be one of joy or leisure. That is still the case today, but speaking from my own experience as a South African, I can assure you that the joy that comes from a successful negotiated process makes all the agony worthwhile.'

Although he did not intend it to be so, much of Currin's prescription was also applicable to Drumcree, a point not lost on many of those present. Some Irish government officials were also impressed, and towards the end of the year, with the Frank Blair process doomed and the Ingram talks going nowhere, Currin's name was put forward as a possible successor in representations to Peter Mandelson. Some informal soundings then began about his suitability and he was probed about his interest in becoming involved by government officials: 'If you were asked would you be willing to help?' As a result of these exploratory preliminaries, he met first senior members of the Orange Order at the organisation's headquarters in Belfast in December, and then Brendan McKenna, for the Garvaghy Road residents, in Portadown.

At first there was significant unease about Currin's potential mediation role within the Orange Order. As joint chairman of the Sentence Review Commission, he was seen as the man letting the prisoners out of jail, and thereby implementing the Good Friday Agreement. To Watson and many others he was therefore suspect. McKenna was made aware of Currin's interest in the issue in late 1999, before the collapse of the proximity talks hosted by Adam Ingram and George Howarth. The Irish government, SDLP and Sinn Fein had all told the coalition about Currin's impressive address to the British–Irish Association. McKenna, who had come to take nothing at face value, contacted a number of lawyers in the United States who had visited Northern Ireland as observers during earlier stand-offs or were helping the campaign for an independent inquiry into the murder of Rosemary Nelson, and asked for their opinion. Their reaction was very positive: Currin was a well-respected human rights lawyer and mediator who had worked in some of the most difficult areas in the world. The clinching factor for McKenna was that his hero, Nelson Mandela, had appointed Currin to oversee the release of prisoners in South Africa.

The evaluation process was not all one-way. Currin had been making enquiries and forming his own impressions about the task he was being lined up to undertake, which had many dreary parallels with the former situation in his own land. There Afrikaners had formed the exclusively white male 'Broederbond', a quasi-religious cultural organisation whose comprehensive influence eventually permeated from the Cabinet, where virtually every minister was a member, all the way through the network of state organisations and the whole of Afrikaner society. Early in the 1990s, when they realised there was going to be political transformation and were confronted with the unwelcome realities of the new constitution, there was a lot of soul-searching. Their dilemma was summed up by a widely acclaimed local satirist: 'Adapt or die.' They chose to adapt, and transformed their organisation into the Afrikanerbond, which now contains many non-white and mixed-race South Africans in its ranks. After five Drumcrees, and with a sixth imminent, Currin wondered if the Orange Order could successfully be persuaded to do the same.

Currin finally decided that if he was to become formally involved then both parties would have to agree to him in advance and, most crucially, that the British government must agree to be treated as a third party to the dispute. Indeed, he considered it was so important to maintain distance and independence from the government that he insisted they must not even fund the initiative. The formalities to enable him to be nominated as mediator were all in place by early June. The Grand Lodge and Portadown District, who had overcome their earlier doubts, and the Residents Coalition all signed up, as did the British government, which accepted it was to be treated as just another party to the problem. To underpin Currin's desire to be seen as totally independent, the philanthropic Joseph Rowntree Charitable Trust agreed to meet the cost of his work. Speaking to BBC Radio Ulster soon after the announcement of his role on 7 June, he said: 'What one really needs to do is try and ensure there is a degree of trust, trust is in short supply, and work on the relationship between the parties. Until such time as one succeeds in improving that relationship, it's very difficult to break deadlocks. Often when you start unpacking the causes of conflict you find it's more to do with the relationship between the parties than the actual issue.'

Although he had been hovering in the shadows of Drumcree since the previous autumn, extensively to all the parties, Currin immediately ruled out any prospect of a resolution in time for the 2000 march. Instead he visited both the Garvaghy and Drumcree areas of Portadown extensively during the fortnight of turmoil, putting in place the first phase of his carefully-thought-out strategy to bring about a mutually acceptable settlement. During what he termed a pre-mediation process he was concentrating on underpinning their commitment to his process despite the ongoing stand-off and getting the parties themselves to set a framework for fuller discussion. For several weeks beforehand he had been engaged in often late-night diplomacy with both sides and other interested parties to try to get agreement on 23 ground rules to govern the mediation process. These included acceptance of an agreed mediator and his powers, the accountability of the mediator and the parties, the degree of confidentiality of the process, the location of talks and a timescale. He believed the deadline should be Easter 2001. With the Orange Order reluctant to meet the residents until there had been a march, and the residents opposed to a march before talks had taken place, the most crucial issue to be thrashed out was whether the talks would be direct or indirect.

Before dealing with parades, Currin wanted both sides to 'unpack' what he described as 'hundreds of years of historical baggage' to come to a better understanding of each other's position and the poor state of community relations and community spirit in Portadown. 'We have to transform a dysfunctional society and town into a forward-looking society and community. We have to cure an ill environment for a healthy environment. If that can happen, there is a chance to deal constructively with marches and a chance to find a local accommodation. The Parades Commission is filling a gap because there doesn't seem to be any other way to resolve the differences. Every time a community dispute is resolved by adjudication, the problem is made worse, the divisions deepen. You have to get agreement. My hope is that this time next year, the way in which the parties deal with each other will be different from what it has been and that they will be able to communicate and negotiate with one another to make their own local arrangements.' In order to improve community relationships in Portadown, Currin proposed to the parties that they, and the broader communities, engage in a relationship-building exercise. This was intended to be a cross-community exercise, to identify problems other than the parade issue and to draw up objectives and action plans for their implementation over an extended period. By August, Portadown District, the residents and the government had agreed to enter a formal mediation process, with Currin's target date of Easter 2001 for resolving the dispute. Two of the ground rules were not agreed: cessation of protest action and the issue of direct engagement.

Before long it became clear that Currin's work was being unwittingly compromised by the Parades Commission. In their determination of 3 July, they had set out their view of the way the dispute could be resolved and had even dangled the prospect of an early parade before the Orangemen:

> Starting with Portadown District, we see it as necessary for them:
> * first to comply with the terms of our determination;
> * to introduce an immediate moratorium on Drumcree-related protest parades and demonstrations;
> * to avoid any actions that could reasonably be perceived as an incitement to break the law or intentionally designed to raise intercommunal tension;
> * and to engage with representatives of the Garvaghy Road residents, both in the Currin initiative and in any civic forum which may be established.
>
> In these circumstances, we believe that a limited parade could take place along the Garvaghy road, in a peaceful and lawful atmosphere, ideally within the next 3–8 months. Let me repeat that: in these circumstances, we believe that a limited parade could take place along the Garvaghy Road, in a peaceful and lawful atmosphere, ideally within the next 3–8 months. The Commission would look to the nationalist residents to demonstrate that they were genuine in seeking a long term resolution of the intercommunal tensions in Portadown by facilitating the proposed parade. As to the future, we cannot envisage circumstances in which any subsequent parade could pass along the Garvaghy Road other than by local agreement, perhaps following discussions in a civic forum.
>
> These are very serious proposals. They are designed
> * to provide real encouragement to all those directly and indirectly involved on both sides, and in the wider communities who are working to achieve a fair and equitable resolution to the Drumcree dispute
> * to end the feeling of tension under which the nationalist residents of the Garvaghy Road have been living

- to recognise the right of the Orange Order to celebrate their culture
- and to create circumstances in which the Currin and other initiatives to improve relationships could flourish.

Let me stress, people will now want to see how Portadown District, the Garvaghy Road Residents and political and civic leaders will react to this. To them we say 'please consider what we are proposing and weigh your response very carefully.' Our proposals are designed to facilitate a sustained and determined effort to build good community relations in Portadown. Everyone has much to gain from that. And we ask all concerned to look to the opportunities for the future, rather than resting on the enmities of the past.

Although the Commission laid down participation in the Currin initiative as one of the tests it would use in deciding to permit a march, Currin was, ironically, unhappy. Writing later in the *Sunday Times*, he questioned the role of the commission and said its July statement was counterproductive. 'By linking to the mediation initiative, the Parades Commission has given the impression to some people that there is a formal connection between the current mediation process and the Parades Commission itself. This is most unfortunate because it called into question the independence of the pre-mediation in which both sides began to participate a couple of months before the Parades Commission's decision. Regrettably, but not surprisingly, the ruling by the Parades Commission on the Drumcree parade has made the situation worse rather that better.' The Orange Order, Currin was aware, was deeply suspicious of the Parades Commission and worried that he was in some way colluding with it. The article was therefore designed to underline his independence and to distance himself from the commission. He also took the opportunity to outline the difference between arbitration and mediation in trying to settle community disputes: 'The lesson from what we have witnessed in Northern Ireland and from community disputes elsewhere in the world is unequivocal: the solution to Drumcree, and to all parades for that matter, does not lie in a state-imposed arbitrating body. The solution must surely lie with the parties and their ability to find their own home-grown solutions. Mediation as a process provides the best possible vehicle to achieve that.'

Holland declined to comment publicly on Currin's intervention, but privately he and other commission members were furious. A short time later the mediator was invited to a meeting on another floor in Windsor House, where he was based. It was an encounter he later described to a friend as one of the most stressful of his entire career. His intervention was immediately welcomed by the Orange Order, and Watson said the remarks reinforced its argument for disbandment. 'We have said all along that this body is not capable of resolving this dispute and it is highly significant that Brian Currin, who is totally independent, should also come to that conclusion. As far as we are concerned it is nothing more than an anti-Order complaints factory.' McKenna was alarmed when he read the comments, fearing that Currin was providing Trimble with valuable ammunition for his continuing campaign to have the Commission abolished. He was also concerned at Currin's criticism of the Commission for insisting on the participation of Portadown District in the mediation process. The next time he met the residents he faced another stressful reception.

Although a number of practical difficulties stood in the way of starting the relationship-building exercise, Currin soon became frustrated by the endless procrastination on all sides. In addition, because the Order would not engage in direct dialogue, he was having to convey messages between them and the residents. This was unsatisfactory, for he felt the words on their own were not enough. Full communication required them to be accompanied by body language, eye contact, shrugs and smiles which could not be conveyed by an intermediary. There were also worrying indications that the Order may not have been negotiating exclusively with him or even with one voice. From the very wide bank of contacts he had now established throughout Northern Ireland, he learned that all sorts of rival channels were in play, some well intentioned and naïve, others more self-serving, dangerously obstructive of his own work and reducing his chances of a successful outcome. At the end of November 2000, just before flying back to South Africa to spend Christmas with his family in Pretoria, Currin issued a statement throwing down a gauntlet to Portadown District to enter direct dialogue with the residents:

> The only legal authority on Parades in Northern Ireland is the Parades Commission. In July this year the Commission reiterated the need for meaningful engagement preferably through direct dialogue. Since June this year one of the major stumbling block to progress in mediation has been the engagement impasse. Having spent many hours during the past six months trying to 'mediate' this impasse I recently informed the parties that I would go back to South Africa and would not return again until the New Year. However, I indicated that I would be willing to return earlier if meaningful engagement becomes possible before then. Since LOL No1 is wishing to exercise what it regards as a right, the onus is on the Orange Order. I have emphasised that it is up to them to

take the initiative. If the dialogue impasse is not broken, I will return to Northern Ireland in the new year to commence a relationship-building process between the broader unionist and nationalist communities in Portadown. Hopefully that will eventually contribute towards meaningful dialogue and a resolution of the parade dispute. Inability to find a quick solution to the parade impasse has prompted a number of voluntary interventions. A common characteristic of these interventions is that they are inclined to emerge from one of the traditions and only the party from that tradition is consulted. The result is that hidden agendas are suspected by the other tradition. My experience of these interventions, irrespective of how well intentioned they may be, is that they tend to undermine what little progress is being made.

For their part, the Garvaghy Road Residents Coalition issued a statement welcoming Currin's comments, and adding its own criticism of Trimble, who was, they knew, still operating in the background. It said: 'Those politically motivated efforts are linked to the wider political process. As such they are self-serving and are not geared towards achieving a solution based on equality or justice. Rather, they are clearly aimed at linking the Portadown issue to unionism's continual demand for political concessions from the British government.'

Currin's challenge to the district officers appeared to have worked. He had to return unexpectedly and urgently to Northern Ireland on Sentence Review Commission work in December, and when they heard he was in town the Orange Order asked for a meeting, which led to Monteith submitting a paper to the residents on behalf of Portadown District. Everything was still predicated on a parade being allowed along the Garvaghy Road, but there was some movement on direct engagement, and encouraging undertakings were given about the ongoing protest action. As a sign of good faith that the protest was effectively at an end, the District proposed that it would remove Gracey's caravan from the church grounds the night before the agreed parade. The authority of the response was doubtful, for its contents had not been cleared by the district members and neither the County Lodge nor Grand Master Saulters was even told about the paper. At a subsequent meeting of County Armagh lodges, David Burrows totally denied its existence.

Nevertheless Currin passed the document to the residents in December and clarified its contents for them in follow-up meetings with both parties. Although the government remained a third party to the Currin process it had remained on the sidelines so far. The residents' response

did not come until mid-February but when it did Currin immediately
identified it as having potential and some of the essential elements of a
long-term solution. In a bold gesture, McKenna and the residents were,
'for the benefit of everyone, both now and for the future', offering a
permanent compromise. The relevant section of the three-page document
reads:

> There is a growing body of opinion within our community which would
> seek the GRRC to argue, quite justifiably, for the banning of the
> Drumcree march in its entirety – a body of opinion which has arisen
> due to the cumulative anger and frustration felt by many as a result of
> the Orange Order's activities in Portadown over the past several years
> in particular.
>
> Indeed, that anger and frustration is, perhaps, to a lesser extent,
> mirrored within the Church of Ireland itself due to the Order's failure
> to give Archbishop Eames the assurances which he sought regarding
> the use, sanctity and integrity of Church property.
>
> Through our meetings with Brian Currin, we have recognised that, in
> order to commence genuine discussion on this issue, there is a clear
> need for all parties concerned to recognise the obvious – that the setting
> of a predetermined outcome will not progress the matter. For one or
> any party to insist that their, and only their predetermined outcome can
> be the sole result of any process is to negate the value and genuineness
> of that process and to undermine completely the meaningfulness of any
> such discussion or dialogue.
>
> In essence the Orange Order's December document seeks to impose
> a mandatory acceptance upon Nationalists that the only outcome must
> be on terms decreed by the Orange Order. That is a march along the
> entire route from Carleton Street Orange Hall to Drumcree returning to
> town via the Drumcree and Garvaghy Roads. We have been informed
> that LOL No 1 does not have a mandate to explore any other option. It
> is a position that the Orange Order has essentially held for a great
> number of years. In that regard, the Orange Order totally rejects the
> right of Nationalists to legitimately hold an alternative viewpoint or
> opinion on this matter.
>
> While acknowledging the opinion of those from within our own
> community urging a total ban, GRRC prefers not to adopt a position of
> seeking an outright ban, however justifiable, on the entire march. Not
> only would such a stance prevent any meaningful and genuine dialogue,
> It would effectively seek to deny the members of LOL No 1 their rights
> to freedom of assembly and expression even on a restricted basis.

It is for that reason that we suggest the following:

In recognition of the Orange Order's right to freedom of assembly (albeit on a restricted basis), and in recognition of the rights of others, the Corcrain Road/Charles Street/Dungannon Road is the route adopted by the Orange Order to and from Drumcree in July 2001 and in future years.

We acknowledge that this initially may appear to create a 'no-win' scenario for the Order. However, that is not our intention. We also recognise that the Order is fearful of a 'domino-effect' situation regarding Corcrain Road, Charles Street and Dungannon Road in the future, particularly in view of proposed housing developments in that general area. Again that is not our intention.

We are sure that the Orange Order realises that there are those who would wish to see an outright ban. Our intention in putting forward this proposal is to reach a compromise that can satisfactorily acknowledge and respect the rights of all parties. It is our belief that if properly validated and endorsed this proposal, unlike the third party assurances of the mid-Eighties and 1995, will be able to withstand the test of time.

We believe, that were a mutual agreement to be reached directly between the three parties involved in the current process regarding the above proposal, this community would publicly acknowledge the generosity of spirit and leadership shown by the Order; and GRRC would, in return, endorse a policy of non-opposition to marches along regarding Corcrain Road, Charles Street and Dungannon Road.

This arrangement, the residents further proposed, could be guaranteed in perpetuity by political, church and community leaders in whatever combination, form and manner would be acceptable to the Order.

Currin helped his Portadown District contacts to read between the lines of the document and use it as the basis for negotiation and, he strongly believed, the shape of a long-term solution. Once again they refused. It is a decision they may well come to regret. The Craigavon Area Plan for 2010 has designated four sites for building around 400 homes in the area bordering Drumcree church and the Garvaghy Road. One of the sites runs from Dungannon Road along the side road used by the Orangemen to march past the Reverend Pickering's rectory to Drumcree church. Given Northern Ireland's rigid sectarian geography and the unwillingness of the majority of people to live in mixed areas, it is inevitable that the people who eventually come to live there will be Catholics. When that happens, the parish church will be isolated from Portadown by a solid Catholic neighbourhood.

McKenna is well aware of this scenario and outlined it to Currin during their discussions. But even the prospect of hundreds of Catholics living in these new housing developments along the outward route to the church, and potentially objecting to the Order marching past their homes, has not persuaded the District to compromise. David Burrows remains defiant: 'It doesn't matter what Brendan McKenna says about guaranteeing the route now because in a few years time there could be a new residents' group with new people involved and they could ignore anything he agrees to. McKenna may think this is a generous offer, but we see it as a threat. They are clearly saying that if we don't agree to end the protest they will object to us getting to the church as well as getting home from it. But we believe it will be much more difficult for them to block our route to church because the human rights convention enshrines the right to worship as well as right to assembly. In a democratic society we don't think any court would uphold a ban on people getting to church'.

Despite the setback, Currin's operation was far from over, for over the winter, as Burrows says, the human rights factor had come into play and was heavily influencing how the Orange Order currently viewed the parading issue. Ever since it had been decided to incorporate the European Convention on Human Rights into British law, the Order believed that its traditional right to march the Queen's highway would be reinforced and put beyond any doubt in the new legal regime. So confident were they that they planned to mount a test case and spent a considerable amount of time during the summer of 2000 gathering evidence with a view to doing so. The courts were given their first opportunity to rule on the matter in October 2000 when David Tweed, a member of Dunloy LOL 496, sought leave to apply for judicial review after the Parades Commission applied restrictions to a parade in the village proposed to be held on 29 October. The legal argument turned upon the relation between the requirements imposed by the 1998 Public Processions Act upon the Parades Commission and the provisions of Article 11 of the European Convention on Human Rights, which provides as follows: '(1.) Everyone has the right to freedom of peaceful assembly and to freedom of association with others including the right to form and to join trade unions for the protection of his interests. (2.) No restrictions shall be placed on the exercise of these rights other than such as are prescribed by law and are necessary in a democratic society in the interests of national security or public safety, for the prevention of disorder or crime, for the protection of health or morals or for the protection of the rights and freedoms of others. This article shall not prevent the imposition of lawful restrictions on the exercise of these rights by members of the armed forces, of the police or of the administration of the State.'

At the High Court in Belfast, Mr Justice Kerr refused leave, a decision upheld on appeal by Sir Robert Carswell, the Lord Chief Justice of Northern Ireland. He decided: 'When one has to consider the impact of the Convention, however, the focus is not on the process of decision-making, but on the substance of the decision itself. The issue then is whether the restriction imposed on the parade can properly be said to be justified on one of the grounds specified in Article 11 (2), whatever factors the commission may have taken into account in reaching its decision. We are quite satisfied that the restrictions in the present case were necessary in a democratic society for the prevention of disorder, and that they were proportionate. We therefore consider that on this basis also the commission's determination was a valid exercise of its powers and was not in breach of Article 11. We accordingly are of the opinion that the decision of the commission to impose conditions preventing the parade from entering any public place in the village of Dunloy was not in breach of the provisions of Article 11 of the Convention and the commission was not in error in law or in its determination.'

Few understood the whole concept of human rights as well as Currin, and he embarked on some research of his own to help persuade the Orange Order to face up, at last, to the problems caused by its parades and to start talking about ways to protect and preserve their deeply cherished marching tradition. He identified seventeen international cases, decided by the European Court of Human Rights, which provided no comfort for the Orange Order. In all cases, the court decided that where any event threatened public disorder it could safely be banned by the government concerned. More worryingly for the Order, five of the cases concerned bans applied by the United Kingdom government outside Northern Ireland. Druids were prevented from celebrating the summer solstice at Stonehenge, and a pressure group, 'Negotiate Now', had been banned from holding a rally in Trafalgar Square. What these decisions showed was that the government applied a far more restrictive policy outside Northern Ireland and that it showed an extraordinary tolerance of potentially violent events there. The way that successive Drumcree protests had been managed and facilitated over recent years was the most telling evidence that a more liberal attitude applied there than elsewhere. Having brought the country to a near standstill in 2000, for example, fuel tax protesters trying to repeat their demonstrations a short time later encountered a far more robust police reaction to thwart them.

Currin embodied all this research in a lengthy document, which he completed by the end of January. He intended that it should be presented to every member of the Grand Lodge of Ireland, who were holding a special meeting at the Ballymacarret Orange Hall in east Belfast on 3 February to discuss a survey gauging attitudes towards a change in policy on at least meeting and discussing issues with the Parades Commission. Because it is such an important pointer to the way ahead for the Orange Order at this point in its history, Currin's document is reproduced in full:

REPRESENTATION TO THE SPECIAL GENERAL MEETING OF THE GRAND ORANGE LODGE OF IRELAND

The honourable Grand Master of the Grand Lodge of Ireland, Mr. Robert Saulters, County Grand Masters, County Officers, District Masters, District Officers and members, I wish to thank you for your willingness to receive from me this written representation. It follows a discussion I had earlier this year with Officers of the Grand Lodge including Mr. Saulters.

As some of you may be aware, I have been tasked by the Portadown District and the other parties to the conflict to try and find a mediated solution to the Drumcree dispute. Some of the policy issues which you will be debating and deciding upon this weekend, go to the very essence of the mediation process. Your final decisions will have a bearing upon the nature and extent of participation in that process by LOL No1. Expressed in another way, your final decisions will have a huge impact on whether or not Drumcree is settled this year and for the future.

Therefore, your meeting this weekend is of monumental significance. The implications of the decisions you make regarding engagement with the Parades Commission and Residents' Groups will be far reaching. I believe that history will judge your decisions this weekend as being of the most important decisions ever taken by the Orange Order. Why do I say that? It is because, in my view, the future of Orange Order parades in NI is in the balance. I would therefore, urge you to be rational and logical in your deliberations. I make this plea not because I hold any special brief for Orangeism and its parades. I also hold no brief against Orangeism and its parades. I come from another country on another continent where we have different issues about which to have sleepless nights. I make this plea because I know that all of you are committed to the preservation of your traditions and culture. I would, therefore, hope that the decisions you take enable you to participate comprehensively and fairly in processes and debates which will undoubtedly impact on the future of Orange traditions and culture in Ulster.

In order to assist you in making these very important decisions I see it as my duty to lay before you relevant facts which might inform the decisions you take.

I am well aware of your current policy regarding engagement with both the Parades Commission and Nationalist Residents' Groups. I have spent sufficient time in meetings with the LOL No 1 Portadown Officers and Grand Lodge representatives to fully comprehend your reasons for this policy. It is not my intention to debate with you the moral issues which inform Grand Lodge policy. The intention of this paper is to table before you objective facts so that when you decide on future policy you do so from an informed position, having due regard to the inevitable practical consequences of your decisions.

What are the facts?

The Parades Commission has, since its inception, issued a number of important determinations in respect of proposed public processions which are perceived by the unionist / loyalist community to be anti unionist / loyalist and anti Loyal Order. A consequence of some of these determinations has been prohibitions against parading along certain traditional routes. Understandably these determinations have gravely hurt the unionists / loyalist community. There is a widespread belief that the Parades Commission was set up to pander to and satisfy nationalist aspirations. It is often referred to as an unelected and illegitimate quango. The Parades Commission is accused of being partisan to such an extent that it is seen to reward violence and threats of violence by nationalist and republicans.

A belief I would want to interrogate in this paper is whether the Parades Commission really does have an anti unionist / loyalist, anti Loyal Order and pro nationalist / republican agenda. To do that I have very carefully studied:

- The Public Processions Act NI 1998 which provides for the establishment and functions of the Parades Commission;
- The Guidelines produced by the Parades Commission as to the exercise of its powers to impose conditions on public processions;
- Many of the contentious determinations issued by the Parades Commission since its inception in 1998; and
- All of the relevant cases decided by the European Commission and European Court of Human Rights dealing with the Right to Freedom of Expression and the Right to Peaceful Assembly during the past 20 years.

The Public Processions Act NI 1998, as its name suggests, does not apply in Great Britain. It is the law relating to public processions in Northern Ireland. As we all know, it was made following the North Review of 1997 which was established as a result of the widespread conflict in the summer of 1996 requiring major intervention by the police under the public order legislation. The broad purpose of the Act is better management of parades in Northern Ireland. It established the Parades Commission in 1998, one of its functions being to issue determinations in respect of proposed public processions. It has many other important functions, including promoting understanding by the general public of the issues concerning parades in the province and a dispute resolution function. As you all know: it requires organisers of parades to give advance notice of parades; it gives the Commission power to impose conditions on parades and it instructs the Commission to have regard to certain factors before making a determination. These factors are: public disorder or damage to property which may result from the procession; potential disruption to the life of the community along the envisaged route; impact on community relationships; past compliance by participants with the Commission's Code of Conduct; and finally, the desirability of allowing a parade along a traditional route. It also imposes a duty on the Commission to issue a set of Guidelines as to the exercise of the above functions.

As far as I have been able to establish, no other country in Europe has an extensive and detailed law of this nature dedicated solely to the issue of public processions.

The Commission Guidelines, and I quote from the Guidelines: 'are based on the fundamental premise that the right to peaceful assembly and freedom of expression as outlined in the European Convention of Human Rights are important rights to be enjoyed by all'. The Guidelines continue then to qualify the above by stating that the right of peaceful assembly, while important, is not absolute. According to the Guidelines, the right is subject to limitations which are to be found both in the international documents (on human rights) and in the general law to protect the rights and freedoms of others or for the prevention of disorder or crime. As will become apparent later in this document, the above statement is an accurate reflection of international and European human rights law.

The Guidelines also instruct the Commission to apply itself to the issue of proportionality. In other words, how important is the parade and compare that with the amount of disruption that it is going to cause. There is also reference to location and route: Is it mainly residential or commercial? What is the demographic balance? What is the significance of Monuments or Churches in the vicinity? Finally, what is the availability of alternative routes which are not controversial? These questions regarding route are asked in the context of the Guidelines recognising the premium attached by many to the concept of tradition.

The Guidelines require the Parades Commission to take account of communication between the parade organisers and the local community aimed at addressing the latter's concerns. The body must also be aware of any long history of inter-community strife which has its roots in the broader political conflict.

The purpose of these Guidelines is to enable the Parades Commission to properly fulfil its very important function of managing controversial processions. To that end the Parades Commission is empowered to impose conditions on parades. It is appropriate to mention here that if one goes by the decisions of the European Commission and the European Court of Human Rights, the tendency in Europe is to ban controversial parades and not to manage them.

The Parades Commission has, since 1998, consistently taken into consideration: attempts by the organisers to reach accommodation with the local residents; the threat of public disorder; the demographic balance along the route and the potential restrictions on the rights and freedoms of local residents; past behaviour of participants; and, the broader political conflict in Northern Ireland. Following its own Guidelines and principles of International Human Rights law, the Commission does not regard the Right to Peaceful Assembly as an absolute right and has not hesitated in restricting that right whenever it believes it is justified in doing so. These decisions, which have impacted on the nature and extent of parades: numbers, bands, music, flags, banners and most importantly, traditional routes, have met the wrath of the Loyal Orders.

The question is whether the anger and passion expressed by you and others within the Loyal Orders, is justifiable. I have no doubt that it is understandable.

The fairest and most effective way of judging the integrity of the Parades Commission would be to test its Guidelines and Determinations against the application of European Human Rights law. It is for that reason that I decided to research European jurisprudence on the relevant points and to that end have identified and analysed all the relevant cases over the past 20 years. For your convenience I have made summaries of these cases, 17 in all, and handed them to the Grand Master so that as an organisation you can, if you so wish, brief your own legal team for another assessment.

I found these cases extremely instructive and have come to the following conclusions:

The Public Processions Act NI 1998 is probably the clearest and most detailed law in Europe providing domestic guidelines on the application of Article 11 of the European Convention on Human Rights, namely the Right to Peaceful Assembly and Freedom of Association.

The Guidelines developed by the Parades Commission, although intended to address the unique problems associated with the right to peaceful assembly and processions in Northern Ireland, are fairly and firmly based on international human rights norms and standards.

Because of the unique problems associated with parades in Northern Ireland, there are, however, significant differences in application between Northern Ireland on the one hand and Great Britain and Europe on the other. Contrary to what you may have expected, the approach adopted in Northern Ireland to public processions is significantly more generous than the norm in Europe.

Procession organisers in England are treated more strictly in the application of English law than their counterparts in Northern Ireland.

The special reference to traditional routes and the premium attached to them in the Parades Commission's Guidelines is not a factor which enjoys any special consideration by the European Commission or the European Court of Human Rights.

To help you understand the basis for these conclusions, I set out in this document the standard approach adopted by the European Commission and Court when deciding whether or not the provisions of Article 11 of the European Convention on Human Rights has been violated by the State party. There is certainly nothing creative or robust in their approach.

They begin by quoting the relevant Article from the Convention.

Article 11 (1): Everyone has the right to freedom of peaceful assembly and freedom of association with others.

Article 11 (2): No restrictions shall be placed on the exercise of these rights other than such as are prescribed by law and are necessary in a democratic society in the interests of national security or public safety for the protection of disorder or crime, for the protection of health or morals or for the protection of rights and freedoms of others.

There is always then the assertion that the right to peaceful assembly is a fundamental one in a democratic society. This statement is immediately qualified with reference to the restrictions in article 11(2). The Commission or Court thereafter proceeds to assess whether or not the ban or restriction imposed on the peaceful assembly or procession by the member State is a violation of the right in question. If the answer is yes then Article 11(2) is applied. If the ban or restriction was not prescribed by law, then it would be unlawful. If it was prescribed by law then there is an investigation into the reasons for the restriction. The question is whether the measures taken by Government were in pursuit of legitimate aims in relation to Article 11(2): public safety, the prevention of disorder or for the protection of rights and freedoms of others. The next question is whether, given the reasons for the restriction – e.g. the prevention of disorder – the measures were necessary. It is not the job of either the European Commission or Court to substitute its judgement on this issue for that of the Government involved. It merely assesses whether the latter exercised its discretion in good faith and in terms of Article 11(2). In determining the issue of necessity, the principle of proportionality is applied. In other words were the measures taken by Government to restrict or ban the procession excessive in the circumstances, taking into account the importance of the event and the reasons for restricting it.

What struck me in particular when reading these decisions is the ease with which both the European Commission and Court uphold total bans on peaceful processions, where in my view member States have not made out particularly strong cases of public disorder or the need to protect the rights of others. It is instructive that in every single one of the 17 cases studied, Government's decision to restrict or totally ban peaceful processions was upheld by either the European Commission or Court.

My own conclusion is that in Europe the right to peaceful assembly is a fairly soft right. The interests of public safety, the prevention of disorder and the protection of the rights of others take relatively easy preference. Now that the European Convention on Human Rights is applicable in the United Kingdom, determinations issued by the Parades Commission and decisions by Courts in Northern Ireland will have to comply with the relevant European law. That means the right to peaceful assembly in Northern Ireland will similarly be subject to the interests of public safety, the prevention of disorder and the protection of the rights of others – which in any event is how the Parades Commission has approached its mandate since 1998.

However, it is my view that the Public Processions Act NI 1998 and the Guidelines of the Parades Commission, although in compliance with the principles of relevant European law, are nevertheless both creative and progressive. Broadly speaking they are aimed, not only at managing contentious parades, but also, in the process of doing that, at promoting cross community tolerance and mutual respect for traditions and cultures. There is an obvious reason for this latter objective and that reason is to be found in the provisions of Article 11 (2) of the European Convention dealing with restrictions.

The stark reality is that the right to peaceful assembly, which covers public processions, is not enforceable in an environment where processions will inevitably result in serious public disorder. The only way of neutralising the basis for such restrictions is through trust building for tolerance and mutual respect.

In my respectful view, the Public Processions NI Act of 1998 and the body it created, the Parades Commission provide a key to the preservation of cultural diversity in Northern Ireland. If that key is thrown away, the consequences for Orangeism, its culture and traditions will be dire.

Ironically from your perspective, given the approach to freedom of assembly in Europe, the Parades Commission could be the saviour rather than the destroyer of the parading tradition in NI. However, for that to happen the approach to parades in NI will have to be a collaborative one, involving both traditions, the Parades Commission and Government.

Brian Currin
February 1, 2001.

Denis Watson arrived at his home in Lurgan at 11.30 pm on Friday 2 February to find that a courier had delivered 150 envelopes, each containing a copy of Currin's legal opinion, which will undoubtedly come to be regarded as one of the most important documents in the Order's history. Watson glanced through it before going to bed. Next morning he brought the package to the Grand Lodge meeting. Currin was anxious for the document to be distributed to everyone attending, believing that his legal arguments would further his Drumcree initiative by persuasively illustrating the need for direct engagement. In the event it was neither distributed nor discussed. Towards the end of the meeting, it was announced with disdain that a document had been received and delegates were asked if they wanted to discuss it. Nobody did, much to the relief of the leadership, who for almost a year had been concealing an equally damaging legal opinion from the membership. This one had been commissioned by William Thompson, an anti-agreement Ulster Unionist who was MP for West Tyrone and an Orangeman for nearly 40 years, and prepared by Austen Morgan, a Northern Ireland-born, London-based barrister who frequently advised Trimble. In late August 2000 his report, running to almost 100 pages, arrived on the MP's desk at the House of Commons. It was uncomfortable reading.

Morgan presented a comprehensive history of parading and an analysis of the implications of human rights legislation for it. In his opinion, the Orange Order could successfully challenge the ban on the Drumcree parade and other contentious routes under the terms of the European Convention on Human Rights, which had recently been incorporated into Northern Ireland law, but two bitter pills would have to be swallowed first: the Order would have to talk to the Parades Commission and to residents' groups. Morgan praised the Apprentice Boys of Derry, who had secured a parade through the predominantly Nationalist city by entering into dialogue with Donnacha MacNiallais, a former IRA prisoner. In contrast, he said, the attitude of Portadown District had 'done considerable damage to the cause of freedom of peaceful assembly for those who commemorate 1689-91.'

The MP submitted a copy of the report to the Northern Ireland Affairs Committee, of which he was a member, and which had just started compiling a report on the parades issue. He also copied it to Robert Saulters, the grand master. Saulters did not like what he read either, and the report was never circulated to Grand Lodge members. Indeed, the majority of them did not even know it existed until many months later when Morgan published his history of parades and his analysis of human rights legislation on his own website, although his recommendations were not posted because Morgan judged it was up to the MP or Grand Lodge to make public his recommendations. These included: that the Loyal Orders should recognize the Parades Commission; that they should challenge Sinn Fein-inspired residents' groups under human rights law; and that it should formulate an overall strategy to deal with trouble spots like Garvaghy Road, the Lower Ormeau and anywhere else it was successfully challenged by residents' groups. Morgan concluded that the Loyal Orders had a choice between two scenarios: 'A stand for principle, involving a boycott of the Parades Commission, a refusal to talk to former republican terrorists, a failure to obey the law and increasing disregard of all legitimate authority, a public relations disaster at home and abroad affecting 'the Ulster people' generally, increasing pro-nationalist stances by the United Kingdom government under pressure from Dublin, more Drumcrees, and a continuing loss of members, leading to a rump organisation at once impotent and despised' on the one hand, or on the other 'an intelligent response to very difficult circumstances, involving engagement with (but not necessarily support for) the Parades Commission, engagement with local residents and genuine community leaders, a complete rejection of all republican and loyalist violence, articulated support for the rule of law in a tolerant, pluralist democracy premised on diversity, undoing some of the damage to Northern Ireland, increasing responsiveness from the United Kingdom government and exposure of surviving intolerance in the Republic of Ireland, tackling the Drumcree issue, and preventing the decline in numbers, and consequent loss of status in the majority community.'

Many liberals and pragmatists within the Order felt betrayed and shared Currin's disappointment when they learned how the Grand Lodge leadership and Portadown District leaders had adopted what one called a 'lunatic, head in the sand' approach to such important and well-grounded advice. There is now a widespread feeling that Grand Lodge leaders actively promote ignorance to pacify unthinking hardliners and traditionalists and prevent unrest. Many senior members of the institution, including the leaders of Portadown District, have privately accepted that they are not likely to succeed with a legal challenge to the parade ban unless they engage in direct dialogue, but have not told the grassroots membership the plain truth. They know that if they do the long-running protest will be exposed as a futile farce and support for them would evaporate.

In February 2001, the Order thus decided to turn again to Trimble in the increasingly vain hope that renewed political pressure from him to abolish the Parades Commission and associated legislation could override the need to submit to the judicial process, which they now perceive to be yet another card in the deck already stacked against them. On 19 February, Richard Monteith told a meeting of county officers that the Currin initiative was finished. Although Monteith shared Currin's analysis, as did other senior Order members, they still dug their heels in as only stubborn old Orangemen can. For his part, Trimble, who prides himself on his knowledge of British constitutional law, argues that Currin, despite his international reputation, is wrong. 'Brian may not know much about the European Commission, but the case law there is very solidly in the Orange Order's favour, because it will not permit the residents to use their right to protest to obstruct the right to freedom of assembly,' he says.

No one in the Orange Order had the manners to tell Currin that his closely-argued document had been rejected without any serious consideration. In February and March, in the belief that there was still a deal to play for, he was travelling to and from Northern Ireland, talking to Orangemen and residents, hoping there would be a breakthrough to head off what would be Drumcree Seven in July 2001. On 8 March, weeks short of his original Easter deadline, while having lunch with an adviser in one of Belfast's best restaurants Currin was finally told his initiative was dead. He was crestfallen. Earlier that day, a meeting with Portadown District officers had been cancelled, ostensibly because of foot-and-mouth disease precautions. After learning from a third party of negative comments about his paper from both Monteith and David Jones, Currin went to the washroom at the back of the restaurant and phoned Monteith, who confirmed that his mediation effort was indeed at an end.

There had been warning signs which Currin had failed to spot. David Campbell, from Trimble's office, who had been in almost daily contact, suddenly stopped phoning after Currin produced his paper on the future of marches. Trimble was privately delighted at Currin's failure, which he had largely engineered. By removing the international mediator from the process, Trimble ensured that Drumcree remained a local political issue. Indeed, the very day that Currin learned of his rejection by Portadown District, Tony Blair and Bertie Ahern were at Stormont for another unsuccessful attempt to resolve the outstanding political issues before the general election. Jonathan Powell and David Campbell had two private meetings, during which Trimble's man again underlined the need to resolve Drumcree in order to achieve agreement in the wider political process. Unionist party sources say the stand-off is mentioned in every substantive conversation between Trimble, Campbell and Downing Street. Trimble himself says: 'People have to realise that it will not be possible to settle this community down without a settlement of Drumcree. You can't implement RUC reform and downsizing without a resolution of Drumcree because if it is not sorted out there will still be a need for thousands of police officers to deal with it.'

Shortly before Easter, when he had hoped to have been announcing a settlement, Currin was instead putting the finishing touches to a report analysing the process and its successes and failures at that point:

> Contrary to the view of the Portadown Officers, I believe that there has been some progress. In December last year the Orange Order tabled a document which was integrative in its language and forward looking in its contents. Due to the confidentiality of the mediation process I am not at liberty to publish the document.
>
> The residents received the document and after careful consideration tabled three questions to the District. The officers answered the questions orally with motivation to me. I conveyed the answers to the GRRC and drafted a written motivation based on my understanding of

what the Portadown Officers were saying. I felt it was important for the process that the Residents should have a thorough understanding of why the District was adopting a particular position in relation to negotiations. Towards the end of February the GRRC tabled a written response to the District. This document contains a number of positive features which in my view created opportunities for further progress. Once again, due to the principle of confidentiality I am not at liberty to publish it.

In my view it is most unfortunate for the people of Northern Ireland, the people of Portadown and for the Orange Order as an institution that the District Officers decided at this critical time to withdraw from mediation. I assume they must have come to the conclusion that their chances of achieving their desired result, namely a parade down Garvaghy Road, would be better served through political intervention. The fact that the First Minister has been calling for the abolition of the Parades Commission and for Government to take the initiative and resolve the impasse by authorising a parade down Garvaghy Road would tend to sustain the strategy adopted by Portadown Officers.

Although I believe history may judge their decision harshly, mediation is a voluntary process and its ultimate success is premised upon the willingness of all parties to engage one another with the objective of reaching a resolution based on compromise. For LOL No1 the dispute is a single-issue dispute, and that is the denial of what they regard to be their right to parade along Garvaghy Road. Seen that way it is for the Portadown Officers a rights dispute and since they are not willing to negotiate their right away there is no room for compromise. It is not surprising, therefore, that they chose to withdraw from mediation and pursue a political intervention aimed at delivering the enforcement of what they regard as their right.

For the GRRC the dispute is not a single-issue dispute. Nor is it a rights dispute. They do not contest that LOL No1 has rights to Freedom of Assembly, Freedom of Expression and Freedom of Religion. The dispute is about how those rights are to be exercised in a way which does not violate the rights of the nationalist community to peace, public order, safety, security and freedom of movement. From their experience the entire July 12 parade, particularly that portion along Garvaghy Road means violence, public disorder, a threat to safety and security and severe restrictions on their movement. To exclude Garvaghy Road from the Orange Order's parade in the interests of balancing reciprocal rights is, they argue, a legitimate restriction and, therefore, not a denial of the Districts rights to Freedom of Assembly,

Expression and Religion. From their perspective this is a community interest based dispute and the only way to resolve it would be through direct meaningful engagement aimed at addressing mutual concerns and balancing reciprocal rights.

The question to which everyone in Northern Ireland wants an answer is whether this dispute is capable of being successfully resolved. There are two answers to that question depending upon how the dispute is defined. If one sees the dispute through the eyes of the Orange Order, i.e. a rights dispute about a parade down Garvaghy Road, the mechanism and process should be through the Parades Commission. It was specifically established to inter alia arbitrate contested parades, which is how rights disputes are best resolved. Therefore, once the Parades Commission has made its decision and determination then for that year the dispute has been resolved. That is how the law operates.

The fact that Parades Commission determinations in respect of contentious parades are widely criticised and rejected by the community/tradition on the losing side, is the best possible evidence that these disputes are not simply rights disputes. Parades disputes in Northern Ireland are quintessential community interest disputes with vast dimensions: historical, political, religious, cultural, social and economic.

Defined in that way, resolution of the broad Drumcree dispute will not happen unless the parties engage in meaningful negotiations and over a protracted period. Should the parties agree to do that there is no reason why a sustainable resolution cannot be found. If mediation is required for that process my door remains open.

The key to unlocking this dispute is finding common ground on the law. It is for that reason that I researched European Convention Human Rights decisions on the right to Freedom of Assembly for the Grand Lodge. Although the Orange Order now seems to accept that Freedom to Assembly is not an absolute right, their interpretation of the term restrictions provided for in Article 11 (2) is at variance with that of the courts. Their interpretation is that a planned assembly/procession may be restricted in format, nature and size. In other words numbers, flags, banners, bands etc. They do not accept that a justifiable restriction could result in re-routing a public procession. It is for that reason that they insist they have a right to parade along Garvaghy Road but subject to restrictions. If the Orange Order were to accept the legal position as expressed by the courts and the Parades Commission that re-routing is legally justifiable in certain circumstances I have absolutely no doubt that progress would be made in resolving this seemingly intractable dispute. They would realise that the only way forward, as the Apprentice Boys of Derry have successfully done, is to attempt to negotiate with objectors the retention of contentious routes.

However, I cannot see this happening until Grand Lodge grasps the nettle.

Brian Currin refuses to call this a signing-off statement. Despite not meeting his original deadline, he insists it is a progress report to date and he says his door is open to an invitation to come back again if and when the Orange Order decides to return to mediation. At Easter 2001, with the Currin initiative apparently stalled, the marching season about to begin again and Drumcree still unresolved after six massive confrontations, a vigil of more than 1000 days on the hill, and no solution even in sight, Northern Ireland was once more holding its breath.

The first omens of the marching season were not encouraging. Shortly before Easter, the Drumcree protagonists emerged from their winter hibernation and embarked once more on a round of talks at Stormont and elsewhere, uttering their uncompromising mantras on the way in and out. Again the process has been dogged by byzantine political sophistry. The deputy leader of the nationalist SDLP, Seamus Mallon, agreed to a meeting with the Portadown Orangemen, but in his SDLP role and with his colleague, Brid Rodgers, as the local assembly member. The Order insisted the meeting should be in his role as deputy first minister of Northern Ireland. Weeks later, it was said, 'a mutually convenient time for the talks has yet to be found'. After a short break in their protest, in deference to the measures imposed to control a serious outbreak of foot-and-mouth disease among farm animals throughout Britain and parts of Ireland, Portadown District announced plans for marches on Downing Street and Hillsborough to draw renewed attention to their grievance. At the same time the Garvaghy Road Residents restated their opposition to a parade. In determining the first flashpoint decision of the year, the Parades Commission decided to let the Apprentice Boys of Derry traverse the Ormeau Road in Belfast on Easter Monday morning. The residents lost a court challenge and announced a major protest. With the police braced for what looked like a bruising encounter, the confirmation of a new foot-and-mouth outbreak forty-eight hours earlier caused the Apprentice Boys to cancel their planned demonstration and the march was called off. The decision was quickly seen as having implications for Drumcree, where the 2001 church parade was scheduled for 8 July.

Portadown District said it was too early to decide and the protest would
go on, leaving the position that only more outbreaks of the highly
contagious disease or an eleventh-hour breakthrough by Currin would
halt Drumcree Seven.

The character and wide-ranging consequences of what one senior
Unionist minister in the Stormont administration uncompromisingly
described as the 'cancer of Drumcree' were graphically summed up by
the chairman of the Parades Commission, Tony Holland, in the
determination halting the 2000 parade:

PRIVATE

The dispute over the Garvaghy Road parade has come to epitomise the
whole public processions conflict in Northern Ireland. It embodies and
magnifies all the fears and concerns, founded or unfounded, which are
present wherever the issue of parades is unresolved. It has great
political and symbolic significance. This dispute has provoked massive
public disorder and damage to property. It has claimed several lives. It
has worsened the already dreadful inter community relationships in
Portadown, and more widely throughout Northern Ireland. And it has
touched the vast majority of ordinary and unconnected people who
simply want nothing to do with it, or who just get out of Northern
Ireland, with their families, at this time each year.

We think the starting point is competing identities, which have
become sharper and more focussed due largely to political events. The
result is a greater sense of identity and more confidence in the
nationalist community; and a commensurate sense of loss – loss of
territory, of influence and of tradition in the loyalist community. In the
birthplace of Orangeism, Drumcree demonstrates all of these. It has
become the touchstone. For Portadown District, as we understand it,
the threat to the Drumcree parade is a threat to everything they stand
for – for civil and religious liberty and the right to demonstrate faith
and culture in a time honoured way. Over the years they have been
asked to give up much, but have reached their limit. They believe the
residents' opposition is politically manipulated and designed to inflict
defeat on their political opinions and religious beliefs as well as their
rights. They do not understand how even a small parade, in silence, can
be offensive to anyone but nor do they believe that they should have to
'seek permission' from anyone in order to get their parade. Furthermore, in what the Orange Order see as a winners and losers situation,
they see the residents in a win-win position: no parade and they win;
parade forced down, and TV pictures around the world of police in full

riot gear in conflict with residents ensure a media victory for the residents' agenda. The Orange Order refuse to talk to the residents' spokesman, albeit an elected representative. And the Order believes that every attempt at even indirect dialogue has been deliberately frustrated – by the tactic of including social and economic demands, which the Order clearly cannot deliver, and by delaying tactics designed to block progress.

On the Garvaghy Road, nationalists feel isolated and under siege from the effects of the Drumcree dispute and the associated parades and rallies. Insensitive sectarian behaviour by bands, hangers-on and supporters fuel their general perceptions of Orange or loyalist parades. These are seen as coat trailing, provocative and devoid of any respect for the community on whom they impinge, often at anti-social hours and over long periods. Moreover, the Orange Order is seen to represent decades of anti-catholic domination symbolised by the loyal orders' insistence on marching through nationalist areas. They resent the lack of respect, lack of equality and lack of parity of esteem towards them as human beings. They have genuine fears about living in Portadown which has become virtually a no go area for many of them. Few of them shop there. Few of them send their youngsters to college or further education there. They want their social problems addressed together with the issues of their rights. Previous attempts to find a resolution have failed for a variety of reasons: the process has on occasions not been carefully enough designed; or has started too late in the day. On the one side, the imperative for dialogue has been to find a way of getting a march down the Garvaghy Road; on the other it appears to have been about respect, equality and righting the social ills of the past. Each sees the agenda of the other as blocking progress.

The mounting social and economic cost of the intractable problem became a grave concern for senior figures within the business community, who realised the violence and the negative image it created was having a significant impact on the economy, especially inward investment. Their message was clear: political stability was a pre-requisite for economic growth. The point was clearly made for them in June 1998, when William Daly, the US commerce secretary, visited Northern Ireland accompanied by the chief executives of eight Fortune 500 companies. The high-powered delegation said they were interested in investing in the local economy, but only if two critical criteria were fulfilled: political stability and security stability. Four weeks later, Drumcree Four erupted and Northern Ireland was engulfed in violence.

Over the years, the accumulation of anecdotal evidence underlines the damage that has been done. One July during the annual stand-off, Stephen Kingon, the president of the Northern Ireland Chamber of Commerce, was in the United States meeting potential inward investors. Sitting in his hotel room before a dinner appointment, he was horrified to see CNN running a story about political difficulties and footage of rioting at home. The first question his guests asked was how he could live in a war zone. As far as they were concerned, Drumcree was not a once a year incident. They thought it was like that all the time. On another occasion, a multinational American company planning to make a substantial investment in Northern Ireland sent over a team of young managers to research the north-west area, around Londonderry, and report back on the feasibility of opening a factory. On their first morning they were trapped in their hotel because of a blockade by Loyalists. The investment never happened.

John Compton, an economic consultant, was on holiday in France another year when he heard that someone from the office of the Comptroller of New York City, who controlled investment funds worth hundreds of millions of dollars, had given an interview to an American television station while wearing a flak jacket standing on the Garvaghy Road. In July 2000, Seamus Mallon, the deputy first minister, and Reg Empey, the minister for enterprise, trade and investment in the Stormont administration, were about to leave for Aldergrove airport to greet a delegation of American businessmen led by the US ambassador in London, when a call came through to say the visit was cancelled because of violence asociated with Drumcree. Later that year a planned investment in north Belfast, which created 900 jobs, almost collapsed because of the Drumcree protest. Empey had to order burned-out cars and other debris of the previous night's rioting to be cleared from the streets on the morning the company executives visited the proposed factory site at Duncairn Gardens to persuade them their investment would be safe and clinch the deal. The scale of the economic impact of Drumcree was revealed during the 1995 stand-off, when the 24-hour blockade of the Port of Larne cost local businesses £1 million in lost exports of perishable food products. The long-term cost in lost orders and confidence was much higher, as companies in Britain and mainland Europe cancelled contracts because of the fear that the supply chain from Northern Ireland was not totally reliable. The crucial link between stability and economic growth was emphasised again by an executive of the American Chamber of Commerce, during a visit to Belfast in 2000, who told an audience of businessmen: 'Money goes where it is welcome, where it is profitable, and where it is safe.'

The local business community was far from complacent about the situation it faced. In 1996, Sir George Quigley, chairman of the Ulster Bank and the Northern Ireland Economic Council, contacted a number of senior business people and told them he believed it was time for them to speak out. During 30 years of violence the business community has been strongly criticised by politicians for failing to play an active role in the peace process. Indeed, in far too many cases, it has indirectly nourished violence and supported the terrorist organisations by paying large sums in protection money to ensure a quiet life. In 1997 Quigley was the prime mover behind the formation of G7, a coalition of leading business figures and trade union representatives with a brief to counter the ill-effects of Drumcree on the economy. The next year, the group tried to convince the government that the way to resolve Drumcree was to improve social and economic conditions in Portadown, which would bring benefits to both Catholics and Protestants in the town. It also tried to persuade Portadown District and the Garvaghy Road residents to compromise in the interests of the wider economy, pointing out that the ripples of their local squabble were tidal waves by the time they reached boardrooms in the European Union and the United States. The pivotal contact in this process was Chris Gibson, chairman of the Northern Ireland Branch of the Confederation of British Industry. In a bid to kick-start such a local economic initiative, he made contact with Ian Milne, a County Armagh Orangeman and funeral director whose philosophy on life is profoundly influenced by the nature of his job. 'Everyone is the same when they go into the ground. No one asks if they are Protestant or Catholic, orange or green,' he says.

Milne spoke to senior members of Portadown District and Archbishop Eames in Armagh. Meanwhile, Gibson, who was also chairman of the Irish School of Ecumenics, fixed an introduction to Father Eamon Stack, the Jesuit priest who worked alongside Brendan McKenna on the Garvaghy Road, and arranged a meeting. Eames came back and said the government wanted some evidence that the group had sufficient clout to influence the Portadown Orangemen, and asked if they could secure a suspension of nightly protests at each end of the Garvaghy Road. Having denied any role in the protests until that point, the Orangemen said they would stop the picket at 6 pm the next day, restarting it at 10 pm, to show that they could control those responsible. When they delivered, Eames said he was satisfied that G7 could have a positive role to play, but Mowlam never delivered her side of the bargain by inviting the group to play a more active role in negotiations.

Undeterred, the group conducted a series of meetings with the Orange Order and went to Iona House, the Jesuit residence in Portadown, hours before the proximity talks in Armagh. Sir George Quigley, Chris Gibson, Stephen Kingon and others outlined plans for improving social and economic conditions: training for the unemployed; inward investment to create jobs; improved recreational and social facilities; and modernisation of houses on the Garvaghy Road and Brownstown, a Protestant estate with similar levels of deprivation. No sum of money was mentioned, but the group was confident it could secure substantial backing from government and the private sector. To their dismay, McKenna appeared uninterested, frequently interrupting the discussions to make or answer calls on his mobile phone. The officers of Portadown District reacted in similar fashion: the package would be welcome, but only after the parade. As Jonathan Powell discovered when he put £15 million on the table, money was not the issue.

Nor was it an issue for some members of the Northern Ireland business community, who shared the suicidal economic instincts of Portadown District. On 8 March 1999, several members of G7 received death threats from a previously unheard of group, styling itself 'The Black Friday Brigade'. The letters stated: 'The Strategic Army Command of the Black Friday Brigade demands that your organisation discontinues all contact with the Republic of Ireland and any joint projects involving organisations from the Republic of Ireland. This instruction must be complied with immediately, with a public statement announcing your full compliance. We cannot guarantee the safety of your staff, members and premises if your organisation fails to comply fully with this instruction. BFB active service units, acting on the standing orders of SAC, will take appropriate measures to end all collaboration with Eire.'

The letters were not simply the work of cranks. Later the wives of several G7 members received defaced photographs of their husbands in the post and customers of some of the businessmen involved were told they would be targeted unless they stopped trading with those the organisation regarded as enemies of the Loyalist people. Sir George Quigley raised the matter with the chief constable and it was decided not to give the people concerned added credibility by making the details public. However, the matter was taken seriously and investigated. At least one senior businessman was warned by police not to use his own car to travel to G7 meetings and to vary his customary route from home to work. Later, working through an intermediary, G7 sent a representative to meet a spokesman for the sinister group. From this contact it was clear that the threats emanated from people closely connected to members of the business community, who made it clear that their uncompromising Loyalist political principles were much more important than the economy. 'After this meeting we had to take it very seriously,' says one of those threatened. 'They had done their research and knew a lot about us. They gave the impression that they meant business and we had to be concerned not only for ourselves, but for our families and staff because they made it clear that they would be targeted too.' G7's role decreased significantly that year, but not only as a result of the threats. The residents and Orangemen made it clear that their efforts were not welcome.

Away from the front line, one of the most visible manifestations of Drumcree is what has become know as the Drumcree exodus, the annual flight of thousands of people departing on holiday to get away from the trouble. One of the most costly effects of the crisis is that, at the height of the annual tourist season, the incoming aircraft are empty. In March 1997, the Economic Council, published the results of a two-year study into the effects of violence on the tourist industry. The annual rate of growth in tourist numbers in Northern Ireland between 1968, when civil unrest began, and 1995, when Republicans and Loyalists declared cease-fires, was just 1 per cent, compared to 3.5 per cent in the Republic of Ireland and 6.1 per cent in Britain. In 1999, despite Drumcree, Northern Ireland enjoyed a record year for tourism, with almost 1.7 million visitors, up 6 per cent on the previous record set in that post-ceasefire euphoria of 1995. However, if visitor numbers had continued to grow at the same rate as in the Republic since the 1960s the number would have been 3.5 million. If they had continued to grow at the same rate as in the rest of the UK, the figure would be 5 million. The impact of the Drumcree factor is clear from hotel occupancy figures for July 2000. During what is the peak holiday season in Northern Ireland it was just 52 per cent. The rate for guesthouses and bed and breakfast accommodation was much worse, at 36 per cent. All this adds up to an annual loss of some £40 million in tourist revenue. The impact on the wider economy is also clear. Analysis of investment announcements by the Industrial Development Board during 2000 reveals no investments between June 29 and August 24. 'In effect, Northern Ireland plc closes down for the month of July and hides its head in shame,' says one senior businessman.'

Economists have not been able specifically to isolate the full cost of Drumcree to the Northern Ireland economy, but it is clearly phenomenal. The additional policing cost is calculated at £50 million since 1995, but the need for the RUC to maintain, train and equip a standing force of some 2000 police officers because of the unique public order problems of Northern Ireland consumes a great proportion of the £650 million annual policing budget. How much the military deployment costs is also unclear, buried deep in the nation's defence budget. However, the bill for moving and deploying at least 3000 troops and their equipment, as well as the expense of operational helicopter flights and the 'Maginot' line construction, must be at least the equivalent of what the police spend. In the financial years 1995/96 and 1999/2000, criminal damage claims totalled £166 million and criminal injury claims amounted to £174 million. A very high proportion of the damage and much of the injury is directly attributable to Drumcree. There are many other costs. In the most recent financial year, the Roads Service had to pay out £250,000 to make good roads damaged by burning vehicles and other disturbances associated with Drumcree. Housing, health, fire and many other public services accrue additional expenditure because of Drumcree. When all is added together and the cost of lost opportunity, jobs, visitors and contracts is taken into account, economists say a figure of £1 billion over six years is a reasonable estimate of the total cost of the cancer of Drumcree. Over the period that equates to about £50,000 for each of the 20,000 citizens of Portadown, three Protestants for every Catholic.

Despite this great burden, much of it on the ordinary taxpayer, many people in Northern Ireland remain unrepentant about the economic and social cost of their continued intransigence. As one Belfast Orangeman told the Parades Commission: 'I can't really see any reason why we should parade around in circles within, you know, a 100 per cent Protestant area. There would be no reason for the parades.'

David Cook, one-time Lord Mayor of Belfast and a former chairman of the Police Authority, says the two must find a way to compromise. 'Such an accommodation would in fact signal a move away from one of the long-standing objectives of Orangemen: that of offending and antagonising Catholics. The sooner that can be achieved the sooner it will become apparent that such an accommodation can actually protect, enhance and even develop the legitimate and inoffensive expression of cultural identity to a point where we can all, with an open heart and a clear conscience, enjoy and celebrate the very diverse cultures of this society.' But others are not so sure. 'Because both sides are now so entrenched, the only solution is utter capitulation by one side or the other, as they see it. With each month that passes that becomes more difficult. It will come down to whichever side blinks first, and both sides seem to have perfected the art of staring,' says a prominent businessman. Brendan McAllister believes the problems over marching have peaked but are far from being resolved and could still lead to some 'nasty, but manageable expressions' of discontent. For him the real challenge is how the cherished tradition of marching can be woven into the tapestry of the new integrated society slowly being created in Northern Ireland.

A widely-travelled senior clergyman believes the problem has become so intractable because of the distinctive nature of Portadown itself. 'It is the most sectarian place on the face of this earth,' he says. A senior British official, a veteran of many bruising negotiations within the EU, in the reunification of Germany and at the United Nations, said, 'Drumcree. Ah! It's in a league of its own.'

Index

Notes:
Names of persons are indexed wherever they occur in the text. Geographical locations are listed only where there is particular significance or detailed description.
The entry 'Twelfth of July' refers to all marches taking place around that date and in commemoration of it, not only those on the day itself.

negotiating position 289–90, 316
public pronouncements 8, 13,
    253–4
suppression of information 352–4
Grattan, Henry, MP 5
Griffin, Donna 247, 313
Guckian, Frank 186, 232
Gunpowder Plot (1605) 32

Hall, Blair 198
Hall, Freddie, ACC 112, 114, 117,
    122
Hamill, Robert, murder of 187–8,
    200, 239, 288, 291
Hamilton, Melvyn 103, 109–10, 112,
    115, 116, 127, 333
    resignation from Order 287
Hamilton, Pamela 127
Hancock, William J 11
Hanna, 'Roaring' Hugh, Rev 12
Harper, Alan, Archdeacon 298
Hatch, Arnold, Cllr xii–xiii, 66, 78–9,
    321
Hayden, Ray 303
Heaney, Seamus 180
Heath, Edward, PM (UK) 261
Henderson, Kevin 75, 76–7, 78–9
Henderson, Michael 75, 76, 78–9
Henry, Ralph 48–9
Hermon, Jack, Chief Con 69, 70–4,
    90–1, 138, 181
    tackling of marching issue 74,
    79–81
Hermon, Lady Jean 85
Hewitt, David 186, 232
Hewitt, John 180
Hibernians, Ancient Order of 3
Highland Paddy (folk group) 90
Hillsborough talks (June 1997)
    205–12, 213–14
History of Ulster (Bardon) 10
Hobson, Paul 188
Holland, Tony 316, 318, 339–40,
    359–60
Home Rule 36
Home Rule, issue of 12–20

Howarth, George, MP 312–13, 335
Hughes, Felix, murder of 54
Hume, John, MP 93–4, 95, 156, 186,
    197, 211, 294, 317–18
hunger strikes (Maze prison, 1981) 3,
    74, 80
Hunt report 70, 71
Hurd, Douglas, NI Secretary 81

Independent Commission for Police
    Complaints 188, 291
Independent Orange Order 14
Ingram, Adam, MP 216, 231, 291,
    312–13, 335
internment 42, 50, 56, 170
Interpoint talks 298–300
Irish language 83, 106, 179
Irish News 171, 234
Irish Republican Army (IRA)
    attacks on Unionist marches 225–6
    bomb attacks (post 1968) 54–5,
    56–7, 68–9, 93, 100, 106–7, 135,
    282, 284
    confrontations with police 41–2, 57
    formation and early campaigns
    20–1, 39, 40–2, 71
    internal differences 21–2, 52
    interrogation methods 97–8
    and marching activities 52–3, 83,
    123, 133–4, 149, 247, 265
    in peace negotiations 93–5 (*see
    also* ceasefires)
Irwin, Barbara, Dr 232

Jackson, Guy, Maj 308
James I, King 25
James II, King 4, 33
Jesuit involvement 136
John Paul I, Pope 61
Johnston, David, murder of 202
Johnston, William, of Ballykilbeg 12,
    34, 128
Jones, David 276–7, 282, 294, 297,
    315, 329, 355
Jones, Lord Justice 49
Kearney, Vincent 258–61, 315